Social Stratification and Career Mobility

Publications of the International Social Science Council

16

MOUTON · PARIS · THE HAGUE

Social Stratification and Career Mobility

edited by
WALTER MÜLLER
and
KARL ULRICH MAYER

MOUTON · PARIS · THE HAGUE

Social stratification and career mobility:
Papers of the International Workshop on Career Mobility, Konstanz, 1971

Printed in France

Contents

Contributors

Bertaux, D.	*Centre National de la Recherche Scientifique, Paris, France*
Bock, E. W.	*Department of Sociology, University of Florida, Gainesville, Fla., USA*
Boudon, R.	*University of Paris-5, Paris, France*
Caserman, A.	*Institute of Sociology and Philosophy, Ljubljana University, Ljubljana, Slovenia, Yugoslavia*
Duncan-Jones, P.	*The Research School of the Social Sciences, The Australian National University, Canberra, Australia*
Fricker, Y.	*Centre for Sociology, University of Geneva, Geneva, Switzerland*
Girod, R.	*Centre for Sociology, University of Geneva, Geneva Switzerland*
Goldthorpe, J.H.	*Nuffield College, Oxford, Great Britain*
Hope, K.	*Nuffield College, Oxford, Great Britain*
Iutaka, S.	*Department of Sociology, University of Florida, Gainesville, Fla., USA*
Körffy, A.	*Centre for Sociology, University of Geneva, Geneva, Switzerland*
Kreckel, R.	*Institute of Sociology, University of Munich, Germany (GFR)*
Mayer, K.U.	*Institute of the Social Sciences, University of Mannheim, Germany (GFR)*
Müller, W.	*Department of Sociology, University of Konstanz, Konstanz, Germany (GFR)*
Ornstein, M.D.	*York University, Toronto, Ont., Canada*
Pasqualini, R.	*Graduate School of Sociology and Social Research, University of Rome, Rome, Italy*
Rossi, P.H.	*Johns Hopkins University, Baltimore, Md., USA*
Svalastoga, K.	*Sociological Institute, University of Copenhagen, Copenhagen, Denmark*
Zloczower, A.	*Department of Sociology, Hebrew University, Jerusalem, Israel*

Introduction *

For almost two decades, social mobility research was guided by a "paradigm" which defined its main theoretical problems, its procedures of data collection and methods of data analysis. The theoretical questions to be answered were those posed among others, by Lipset, Bendix and Zetterberg (1959): do societies differ in the extent of social mobility according to their degree of industrialization? And the counter-question was: is the (American) class structure becoming more rigid and less permeable? And secondly, do different value-systems of societies, especially in regard to emphasis on status vs. equality and ascription vs. achievement, entail different levels of social mobility? These questions were to be answered by the collection of nationally representative data on mobility between generations of men within hierarchies defined in terms of occupational prestige, the analysis of such data by summary statistical measures derived from father-son transition matrices and their cross-national as well as historical comparisons.

It is now generally acknowledged that this strategy for discovering relationships between structural or normative features of societies and levels of social mobility has failed, despite the fact that some studies belonging to this tradition count among the best examples of empirical sociology. The provisional results of this research tradition — no marked differences in mobility rates (except perhaps in elite mobility) between countries at different levels of economic development, societies with different normative orientations and with

* The editors would like to acknowledge the support of the Department of Sociology and the Research Council of the University of Konstanz in the organization of the Workshop, the Baden-Württemberg Ministry of Cultural Affairs, the Verein der Freunde und Förderer der Universität Konstanz and the Deutscher Akademischer Austauschdienst (DAAD) for their financial assistance. For their efforts in making a publication of the workshop papers possible we wish to express our profound appreciation to Prof. Kaare Svalastoga and Prof. Stein Rokkan. Further we should like to thank Christa Labuske, Christine von Prümmer, Karin Schaab, Klaus Schröter and Ingrid Starke for their technical and secretarial assistance.

differential class structures; no marked differences for individual societies within the last 40-50 years — lead to an impasse, whether one accepts them or rejects them for well-grounded methodological reasons. Either the hypotheses concerning the societal conditions which should explain various levels of social mobility are to be discarded, since the empirical tests did not show the expected results, in which case one is left without a satisfactory theoretical account for the observed rates, or, the methods used to produce estimates of national mobility rates are to be judged inadequate for this purpose.

A few, among the many methodological problems in the study of inter-generational mobility rates, illustrate the limitations of the paradigm.

Inter-generational mobility data provide observations on positions at two points in time, father's status and son's status or, in other words, status of origin and status of destination. Since in cross-sectional investigations, information on father's status is obtained by asking the son, the fathers do not constitute a representative sample of their generation, even if the sons do (Duncan, 1966). On the basis of such data it is therefore impossible to make reliable inferences concerning structural parameters (distribution of fathers and distance between status groups) or to link observed mobility rates to changes of structure (Sorensen, 1971). This precludes, for instance, the accurate identification of the extent of mobility engendered by changes in the size of status categories between father- and son-generation and "*free*" or *exchange* mobility.

Measurements of social mobility cannot easily be aggregated, since equivalence classes of social distances between positions of different status are difficult to establish. Furthermore, mobility indices yield ambiguous results in testing relationships, in which mobility is an independent variable. Mobility effects can either result from the additively combined influence of origin and destination status or exclusively from the condition of having been mobile or from both (Blalock, 1967). In recent analyses, attempting to control for the influences of origin and destination status, it has been shown that many of the hitherto assumed effects of mobility cannot be validated (Blau and Duncan, 1967; Kessin, 1971; Laslett, 1971).

The measurement of social mobility as moves of individuals between groups of positions with differential occupational prestige limits observations to an ambiguously defined dimension of social inequality and leaves the characteristics of the stratification system, in which mobility processes take place, largely unexplored. The validity of the occupational prestige hierarchy as an indicator of class structure is controversial and its varying adequacy in different societies makes cross-national analyses of the extent of social mobility and its effects a highly inferential undertaking.

The comparison of fathers and sons on the basis of information on their status at only one point in time for each implicitly assumes that status, as usually defined in occupational terms, is more or less invariant over the life-cycle after a certain age period. Both for fathers and sons, however, the occupational status varies even for older age groups to an extent which introduces considerable leeway in the estimation of mobility parameters.

Despite such objections, the inter-generational mobility matrix may still give a relatively good picture of the gross inequality of opportunity of access to the status assets measured. Yet, as concerns the consequences of mobility, comparisons with one's own father may become less and less salient as a basis for self-evaluations and thus for determining the gratification and deprivation experienced. Parents and families of sons live less often in the same communities where the "significant others" of the son will evaluate him according to the social standing of the father. The emergence of new and more numerous qualified occupations, the upgrading of occupations by higher levels of training and, in some countries, the taking over of manual jobs by foreign workers produce a general upward push. Also, general rises in income and standard of living set all sons in a position hardly comparable to that of their fathers. Due to the expansion of formal education, differences of educational levels between parents and children will occur quite frequently. Together with other cultural cleavages between generations this will also contribute to a decrease in the salience of father-son comparisons.

Furthermore, given widespread mobility and the normative impact of a success ideology, the comparisons made in assessing one's status are age-specific and the comparison with the father may be predominant only among younger men with short occupational experiences. Later, the major reference points are one's peers, acquaintances in the same line of work and one's own past. Even with respect to comparison with parental status, occupation as such may be much less a standard for comparison than cultural patterns of behavior in the family of origin (Wilensky, 1966). Thus, father's occupational status as a convenient indicator of social origin turns out to be just one among several possible anchorings of career experiences.

In analogy to Kuhn's (1964) observations on the development of the natural sciences we may say that the once established mode of mobility research has ceased to be a paradigm. In contrast to initial expectations, many theoretical problems it posed could not be decided empirically.

Kuhn remarks that when the weaknesses of a paradigm become apparent, its necessarily narrow definition of the problem area comes to be called in question, new and forgotten issues are being raised. On a wide scale, criticisms of the old paradigm arise which its promoters knew well, but found less significant than its promises. Scientists redefine their problem area and thereby, in many ways, redefine the world.

The collection of papers in this volume reflects such a stage in the development of mobility research.

During the Seventh World Congress of Sociology in Varna, 1970, many participants in the session on theory, research and simulation studies on social mobility of the Research Committee on Social Stratification and Mobility felt that the new heterogeneity of ideas and approaches had not emerged distinctly enough and had not been sufficiently discussed.

Consequently, and with the kind support of Prof. Svalastoga, the editors of this issue organized a meeting of sociologists working in this field at the University of Konstanz in April 1971. Its title "Workshop on Career Mobility" indicates one of the routes which mobility research might follow.

With the exception of Raymond Boudon's article all the contributions to this issue of *Social science information* were read at the Workshop or arose out of discussion statements. Their authors represent research groups working on problems of social mobility in Denmark, France, West Germany, Great Britain, Ireland, Israel, Italy, Switzerland, Yugoslavia and the United States. Unfortunately, colleagues invited from the GDR (German Democratic Republic), Czechoslovakia and Poland were not able to participate.

The following brief comments are intended to indicate the way in which each paper is contributing to the assessment, reorientation and development of the study of social mobility. They may also explain the order in which the articles are printed and thus serve as a preliminary guide to the reader. Sketchy and selective as they are, these remarks cannot, of course, do full justice to the great variety of opinions, procedures and findings assembled. Another, more amusing and highly recommendable way to whet one's appetite for the content of the papers would be to follow the selection of the discussion statements from the Workshop, which are reproduced below at the end of this issue

A necessary prerequisite of the measurement of social mobility is a conception of the structure and major components of the stratification system. The way in which the researcher commits himself in this regard and the extent to which he is able to establish valid and feasible indicators determines almost completely the possible theoretical substance of the results mobility analyses may yield. It is therefore not surprising that in a period of re-appraisal and of quests for alternative developments, considerable attention is paid to these "a prioris" and their customary solutions.

In their paper, Goldthorpe and Hope contrast the theoretical implications of the sociological concept of prestige with the measurement and interpretation of occupational prestige in mobility studies. They maintain that occupational prestige scales do not measure prestige rankings, but represent diffuse cognitions of the relative goodness of occupations in respect to their requirements and rewards. Occupational position is retained as a basic unit of stratification and a convenient indicator of social rank in large-scale mobility surveys. However, in discussing material provided by pilot studies, the authors propose to establish the hierarchy of occupations in regard to three dimensions of inequality, "standard of living", "prestige in the community", "power and influence over other people". Their theoretical and empirical efforts pave the way towards conceptually more valid multi-dimensional measures of social mobility.

Svalastoga's article addresses itself to a problem crucial for empirical research employing occupational prestige as a stratification variable: estimating scores for positions on the basis of more readily available information than respondents' grading of occupational titles. The author proposes task difficulty and responsibility as principal determinants of occupational prestige. Difficulty of task can conveniently be related to the amount of education incumbents of specific occupations have received. Svalastoga discusses several approaches to the more difficult measurement of responsibility, for which he then proves size of enterprise and hierarchical position in the work organization to be a viable empirical referent. As a result, he provides a regression equation, which permits us to estimate the occupational prestige of any respondent for which these two elements of information are available.

Even if theoretically valid and empirically feasible, do the current concepts of social mobility have any meaning for the actors whose movements they are to describe? Do these actors define past mobility experiences, expectations and aspirations by means of vocabularies which justify a general and unidimensional notion of mobility? Mayer's empirical observations corroborate the predominant significance of occupational position as a dimension of subjective mobility experience. They indicate, however, not only that security, income, home ownership and relations to fellow workers are the more important criteria by which improvements in this sphere are being evaluated, but also that the articulation of concerns varies with type of and relative position in a career.

More fundamentally, Bertaux and Kreckel object that the use of occupational prestige scales as continuous or hierarchical representations of stratification leads to the neglect of the objective inequalities in life-chances, limits analysis to merely distributive aspects of class structure, by definition rules out the problem of class conflict and necessarily creates the impression of high mobility rates. The very preoccupation with social mobility is here seen as an option in favour of the liberal political ideology and its ideal of equality of opportunity. It leaves, the authors argue, the degree of inequality and the basic relationships of dominance, exploitation and dependency unexplored and unchanged. In this view, both mobility studies and the mobility they observe obscure the existing range of inequalitites and contribute to their maintenance and stabilization. Equality of opportunity might have been a potent political demand when directed by the rising bourgeoisie against the feudal aristocracy. Yet, as a guiding idea of contemporary mobility research, it is looked at as harmless at best and as a tool of appeasement at worst.

In these introductory notes there is no space to argue for or against such strong verdicts. This has been done lucidly in several contributions to the discussions during the Workshop which are reproduced below at the end of this volume.

However, if one proceeds from a position which holds that a more advanced knowledge of mobility processes is an indispensable instrument for the comprehension and thus for the political transformability of present stratification systems, efforts to perfect the mathematical tools used in the field are of no minor relevance. The extracts from the work of Boudon and Duncan-Jones belong to a long series of methodological proposals which have led, step by step, to more refined modes of analysis.

Boudon reviews several mover-stayer models of mobility based on the statistics of Markov chains. He thereby develops a generalized version which has an important characteristic: by applying the generalized model one is likely to find, empirically, the structures underlying the transitions described by a given mobility matrix. This is a further advance in the attempt to describe the stratification system precisely by analyzing mobility data in terms of a rigorously defined model.

Duncan-Jones' paper on "Preparing social stratification data for path analysis" is of particular relevance, since, in recent years, path analysis has enjoyed a veritable boom in stratification and mobility research. The author takes up a crucial problem encountered in applying path analysis: the necessity of giving scores to variables which generally have "no in-built metric". Various canonical scoring methods are shown to be useful for this purpose and applicable to stratification data.

The remaining papers report on empirical studies in various countries. Seen together, they manifest a distinct trend away from the inter-generational point of view to accentuation in issues of career mobility, this term being understood in the wider sense of mobility in the course of the whole life-time of an individual. Such a change is clearly revealed in the studies of the status attainment process presented by Iutaka/Bock, Müller, Girod/Fricker/Körffy and Rossi/Ornstein. These contributions also reflect the turning away from indices of the amount of mobility observed between given time intervals. The primary interest of the authors is the assignment of relative weights to a number of variables assumed to determine the occupational status attained at succeeding stages of a person's life cycle.

Iutaka and Bock attempt a comparison of the American and Brazilian stratification process with the aid of Blau and Duncan's basic path-analysis model. Despite the fairly differentiated approach, no crucial differences emerge in the pattern of career determinants in American society and the most advanced sectors of the *Brazilian* social system. The only notable difference which the authors point out is the finding that, in an industrializing society, father's occupation is more important than his educational background in determining the son's attainment.

Müller's contribution reopens the question as to whether the educational system effectively alters inequalities resulting from the family of origin. On the basis of data gathered in a *West-German* city, it is found that the independent influence of education is reduced to a very low proportion once a complete account of family background influences is made. On the other hand, the educational efforts which produce a compensating effect are most probably those undertaken during the occupational career and related to specific work requirements. Adult education is shown to be of particular importance for intra-career promotion of persons disadvantaged by their social origin.

Opposing patterns of career mobility for sons of white-collar and sons of blue-collar fathers are clearly revealed in the *Geneva*-study by Girod/Fricker/Körffy. For blue-collar sons, promotion chances during the course of their career are fairly limited. If they are inter-generationally mobile, blue-collar sons have usually accomplished this step when they enter their first occupation. On the contrary, many sons of white-collar fathers are "counter-mobile"; they begin work life in a manual occupation, but to a great extent reach white-collar occupations later on, *i.e.* they return to the milieu of origin, which socially they may never have left.

Whereas equality of opportunity in the occupational system for many authors is *the* criterion of social justice, for Rossi, Coleman and their associates, occupational promotion chances constitute only *one* "social account" in a long inventory of deficits and assets of the black and white population of the *American* society. A long-standing demand for data on occupational histories has been fulfilled by the Johns Hopkins Social Accounts Project in an exemplary manner. The methods introduced by this project for collecting and analyzing detailed retrospective data on life histories must be considered an important breakthrough in social mobility research. In a variety of ways, the report by Rossi and Ornstein provides evidence on a great many aspects of occupational attainment in which blacks are disadvantaged in relation to whites. Blacks lag behind whites when entering the labour force and their experiences of discrimination continue thereafter, so that "the longer they work, the further behind whites they fall".

An important point is raised by Pasqualini in her note on a current research project in Italy. Upward mobility in occupation must be seen in relation to differential opportunities in various sectors of the economy and their change and as often embedded in processes of migration and particular job-sequences. In her study of construction workers in Rome she hypothesizes a "two-step flow of sectorial relocation from agriculture to manufacturing industry" and discusses the close dependency of these processes on economic cycles, the situation and rules of the local labor market and the age of the mobile workers.

Few of the papers reviewed up to now explicitly make use of a political frame of reference. This, however, should not obscure the fact that the ultimate interest of almost any mobility study is political. The descriptive use of mobility matrices, as well as the more explanatory analyses of the status attainment process, must be understood in this light as a — not always conclusive — means of demonstrating the extent to which initial disadvantages and privileges violate standards of social justice and the extent to which public institutions such as the school are able to counteract this. More often than not such studies focus on the attributes and capacities of individuals as though these were unaffected by concrete political actions. Evidence to the contrary is presented by Caserman, who for a *Yugoslavian* sample, examines how, as a consequence of political transformations, career assets are redistributed and now work in favour of Communist party members and members of the Association of Veterans.

The main theoretical issue regarding the political implications of social mobility concerns its effects, *e.g.* the weakening of working class solidarity and the prevention of class conflicts. As a modern version of this problem formulation, it may be asked why persons upwardly mobile out of the working class retain or change the generally more "leftist" orientation of their class of origin. On the basis of contradictory evidence from the United States on the one hand, Israel and Western European states on the other, Zloczower rejects explanations in terms of over-conformity to the class of destination or varying discrepancy between occupational position and class position. He considers, rather, the strength of the political and economic organization identified with the working class to be a crucial variable which determines the extent to which the occupationally upwardly mobile orient themselves toward middle class political norms and values.

What will be the outcome of the conceptual clarification, sensitivity to indicator problems, methodological innovations, substantial studies of mobility processes and "Ideologiekritik" which are exemplified by the main concerns of the papers of this volume?

It would seem that, along with the critique of its methods, the main theoretical issues arising out of the earlier paradigm have also lost much of their interest. We would conjecture that, in their further development, mobility studies will not be focussed primarily on explanations of overall societal rates of mobility and, most likely, will not come up with any more definitive answers concerning the societal conditions which entail such differential rates.

There is not much left of the optimistic belief in a quasi-automatic secular trend in which social background exercises an ever decreasing impact on life chances due to various facets of the modernization process. In contrast, it is argued that inequalities will only be reduced by determined political action and that the mechanisms which bring them about continually tend to replace each other.

If a new paradigm does at all achieve acceptance among researchers in the field, it will again concern the political objectives and uses of their empirical investigations. But, as, for instance, the Social Accounts Project foreshadows, mobility researchers will not content themselves with merely describing and explaining the inequality of conditions and opportunities from the point of view of uninvolved observers from outside. Rather, with increased policy orientation, they will concentrate on how the social standing, economic situation and political participation of specific groups can be enhanced.

WALTER MÜLLER KARL ULRICH MAYER

REFERENCES

Blalock, H.M.
1967 "Status inconsistency, social mobility, status integration and structural effects", *American sociological review* 32, October: 790-801.

Blau, P.M.; Duncan, O.D.
1967 *The American occupational structure.* New York, Wiley.

Duncan, O.D.
1966 "Methodological issues in the analysis of social mobility", in: N.J. Smelser; S.M. Lipset (eds.). *Social structure and social mobility in economic development.* Chicago, Ill., Aldine.

Kessin, K.
1971 "Social and psychological consequences of intergenerational occupational mobility", *American journal of sociology* 77 (1): 1-17.

Kuhn, T.S.
1964 *The structure of scientific revolutions.* Chicago, Ill., University of Chicago Press.

Lasslett, B.
1971 "Mobility and work satisfaction: A discussion of the use and interpretation of mobility models", *American journal of sociology* 77 (1): 19-35.

Lipset, S.M.; Bendix, R.
1959 *Social mobility in industrial society.* Berkeley, Calif., University of California Press.

Miller, S.M.
1971 "The future of social mobility studies", *American journal of sociology* 77 (1): 62-65.

Sorensen, A.B.
1971 *Models of social mobility.* Baltimore, Md., Johns Hopkins University, Center for Social Organization of Schools. (Report No. 98.)

Wilensky, H.L.
1966 "Measures and effects of social mobility", in: N.J. Smelser; S.M. Lipset (eds.). *Social structure and social mobility in economic development.* Chicago, Ill., Aldine.

JOHN H. GOLDTHORPE • KEITH HOPE

Occupational grading and occupational prestige*

Introduction

A cursory glance at the form and content of this paper would suggest that the first part contains a sociological analysis of the concept of occupational prestige and its uses, which generates certain propositions amenable to empirical test, and the second part consists of a small-scale sketch of methods of testing those propositions. However, while such a sequence does occur, it is at the same time important for the reader to recognize that *both* parts of the paper are intended as conceptual analyses of the field of occupational grading; the one being linguistic in form, based on a reading of previous empirical work, while the other seeks conceptual clarification by imposing a design on possible data. The emphasis of Part 1 is on the nature of the components of occupational grading. Part 2 takes certain components as given and shows how one can define a set of quantifiable concepts covering all aspects of the employment of those components. This set is in an important sense complete, in that it exhausts all possible sources of variance.

In the first part of the paper we begin with an attempt to explicate the concept of prestige in what seems to us to be the sociologically most meaningful sense, and that generally found in the classical literature on social stratification. Specifically, we suggest that prestige should be understood as a particular form of social power and advantage that is of a symbolic rather than of an economic or political character, and which gives rise to structured relationships of deference, acceptance and derogation. We then consider whether such a concept of prestige has been that usually adopted in conventional studies of the prestige of occupations. We conclude that in fact the theoretical basis of these studies has been often confused, and that the occupational

* This paper was first published in: K. Hope (ed.), *The analysis of social mobility: Methods and approaches*. Oxford, Clarendon Press, 1972. (Oxford studies in social mobility, Working papers 1.)

gradings they produce cannot be safely regarded as a valid indicator of a prestige order in the sense previously established. Rather, we argue, conventional occupational "prestige" ratings are better interpreted as representing popular evaluations of the general "goodness" (in the broad sense of "desirability") of occupations. This interpretation is consistent both with respondents' accounts of the considerations they actually have in mind when performing conventional occupational grading tasks and with the pattern of individual and group variation that the results of such grading exercises typically reveal. Finally, on the basis of this interpretation, we examine critically the appropriateness of the uses to which occupational "prestige" ratings have been put in both theory and research. As regards the former, we question whether these ratings can offer any firm empirical support for a functionalist theory of social stratification. As regards the latter, we conclude that occupational classifications or scores derived from "prestige" ratings are likely to provide a sounder basis for studies of specifically occupational mobility than for studies concerned with social mobility in any wider sense.

Although the burden of the research reviewed in Part 1 is that in conventional occupational prestige studies a strong "general factor" in the grading of occupations is present, the research design expounded in Part 2 starts from the position that there may still be discriminable strands in the grading activity. Some of these, admittedly, may be idiosyncratic in the sense that they are not shared by all persons, and the design allows for the estimation of such effects; but it also seeks out other effects, where there is agreement among respondents but distinctions are made between different aspects or dimensions of grading. A pilot analysis of data obtained from a small number of respondents provides some tenuous evidence that both these factors are at work, but we do not wish to ascribe substantive significance to the analysis of these data — the reader is asked to consider the numbers employed as simply there to give content to the quantitative conceptual analysis which is the real substance of Part 2.

In addition we show how the method of analysis proposed may provide a basis for the representation of cognitive maps of the occupational structure, and we briefly indicate how, with adequate data, it might be possible to investigate the social determinants, or at least concomitants, of aspects of the perception of occupations.

The preliminary nature of the analysis is further emphasized by the inclusion of an Appendix describing the findings of an identical analysis of results from a different set of respondents. The reports of these pilot studies are in fact prolegomena to another study, now under way, in which a moderate-sized random sample of the electors of Oxford is being asked to undertake a slightly different version of the task performed by our pilot respondents. The purpose of the study is to illustrate what it is that people are doing when they assess the standing of occupations, and to tease out some of the social determinants or correlates of aspects of this activity. Having cast some light on the processes of occupational perception and discrimination, we hope, if the technical difficulties are not too great, to undertake yet one more study, in which we shall provide a means of assigning a grade or score to any occupation.

1. Occupational prestige: uses and abuses

Introduction

Over the last forty years or so, there has accumulated in the literature of sociology and social psychology a relatively large number (probably several score) of studies in which respondents have been required to grade a selection of occupations in some hierarchical fashion. It has become customary to refer to such studies as being ones of "occupational prestige". Indeed, when the matter of occupational prestige is now considered, it is almost invariably in terms of studies of the kind in question. Furthermore, the data provided by these enquiries have come to play an important part both in theoretical discussion and in the conduct of empirical investigation in the general problem-area of social stratification and mobility. Yet, oddly enough, "occupational prestige" studies have rarely been subjected to critical examination other than from a technical point of view.

In this paper, therefore, we begin in Part 1 with some critical observations which are chiefly concerned with theoretical matters. They lead on, however, to a number of issues of a kind amenable to empirical research. We proceed, then, in Part 2 to report an investigation which we designed and carried out as a "pilot" for more extensive and refined studies relevant to these issues.

The meaning of prestige

An appropriate starting point for a more radical appraisal of "occupational prestige" studies that seems hitherto to have been made is with the concept of "prestige" itself. In a sociological context, we would suggest, prestige can be most usefully understood as referring to a particular form of social advantage and power, associated with the incumbency of a role or membership of a collectivity: specifically, to advantage and power which are of a *symbolic*, rather than of an economic or political nature. That is to say, such advantage and power imply the ability of an actor to exploit — in the pursuit of his goals — *meanings* and *values* rather than superior material resources or positions of authority or of *force majeure*.

From this conception it follows that a hierarchy of prestige is constituted by intersubjective communication among actors, and must therefore be characterized in attitudinal and relational terms. It cannot be characterized —

other than misleadingly — as a distribution in which units have differing amounts of some particular substance or quality. As a provisional statement, a prestige hierarchy might be one in which actors:

1) *defer to* their superiors — that is, acknowledge by speech or other action their own social inferiority — and seek, or at least appreciate, association with superiors;

2) *accept* their equals as partners, associates, etc., in intimate social interaction — entertainment, friendship, courtship, marriage, etc.;

3) *derogate*[1] their inferiors, if only by accepting their deference and avoiding association with them other than where their own superiority is confirmed.

The attributes of roles or collectivities which differentiate actors in respect of their prestige are various. What they have in common is some symbolic significance — some generally recognized meaning — which, in conjunction with prevailing values, constitutes a claim to social superiority or, conversely, some stigma of inferiority. For example, having the role of doctor and working in a hospital or clinic implies having knowledge of, control over and close involvement with matters which are generally regarded as ones of ultimate concern — matters of life and death. Belonging to an aristocratic family and owning a landed estate signifies descent from illustrious forebears and participation in an historically-rooted, distinctive and exclusive way of life. Working as a clerk in a bank evokes such generally valued characteristics as honesty, trustworthiness, discretion and dependability, and again in relation to "important" — in this case, financial — matters. In all of these cases, then, "deference-entitlements" (Shils, 1968) exist, and are likely to be honoured at least by some actors in some contexts. In contrast, being, say, a gypsy scrap-metal dealer or a West Indian refuse-collector is likely to mean relatively frequent exposure to derogation, on account both of the symbolic significance of the ethnic memberships in question and of the implied occupational contact with what is spoiled, discarded and dirty[2]. In other words, prestige positions do not derive directly from the attributes of a role or collectivity "objectively" considered, but rather from the way in which certain of these attributes are perceived and evaluated in some culturally determined fashion.

The particular modes in which prestige is manifest as a form of advantage and power in social relationships are ones conditioned by its symbolic character. The following are perhaps the most obvious:

1) by creating favourable presumptions: *e.g.* that an aristocrat will be an honourable man, that a bank clerk will be credit-worthy;

2) by providing a basis for exerting influence: a high prestige actor is in a

1. We use "derogate" in this context following Shils (1968). Were it not that its usual connotations go beyond its strict meaning, "disparage" — literally "to make unequal" — might be a preferable term.

2. On "stigma symbols" as the obverse of "prestige symbols", see Goffman (1963).

position to offer his (prestige-giving) association and support to those who are prepared to be guided by him, accept his "advice", think as he thinks, etc.; 3) by giving the ability to determine standards, tastes and styles — in the arts, manners, leisure pursuits, dress, speech, etc.: the high valuation set on some symbolic aspect of a social role or collectivity tends to "spill over" and lead to emulation of the total life-style thought to be characteristic of the incumbents of the role or members of the collectivity.

It is not difficult to envisage how, through modes of expression such as the above, prestige can be "converted" into advantage and power of an economic or a political kind — just as the latter may of course in turn be utilized in order to gain increased prestige. However, it is still important to recognize that advantage and power in the form of prestige remain distinctive in that they *entirely depend upon* the existence of some shared universe of meaning and value among the actors concerned. One cannot have an objective or "factual" hierarchy of prestige *in the same sense* as one can a hierarchy of, say, wealth or bureaucratic authority: one, that is, which can exist and maintain its force independently to some important degree of the subjective dispositions of the individuals involved in it, at any one point in time. If the symbolic significance of roles and collectivities is not recognized, or if what is symbolized is subject to divergent evaluations, then no consistent basis for deference, differential social acceptance or derogation is present. While one may talk of an actor pursuing his ends through the exercise of "sheer money power" or "naked force", it would be meaningless to speak of "naked" prestige. Wherever and however ego expresses his prestige in a social relationship, the "complicity" of alter is always entailed. In other words, a prestige hierarchy is part of "socially constructed" reality. It is as it is because the actors implicated in it make it that way through their own actions — although not necessarily, of course, in a fully conscious or intended manner [3].

Recognition that prestige hierarchies are analytically distinct from economic or political hierarchies and are, moreover, not merely epiphenomena of the latter is in fact widely revealed in the "classical" literature of social stratification (Pareto, Weber, Michels, etc.). It is evident, for example, in discussions of "old aristocracies", or of the situation of *nouveaux riches* or *parvenus*, or of the emergence of "new men of power" such as political bosses

3. That prestige is a phenomenon of the kind in question can be elucidated by considering the way in which in interpersonal relations its force may be annulled by that of esteem. Following Davis (1945) one may regard esteem as deriving not from attributes of a role or collectivity but from what an individual actually does and achieves as an incumbent or member. Among persons having close knowledge of each other's performances, therefore, esteem is also a possible basis for deference, etc. And where performances are recognized as incongruent with the expectations associated with roles or memberships (the aristocrat is a boor and a cheat; the bank clerk an embezzler) prestige structures tend to collapse. Persons are seen "for what they are". It is not entirely misleading to keep in mind the etymological connections between "prestige" and "illusions" (*prae-stigiae*) or the act of blindfolding or dazzling (*praestringere oculos*).

or trade union officials. In all these cases, the focus of interest is on the discrepancy that exists between the position of certain groups within a prevailing prestige hierarchy and their position in terms of economic or political power and advantage. By what means does an aristocracy maintain its superior prestige once it has lost its economic and political dominance? What are the consequences of the non-acceptance of newly-risen entrepreneurs or other "men of talent" by established status groups? Can popular leaders who achieve political pre-eminence resist *embourgeoisement* and the embrace of the existing prestige order? — and so on. Obviously, the very posing of such questions implies a conception of prestige similar to that we have proposed (though some other term — *e.g.* "honour" or "respect" — may be used) in which the relation of prestige to other forms of social advantage and power is taken as problematic.

In more recent sociological writing, it should be added, this perspective has often been blurred, or lost, as a result of one or other of two tendencies: first, the tendency to think (for theoretical — or ideological — convenience) of stratification as comprising no more than an "evaluative" hierarchy of prestige or status groups, and thus to leave out of account the sheer "facticity" of inequalities in life-chances; and secondly, the tendency to think (for methodological convenience) of stratification as being unidimensional and to construct scales of "socio-economic status" in which prestige is amalgamated with other components that are deemed to be relevant. However, both of these tendencies are open to, and have met with, strong objections on empirical and analytical grounds alike. Although aimed at simplification, conveniences of the kind in question often in fact lead to greater rather than less difficulty in comprehending stratification phenomena. Indeed, it would seem that if prestige is not to be understood in something approximating the way we have suggested, then certain fairly obvious and intrusive problems — of the kind illustrated in the classical literature — cannot even be raised, let alone investigated.

Occupational prestige

Assuming, on the other hand, that a conception of prestige consistent with classical analyses *is* adopted, then the reference of "occupational prestige" follows from it directly: it is to the chances of deference, acceptance and derogation associated with the incumbency of occupational roles and membership in occupational collectivities. Such prestige will be related to the "objective" attributes of occupations — their rewards, requisite qualifications, work-tasks, work environments, etc. — but only indirectly: only, that is, insofar as these attributes carry symbolic significance of a kind that is likely to be interpreted as indicative of social superiority or inferiority, with corresponding interactional consequences.

We may, therefore, now go on to ask such questions as: *a*) whether such a conception of occupational prestige has been that generally held by the authors of conventional occupational prestige studies; *b*) whether the results of such studies provide valid indicators of prestige in the sense in question; *c*) whether the uses to which results have been put have been appropriate ones.

The conception of occupational prestige in conventional studies

The two investigations which have undoubtedly had greatest influence in setting the pattern for occupational prestige studies generally in the period after the Second World War are those of NORC (National Opinion Research Center) in the US (1947) and of Hall and Jones in the UK (1950). The findings of both of these investigations have, moreover, been subject to further detailed analyses and review subsequent to their initial presentation (Reiss, 1961; Moser and Hall, 1954). It will therefore be convenient, and not seriously misleading, to concentrate chiefly on these two studies in considering questions *a*) and *b*).

Whether or not the conception of prestige which guided the authors of these studies is similar to that we have previously discussed is an issue which cannot easily be settled on account of some lack of clarity in the research reports in question. In both studies alike there is certainly recognition of the fact that "prestige", may well be used in different senses; but there is no sustained attempt at specifying these senses and at making clear which is being employed at any one time. Some considerable confusion results.

For example, Hall and Jones state that their classification "aims at distinguishing between occupations according to their social prestige" (p. 33) and go on to suggest that the prestige of an occupation is chiefly indicated by "the class of people with whom the person so occupied would normally associate, whether at leisure or at work" (p. 36). This would seem to imply something close to the "classical" idea of prestige as being manifest in relational terms through participation in status groups. However, in the later presentation of the Hall-Jones scale by Moser and Hall this viewpoint is not consistently maintained. Although sometimes "social prestige" and "social status" are apparently treated as synonymous, social status is also used as some kind of generic term to refer to the "overall" position of a social unit within a total stratification structure: as, for instance, when it is argued (p. 46) that social status involves "associational, prestige and allied matters" *and not simply* objective characteristics such as income, working conditions, responsibility, educational standards, etc. Moreover, it becomes evident that "occupational prestige" is in fact most frequently interpreted as "occupational social status" in this last-mentioned, broad sense of social status, and that consequently it is as an indicator of the *latter* that the Hall-Jones scale is effectively intended. This is perhaps most clearly revealed when, in discussing occupations such as "Nonconformist minister" on which respondents showed considerable disagreement, Moser and Hall write: "They are occupations for which material rewards and traditional social prestige are at variance" (p. 40). Obviously, *if* the Hall-Jones scale were seriously meant as a measure of prestige in the "classical" sense — as something distinct from economic position (and always in some degree "traditional") — then a suggestion of this kind would imply that the scale was of very dubious validity, and it would not do merely to observe that "the spread in ranking in such cases indicates that different rankers may employ different criteria as a basis for their judgment" (*ibid.*).

In the case of the NORC study, it is recognized, at least by Reiss in his re-presentation of the enquiry, that "the term 'prestige' [...] is perhaps used more loosely in this monograph than would be consistent with the definition of it in theories of social stratification" (p. 1). This recognition is a wise one, and what is surprising, in view of data later discussed, is that it is not made far more emphatically. After they had rated ninety occupations in terms of their "general standing", respondents in the NORC study were immediately asked: "When you say that certain jobs have excellent standing, what do you think is the *one main* thing about such jobs that gives them this standing?" In the outcome, the answers given were quite varied, and, most notably, only 14 % of responses were classified as referring to "social prestige" — as against 40 % referring to potential occupational rewards and 32 % to job or occupational requirements. For the most part, then, as Reiss concludes, respondents "do not appear to have made their evaluations in terms of a conscious awareness of the social prestige attached to the occupation. They are more likely in fact, to emphasize the relevance of indicators sociologists use to measure socio-economic status" [4]. However, despite this significant result, the fact that Reiss continues to speak of the NORC ratings as ones of occupational "prestige" leads to a number of quite unwarranted shifts back to the use of this term in a stricter sense. For instance, Reiss spends some time (pp. 75-77) on the question of why, "contrary to conventional views on the prestige of white-collar work", the occupational group of sales, clerical and kindred workers has a score below that of craftsmen, foremen and kindred workers. But since it appears that most respondents in the NORC study were rating on the basis *not* of social prestige, but rather of occupational rewards or requirements, there is in fact no particular problem here, or at least not of the kind that Reiss raises.

We may then conclude that in the two studies of "occupational prestige" in question — on which nearly all subsequent work has been modelled — underlying theoretical conceptions were, to say the least, uncertain; and further, that whatever interpretation of "prestige" their authors had in mind,

4. Taft (1953) and Tiryakian (1958) also investigated the criteria used by respondents in "occupational prestige" ratings, and in these cases a greater variety of criteria were reported than in the NORC study; also, it was found that respondents used different criteria at different ranges in the scale. However, the NORC findings were confirmed in that only a small minority reported using specifically "prestige" criteria.

it seems most unlikely that the occupational gradings that were produced do in fact measure the relative prestige of occupations in what we would regard as the most sociologically useful sense.

The validation of occupational prestige ratings

In this last connection, some few remarks specifically on the matter of validation might appropriately be added, since the issue of the relationship between concept and empirical indicator is thus, of course, directly posed.

In the British enquiry, it is noteworthy that the validity of the Hall-Jones scale as a measure of prestige is never explicitly considered. This further confirms the view that it is intended to serve as some kind of "composite" social status measure rather than as, say, an indicator of the probability of differential association as initially implied. Assuming this is so, it might be argued that the only validation required is sufficient consensus among respondents to make possible the claim that a publicly recognized hierarchy of "occupational prestige" does exist. Such an argument is in fact advanced by Reiss in regard to the NORC scale: "The validation of a construct like 'general standing' or 'prestige-status structure' rests upon the convergence of evaluations apart from any general agreement upon the criteria for making the evaluations. The high correlations among the ratings for occupations by individuals with ostensibly different evaluative criteria strongly suggest the existence of an underlying and agreed upon structure of occupational prestige" (p. 195) [5].

Consideration of this position will be deferred until later: for the moment, it may be said simply that it appears to be that adopted, implicitly or explicitly, in most other "occupational prestige" studies. The one exception which deserves to be mentioned occurs in the work of Svalastoga (1959). Svalastoga clearly wishes to work with a conception of prestige which approximates the "classical" notion, and in a section of his book specifically devoted to the question of the validity of ratings of occupational prestige gained through conventional methods, he writes (p. 120): "Occupational prestige ratings may be considered valid to the extent, that they correlated with verbal or non-verbal deferential behaviour, shown towards persons having the rated occupations. " The problem then is, of course, that of finding some reliable direct measure of such behaviour, by reference to which validation may be attempted. The approach that Svalastoga adopts, *faute de mieux*, is to examine those occupations included in his study which are embraced

5. This follows Duncan and Artis (1951): "The validation of a construct like general standing, prestige structure or community reputation is not to be found in the uniform conceptualization of a social system by its members, but in the convergence (if it exists) of their several schemes of evaluation upon the same individuals. The problem is not one of a consensus in the realm of values, but of the inter-correlations of the several dimensions of stratification" (p. 21).

by major social organisations such as the civil service, the church, the military, etc. Since positions within these organisations have a formally recognized rank order, prestige ratings may be considered as invalid if they are in contradiction with this order — if, for example, they result in a lower-grade civil servant being rated above a higher-grade one, a dean above a bishop, a captain above a colonel, etc. On the basis of such a test — involving paired comparisons among 13 of his 75 occupations falling into five formal hierarchies — Svalastoga arrives at a best estimate of "the average invalidity of all occupational prestige ratings, reported in this study" of 6 % (p. 120). However, while applauding the way in which Svalastoga faces up to the real issue, one must be highly sceptical about whether he has come at all close to resolving it. First, the occupations to which Svalastoga can apply his test, by virtue of their being incorporated within some formal hierarchy, may well be *ipso facto* less likely to give rise to invalid ratings than other occupations. Secondly and again because of the principle by which the occupations have to be selected, the test can in any case provide only negative results: the fact that the occupations in question are generally rated according to their position in a formal rank order cannot constitute a positive indication that prestige is the basis of the rating, rather than, say, occupational rewards or requirements; for within a bureaucratic organisation *all* these attributes will tend, of course, to be very closely intercorrelated. In other words, Svalastoga's test provides no good grounds for rejecting the view formed on other evidence that conventional "occupational prestige" studies do not specifically tap a distinctive prestige dimension of stratification.

Accepting this conclusion, then, the question which obviously follows is: how should the results of such studies be interpreted? Some answer must be formulated before our third issue, concerning the appropriateness of the uses of these results, can be broached.

The interpretation of occupational prestige ratings

It has been regularly remarked that in occupational prestige ratings, as conventionally carried out, both cognitive and evaluative processes are involved. However, precisely what are supposed to be the objects of these processes has rarely been made clear. For example, if it really were occupational prestige in the sense we would favour which was being assessed, then what would have to be cognized (or, rather, recognized) and evaluated would be the symbolic significance of certain features of an occupation with regard to the chances of those engaged in the occupation meeting with deference, acceptance or derogation in their relations with others. If, for instance, the occupational "stimulus" given were that of "coal miner", a possible response might be on the lines of

"dirty, degrading work" ⟶ "rough, uncultivated men" ⟶ "likely to be looked down on by most groups" or, alternatively perhaps

"difficult, dangerous work" → "able, courageous men" → "likely to be respected by many groups"

But is this in fact the kind of thing that usually happens? As we have seen, there is little reason to believe so, at least if we are guided by respondents' own accounts of what chiefly influenced their ratings. Rather, we would suggest, the operation that most respondents have tended to perform (perhaps in accordance with the principle of least effort) is a far more obvious and simple one: namely, that of rating the occupations on the basis of what they know, or think they know, about a number of objective characteristics, evaluated in terms of what they contribute to the general "goodness" of a job. In other words — and consistently with their own accounts — respondents in occupational prestige studies have not typically been acting within a distinctively "prestige" frame of reference at all. The sensitivity to symbolic indications of social superiority and inferiority which this would imply has not usually been evoked by the task of grading set them. Rather, this task has led them to assess occupations only in some far less specific fashion, according to a composite judgment on an assortment of their attributes which might be thought of as more or less desirable [6].

Such an interpretation of what "occupational prestige" ratings are actually about would seem, moreover, to fit far better with what is known of the pattern of variation in such ratings than would the idea that they relate to prestige *stricto sensu*. The basic feature of this pattern is that while some considerable amount of disagreement in rating occurs as between *individuals*, differences between the mean ratings of age, sex, regional, occupational and other collectivities are never very great. If one assumes that in making their judgments, respondents more or less consciously *a*) consider a number of different occupational attributes which they take as determining how "good" a job is; *b*) attach some subjective "weight" to each of these; *c*) for each occupation presented apply their rating "formula" to what they know about the occupation, and thus; *d*) come to some overall assessment of it — then one might well anticipate some appreciable degree of variation in ratings at the individual level. Individuals are likely to differ in their familiarity with particular jobs and in their priorities as regards what makes a job "good". However, one would not expect — other than in somewhat special and limited cases [7] — that such differences would be socially structured in any very striking way. Knowledge about the more general characteristics of other than rather eso-

6. As regards the NORC study, it is worth recalling what is usually forgotten: that this enquiry, at least in the view of those who devised it, was in fact specifically aimed at finding out what people thought were the best jobs, in the sense of the most desirable. Where "prestige" and "standing" are referred to in the initial report on the study, they are obviously equated with desirability. See NORC (1947).

7. *E.g.* where respondents are rating occupations within their own status or situs areas, *cf.* Gerstl and Cohen (1964).

teric occupations is relatively "open"; and, again in general terms, the kinds of thing thought of as "good" in a job are unlikely to give rise to systematic differences in ratings, especially since there is, in any case, a clear tendency for such advantages to go together. To take a particular example — from the NORC data — it is not surprising, given an interpretation of the kind we have proposed, that individuals should quite often disagree about the ratings of "building contractor" *vis-à-vis* "welfare-worker" — nor that, at the same time, in the case of age, sex, regional, occupational or other categories, the former job should invariably have the higher *mean* rating (*cf.* Reiss, 1961, pp. 55-56; 225-228) [8].

On the other hand, if we were to suppose that "occupational prestige" scores did give a valid indication of a structure of prestige relations, then the degree of consensus that is shown among different social groups would indeed be remarkable, at least in those societies where other research has indicated some notable diversity in value systems and in particular between members of different social strata. For in this case it would not be a matter of evaluative consensus simply on what attributes make a job "good", but rather on certain symbolic criteria of generalized superiority and inferiority, with all their attitudinal and behavioural implications. As Shils has observed, the conditions necessary for an entirely, or even a largely, "integrated" prestige order to exist are in fact demanding ones. It would seem, therefore, the safest assumption to make that, within modern industrial societies, such conditions will prevail only locally, transiently, or imperfectly, and thus that social relations expressive of a prestige order will occur only in an intermittent or discontinuous fashion. On the basis of available empirical data, one might suggest that while derogation is still quite widely manifest — as, for example, in the form of differential association or status-group exclusivity — the claim to superiority thus made by one group is not necessarily, or even usually, acknowledged by those regarded as inferior; that is to say, the latter are often not inclined to display deference [9]. This refusal may be revealed passively — by disregard for the claim to superiority, in that no particular "respect" is shown, and little concern to reduce social distance from the "superior" group; or, perhaps, some direct challenge to the claim may be made where

8. Our interpretation of the meaning of "occupational prestige" ratings is also consistent with the fact that certain variations in the task set to respondents appear to make little difference to the results achieved: *e.g.* whether respondents are asked to rate occupations according to their "social prestige", "social standing", "social status", "general desirability", etc.: or whether they are asked for their own opinions or what they believe are generally prevailing opinions. It seems reasonable to suppose that if respondents are required to grade occupations according to any one criterion, which, while rather imprecise, implies a "better-worse" dimension, they will produce results of the kind in question; and further, that the level of consensus in this respect is such that the distinction between personal and general opinion is of little consequence — provided that there is no suggestion of a normative judgment being required, that is, one in terms of which jobs *ought* to be the best.

9. *Cf.* for example, Goldthorpe, Lockwood, Bechhofer and Platt (1969), chapters 4 and 5.

real interests are felt to be threatened by it — as, say, by "exclusivity" in housing areas, use of amenities, etc.

In the light of the foregoing we may now move on to consider the third issue that we raised in regard to occupational prestige studies — that of how far the uses of their results in stratification theory and research have been appropriate ones.

The uses of "occupational prestige" ratings

One notable use of the data in question results from the fact that over the last two decades occupational prestige studies have been carried out in a steadily increasing number of countries at different levels of economic development. The opportunity has therefore arisen of making cross-national comparisons which, it has been supposed, can throw light on the relationship between value systems and social structural characteristics and are thus relevant to the thesis of the "convergent" development of societies as industrialism advances. For example, Inkeles and Rossi (1956), comparing occupational prestige ratings in studies from six industrial societies, showed that a high degree of similarity prevailed. On this basis, they concluded that common structural features of these societies were of greater influence on the evaluation of occupations than were differences in cultural traditions. Subsequently, however, occupational prestige ratings from several countries as yet little industrialized have *also* been shown to be broadly in line with the hierarchy found in economically advanced societies — insofar, that is, as comparisons can be made. This result has then led to the modified argument (Hodge, Treiman and Rossi, 1966) that what is chiefly reflected in prestige ratings is the set of structural features shared by national societies of *any* degree of complexity — "specialized institutions to carry out political, religious, and economic functions, and to provide for the health, education and welfare of the population". Occupations at the top of these institutional structures, it is suggested, are highly regarded because of their functional importance and also because they are those which require the most training and ability and those to which the highest rewards accrue. Thus, "any major prestige inversion would produce a great deal of inconsistency in the stratification system" (p. 310).

In this way, therefore, it is clearly indicated how occupational prestige data may further be employed in support of a general theory of social stratification of a structural-functional type. Such an application has in fact been made quite explicitly in the work of Barber (1957). Following a Parsonian approach, Barber takes the results of the Inkeles-Rossi study as the main empirical foundation for the view that the factual order of stratification in modern societies tends in the main to be consistent with the dominant normative order. Inequality in social rewards and relationships, it is held, is structured in accordance with functional "needs", and this arrangement is then seen as receiving general moral support: "functionally important roles are congruent with or partly determine a system of values" (p. 6).

Clearly, for occupational prestige data to be used in the ways in question, it is necessary to assume that such data reflect prevailing values and norms *of a particular kind*: ones pertaining to the "goodness" — in the sense of the "fairness" or "justice" — of the existing distribution of social power and advantage. However, in view of our previous discussion, it is difficult to regard such an assumption as a valid one or indeed to understand why it ever should have been made. Even if it were to be supposed that data on publicly recognized occupational hierarchies do indicate a prestige order in something approximating the classical conception, it still then would not follow that they can provide evidence that the objective reality of stratification is morally legitimated. For while prestige relations do depend upon a certain range of shared understandings, consensus on principles of distributive justice is not necessarily involved [10]. Moreover, as we have argued, by far the most plausible interpretation is that occupational prestige ratings reflect prevailing ideas at a much lower level of abstraction: that is, ideas of what is "good" in the sense simply of what is generally found desirable in an occupation. And if *this* is the case, then the consensus that exists is obviously of no very great moral or legitimatory significance at all. Apart from quite unsurprising agreement on such matters as, for example, that high pay is preferable to low pay, more security to less, qualifications to lack of qualifications, etc., the consensus that is implied is of a cognitive and perceptual kind, not an evaluative one. The fact that, on average, all groups and strata agree that certain occupations should be rated higher than others tells one nothing at all about whether the occupational hierarchy that is thus represented is regarded as that which *ought* to exist. And insofar as the publicly recognized hierarchy corresponds to that proposed by structural-functional theorists, this would seem to indicate no more than that broadly similar sets of rating criteria are being applied: *i.e.* occupational rewards and occupational requirements [11].

Thus, as regards the utilization of occupational prestige data in the advancement of stratification theory, our view must be that this has been fundamen-

10. In fact, one might suggest the hypothesis that societies of the kind in which an integrated and stable prestige order is to be found will tend to be ones in which the factual order of stratification is not commonly appraised in terms of distributive justice, or indeed envisaged as capable of being in any way substantially different from what it is.

The distinction between the recognition of prestige and the attribution of justice is foreshadowed — as are several other points in the above paragraph — by Gusfield and Schwartz (1963) in a paper that has been curiously neglected by subsequent American writers on occupational grading.

11. It is a well-known problem of the structural-functional theory of stratification that other usable criteria of the functional importance of occupational roles are hard to find: employing the two criteria in question does, of course, introduce a serious degree of circularity into the argument.

tally misguided. What, now, of their application in research? Primarily, of course, occupational prestige ratings have been used in studies of social mobility, in which they have constituted the hierarchy — scalar or categorical — in the context of which mobility has been assessed. Assumptions about what prestige ratings rate are thus necessarily involved in the interpretation of mobility patterns, and the crucial issues that arise are once more ones of "validity".

Concerning the question: What, in mobility studies, may occupational prestige ratings be taken to indicate? — three main positions can be distinguished. These can be usefully considered in turn, together with their implications and problems.

1) Ratings may be taken — as, for example, by Svalastoga — as indicative of the position of an occupation within a prestige order; that is, as indicative of the chances of those holding that occupation encountering deference, acceptance or derogation in their social lives. In this case, therefore, mobility between different occupational levels, other than of a marginal kind, may be interpreted as involving the probability of subcultural and relational discontinuity. While such a perspective does not necessarily mean that society is seen as divided up into more or less discrete strata, it does imply that social mobility, as measured, is not just a matter of individuals gaining more qualifications, more income, more interesting work, etc., but further of their experiencing changes in their life-styles and patterns of association. The difficulty is, however, as already remarked, that the validity of occupational prestige ratings construed in this way has never been established, and that there are indeed strong grounds for doubting their validity. In other words, we are simply not in a position to infer, with any acceptable degree of precision and certitude, what are the typical consequences of mobility, as measured via occupational prestige ratings, for the actual social experience of those deemed to be mobile.

2) Prestige ratings may be taken as indicative of the status of occupations in the generic sense earlier distinguished — that is, as being in effect comparable with composite measures of "socio-economic" status, derived from data on income, education, housing, possessions, etc. Justification for this position is twofold: first, to repeat the observation of Reiss, respondents in prestige-rating studies appear "to emphasize the relevance of indicators sociologists use to measure socio-economic status"; secondly, as shown by Duncan (1961), it is possible, at least in the American case, to predict prestige ratings fairly accurately from census data on occupational income and education. If, then, "occupational prestige" is understood in the way in question, some reasonable basis may be claimed for interpreting occupationally-measured mobility in terms of movement between grades of occupation differentiated chiefly by their levels of rewards and requirements. At the same time, though, it must be emphasized that in this case no good grounds exist for any interpretation in terms of prestige *stricto sensu*, and, of course, no basis at all for any conside-

ration of how far mobility may be incongruent from one form of stratification to another. Precisely because of the inevitably "synthetic" nature (Ossowski, 1963) of socio-economic status, as indicated by prestige scores, the analysis of mobility must be strictly unidimensional. These limitations would lead one to suggest, therefore, that if it is accepted that occupational prestige ratings are not valid indicators of a prestige order but are being used simply to stand proxy for socio-economic status, then it would be preferable, where possible, to seek to measure the latter more directly — and without any concern to combine components so that a good "fit" with prestige scores may be obtained. To discard the notion of prestige altogether would, in this case, mean losing nothing but the possibility of terminological confusion; and developing separate indices of occupational income, education, etc., as well as some composite measure, would permit the analysis of mobility in a multi-dimensional manner. In short, there seems no good argument for basing mobility research on occupational prestige ratings, interpreted as socio-economic status scores, other than where a lack of data on the socio-economic attributes of occupations makes this procedure an unavoidable *pis aller*.

3) Prestige ratings may be taken as indicating popular evaluations of the relative "goodness" of occupations in terms of the entire range of prevailing criteria. In this case, related mobility data are open to interpretation as showing, basically, the chances of individuals entering more or less desirable grades of occupation, given certain grades of origin. While an interpretation of the data on these lines has rarely, if ever, been pursued consistently throughout a mobility study, it is that which, on grounds of validity, could best be defended. First, as we have already argued, grading occupations according to notions of their general "goodness" is what respondents in occupational prestige studies appear, in the main, to be doing. Secondly, it is in regard to *this* understanding of prestige scores that it would seem most relevant to claim, following Duncan and Artis and Reiss, that their validity lies in the degree of consensus which emerges, despite the use of quite various criteria of evaluation. The argument that this consensus points to "the existence of an underlying and agreed upon structure of occupational prestige" is difficult to sustain once it is recognized just what consensus on a prestige order entails. But the idea of a broadly agreed upon ordering of occupations in terms of "goodness" does, on the evidence in question, receive some clear — and not very surprising — support. Furthermore, if prestige ratings are taken as indicative of an occupational hierarchy of this kind, then the fact that they represent synthetic judgments and cannot be "disaggregated" is no longer a problem in the analysis of mobility patterns. For if mobility is being interpreted as being simply between grades of occupation of differing desirability in some overall sense, a unidimensional approach would appear the appropriate one. However, it must be added that what would then be a dubious and potentially dangerous step would be to shift from such an interpretation of specifically occu-

pational mobility to one in which conclusions were drawn regarding the stability of status groups, income classes, or social strata in any sense whatsoever; that is, conclusions regarding *social* mobility as generally understood. In effect, of course, a shift of this nature has been made in most large-scale mobility studies carried out in the recent past. But while it might reasonably be held that such a manoeuvre is unlikely to be very misleading so far as the "gross" patterns of social mobility are concerned, the difficulty is (apart from the limitation of unidimensionality) that we have no way of knowing at just *what* point and in *what* ways it might turn out to be quite deceptive. Yet again, the problem of validity recurs.

The general — and rather pessimistic — conclusion to which one is led is, therefore, the following: that to the extent that the meaning of occupational prestige ratings is correctly construed, the less useful they appear to be as a basis for mobility studies which pursue the "classical" sociological interests of mobility research.

Empirical questions which arise

The discussion of the foregoing paragraphs has to a large extent been concerned with conceptual and methodological issues. However, it is possible to think of a number of questions which are relevant to the arguments we have deployed, which could be determined — or at least explored — empirically, and which remain so far unanswered. It is to *some* of these questions that we now turn.

To begin with, it would obviously be of value to know more on the matter of just how individuals do grade — or are capable of grading — occupations when occupational titles are in some way presented to them. We have argued that occupational prestige ratings, as collected via conventional methods, should be interpreted as indicating popular conceptions of the general "goodness" of occupations. But is this the only kind of grading that can be reliably elicited? If our view is correct, then the possibility should exist, in principle at least, of obtaining gradings on various more specific criteria, which would differ systematically, even if not perhaps substantially, from conventional occupational prestige ratings — as well, of course, as from each other. And of particular interest here would be to investigate whether such discrimination can be achieved on criteria relating to dimensions of stratification which, in the classical literature and subsequently, it has been found theoretically important to distinguish — including, perhaps, that of prestige in the classical sense [12].

Furthermore, our interpretation of conventional occupational prestige ratings is specifically opposed to the idea that these ratings are evaluative in

12. Assuming, that is (which may well be doubtful) that in modern societies a recognizable prestige order actually exists to be "tapped" in this way.

the sense that they imply moral approval of the occupational hierarchy which they serve to constitute. For example, we would hold that this hierarchy cannot be taken — as it is by structural-functional theorists — as indicating how occupations are seen as receiving legitimately differentiated rewards in accordance with their relative importance in meeting societal needs. If, then, our argument is sound, it should be possible for us to show that there exists some significant degree of discrepancy between ratings of the kind in question and those that result when respondents' specifically normative assessments *are* obtained.

Further still, if we assume that individuals *do* in general have the ability to grade occupations on different dimensions in some meaningful fashion, then another whole set of questions can usefully be posed. One can ask not only how far particular occupations or groups of occupations are "in line" or discrepant when "normative" and "non-normative" assessments are compared, but also about discrepancies in their ratings on different non-normative dimensions. In other words, one could, in principle, investigate the *perceived* degree of "status crystallization" throughout the occupational structure. From this, it is not a long step to thinking in terms of typologies of occupations based on their differing "profiles" across the dimensions considered. Such typologies, if they could be established, could then be taken as reflecting "cognitive maps" of the occupational structure which popularly prevail, and could obviously be used in the analysis of occupational mobility data to investigate the advantages of working on a multidimensional basis, rather than with the unidimensional notion of occupational "goodness".

Finally, exploring issues of the kind in question must in turn reopen the whole matter of consensus. We have previously used our interpretation of the meaning of conventional occupational prestige ratings to suggest an explanation of the patterns of consensus (and dissensus) which these ratings display. Specifically, we have claimed that the consensus which is in evidence at the level of groups and strata has far more a cognitive than an evaluative character. If a primarily normative assessment of the occupational hierarchy could in some way be obtained, then, following our arguments and in the light of existing data on subcultural differences, we would expect far more structured (as well as individual) disagreement to be revealed. Moreover, even with the ostensibly non-normative grading of occupations, one might anticipate some increase in dissensus of this kind where respondents were required to make their ratings multidimensionally. For one thing, there would then of course exist the possibility of disagreement not only about the rating of occupations on any one dimension but also about the shape of their profiles across a number of them. And, in addition, socially patterned differences in values could conceivably show more influence on judgments relating to fairly specific criteria than on ones of a more comprehensive kind, where possibilities for "cancelling out" would be the greater.

The conception of a pilot study

Chiefly to investigate how empirical issues such as those raised above might best be approached, we planned a pilot study in multi-dimensional occupational grading on the following lines:

1) Forty occupational titles were selected. These included 28 out of the 30 titles used in the Hall-Jones study, for which there exists a known ordering on the basis of a conventional prestige-rating task. The two titles omitted were both ones which had become rather archaic: coal hewer and carter. The remaining 12 titles were chosen mainly so as to compensate for the under-representation in the Hall-Jones list of manual factory jobs or because they seemed ones very likely to provide instances of "discrepant" ratings (*e.g.* psychiatrist, ballet dancer).

2) Four rating criteria were selected. Three were chosen with the familiar distinction among the "economic", the "prestige" and the "power" aspects of stratification in mind. They were: "Standard of living", "Prestige in the community " and "Power and influence over other people". As the fourth criterion, we sought one which would induce respondents to make primarily normative assessments, rather than ones which might be supposed to be largely descriptive. Previous investigations have suggested that if respondents are asked directly to rate occupations according to what *should* be their "general standing", etc., they tend to experience some difficulty in maintaining a normative stance throughout the exercise (Turner, 1958). We decided, therefore, to adopt a rather different approach and to ask respondents to rate occupations according to their "Value to society". In this case, we believed, it could be argued that, regardless of how respondents themselves construed what they were doing, the judgments they made must be determined primarily by values which they held rather than directly by their perception of some aspects of social fact. Notions of the Standard of living, Prestige in the community and Power and influence over other people which attach to occupations are ones with some generally accepted empirical referents (although arguably in differing degree). This is not so with Value to society: one could not, for example, "refute" ratings on this criterion by recourse simply to logic and evidence. Thus, in this case, it is difficult to see how the makings of relatively "pure" value judgments can actually be avoided [13].

3) Ten respondents were selected. Because we thought it premature at this stage to tackle questions of variation in ratings between different groups, strata, etc., we did not aim for a large number of respondents nor to have a

13. This is not to claim, of course, that one will necessarily or even probably get respondents' considered, personal judgments, rather that some more or less "stock" cultural or subcultural response. But the *form* of the response will be an evaluative one.

sample of any particular population. Rather, we chose individuals from among our relatives, friends and acquaintances of both sexes so as to have as socially heterogeneous a group as could be arranged[14].

4) It was decided that respondents should perform the same rating task on two different occasions, separated by an interval of a week. In this way we would have some opportunity for checking on how far the occupational gradings produced by our respondents did appear to reflect their actual perceptions, evaluations, etc., rather than being the result of operations more or less arbitrarily performed simply in order to satisfy the investigators.

Table 1. *The forty occupational titles ranked by the respondents*

1. Agricultural labourer	21. Insurance agent
2. Ambassador to a foreign country	22. Jobbing master builder
3. Ballet dancer	23. Medical officer
4. Barman	24. News reporter
5. Bricklayer	25. Newsagent and tobacconist
6. Bus driver	26. Nonconformist minister
7. Business manager	27. Policeman
8. Car worker	28. Primary school teacher
9. Carpenter	29. Psychiatrist
10. Chartered accountant	30. Quarry worker
11. Chef	31. Railway porter
12. Civil servant (Executive)	32. Road sweeper
13. Commercial traveller	33. Routine clerk
14. Company director	34. Sheet metal worker
15. Country solicitor	35. Shop assistant
16. Dock labourer	36. Social worker
17. Farmer (over 100 acres)	37. State registered nurse
18. Fireman	38. Tractor driver
19. Fitter	39. TV announcer
20. Foreman in a factory	40. Works manager

In Part 2 of this report, the methods and results of the pilot study are presented in detail. The potential relevance of the type of data and the analytical technique to the issues set out above should be evident. This potential will, it is hoped, be realized when more adequate data have been collected.

2. Results from a pilot experiment

Method

Each occupational title in Table 1 was typed on a 5″ × 1½″ piece of card, and the corresponding number from the table was written on the back of the

14. The Appendix describes a subsequent study of ratings by ten persons drawn from the electoral register of Oxford. An enquiry based on a larger sample is under way at the time of writing.

card. Each respondent was asked to rank all occupations on each of four dimensions. In some cases the respondent rated Standard of living before Prestige in the community. Other respondents took these two dimensions in the opposite order (see Table 2; the order for a particular subject was randomly determined). These were always the first two dimensions to be employed. In every case Power and influence over other people came third and Value to society came last.

Table 2. *Characteristics of the ten respondents*

Respondent	Sex	R.G.'s social class 1966	Order of presentation*
—	—	—	—
A	M	I Nm	S
B	F	I Nm	P
C	M	I Nm	S
D	F	I Nm	P
E	M	III Nm	S
F	F	III Nm	S
G	M	III M	S
H	M	IV Nm	P
I	F	V M	P
J	F	V M	P

* S indicates that the respondent rated "Standard of living" first; P indicates that the respondent rated "Prestige in the community" first.

The respondent was seated at a large table. The experimenter shuffled the cards and handed two or three to the respondent saying:

Here you have forty cards. On each is the name of an occupation. I'm going to ask you to rate these forty occupations in a number of different respects. The first of these is *standard of living*[15]. I would like you to arrange the cards in a column, so that the occupation which you think carries *the highest standard of living* is at the top, with the rest following in order until you have the occupation carrying *the lowest standard of living* at the very bottom. If you think that any two or more occupations have the same *standard of living*, just put their cards side by side in the column. You can put as many cards side by side as you like. Try to think of the occupations generally, and *not* of particular people in them. Take as much time as you need and change your mind as much as you want as you go along. Have you any questions? Shall I repeat that?

The cards were spread out on the table and the respondent was left to sort them at his leisure. He was occasionally reminded of the name of the dimension he was employing. When he had finished, the experimenter recorded the results on a schedule. Starting from the top of the column, he picked up the cards in order, recording a 1 against the occupational title(s) in the top rank, a 2 against the title(s) in the second rank, and so on. The highest number recorded was the number of separate ranks employed by the respondent.

The cards were shuffled and the subject was asked to rank the titles on the

15. "Prestige in the community" for some respondents.

second dimension (Prestige in the community or Standard of living); then again on Power and influence over other people; then on Value to society.

During the course of the experiment a respondent was sometimes asked what he had in mind as he ranked the occupations on a particular dimension and his observations were recorded. At the end of the session it was arranged that he would attend again one week later "to discuss results". At the second session the task was repeated exactly as on the first occasion. The respondent was asked not to think back to how he rated the occupations on the previous occasion but to rate them as he felt now. The order of presentation of Standard of living and Prestige in the community was the same on both occasions for each individual.

Distribution of ranks

On each dimension a respondent could utilize up to forty ranks or grades. In fact, on the first occasion of testing, this number was used in only two out of forty sets of rankings. The mean number of grades employed by the ten respondents was 27.9 for Prestige, 24.2 for Standard of living, 21.8 for Power and influence, and 17.9 for Value to society. On the second occasion the corresponding means were, respectively, 20.5, 20.3, 18.4 and 16.5. Ties were more frequent in the ascription of value than they were in the assessment of the other three characteristics. The nature of the ties was explored further by calculating, separately for each set of rankings, the correlation (tau_h [16]) between the grade to which an occupation or occupations were assigned and the number of occupations assigned to that grade. Insofar as ties tend to occur in the upper levels of the occupational distribution tau is positive, and insofar as ties occur among the low-ranking occupations tau is negative. The nearer the ties congregate towards one extreme the higher is the absolute value of tau.

16. tau_h (Hope, 1968, p. 278) is a rank correlation coefficient which always has attainable limits of ± 1. It has as its numerator Kendall's (1962) S. Its denominator is the maximum value S can take subject to the constraint that the marginal totals of the contingency table from which S_{max} is calculated are identical with those of the observed table.

The application of tau_h in the text is rather unusual and may be illustrated by an example in which a respondent, grading occupations on a certain dimension, groups the forty cards into only seven rows or ranks. The frequency distribution might then be

Rank	Number of occupations
1	9
2	6
3	6
4	7
5	3
6	5
7	4
	40

The mean of all eighty values of tau is -0.28, and the mean of the eight values for a respondent is negative for each of the ten respondents. We conclude, therefore, that tying tends to occur among the occupations which the respondent assigns to the lower end of a dimension. It must, however, be remembered that the tenor of the instructions encouraged respondents to begin their ranking task at the top end of the scale.

A mean tau was computed for each of the four dimensions. There is some evidence here that Power and influence (mean tau -0.44) shows greater skew than the other three dimensions (for which the means lie between -0.21 and -0.25). There was little difference between mean taus for the two occasions.

Isolating the elements of occupational status[17]

The preceding analysis has explicitly taken into account differences among respondents and among dimensions in the shape and scatter of the frequency distributions. The analysis to which we now come deliberately irons out all such differences, so far as this is possible. The ten respondents, each employing four dimensions on two occasions, supplied eighty columns of ratings, each column containing rankings of forty occupational titles. In the following analysis the rank assigned to an occupation is treated as a score, and a mean and standard deviation are calculated for each of the eighty columns of scores. Each score is then centred and standardized by, firstly, expressing it as a deviation from its column mean and, secondly, dividing this deviation by the column standard deviation. The standard deviations were calculated with 40 - 1 = 39 degrees of freedom. The resulting 40 × 80 matrix of centred and standardized scores has a sum of squares of 39 × 80 = 3 120.

The justification for these preparatory procedures is implicit in the design of the experiment. The collection of the data was planned in such a way that they conform to the pattern of a completely-crossed four-factor design in the

This distribution may be laid in the form of a contingency table as follows:

		Frequency					
		9	7	6	5	4	3
Rank	1	9	0	0	0	0	0
	2	0	0	6	0	0	0
	3	0	0	6	0	0	0
	4	0	7	0	0	0	0
	5	0	0	0	0	0	3
	6	0	0	0	5	0	0
	7	0	0	0	0	4	0

Kendall's S and tau_h are then computed from the elements of the table in the usual way. In this example they are clearly positive in sign.

17. Throughout the second part of this paper "status" is used in the purely locational sense of position on an axis.

analysis of variance. The virtue of the analysis of variance in a rating experiment is that it enables the research worker to identify a number of possible elements or sources of variance and to uniquely ascribe a quantity to each source which is an indication of its relative importance. This quantification of importance is possible so long as the experimenter is able to specify a model which may be supposed to generate the data.

The terms and procedures of the analysis of variance are not, of course, primarily designed for data-reduction in rating experiments, and it is not pretended that the model which is adopted can be defended in the same terms as in the analysis of a more typical experimental design, where independent errors may be supposed to be generated by a truly random process. Nevertheless, at several points in the analysis the results of the application of the model are examined to see whether or not the data are behaving as if they conformed to the canons of analysis of variance. The fact that no noticeable malfunctioning of the model is detected is at least negative evidence for its appropriateness and may stimulate theoretical workers to elaborate a rationale for this kind of application.

The design to which the data conform is a four-factor Occupations × Respondents × Occasions × Dimensions (40 × 10 × 2 × 4) design. Because the data have been centred for all factors except the first the variance of the remaining three terms, and the variance of all possible interactions among the three, is necessarily zero. The justification of this brutal elimination of so many possible effects is simply that the mean of a column of ranks is an artefact, and comparison among such means would be comparison of artefacts. The justification for standardizing every column of ranks is that, although differences in column variances are of interest, we do not wish to give greater weight to a particular column simply because it has a high variance. By equating the variances we equate the contribution of each column to the analysis.

Factors involved in the ascription of status

The sums of squares and mean squares of the effects which have not been eliminated are shown in Table 3. It will be seen that the analysis accounts for the total sum of squares of the 40 × 80 matrix of scores. In order to estimate the relative importance of the terms we must specify a model which indicates the components of variance which, when weighted and linearly combined, constitute the mean squares. The model we have employed is of the kind which is known as mixed because it comprises effects of two different sorts: random effects and fixed effects. We propose to regard Occupations [18], Respondents and Occasions as random effects. It must be admitted that the occupational titles and the respondents were not, in fact, chosen randomly

18. The nature of the Occupations terms is disputable. However, it is not in fact necessary to specify whether Occupations is fixed or random since, in their present application, the equations of the model are identical whichever view we take.

from a population of titles and persons, but they were chosen with an eye to their representativeness. We are not simply interested in conclusions about these particular occupations and these particular persons, rather we wish to use the evidence of the study for which this is a pilot as a means of gaining information about general attitudes to the whole range of occupations. If we are mistaken in treating the occupations and respondents as if they were random samples from wider populations the data may belie us by throwing up negative estimates of variance. In the event we shall see that no negative variance of any size does, in fact, occur in our pilot analysis, and this is encouraging, though it is not a sufficient proof of the adequacy of our model.

Dimensions differs from the other three factors in that we are interested in drawing conclusions about these specific axes of stratification, so we regard Dimensions as a fixed effect. (In fact, the estimates of variance would be very little altered if Dimensions too was treated as random.)

In this analysis there is no estimate of random error other than the third-order interaction term, that is the interaction of all four main terms. In a mixed model it is necessary to distinguish these two components because it is not the case, as it is with a completely random model, that both contribute to the mean square of every other term. In carrying through the analysis it has been assumed that the third-order interaction variance is zero and the whole of the mean square for this effect is attributable to error [19].

Having specified the model it is a simple matter to write the equations using Schultz's (1955) rules of thumb, and to estimate the component of variance attributable to each term in the analysis (Table 3). It can be seen that two of the estimates are negative. If these quantities had been large we should have had reason to doubt the appropriateness of the model; the fact that they are practically zero is reassuring.

The structure of the social status of occupations

Examination of the components reveals a fairly simple hierarchy of three levels of importance:

a) Occupations, which accounts for over half the total variance,

b) Occupations × Respondents, Occupations × Dimensions, and Occupations × Respondents × Dimensions, each of which accounts for about ten percent of the variance,

c) the remaining three terms (apart from error) which have practically zero importance [20].

19. Stanley (1961) writes : "Probably we are well advised to design fuller studies, in which each rater rates each ratee (occupation) at least twice on each trait (dimension). Then there will be a third-order interaction mean square whose mathematical expectation more nearly approaches pure measurement error than does the expected mean square for the second-order interaction." The examination of the third-order term which we carry out below tends to bear out Stanley's advice.

20. The sum of the variance components in Table 3 is 1.0570. If we had assumed a completely random model then the sum would have been unity.

Table 3. *Analysis of variance and estimates of components of variance. "Occupations", "Respondents" and "Occasions" are assumed to be random and "Dimensions" is assumed to be fixed*

Source	d.f.	Sum of squares	Mean square	Variance component
Occupations	39	1868.2842	47.9047	0.5853
Occupations × Respondents	351	380.8301	1.0850	0.1164
Occupations × Occasions	39	5.9333	0.1521	-0.0000
Occupations × Dimensions	117	318.2015	2.7197	0.1195
Occupations × Respondents × Occasions	351	53.9829	0.1538	0.0088
Occupations × Respondents × Dimensions	1053	355.0089	0.3371	0.1093
Occupations × Occasions × Dimensions	117	13.0362	0.1114	-0.0007
Error	1053	124.7228	0.1184	0.1184
Sum	3120	3119.9999	-	1.0570

As a shorthand means of referring to the terms of the analysis let us assign the letters J (for "Jobs"), R, O and D respectively to the factors Occupations, Respondents, Occasions and Dimensions. Then a combination of letters will refer to the interaction of the factors signified.

The terms which have negligible variance indicate: (JO) that, taking the sample of ten persons as a whole, there is no systematic tendency for some occupations to rise in status between first and second testing while others fall; (JRO) that neither is there any such tendency in the ratings of the individual respondents; nor (JOD) is there any such tendency for the sample as a whole when dimensions are looked at individually. We cannot ask whether there is systematic change in the ratings of individual occupations by individual respondents on individual dimensions because we have set the variance of the third-order interaction term to zero by assumption. The fact that the reliability of the individual element of our 40×80 score matrix is $(1/0.1184) - 1.0570 = 0.89$ is an indication that further scope for the reduction of error is limited.

The lesson of the preceding paragraph is that there is no systematic change of mind between the two occasions of testing. In future work retesting of respondents may well prove unnecessary, unless for the purpose of estimating random error.

The three terms which each contribute about ten percent to the total variance of an individual score indicate (JR) that different persons do have different ideas about the relative ranking of occupations, considered as an average over the four dimensions, and that these idiosyncrasies persist from one occasion to the next; (JD) that the sample as a whole, in the sense of the average respondent, discriminates in its use of the four dimensions, in other words that the four dimensions are not treated as synonymous; (JRD) that individual respondents make idiosyncratic differentiations among the dimensions, over and above those made, on average, by the sample.

Although these effects have been shown to exist and they merit discussion, their quantitative importance should not be exaggerated. The size of the variance attributable to Occupations indicates that the most important single effect is simply the mean of an occupational title over all ten respondents, both occasions and all four dimensions. This effect is a vector of forty terms, each being a mean for an occupation over the eighty columns of the centred and standardized data matrix. These occupational means are reported in Table 4, in the column headed "Four dimensions". They have been themselves standardized so as to have a mean of 100 and a standard deviation of 15. This is, in fact, the "general factor" of our four dimensions of social standing. In crude terms its proportionate sum of squares is 1868/3120 or 60 percent of the total sum of squares (Table 3). The refinements introduced by the model assign to it a contribution of 55 percent to the total variance [21].

21. These assessments of its importance differ from that which would be made by a factor analysis in two respects. In the first place the general factor of our analysis is an unweight-

The term "general" is here used in a double sense, since it signifies variance shared by respondents and by dimensions. The factors which we have called idiosyncratic are also general in that they represent variance common to the four dimensions, but they are specific to respondents. Since psychologists have arrogated the term "general" to variance common to several tests or dimensions we propose to refer to the variance of occupations as "common-general" variance, that is, variance which is common to all persons and general over all dimensions. We may then refer to the idiosyncratic variance (the term JR) as "personal-general" variance. The term "personal" should not be taken to imply "unshared", since two or more persons may deviate from the common-general assessment of status in very similar ways. To sum up: "general" implies average status over a number of dimensions, "common" implies average status over all persons, and "personal" implies aspects of status which are not common (*i.e.* universal) but may be shared.

Stability of the structure of occupational gradings

It has been shown that the variance components are of considerable interest in themselves. They may, however, be put to further use in the construction of a number of coefficients which estimate the stability of the structure which the analysis has uncovered. Coefficients of this nature are an elaboration of Fisher's (1958) intraclass correlation coefficient[22]. Previous work has thrown up two basic types of coefficient. These are Mahmoud's (1955) coefficient of person stability and Hope's (1964) coefficient of pattern stability. The title appropriate to either coefficient varies according to the context in which it is employed. We shall here use Mahmoud's coefficient as a measure of the reliability or "function stability" of the status of occupations. It should be noted that the reference of this coefficient is to the stability of the status of occupations rather than to measurement of that status. Hope's coefficient likewise is an index of stability of the effect measured, irrespective of errors in the means of measuring it.

We shall refer to Mahmoud's coefficient as a coefficient of stability of the status or rank of occupations and to Hope's coefficient as a coefficient of stability of status profiles of occupations. Sociologists are accustomed to think

---

ed sum or mean of the four dimensions. The introduction of differential weighting, as by a principal component analysis, would increase its importance somewhat (though experience with the two kinds of analysis in circumstances similar to the present suggests that the increase would not be great). And in the second place the employment of a model takes account of the fact that the sum of squares of the general factor is inflated by higher-order terms in the analysis. In this respect our estimate of 55 % is a double deflation of the comparable figure which would be derived from a principal component analysis. Nevertheless it remains high and is in fact very similar to the value which a psychologist would expect to find for "general ability" in the analysis of variance of a battery of cognitive tests (*cf.* Mahmoud, 1955).

22. The groundwork of this elaboration is largely due to Sir Cyril Burt and it is accessible in Burt (1955) and Mahmoud (1955).

Table 4. *Mean ratings of each occupation. The means have a mean of 100 and a standard deviation of 15*

Occupation	Four dimensions (SPIV)	Three dimensions (SPI)	Difference
	—	—	—
1. Agricultural labourer	82	78	+ 4
2. Ambassador to a foreign country	130	131	— 1
3. Ballet dancer	96	99	— 3
4. Barman	80	84	— 4
5. Bricklayer	86	86	0
6. Bus driver	87	85	+ 2
7. Business manager	117	119	— 2
8. Car worker	92	93	— 1
9. Carpenter	87	87	0
10. Chartered accountant	116	118	— 2
11. Chef	92	93	— 1
12. Civil servant (Executive)	119	119	0
13. Commercial traveller	94	97	— 3
14. Company director	126	129	— 3
15. Country solicitor	118	119	— 1
16. Dock labourer	90	88	+ 2
17. Farmer (over 100 acres)	105	103	+ 2
18. Fireman	100	95	+ 5
19. Fitter	87	87	0
20. Foreman in a factory	102	102	0
21. Insurance agent	97	99	— 2
22. Jobbing master builder	101	102	— 1
23. Medical officer	123	119	+ 4
24. News reporter	113	113	0
25. Newsagent and tobacconist	89	91	— 2
26. Nonconformist minister	106	107	— 1
27. Policeman	112	107	+ 5
28. Primary school teacher	111	106	+ 5
29. Psychiatrist	121	119	+ 2
30. Quarry worker	82	83	— 1
31. Railway porter	79	80	— 1
32. Road sweeper	76	75	+ 1
33. Routine clerk	82	84	— 2
34. Sheet metal worker	90	91	— 1
35. Shop assistant	84	85	— 1
36. Social worker	109	106	+ 3
37. State registered nurse	110	105	+ 5
38. Tractor driver	82	82	0
39. TV announcer	117	121	— 4
40. Works manager	110	111	— 1

of the status of a person or an occupation as more or less "crystallized" (Lenski, 1954). The profile stability coefficient tells us how far we may regard the pattern of departure from crystallization as a constant feature of the occupations. Naturally, we should be surprised to find any ponderable inconstancy over the space of one week.

Earlier factorial studies employing these coefficients (Mahmoud, 1955; Hope, 1964; Pilliner, 1965; Hope and Caine, 1968; Hope, 1969) have been less complex than the four-factor design of the present investigation. The complications of this analysis imply that we must distinguish two forms of each of the coefficients, one which is common in that it refers to averages over all the respondents, and the other which is personal in that it refers to the individual respondents. Let us write lower-case j, r, o and d, and combinations of these letters, for the estimated components of variance in Table 3. Then the coefficient

$$\frac{j}{j + jo} = \frac{0.5853}{0.5853 + (-0.0000)} = 1.00$$

is an index of the stability of the social ranks of occupations (insofar as our respondents form a representative sample of society) over the short interval of one week. We freely concede that this value serves more as a test of our method and our model than as a source of information about society, but we commend the coefficient for future research into status stability over longer periods.

The second version of Mahmoud's coefficient is

$$\frac{jr}{jr + jro} = 0.93$$

which is an index of the stability of an individual's assessment of occupations insofar as that assessment differs from the sample average. It must be allowed, that since this is a measure of idiosyncratic or personal-general deviations from a collective norm of occupational assessment (as represented by the scores averaged over all the respondents), the coefficient is higher than might have been expected. But it would be unwise to place much weight on a ratio of estimates computed for our miscellaneous collection of respondents over a short time interval.

The following two coefficients are, respectively, the common and the personal version of the coefficient introduced by Hope (1964), and they indicate the stability of pattern of ratings over the four dimensions. For example, an occupation with a mean of 120 over the four dimensions (on the standardized scale of Table 4) might have values on the individual dimensions of 125, 115, 110 and 130. Its pattern or profile may be represented in terms of deviations about its mean as +5, —5, —10 and +10. The question which the coefficients of profile or pattern stability seek to answer is, how far do patterns such as this reproduce themselves from occasion to occasion (leaving out of account random measurement error)?

First, we calculate

$$\frac{jd}{jd + jod} = 1.01$$

which is slightly in excess of unity because jod is slightly on the wrong side of zero. This is an estimate of the constancy of the differentiation among the four dimensions which is made by the average respondent. Again, computed for a truly representative sample over a longer time interval it would serve to indicate the degree of change within the "stratification space" of the society which is not simply vertical movement up or down the common-general factor of social standing [23]. So far as the evidence for our respondents goes, stability is complete.

The second version of the profile stability coefficient is conceptually obvious but practically incalculable. It is

$$\frac{\text{jrd}}{\text{jrd} + \text{jrod}}$$

The reason why it is incalculable is that we have explicitly assumed that the third-order interaction term is zero and assigned all its variance to error. Thus, so long as jrd is positive we have, as it were, defined the value of this coefficient as unity.

It would, of course, be useful to be able to assess these coefficients in the light of their standard errors. However, little is known of the standard errors of estimates of components of variance, and still less is known of the properties of ratios of such estimates. In the absence of theory, the sociologist must rely on experience and replication. The three levels of variance components (0 percent, 11 percent and 55 percent) are so clearly differentiated in these data that we are inclined to give credence to the coefficients derived from them.

Dimensions of occupational grading

So far the analysis has been of the four specified dimensions, with each contributing equally to the general factor of the social assessment of occupations. However, in choosing these dimensions we considered that the fourth — Value to society (V) — and possibly also the third — Power and influence over other people (I) — would behave more eccentrically than the first two — Standard of living (S) and Prestige in the community (P). The present analysis has not yet taken account of this possibility. In calculating a mean for an occupational title by averaging over all four dimensions we are implicitly assuming that the four dimensions are symmetrically related to the mean. In fact, the correlations between the four dimensions (each being averaged over all ten respondents and both occasions) and the grand means (averaged over all

23. The concept of a stratification space which is elaborated in the editorial Introduction (*cf.* Hope, ed., 1972) has been found to be most helpful in distinguishing the sorts of ways in which a society may change over time. The statement in the text refers to movements of occupations within the space defined by a set of stratification axes which do not themselves move in relation to one another. It should be noted that in this paper "dimension" is used to mean the same as "axis" in the Introduction.

Table 5. *Correlations among the four dimensions and their correlations with the grand means over all respondents, occasions and dimensions (Table 4)*

	S	P	I	V
Standard of living (S)	1.0000			
Prestige (P)	0.9324	1.0000		
Power and influence (I)	0.8614	0.9484	1.0000	
Value to society (V)	0.5458	0.7401	0.7842	1.0000
Grand mean	0.9144	0.9842	0.9747	0.8166

eighty columns of the data matrix) are (S) 0.91 (P) 0.98 (I) 0.97 and (V) 0.82[24].

These correlations, and the correlation of each pair of dimensions, are shown in Table 5. When the grand mean is partialled out S retains 16 percent of its variance, P retains 3 percent, I retains 5 percent and V retains 33 percent. This suggests that we are correct in supposing that value to society is rather different from the other three dimensions. When V is omitted and the grand means are calculated from the remaining three dimensions (second column of Table 4) S retains 8 percent of its variance, P retains 2 percent and I retains 7 percent.

It will be recalled that twenty-eight of our forty occupations were taken from the list of occupations employed by Hall and Jones (1950). For each of these twenty-eight we converted average rating on each dimension into a rank and we similarly recorded the rank of each occupation in the Hall-Jones study. Both sets of ranks run from 1 to 28; there are no ties. Each of our dimensions was then correlated with the Hall-Jones ranking. The product-moment correlations (with the corresponding value of Kendall's tau in brackets) are: (S) 0.94 (0.81), (P) 0.96 (0.87), (I) 0.85 (0.70), and (V) 0.70 (0.52). We conclude that our non-normative dimensions, particularly Prestige and Standard of living, approximate closely to the dimension which our predecessors measured twenty years ago, but that our normative dimension stands somewhat apart from the non-normative dimensions.

The analysis of variance was repeated for the three dimensions S, P and I (Table 6). Examination of the variance components reveals a distinct increase in the variance due to the common-general factor for occupations, and a corresponding decrease in two of the three middle-ranking variance components. The error component also falls to about 8 percent. The net effect of the changes is to leave the stability of the common-general factor unchanged at 1.00, to reduce the stability of the personal-general factors from 0.93 to 0.88, and to reduce the estimated stability of the status profiles of the occupations from 1.01 to 0.95.

In fact, all possible combinations of two, three and four dimensions were analysed (Table 7). Negative variance components occur in, and only in,

24. The lower correlation for V must in part be due to the difference in distribution between V and the other three dimensions.

Table 6. *Repeat of the analysis reported in Table 3 with one of the dimensions omitted*

Source	d.f.	Sum of squares	Mean square	Variance component
	—	—	—	—
Occupations	39	1677.1405	43.0036	0.7032
Occupations × Respondents	351	276.4568	0.7876	0.1103
Occupations × Occasions	39	5.9327	0.1521	0.0009
Occupations × Dimensions	78	102.1371	1.3095	0.0522
Occupations × Respondents × Occasions	351	44.1437	0.1258	0.0144
Occupations × Respondents × Dimensions	702	167.8402	0.2391	0.0783
Occupations × Occasions × Dimensions	78	8.4425	0.1082	0.0026
Error	702	57.9065	0.0825	0.0825
Sum	2340	2340.0000	-	1.0444

Table 7. *Items drawn from each of the analyses of all possible combinations of four dimensions*

Dimensions	Variance Components: Largest negative	Occupations	Error	Sum	Coefficients: $\frac{j}{j + jo}$	$\frac{jr}{jr + jro}$	$\frac{jd}{jd + jod}$
—	—	—	—	—	—	—	—
SPIV	-0.0007	0.5853	0.1184	1.0507	1.00	0.93	1.01
SPI	-	0 7032	0.0825	1.0444	1.00	0.88	0.95
SPV	-0.0033	0.5464	0.1297	1.0928	1.00	0.99	1.02
SIV	-0 0008	0.5465	0.1250	1.0955	1.00	0.91	1.00
PIV	-0.0019	0.5848	0.1365	1.0715	1.00	0.95	1.02
SP	-	0.7135	0.0831	1.0529	1.00	0.97	0.98
SI	-	0.6975	0.0763	1.0928	1.00	0.84	0.95
PI	-	0.7246	0.0880	1.0539	1.00	0.87	0.92
SV	-0.0040	0.4739	0.1416	1.2168	1.00	0.96	1.01
PV	-0 0077	0.5302	0.1644	1.1478	1.00	1.05	1.04
IV	-0.0029	0.5512	0.1572	1.1201	1.01	0.94	1.01

analyses which include Value to society. But in none is a negative component as large as 1 percent of the total variance. In every case the constancy of the shared-general assessment of the social standing of occupations is 1.00 or 1.01. The personal assessments have stabilities ranging from 0.84 to 1.05, and the status profiles have stabilities ranging from 0.92 to 1.04. Analyses which include Value to society have variance components for the common-general factor which range between 0.47 and 0.59. Those which do not include this dimension have components ranging between 0.70 and 0.73. The implication of Table 7 is that the first three dimensions form a cluster or sheaf while Value to society lies somewhat apart. This is not, of course, to say that S, P and I are indistinguishable. On the contrary, although they are highly correlated (Table 5)[25], the analyses of variance have shown that respondents agree with one another, and with themselves over time, in the differential ranking of occupations along the dimensions.

The choice of Value to society as one of the four dimensions was made in the explicit expectation that there would be less inter-respondent, and perhaps less intra-respondent, agreement on this dimension than on the other three. The findings of this section are consistent with either or both of these suppositions, but it is possible, by analysis of the dimensions severally, to make a direct test of our expectation. A three-factor, Occupations × Respondents × Occasions, analysis of variance was carried out on each of the dimensions. The results for the first three dimensions are remarkably uniform, with the second-order interaction variance component being (S) 0.0800, (P) 0.0950 and (I) 0.1157 and the Occupations component being (S) 0.7391, (P) 0.7280, and (I) 0.7468. But in the analysis of Value to society the second-order interaction component is 0.2184 and the Occupations component is only 0.4856. (These values of the components represent proportions of total variance because the data have been standardized and because each of the three factors of the analysis is random.) The relative extent of evaluative dissensus is indicated by the Occupations × Respondents component of 0.3061 for Value to society compared with not more than 0.18 for any of the other three dimensions. All four Occupations × Occasions components are virtually zero.

We conclude, therefore, that the lower degree of consensus (49 percent compared with 74 percent) on Value to society is partly explained by a greater degree of intra-respondent disagreement (22 percent as against about 10 percent) and partly by a higher degree of dissensus (31 percent as against 13-18 percent). The second-order interaction variance of 22 percent indicates a greater amount of intra-respondent disagreement on the normative dimension, but it is not possible to say whether this is entirely random or whether it includes an element of systematic changes of mind by individual raters.

25. The correlations in Table 5 are for the dimensions averaged over the sample. Their size, therefore, dissembles the personal-general components in the assessment of occupational status.

A surrogate for mean status

One of the purposes of this enquiry was to throw light on the practical problem of assessing occupational status. Two main kinds of relations among the various possible dimensions of such status may be envisaged. In their idealized forms these two possible situations may be represented as follows. On the one hand, we may have a set of dimensions all of which are equidistant from a central dimension, like the ribs of a partly-opened umbrella round its stock, or like the feathers of a fan, one of which is at the centre of the arc. On the other hand, we may have a situation in which no one dimension is central to all the others. If a central dimension exists it is important to find it, because it may be supposed to represent a general measure of the status of occupations. If no central dimension exists then status can be measured without bias only by a careful choice of dimensions which are symmetrically arranged with respect to their centroid.

The problem of finding the central dimension or centroid of status is not an easy one. A full empirical solution might be said to involve the specification of all possible dimensions of status and the measurement of each with the same degree of reliability. But dimensions are, operationally, only forms of words. And a new dimension may be produced from an old one by a very slight alteration in wording. Even the theoretical specification of possible dimensions of status is fraught with conceptual difficulties, and these are of two kinds: those which arise on the borders of the stratification space and those which arise within that space. If we think of a conical space, bounded by axes like the ribs of a partially-opened umbrella, we can always, in imagination, insert an axis which lies at a slightly greater angle to the umbrella stock than do the ribs. So long as it is not at right angles to thc stock this axis will be a correlate, and, therefore, to some extent a measure, of status. And, secondly, if we imagine our space as traversed by axes having no symmetrical relation to one another we may suppose that in our choice of dimensions we inadvertently introduce a bunched axis-set which, in the determination of the position of the central axis of the space, gives undue weight to the part of the space though which it passes. The search for *the* measure of status is not unlike the corollary of universal symmetry which posed such a problem for Newton's cosmology.

The shot-gun method of inventing as many dimensions as possible and getting respondents to rate them is probably impracticable. It may also be theoretically indesirable in that local bunching[26] may occur, and the effect of this bunching may be exaggerated by differential reliability of the ratings of the various dimensions.

26. Some kinds of bunching would be worse than others. There is always the possibility that the bunches may be symmetrically arranged with respect to the general factor of status. Furthermore, distortions are less serious if the angles between the most dissimilar axes are of only moderate size, that is if the dimensions are highly correlated.

Table 8. *Percentages of variance remaining to each dimension after partialling out the grand mean in every possible combination of the dimensions*

Dimensions	S	P	I	V
SPIV	16	3	5	33
SPI	8	2	7	-
SPV	15	3	-	33
SIV	19	-	5	30
PIV	-	8	5	22
SP	3	3	-	-
SI	7	-	7	-
PI	-	3	3	-
SV	19	-	-	27
PV	-	11	-	15
IV	-	-	9	13

The alternative approach is to choose a few theoretically significant dimensions as carefully as possible with the aim of spanning the space in a regular fashion. Whether we have succeeded in our attempt to accomplish this we cannot know until other possible sets have been tried. What we can say is that, of the three dimensions S, P and I, the second, Prestige in the community, comes very close to being the central axis of the space of all three. This emerges from a repetition for all possible dimension-sets of the correlational procedure which was described in the preceding section for two dimension-sets. Table 8 shows that, over the four analyses from which Value to society has been omitted, Prestige in the community comes closer to the grand means than do its two rivals [27].

In the light of the discussion of the first part of this paper, the interpretation of this finding calls for some comment. We had entertained hopes that by asking about prestige "in the community" — and in the context of a multi-dimensional grading task — we might achieve more obvious success than in conventional enquiries in inducing respondents to grade occupations within a distinctively "prestige" frame of reference. However, given the results produced, we are doubtful if we made any significant advance in this respect [28]. The very high correlation between ratings on Prestige in the community and the grand means strongly suggests to us that again "prestige" was

27. It is unlikely that this is a position-effect since P sometimes preceded and sometimes followed S in the administration of the task. A more adequate elimination of such possible effects would involve balanced ordering of all the dimensions which are intended to span the stratification-space.

28. We would again make the point that it may well be that in modern societies no sufficiently integrated and stable ordering of prestige relationships exists to make the prestige rating of occupations (or other roles or positions) at all a feasible proposition.

being usually construed as generalized "goodness" or "desirability" in a process something like that indicated earlier. It is in this manner, that is to say, that we would interpret its "central" position. For if some central dimension of occupational status can be shown to exist, it seems to us far more plausible that it should be a general "goodness" or "desirability" one, rather than one relating to prestige in the classic sociological sense. Thus, what one would ideally like to be able to show is that one can pick out a number of theoretically relevant dimensions on which the status of occupations is not especially highly correlated but across which *mean* ratings of occupations are produced that correlate very highly indeed with those resulting from conventional "prestige" rating tasks.

The status indeterminacy of occupations

In the following part of the analysis we omit the dimension Value to society, we take the common-general factor of occupational status (defined by the analysis of the three dimensions, S, P and I) as given, and we look at the contribution of individual occupations to various kinds of deviation from their mean status.

Table 9 lists the occupations in order of their common-general status as recorded in the second column of Table 4. It also lists the contribution of each occupation to each of four sums of squares, followed by the sum of the contributions to all sums of squares except that for Occupations. The first four sums of squares colums add up, apart from rounding errors, to the equivalent sums of squares in Table 6, and the last column adds up to 2 340 — 1 677 where 2 340 is the total sum of squares and 1 677 is the sum of squares for Occupations.

In previous sections of this report we have defined the terms "general", "common", "personal" and "profile" by reference to certain features of assessments of occupational status. Now we are going to consider these same features as sources of uncertainty or heterogeneity in the determination of status. We shall, therefore, assign an appropriate name to each feature which indicates the sort of indeterminacy which it reflects, and we shall refer to the features collectively as sources of *status indeterminacy* of occupations.

The first of the four features is the term JROD which is an indicator of *random measurement error*. Looking at the JROD column of Table 9 we see that the sums of squares are pretty uniform from occupation to occupation, which gives us no cause to retract our assumption that the variance of this term is largely error.

Each of the remaining three sources of status indeterminacy is related to a sum of squares in Table 9, but the relationship is not straightforward. It will be recalled that the model to which we are working assumes that higher-order terms in the analysis enter into lower-order terms and inflate their mean

Table 9. *Contribution of each occupation to certain sums of squares in the analysis of the three dimensions S, P and I (Table 6)*

Occupation	Mean status	JR	JD	JRD	JROD	All except J
		Sums of squares				
2. Ambassador to a foreign country	131	2	0	6	1	11
14. Company director	129	1	1	2	1	6
39. TV announcer	121	4	5	7	1	18
7. Business manager	119	6	1	3	2	11
15. Country solicitor	119	5	1	4	3	14
12. Civil servant (Executive)	119	16	1	5	3	26
29. Psychiatrist	119	3	0	5	1	10
23. Medical officer	119	10	0	3	1	16
10. Chartered accountant	118	11	2	5	1	21
24. News reporter	113	13	2	3	2	22
40. Works manager	111	11	0	3	2	18
26. Nonconformist minister	107	9	2	9	2	25
27. Policeman	107	5	21	3	2	32
28. Primary school teacher	106	3	7	6	1	20
36. Social worker	106	3	7	2	1	16
37. State registered nurse	105	5	6	9	2	24
17. Farmer (over 100 acres)	103	21	6	6	2	39
22. Jobbing master builder	102	10	1	6	2	20
20. Foreman in a factory	102	4	2	8	1	17
21. Insurance agent	99	7	0	5	2	16
3. Ballet dancer	99	13	11	13	2	42
13. Commercial traveller	97	8	2	8	0	20
18. Fireman	95	7	3	5	2	18
11. Chef	95	7	1	3	3	16
8. Car worker	93	12	5	4	1	25
25. Newsagent and tobacconist	91	8	1	3	2	15
34. Sheet metal worker	91	4	2	2	1	10
16. Dock labourer	88	12	3	9	1	29
9. Carpenter	87	4	1	2	1	8
19. Fitter	87	3	1	2	2	8
5. Bricklayer	86	6	1	3	1	11
6. Bus driver	85	2	0	1	1	5
35. Shop assistant	85	4	1	4	2	11
33. Routine clerk	84	4	0	2	1	8
4. Barman	84	9	0	1	1	12
30. Quarry worker	83	9	0	1	1	11
38. Tractor driver	82	2	0	1	2	8
31. Railway porter	80	3	1	1	1	6
1. Agricultural labourer	78	5	1	2	1	12
32. Road sweeper	75	3	0	1	1	7
Sum	-	274	99	168	60	664

squares and sums of squares. The equations of the model specify which higher-order terms contribute to which lower-order terms and with what weighting. We propose to define each species of status indeterminacy for an occupation in terms of the contribution of that occupation to the appropriate variance component in Table 6. We write s_k for a sum of squares of term K (and s_{kl} for the sum of squares of the interaction of K and L, and so on) Table 9, and n_j, n_r, n_o and n_d for the number of levels of each of the factors (40, 10, 2 and 3 respectively). We append the subscript i to our variance components to indicate that we are now calculating the contribution to a variance component of a specific occupation i.

Then, taking the personal-general component jr we define our measure of *status disagreement* as

$$jr_i = \frac{s_{jr} - s_{jro}}{(n_j - 1)\,(n_r - 1)\,n_o n_d}$$

Taking the common-profile component jd we define a measure of *status discrepancy* as

$$jd_i = \frac{(n_r - 1)\,(s_{jd} - s_{jod}) + s_{jrod} - s_{jrd}}{(n_j - 1)\,(n_d - 1)\,n_r n_o}$$

Thirdly, taking the personal-profile component jrd we define a measure of a new concept, for which we propose the name *status profile disagreement*

$$jrd_i = \frac{s_{jrd} - s_{jrod}}{(n_j - 1)\,(n_r - 1)\,(n_d - 1)\,n_o}$$

The measure of random error may be brought into line with the other measures of status indeterminacy by defining

$$e_i = \frac{s_{jrod}}{(n_j - 1)\,(n_r - 1)\,(n_d - 1)}$$

It should be noted that these definitions have been simplified slightly because Occasions has only one degree of freedom.

Table 10 contains the indices of status indeterminacy. Each index has been multiplied by one thousand, and so the columns sum to one thousand times the appropriate variance component in Table 6. The last column, which is headed "Status indeterminacy" is a sum, not merely of the four indices which have been explicitly defined and which form the first four columns of the table, but also of similar indices which may be defined for the remaining interaction terms in Table 6. Thus the sum of the status indeterminacy column is one thousand times (1.0444—0.7032), which is the variance not accounted for by the common-general factor. The table may be read both horizontally and vertically, that is, we may compare different types of indeterminacy for the same occupation, or we may compare occupations on a given measure of indeterminacy.

It will be appreciated that no standard errors of these indices are available and that the caveats which apply to the estimates of components of variance apply with even greater force to these partitions of those estimates. Nevertheless, we are encouraged by the negligible number and size of negative indices. In the absence of statistical theory the sociologist's resource must be to replication. In future work with the design it will be desirable to employ a sample of respondents which is large enough to be split into several sub-samples, each of which may be analysed separately.

The status indeterminacy column of Table 10 indicates the extent to which ratings of an occupation vary about the grand mean. It can be seen that occupations with the highest status indeterminacy tend to lie toward the middle of the status range. An exception to this tendency is civil servant (executive), about which respondents evinced much uncertainty, most of them not being familiar with civil service grades. We suspect that the high mean status of this occupation is a consequence of the confusion of executive with administrative functions. The occupations with the highest indeterminacy are ballet dancer, farmer (over 100 acres) and policeman. Dock labourer also has high indeterminacy. A remark by one of our respondents suggested that there is uncertainty about this occupation because its apparently low-status work contrasts with reiterated assertions of its national importance when a stoppage is threatened. Another respondent thought that dock labourers and car workers have the income to support a high standard of living but that they do not spend their money wisely. The implied contrast between two senses of "standard of living" could contribute to indeterminacy. Non-conformist minister, SRN, and car worker also have high indeterminacy.

The error column of Table 10 is proportional to the JROD column of Table 9 and so yields no new information when read vertically.

Occupations about whose status there is much disagreement are farmer (over 100 acres), civil servant (executive), news reporter and ballet dancer. It would in principle be desirable at this point to explore the data further in a search for the determinants of status disagreement. We might, for example, classify the respondents by age, sex and social status and calculate the mean of each category of respondent for each disputed occupation on the JR term of the analysis. Or, taking an alternative approach, and writing **A** for the JR matrix of mean deviation ratings of each occupation by each respondent, we might calculate the pairs of latent vectors $\mathbf{q}_j'$ and $\mathbf{u}_j$ such that $\mathbf{q}_j' \mathbf{A}\mathbf{u}_j = \lambda_j$ (a latent root), which represent patterns of relations between respondents and occupations [29]. Similar analyses might be made of each index of status indeterminacy (apart from error). However, the num-

29. An example of the factorization of an interaction matrix is reported in Hope, 1969.

Table 10. *Indices of status indeterminacy for each of the occupations* ($\times$ *100*)

Occupation	Status disagreement	Status discrepancy	Status profile disagreement	Error	Status indeterminacy
	—	—	—	—	—
2. Ambassador to a foreign country	0.70	0.48	3.32	1.62	5.81
14. Company director	0.08	0.45	1.14	1.13	3.05
39. TV announcer	1.38	2.20	4.29	1.60	10.26
7. Business manager	2.59	0.19	1.26	2.26	5.60
15. Country solicitor	1.51	0.39	0.96	3.79	6.33
12. Civil servant (Executive)	6.68	0.68	1.38	3.84	12.30
29. Psychiatrist	1.40	-0.12	3.07	1.12	5.57
23. Medical officer	4.09	-0.00	1.05	1.83	7.85
10. Chartered accountant	4.97	1.12	2.26	1.99	10.42
24. News reporter	6.15	1.20	0.95	2.43	10.70
40. Works manager	4.62	0.08	0.80	2.89	8.36
26. Nonconformist minister	3.67	0.69	5.13	2.98	13.26
27. Policeman	2.20	13.41	0.98	2.66	18.81
28. Primary school teacher	1.08	4.39	3.46	1.89	11.07
36. Social worker	0.61	4.44	0.47	1.64	8.43
37. State registered nurse	1.84	3.04	4.98	2.54	13.07
17. Farmer (over 100 acres)	9.06	2.60	2.82	2.49	19.70
22. Jobbing master builder	4.14	0.36	2.48	2.93	10.18
20. Foreman in a factory	0.82	0.88	4.59	1.63	9.26
21. Insurance agent	2.74	0.03	1.95	2.98	8.12

Table 10. *(continued)*

3. Ballet dancer	5.50	5.77	7.77	3.40	23.36
13. Commercial traveller	3.02	0.95	5.63	0.49	11.01
18. Fireman	2.85	1.52	2.58	2.23	9.62
11. Chef	3.18	0.45	-0.06	4.08	7.25
8. Car worker	4.29	3.09	1.94	1.61	12.73
25. Newsagent tobacconist	3.72	0.56	0.93	2.23	7.09
34. Sheet metal worker	1.67	1.33	0.53	1.49	5.13
16. Dock labourer	4.08	1.09	5.32	2.00	15.34
9. Carpenter	1.76	0.28	1.09	1.01	4.12
19. Fitter	1.23	0.31	0.16	2.61	3.54
5. Bricklayer	2.43	0.27	1.67	1.18	5.49
6. Bus driver	0.85	0.13	0.27	1.04	2.39
35. Shop assistant	1.32	0.01	0.92	3.18	5.23
33. Routine clerk	1.68	-0.16	0.85	1.12	3.87
4. Barman	4.00	-0.14	0.36	0.89	5.77
30. Quarry worker	4.20	0.09	0.41	0.80	5.44
38. Tractor driver	0.54	-0.03	-0.04	2.17	3.68
31. Railway porter	1.02	0.45	0.08	1.35	2.86
1. Agricultural labourer	1.39	0.52	0.63	1.14	6.16
32. Road sweeper	1.24	0.20	-0.05	1.96	3.00
Sum	110.30	52.24	78.33	82.49	341.23

ber and method of selection of the respondents in the present study do not justify such detailed explorations.

The indices of status *discrepancy* are more heterogeneous than the indices of status disagreement. The outstanding occupation is that of policeman, whose power is well above his mean status, while his standard of living is well below. For the ballet dancer, by contrast, standard of living and, to some extent, prestige are thought to exceed power and influence. The social worker and the primary teacher are regarded as having a relatively low standard of living and relatively high power and influence [30].

Coming now to the index of status *profile disagreement* we must first explain what we mean by the term. The index corresponds to the personal-profile component jrd and it indicates the extent to which people have profiles of the occupation over the four dimensions which differ from the average profile in the sample as a whole. Profile disagreement, therefore, means "disagreement about discrepancy". Ballet dancer is again the subject of considerable disagreement. A group of occupations which manifests a fair degree of disagreement consists of: commercial traveller, dock labourer, non-conformist minister, SRN, foreman and TV announcer. These differ from ballet dancer in that none, except possibly nurse, has high discrepancy over the sample as a whole. The low value of the index for policeman indicates little disagreement over the discrepant profile of that occupation.

Seeking the determinants of status indeterminacy

Ballet dancer is the only occupation which has been high on each of the three measures of status indeterminacy. It is, therefore, analysed in Table 11 for illustrative purposes. The body of the table contains mean ratings of the occupations on each dimension, averaged over the two occasions. The sum of every row and every column is, apart from rounding errors, zero. If each element of the 10 × 3 matrix is squared and multiplied by the number of occasions the resultant values sum to the sum of squares JRD for ballet dancer in Table 9. Similarly, the eleventh row of the table sums to zero and is the source of the JR sum of squares for ballet dancer. The fourth column sums to zero and is the source of the JD sum of squares. The grand mean (in brackets) is the mean rating of ballet dancer over all eighty columns of the standardized data matrix. It is a non-standardized version of the mean 99 in Table 9.

30. One of our respondents, when asked to say what he had in mind in ranking occupations for their "power and influence over other people" drew a clear distinction between the influence of a psychiatrist or a shop assistant and the power of a trade union leader. This respondent also distinguished between intensive power or influence brought to bear on few people, as by a psychiatrist, and extensive power or influence. Having ranked the occupations on three dimensions and being told that another was to be employed he guessed that it might be "how their health is affected".

Table 11. *Position of " ballet dancer" in terms of three analyses which represent aspects of status indeterminacy*

	Term JRD			
	Dimension			
Respondent	S	P	I	Term JR
A	0.13	0.16	-0.30	-0.11
B	0.04	-0.23	0.19	0.10
C	-1.12	0.23	0.89	0.52
D	-0.27	0.99	-0.72	0.21
E	0.35	-0.17	-0.17	0.02
F	0.03	-0.02	-0.00	0.18
G	1.03	-0.39	-0.63	0.18
H	-0.40	-0.37	0.77	-1.16
I	0.16	-0.06	-0.10	0.52
J	0.05	-0.13	0.08	-0.47
Term JD	0.44	0.13	-0.57	(Term J = -0.06)

In Table 11 it is possible to see that respondent H, who has a low opinion of the status of ballet dancers, credits them with about equal power, prestige and standard of living, that is, his profile is roughly equal and opposite to the overall profile given in the bottom row of the table. The two profiles iron one another out. Respondent J, on the other hand, who also has a fairly low assessment of the occupation, follows the sample profile closely, and G, who is a little above average in his overall assessment, displays a much-intensified version of the sample's profile.

Analyses of this sort are of no more than psychological interest so long as we are not in a position to relate them to social characteristics of the respondents. However, with a large sample of respondents, each of whom would be assigned to a position on each member of a set of social variates, we could explore the extent and nature of the social determination of the perception of occupational status. An appropriate analysis would involve a multivariate non-orthogonal design in the analysis of variance supplemented by the extraction of "explanatory variates".

The evaluation of occupations

Most of the preceding analysis has been of the three dimensions S, P and I. In this and the following section we look at the relations among all four dimensions, and first we look at the discrepancies between non-normative and normative gradings.

An examination of the difference column of Table 4 shows the effect of introducing Value to society into the criteria of status. There are no surprises here. Those occupations whose "value" exceeds their non-normative status are the life-giving (agricultural labourer), life-saving or protecting (fireman, policeman, medical officer, nurse), and life-enhancing (teacher, social-worker) occupations, all of which are associated with central social values. The craft occupations undergo little revaluation. The most disvalued occupations are barman and television announcer, occupations associated with leisure and entertainment. We may surmise that the former suffers because his trade is thought to be noxious whereas the latter is downgraded because his non-evaluated status is thought to be excessive. Occupations which also suffer disvaluation (clerk, company director, insurance agent, newsagent, accountant) are commercial service functions which lack immediate biological or welfare relevance. Foreman and works manager change little.

A typology of occupational profiles

The element of Table 3 which reflects the extent to which the sample as a whole attributes different profiles to the various occupations is the Occupations × Dimensions (JD) term. The sum of squares of this term is derived from a 40 × 4, Occupations by Dimensions, matrix, each of whose elements is a mean over the ten respondents and the two occasions. The JD sum of squares is the sum of this matrix multiplied by 10 × 2 = 20. The matrix, therefore, contains the averaged profiles of the occupations.

An empirical classification of occupations in terms of the extent to which they share a profile, irrespective of their general ranking in the status hierarchy [31], may be obtained by treating the columns of the matrix as axes of a space in which each occupation is represented by a point, and examining the clustering of these points. The method used to identify the empirical clustering is that known as Complete Analysis, which incorporates an approximately minimum-variance taxonomic procedure applied to a Euclidean metric (Hope, 1969*b*).

Table 12. *Latent roots and vectors of the Occupations × Dimensions matrix of means*

Dimension	Component		
	1	2	3
Standard of living (S)	0.57	-0.52	-0.39
Prestige in the community (P)	0.20	0.08	-0.84
Power and influence (I)	0.02	0.78	0.37
Value to society (V)	-0.79	-0.34	0.07
Latent root	0.31	0.07	0.02
% variance	77.65	16.68	5.67

31. This is a particular case of taxonomic analysis after the elimination of the "size" factor, which is discussed in Hope, 1970.

The variances of the four dimensions in the Occupations × Dimensions matrix are: (S) 0.12 (P) 0.03 (I) 0.04 and (V) 0.20. The mean of these variances is 0.10. There are three non-zero latent roots accounting respectively, for 78 percent, 17 percent and 6 percent of the variance. The latent vectors

Figure 1. *Plot of forty occupations in a two-dimensional space which contains 94 percent of the sum of squares of their profiles*

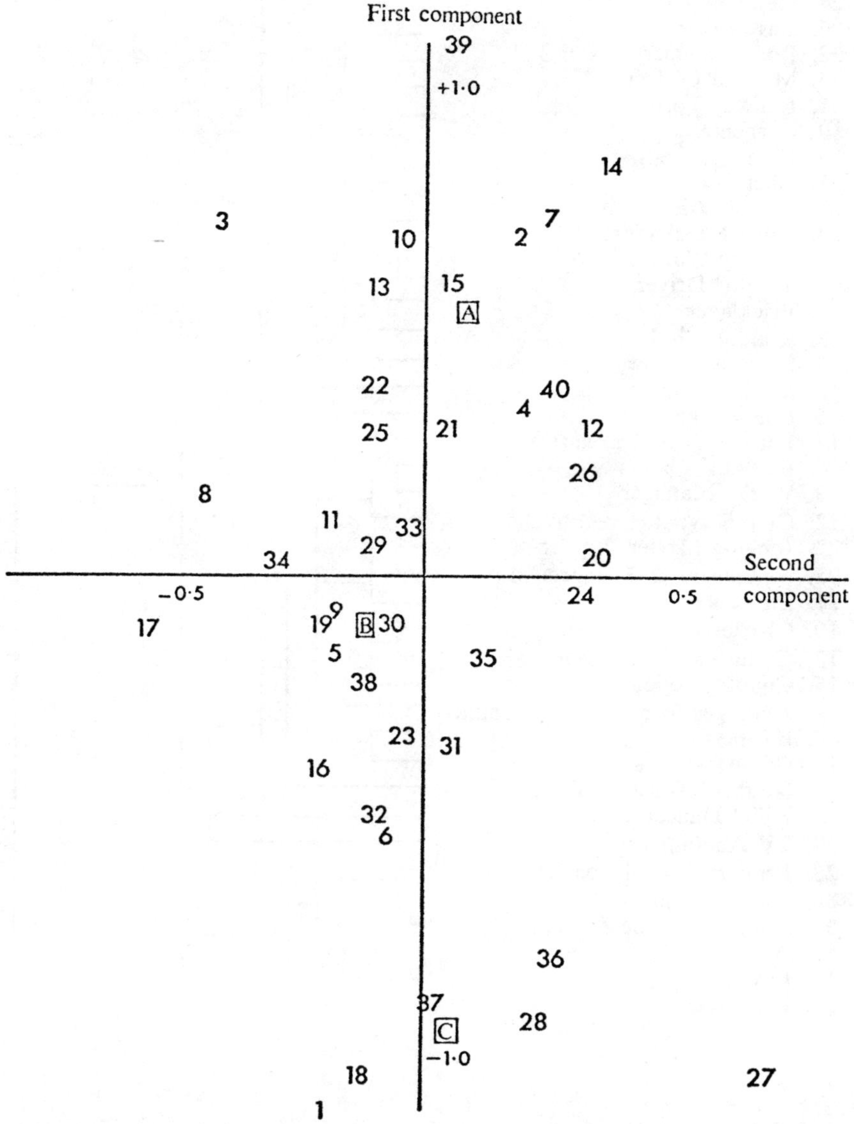

Figure 2. *Dendogram showing the clustering of occupations according to the similarity of their profiles across four dimensions of occupational status*

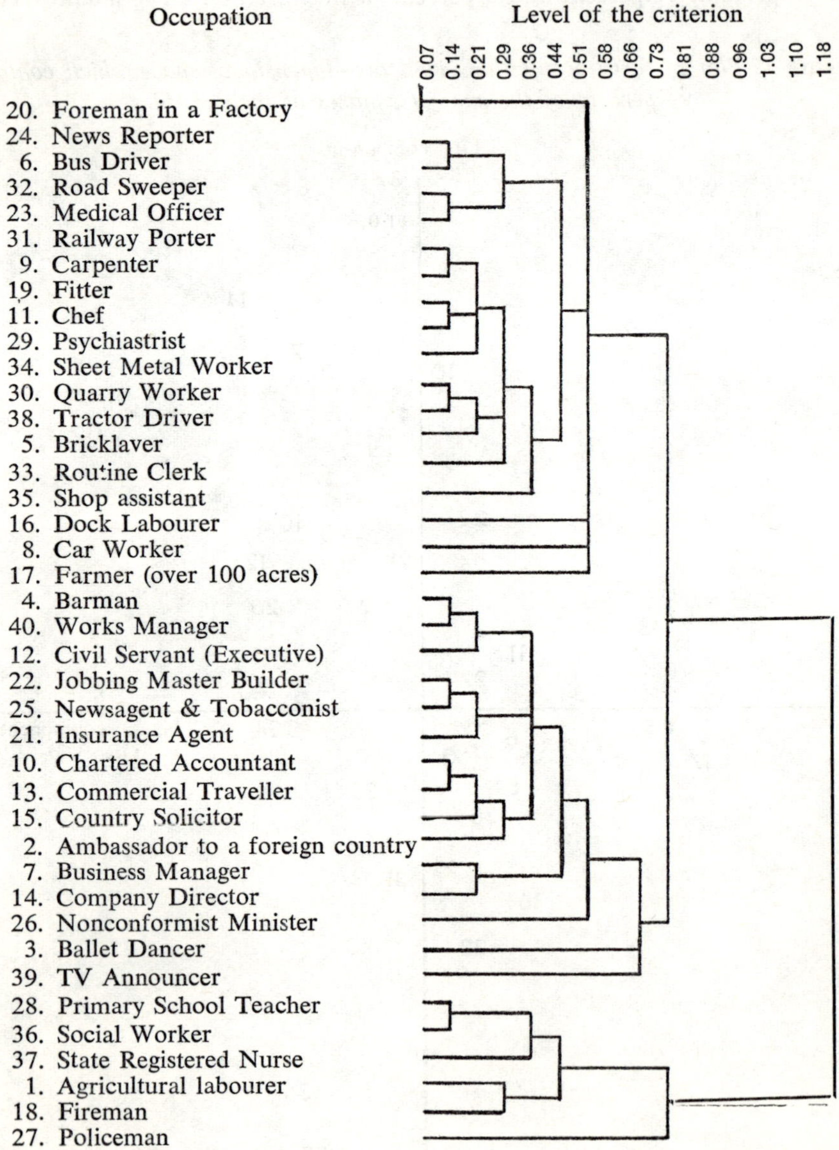

are shown in Table 12. The positions of the occupations in the space of the first two components are shown in Figure 1 and the clustering of the occupations in the space of all three components is shown in Figure 2.

If we look at level 0.66 of the dendrogram we see that the taxonomic analysis finds three clusters, whose means have been indicated in Figure 1 by the letters A, B and C. Policeman is not included in this taxonomy, though it joins cluster C at the next level of the dendrogram. The tightness or looseness of a cluster may be indexed by a coefficient of dispersion which is the sum of squared distances of constituent occupations from the mean of their cluster, divided by the number of occupations in a cluster and also by the number of dimensions = 4. (The index of dispersion for all forty occupations considered as a single cluster is 0.10, the mean of the variances of the dimensions.) The dispersion of each cluster is given in Table 13. When A and B unite to form a single cluster at level 0.73 the dispersion of this larger unit is 0.06.

Table 13. *Relations of three clusters of occupations to the four dimensions in the Occupations × Dimensions matrix**

Cluster	n	Index of dispersion	Distance of cluster mean from the origin	Mean of cluster on S	P	I	V
A	15	0.03	0.56	0.27	0.14	0.07	-0.47
B	19	0.03	0.18	0.00	-0.08	-0.07	0.15
C	5	0.02	0.95	-0.62	-0.06	-0.05	0.72

* Note that one occupation does not belong to any of the clusters.

Table 14. *Mean of each cluster on each principal component of the Occupations × Dimensions matrix*

Cluster	n	Component 1	2	3
A	15	-0.56	0.08	-0.02
B	19	-0.14	-0.11	0.05
C	5	-0.94	0.04	-0.16

The means of the clusters on the original dimensions are given in Table 13 and their means on the components are given in Table 14. It can be seen that the taxonomy is effected mainly in terms of the first component, which contrasts relatively affluent with relatively valued occupations.

Reliability of the ratings

We have already examined the stability of the functions measured by the ratings but we have not yet assessed the reliability with which those functions may be measured. Several types of reliability may be specified in a design of this nature and these may be introduced by the device of a pooling square which is a more complex version of that employed by Mahmoud (1955) and Hope (1969). The elements of the pooling square (Table 15) represent variances and covariances. Two conditions are distinguished for each of three terms of the analysis. For example, taking the term Respondents, in estimating the covariance of two sets of ratings we distinguish two cases, one in which both sets were obtained from the same respondent and one in which the sets were obtained from different respondents. It is sufficient, therefore, to represent Respondents in the pooling square by only two states, R_1 and R_2. Similarly, Occasions is represented by O_1 and O_2 and Dimensions by D_1 and D_2. In the square variancces are symbolized by the letter v and covariances by c. The subscripts of an element are determined by the concomitance or lack of it of the row and column symbols for that element. For example, in the first row and second column we write c_{ro} because this term stands for a covariance in which the same respondent has rated occupations [32] on the same occasion. The subscript d is omitted because the ratings are on two different dimensions. The term c without subscript signifies the covariance between different respondents rating different dimensions on different occasions. The symmetry of the square (or rather half-square as it is given in Table 15; the missing lower triangle is of course the mirror image of the upper triangle) is such that every covariance appears four times, but no distinction is to be drawn among these four appearances. In every case a particular covariance represents the same number, namely the average of all

Table 15. *Pooling square*

Respondents	R_1				R_2						
Occasions	O_1		O_2		O_1		O_2				
Dimensions	D_1	D_2	D_1	D_2	D_1	D_2	D_1	D_2			
	v_{rod}	c_{ro}	c_{rd}	c_r	c_{od}	c_o	c_d	c	D_1	O_1	R_1
		v_{rod}	c_r	c_{rd}	c_o	c_{od}	c	c_d	D_2		
			v_{rod}	c_{ro}	c_d	c	c_{od}	c_o	D_1	O_2	
				v_{rod}	c	c_d	c_o	c_{od}	D_2		
					v_{rod}	c_{ro}	c_{rd}	c_r	D_1	O_1	R_2
						v_{rod}	c_r	c_{rd}	D_2		
							v_{rod}	c_{ro}	D_1	O_2	
								v_{rod}	D_2		

32. No subscript for Occupations is employed because Occupations is universally present in every element of the pooling square.

covariances which satisfy the subscripts of c. It is easy to see that, with three dimensions [33], there are 3(3 — 1)/2 = 3 covariances for each person on each occasion which satisfy the subscripts of c_{ro}. And so, taken over all ten respondents and both occasions, c_{ro} stands for a mean of $10 \times 2 \times 3 = 60$ covariances.

It is a simple matter to compute the value of each element of the pooling square from a consideration of the variance components which do and do not contribute to it. All elements involve component j for Occupations. In addition c_{ro}, for example, involves the interaction components j_r, j_o and j_{ro}, so that we write

$$c_{ro} = j + j_r \times j_o + j_{ro}$$

The constitution of each element of the pooling square is indicated by plus signs in Table 16.

Table 16. *Elements of the pooling square in terms of variance components*

	Variance component							
Element	j	jr	jo	jd	jro	jrd	jod	jrod
c	+							
c_r	+	+						
c_o	+		+					
c_d	+			+				
c_{ro}	+	+	+		+			
c_{rd}	+	+		+		+		
c_{od}	+		+	+			+	
v_{rod}	+	+	+	+	+	+	+	+

It can be seen that v_{rod} is simply the sum of all variance components. In the case of a design in which all four factors are random the value of v_{rod} is necessarily unity (when all the columns of the matrix of ratings have been standardized), and the covariance elements of the pooling square represent means of product-moment correlations among appropriate columns of the data matrix. Having assumed that Dimensions is a fixed effect we find that $v_{rod} = 1.04$ and we divide this into each covariance to obtain a correlation coefficient r (Table 17). These correlations may be employed as estimates of reliability. For example, $r_{nd} = 0.90$ is the reliability with which a respondent will repeat his ratings of occupations on a given dimension. The reliability or extent of agreement between different respondents rating the same dimension on the same occasion is $r_{od} = 0.73$, which scarcely differs from the correlation between two different respondents rating the same dimension on two different occasions $r_d = 0.72$. The degree of correlation between a par-

33. It will be noted that Value to society is omitted from the calculation of reliability.

ticular respondent's assessment of different dimensions is given by $r_{ro} = 0.79$ and $r_r = 0.78$. The correlation between different respondents' ratings on different dimensions is $r_o = 0.67$ and $r = 0.67$.

Table 17. *Elements of the pooling square and corresponding correlation coefficients*

Coefficient	Element	Correlation
—	—	—
c	0.7032	0.6733
c_r	0.8135	0.7789
c_o	0.7040	0.6741
c_d	0.7554	0.7233
c_{ro}	0.8288	0.7936
c_{rd}	0.9440	0.9039
c_{od}	0.7588	0.7266
v_{rod}	1.0444	1.0000

The negligible influence of Occasions enables us to simplify the findings of this section. Table 18 contains a reduced pooling square, lacking the factor of Occasions, with Dimensions and Respondents interchanged, and with r_{rd} in the diagonal. The other elements of the square are r, r_d and r_r. In interpreting these coefficients it must be borne in mind that they estimate the reliability of a single set of ratings by a single rater. The reliability of the mean of several sets of ratings is of course higher than the reliability of the individual sets which have been averaged.

Table 18. *Reduced pooling square with reliabilities rather than unities in the diagonal*

Dimensions	D_1		D_2		
Respondents	R_1	R_2	R_1	R_2	
	0.90	0.72	0.78	0.67	R_1 D_1
		0.90	0.67	0.78	R_2
			0.90	0.72	R_1 D_2
				0.90	R_2

Each of the seven estimated correlations in Table 17 may be compared with the corresponding estimate derived from the completely random model (which is a mean of product-moment correlations among the appropriate columns of the standardized data matrix). Discrepancies between corresponding estimates derived from the two models vary within the limits -0.015 and + 0.010, that is, they are negligible.

The coefficients in Table 18 may be used to determine the "true" correlation between different dimensions, that is, to find the extent to which the three dimensions splay out from one another, on average. The coefficient $r_r = 0.78$ indicates the mean correlation between ratings of different dimensions by the same person, but we would expect this to contain a halo effect.

The coefficient r = 0.67 represents the mean correlation between different dimensions rated by different persons, and the difference between the two, 0.11, is an indication of the extent to which halo effects occur (Chi, 1937). Since r_{rd} is the reliability with which an individual respondent rates occupations in a particular dimension we may use it to correct r for attenuation due to unreliability. Then r/r_{rd} = 0.74 represents an estimate of the average "true" or "objective" correlation between different dimensions of occupational status, an estimate which discounts both halo effects and effects of unreliability.

APPENDIX

A further pilot study

The data which have been analysed in the second part of this paper were derived from relatives and acquaintances of the authors who were socially fairly heterogeneous. To try the procedure under different, and in some ways more testing, conditions another pilot study, also of ten persons, was carried out on a sample drawn randomly from the electoral register for a working class area of Oxford. The sample was constrained to contain equal numbers of men and women. Eighteen people had to be approached before ten respondents were obtained. The administration of the task was undertaken by Miss Anne Sharp.

Apart from the nature of the sample, the only difference between the two tasks was the omission from the second of "Prestige in the community" (P) and its replacement by the "interest of the work" (W). The dimensions were always administered in the order S, W, I and V, and the interval between the first and second occasions was again about one week.

Table 19 shows the analysis of variance of the three dimensions S, W and I, and is comparable with the analysis of S, P and I shown in Table 6. The two outstanding changes are first, an increase of about 20 percent in error (from 8 percent to 27 percent) and second, a decrease of 28 percent in the common-general term (from 67 percent to 39 percent). Apart from these two changes the only differences worthy of mention are that the Occupations × Respondents term is rather larger and the Occupations × Respondents × Occasions term is not as close to zero as it was in the original analysis. These two differences suggest that there is more personal-general variance but that it is not as stable as in the former analysis (the coefficient of stability is 0.83, as against 0.88 formerly). The stability of the sample's common-general ratings is again 1.00.

However, the most important feature of the second pilot study is the relatively large second-order interaction for the new dimension, W, analysed in isolation from its companions. In the comparable analyses of the previous study S, P and I had error (second-order interaction) variances of 8-12 percent and V had an error variance of 22 percent. In the new study the error variances of the individual dimensions are (S) 21 percent, (W) 49 percent, (I) 26 percent and (V) 44 percent. While all errors have increased, in consequence of the nature of the sample, the substitution of W for P has introduced a dimension whose error is of the same order of magnitude as the error of V. The analysis of S, W and I is less valid than the analysis of S, P and I because the former is heterogeneous with respect to error while the latter is homogeneous. We may surmise that people find it hard to grade the "interest of the work" because they are at two removes from the characteristic they are being asked to consider. In the first place they are only imperfectly aware of the nature of the tasks undertaken in a particular job, and in the second place they find the estimation of the subjective interest of those tasks difficult. Indeed, they may not con-

Table 19. *Analysis of gradings of occupations by ten respondents (randomly sampled from a working class area) on three dimensions: "Standard of living" (S), the "interest of the work" (W), and "power and Influence over other people" (I)* *

Source	d.f.	Sum of squares	Mean square	Variance component
Occupations	39	1019.1755	26.1327	0.4124
Occupations × Respondents	351	507.1394	1.4448	0.1757
Occupations × Occasions	39	13.1106	0.3362	-0.0018
Occupations × Dimensions	78	121.6800	1.5600	0.0580
Occupations × Respondents × Occasions	351	137.1089	0.3906	0.0359
Occupations × Respondents × Dimensions	702	326.1421	0.4646	0.0909
Occupations × Occasions × Dimensions	78	17.0990	0.2192	-0.0064
Error	702	198.5446	0.2828	0.2828
Sum	2340	2340.0001	-	1.0475

* *Cf.* Table 6 for an identical analysis of gradings on S, P, and I by ten selected respondents.

cede that there can be an agreed assessment *in abstracto* of the subjective and interactive relations between a man's character and the tasks he is called upon to perform in fulfilling his occupational roles.

There is no reason to suppose that P would not have behaved like S and I if it had been included in place of W. The main contrast, therefore, between our first, highly selected, respondents and a random sample of a working class area is an increase of the error variance of the non-normative dimensions from about 10 percent to about 25 percent. An increase was to be expected and the existence of about 25 percent error in the grading of an occupation by a single respondent is not discouraging, since it implies that a very high degree of reliability may be obtained by averaging over only a small number, say ten or fifteen, of respondents.

Besides giving us a more realistic estimate of error the second pilot study has warned us to pick our dimensions with an eye to the uniformity of their error components. This admonition emerged from the data only after they had been subjected to lengthy and detailed analysis. We feel that this point illustrates the value of our rather unusual proceeding in which we have, as it were, carried out the analysis in advance of collecting the data. It is our contention that piloting the analysis is at least as important as piloting the data-collection procedures, and that both must be carried out if the suitability of the one to the other is to be adequately assessed.

REFERENCES

Barber, B.
1957 *Social stratification.* New York, Harcourt and Brace.

Burt, C.
1955 "Test reliability estimated by analysis of variance", *British journal of statistical psychology* 8: 103-118.

Chi, P. L.
1937 "Statistical analysis of personality rating", *Journal of experimental education* 5: 229-245.

Davis, K.
1945 "Some principles of stratification", *American sociological review* 10: 242-249.

Duncan, O. D.
1961 "A socio-economic index for all occupations", in: A. J. Reiss (ed.). *Occupations and social status.* New York, Free Press of Glencoe.

Duncan, O. D.; Artis, J. W.
1951 *Social stratification in a Pennsylvania rural community.* University Park, Pa., Pennsylvania State College. (Agricultural experiment station bulletin 543.)

Fisher, R. A.
1958 *Statistical methods for research workers.* Edinburgh, Oliver and Boyd. (13th ed.)

Gerstl, J.; Cohen, L. K.
1964 "Dissensus, situs and egocentrism in occupational ranking", *British journal of sociology* 15: 254-261.

Goffman, E.
1963 *Stigma.* Englewood Cliffs, NJ, Prentice-Hall.

Goldthorpe, J. H.; Lockwood, D.; Bechhofer, F.; Platt, J.
1969 *The affluent worker in the class structure.* Cambridge, Cambridge University Press.

Gusfield, J. R.; Schwartz, M.
1963 "The meaning of occupational prestige: Reconsideration of the NORC scale", *American sociological review* 28: 265-271.

Hall, J.; Jones, D. C.
1950 "The social grading of occupations", *British journal of sociology* 1: 31-55.

Hodge, R. W.; Treiman, D. J.; Rossi, P.
1966 "A comparative study of occupational prestige", in: R. Bendix; S. M. Lipset (eds.). *Class, status and power.* New York, Free Press of Glencoe. (2nd ed.)

Hope, K.
1964 *The constancy of hostility.* (Paper delivered to the Edinburgh University Group for Defence Studies, Conference on aggression.)
1968 "Handbook of multivariate methods programmed in Atlas Autocode", appendix to the hardbacked edition of *Methods of multivariate analysis.* London, University of London Press.
1969*a* "The study of hostility in the temperaments of spouses: Definitions and methods", *British journal of mathematical and statistical psychology* 22: 67-95.
1969*b* "The complete analysis of a data matrix", *British journal of psychiatry* 115: 1069-1079.
1970 "The complete analysis of a data matrix: Application and interpretation", *British journal of psychiatry* 116 : 657-666.

Hope, K.; Caine, T. M.
1968 "The hysteroid-obsessoid questionnaire: A new validation", *British journal of social and clinical psychology* 7: 210-215.

Inkeles, A.; Rossi, P.
1956 "National comparisons of occupational prestige", *American journal of sociology* 61: 329-339.

Kendall, M. G.
1962 *Rank correlation methods.* London, Griffin. (3rd ed.)

Lenski, G. E.
1954 "Status crystallization: A non-vertical dimension of social status", *American sociological review* 19: 405-413.

Mahmoud, A. F.
1955 "Test reliability in terms of factor theory", *British journal of statistical psychology* 8: 119-135.

Moser, C. A.; Hall, J.
1954 "The social grading of occupations", in: D. V. Glass (ed.). *Social mobility in Britain.* London, Routledge.

NORC
1947 "Jobs and occupations: A popular evaluation", in: R. Bendix; S. M. Lipset (eds.). *Class, status and power.* New York, Free Press of Glencoe.

Ossowski, S.
1963 *Class structure in the social consciousness.* London, Routledge.

Pilliner, A. E. G.
1965 *The application of analysis of variance in psychometric experimentation.* Edinburgh, University of Edinburgh. (Unpublished Ph.D thesis.)

Reiss, A. J.
1961 *Occupations and social status.* New York, Free Press of Glencoe.

Schultz, E. F.
1955 "Rules of thumb for determining expectations of mean squares in the analysis of variance", *Biometrics* 11: 123-135.

Shils, E. A.
1968 "Deference", in: J. A. Jackson (ed.). *Social stratification.* Cambridge, Cambridge University Press.

Stanley, J. C.
1961 "Analysis of unreplicated three-way classifications, with applications to rater bias and trait independence", *Psychometrika* 26: 205-220.

Svalastoga, K.
1959 *Prestige, class and mobility.* Copenhagen, Gyldendal.

Taft, R.
1953 "The social grading of occupations in Australia", *British journal of sociology* 4: 181-188.

Tiryakian, E.
1958 "The prestige evaluation of occupations in an underdeveloped country: The Philippines", *American journal of sociology* 63: 390-399.

Turner, R.
1958 "Life situation and subculture", *British journal of sociology* 9: 299-320.

KAARE SVALASTOGA

Measurement of responsibility

The prestige attributed to an occupation by a population is assumed to be mainly determined by two occupational characteristics:

1. The difficulty of the occupation, for which the amount of schooling required is a usable operationalization;

2. The responsibility of the occupation for which several operationalizations will be discussed below.

To the extent that information about occupations is generally available, and to the extent that ideological bias is absent in the population, prestige would be expected to depend only upon difficulty and responsibility. Relative weight to be attributed to each of the two factors would still be problematic. The author tends to favor the view that, in general, responsibility is given more weight than is difficulty. It is very difficult to perform the feats of some circus artists, but the occupation "circus artist" does not imply much responsibility either in terms of persons supervised, or in terms of material values controlled. Hence, the prestige of the occupation tends to be modest. In contrast, the entrance requirements to top political positions typically do not require university degrees, but the responsibility resting upon a governmental minister exceeds by far the responsibility of occupations demanding high educational levels for entrance, *e.g.* civil service occupations in many countries [1]. Because of its high responsibility the prestige of a position as governmental minister tends to surpass that of most other positions, where information is complete and bias absent.

1. On the prestige of the businessman, C. Wright Mills (1956) had this to say: "The prestige of the businessman is measured less by his wealth or his income — although, of course, these are important — than by the size of his business. He borrows his prestige from the power of his company as measured by its size and from his own position in its hierarchy" (pp. 83-84). He also pointed out the higher prestige of the head of a major corporation who earns $ 200 000 a year as compared to that of a small businessman, earning $ 1 000 000 a year.

We may write:

$$z = f(x, y; a, b, c) \tag{1}$$

where

z = occupational prestige
x = occupational responsibility
y = occupational difficulty
c = constant denoting relative weight of x
a = ideological bias parameter
b = bias parameter due to ignorance

One possible interpretation of (l) is the following

$$z = ax^{bc} y^{b(1-c)} \tag{2}$$

$$\log z = \log a + bc \log x + b(1\text{-}c) \log y \tag{3}$$

Here log a may be interpreted as an ideological bias parameter, b may be interpreted as bias due to ignorance with range

0 = minimum information
1 = full information, and

c indicates the weight attributed to factor x.

Hence, in the absence of bias due to ignorance or ideology, we obtain

$$\log z = c \log x + (1\text{-}c) \log y. \tag{4}$$

The main concern of this paper is the problem how to measure the factor x. The importance of such measurement is connected with the fact that prestige rarely can be measured directly for more than some hundreds of occupations and customarily much fewer occupations are involved. Hence, there is always a need for some estimation procedure in order to assess prestige for occupations not submitted for prestige measurement. Since education of incumbents customarily functions as an acceptable operationalization of occupational difficulty there is an excellent chance of solving the problem once an acceptable indicator of responsibility may be developed.

In fact, the sociological research tool market already offers several operationalizations. A distinction should be made between micro-approach and macro-approach, since techniques of measurement developed for microsystems frequently may not be used in macrosystems.

Two major microsociological approaches may be distinguished:

1) Those that rely on variants of so-called job analysis (Lanham, 1955);

2) Those that rely on measurement of "time span" (Jaques, 1956).

Macrosociological approaches to responsibility measurement may be classified as follows:

1) Expert judgment of occupations with respect to factors indicating responsibility;

2) Reliance on correlation of responsibility with other factors, chiefly number of subordinates, and income;
3) Utilizing deductions from organizational models.

Job analysis typically deals with ranking and rating of job components rather than with actual observation of job execution and job interaction (Lanham, 1955). A typical procedure and also the most popular is the so-called point method. One starts with a list of factors or job components. These components are next weighted so that the total of weights adds to 1 or 100. Then the jobs that are to be evaluated are separately graded or ranked in terms of how much they demand of each.

Lytle (1954) contended that there were really only four major job characteristics, namely: 1) Skill, 2) Effort, 3) Responsibility, 4) Working conditions.
— Skill: that which must already be possessed by worker, and additions which must be required.
— Effort: that which the worker must be able to exert in use of both physique and skill.
— Working conditions: that which the worker must hazard or endure.
— Responsibility : that which the worker must be able to assume.

These four may of course be subdivided as needed. A tentative, partly empirically based, rank order given by Lytle (Lanham, *op. cit.*) gives the following result:

	Approximate median importance in proportion of total importance
	%
Skill	50
Responsibility	25
Effort	15
Working conditions	10
Total importance	100

For each factor or subfactor levels (degrees or grades) are described, and a common practice is to let the lowest level on a factor or subfactor receive the number of points corresponding to the rated relative importance of the factor or subfactor. If the relative importance of responsibility is 25 then we attribute 25 points to the occupation having the very lowest level of responsibility, 50 points to the second level, 75 points to the third level, and so on up.

Some prefer to let points increase in constant proportion rather than with constant number as above. The method gives a total number of points for each job. This number may then be converted to a smaller number of job grades (*ibid.*, p. 91).

It seems clear that neither this method nor other commonly used job analytical methods go beyond the ranking or rating of occupations by experts with respect to any component of interest. However, because job analysts usually work in environments, where rather full information on the jobs concerned may be available to experts, the outcome of the rankings or ratings may be quite realistic.

A promising new variant of job analysis was developed by Guttman (1964) in connection with grading of the Israeli civil service. Guttman stressed that criteria for the analysis of jobs should be sufficiently general so as to apply equally well at all levels of an organizational hierarchy and regardless of type of work. Among such factors he stressed the following [2]:

1) Oral and written expression called for,

2) Initiative originality,

3) Independence of judgment,

4) Institutional level of persons with whom job holder interacts,

5) Amount of supervision by others.

All factors were operationalized through self ratings, superior ratings, and interviewer ratings.

One of the most impressive contributions towards the measurement of responsibility is due to the British researcher Jaques, who in several publications, outlined his method of time span analysis (Jaques, 1956; 1961; 1964). Jaques has written three books to explain what time span analysis is, and we cannot expect to do full justice to his method in this brief outline.

It is a method of measuring occupational responsibility solely by reference to a definite temporal characteristic of the role associated with an occupational position. This temporal aspect is simply the maximum length of time between the execution of a task and its control, although the attempt to obtain the necessary information may encounter numerous difficulties (see in particular Jaques, 1964). A task is defined as a job assignment that entails both requirements as to quality and maximum allowable time for completion, Tasks are distinguished from general responsibilities (*e.g.* whenever situation X occurs to Y), which simply apply indefinitely unless amended. The time span measured from initiation of a task until its review covers the time where the person in charge of the task has to exercise satisfactory discretion towards proper fulfilment of the task. It is definitely not a technique usable in macro-analysis like survey research. This must be so, because Jaques' preferred source for information regarding the time span characterizing the occupation of a respondent would typically be not the respondent, but the manager, if any, responsible for assigning work to the respondent. An interesting feature about responsibility measured in terms of time span is its enormous range from about 1/300 000 year to 20 years.

An interesting side-finding was the fact that time span correlated positively with a measure of what role incumbents felt to be fair pay for a given

2. I am indebted to Prof. Erling Schild for supplementary information on the factors and their operationalization.

position (see in particular the chart in Jaques, 1961, p. 125). Using logarithmic measures of both variables Jaques documented a curvilinear relationship suggesting a rather modest and constant relative increment in fair pay for a given relative growth of values of time span below one month. At higher values of time span, relative increment in fair pay is considerably larger for a given relative increase in time span.

Jaques suggested an optimal hierarchy as existing when ranks are thus distributed:

Rank	Time span years
7	20
6	10
5	5
4	2
3	1
2	1/4
1	Not indicated

Hill (1956) noted that some jobs might possess a range of maxima rather than a single maximum value of discretionary time span. He also stressed that the informal and indirect review of work done by subordinates creates special problems for the time span analyst.

Two recent empirical investigations have attempted to secure measures of occupational responsibility or variables closely related (authority, participation in management) for use in survey research.

Slomczyń (1970) presented results of studies in three Polish cities, where authority was measured by expert ranking. He reported that his sample produced a much higher correlation between education and prestige (.35) than between authority and prestige (.20). This finding may be highly specific and not generalizable (*cf.* above).

Machonin (1969) measured "participation in power and management" in a large scale Czechoslovakian survey. His indicators were: type and size of organization in which respondent worked, respondent's hierarchical position within the organization, and respondent's participation in the Communist Party, elected state organizations, and other organizations. A highly skewed distribution was found.

Number of subordinates has frequently been used in survey research as an indicator of responsibility. The indicator has, however, certain weaknesses, which limit its usefulness. Thus, it is probably much more meaningful as applied to employers than in its application to employees. In general it suffers from the basic weakness that the unit does not seem to represent an invariant amount of responsibility either at different levels of a hierarchy or in different institutional fields. Many high ranking occupations can count only very few direct subordinates, whereas many positions of modest rank (foreman) can be credited with a considerable number.

The most useful substitute for responsibility measurement in survey research seems to be income. This seems particularly to hold:

a) When income is assessed for classes of occupations rather than individual occupations;

b) When income is measured in terms of proportion earning an income above a certain level rather than in terms of average income.

For persons employed in the same organization income is expected to vary quite closely with amount of responsibility associated with the income-giving occupation. However, due to the dependence of income on market demand, interorganizational comparison of incomes may not reflect responsibility so faithfully. It is notable that the heads of governments rarely receive maximum income, although the responsibility associated with their positions can be matched by very few if any other occupations. Still, Duncan's index of socioeconomic status showed the usefulness of income when used as predictor of occupational prestige together with an indicator of educational requirement (Reiss, 1961).

The method of measuring responsibility to be suggested in this paper takes its departure from Simon's model of organization (Simon, 1957). Let us briefly introduce this model. We begin by making two rather strong assumptions:

1) Invariant number of subordinates (n) for given superordinate,

2) Invariant rate b, where

$$b = \frac{\text{superordinate pay}}{\text{immediate subordinate pay}}$$

The size S of the organization (in terms of number of persons) may now be written:

$$S = 1 + n + n^2 \ldots\ldots n^L - 1 = \frac{n^L - 1}{n - 1} \doteq \frac{n^L}{n - 1} \qquad (5)$$

where L is the number of hierarchical levels.

Define

A = pay at bottom level
C = pay at top level

then

$$C = Ab^{L-1} = Bb^L, \text{ where} \qquad (6)$$

$$B = \frac{A}{b}$$

From (5) we obtain

$$\log S = L \log n + \text{constant, and} \tag{7}$$

$$L = \frac{1}{\log n} \log S + \text{constant}$$

From (6)

$$\log C = L \log b + \text{constant} \tag{8}$$

$$\log C = \frac{(\log S + \text{constant})}{\log n} \log b + \text{constant} = \frac{\log b}{\log n} \log S + \text{constant} \tag{9}$$

Roberts (1956) obtained this equation with $\frac{\log b}{\log n} = .37$ as least square estimation of the pay of top executives.

Roberts worked with a different interpretation of S, however. He operationalized S as annual value of sales of the business. The number of persons at a given level α is

$$n^{\alpha\text{-l}} = N(\alpha) \tag{10}$$

Their mean pay must be

$$C'(\alpha) = \frac{C}{b^{\alpha} - 1} \tag{11}$$

$$\log C' = (1 - \alpha) \log b + \text{constant}$$

From (10)

$$(\alpha - 1) \log n = \log N$$

Hence

$$\log C' = - \frac{\log b}{\log n} \log N + \text{constant} \tag{12}$$

Davis (1941) found for General Motors that this equation with $\frac{\log b}{\log n} = .33$ fitted the empirical data regarding the relationship between mean pay at a certain level of responsibility and the number of workers at that level.

The mean pay at any level α may also be written (generalizing from eq. 6)

$$C_\alpha = A\, b^{L\text{-}\alpha} \tag{13}$$

where C α is pay at level α, when top level is indicated with $\alpha = 1$.

We may rewrite (13) as follows :

$$C_\alpha = A\, b^{L-1-(\alpha-1)} = k\, S^a\, b^{-\alpha}$$

$$\text{with } a = \frac{\log b}{\log n}$$

$$\log C_\alpha = \frac{\log b}{\text{lob } n} \log S + \log b\,(1 - \alpha) \tag{14}$$

We have been working under the assumption that b and n are invariant. In fact, we know that they may vary within limits, even at administrative levels (*cf.* above). Starbuck (1965) pointed out the higher value of n at the manual level, foremen typically having larger spans of control than chief executives.

It follows from the postulate of invariant b in this model that responsibility as measured by the administrative level α is a necessary function of income and vice versa. Hence, it is permissible to use equation 10 as a measure of occupational responsibility.

With $\frac{\log b}{\log n} = \frac{1}{3}$ and $\log b = \frac{1}{5}$ we obtain

$$\log C_\alpha = \frac{1}{3} \log S + \frac{1}{5}(1 - \alpha) \tag{15}$$

While the first constant may be a rather realistic estimate, the second may be too high at least for Danish applications. It follows that for employers and self-employed the only relevant information for the measurement of responsibility is a measure of the size of the enterprise. For employees we need the same information and additional information regarding position in the organizational hierarchy.

In an ongoing longitudinal study described in Svalastoga (1970) information was collected in a subsample regarding organizational size as measured by the number of persons employed and the hierarchical position of all persons who were employees.

We also have educational data for these persons and, on the basis of information on their occupational titles, it is possible to assess the relationship between the three variables initially listed and thereby also to obtain an evaluation of the responsibility measure [3].

The sample consists of 296 Copenhagen metropolitan fathers all having sons aged 15 years. All fathers selected are employees unless otherwise mentioned. The occupation of these fathers was coded according to a Danish adaptation of the international scale worked out by Danmarks Statistik. This scale as applied here consisted of 20 categories. Tom Rishoj next converted this scale into the Svalastoga 1 — 9 scale (Svalastoga, 1959) by using a specification of the position of 590 occupations on the international scale [4].

For each international scale category, the average prestige score on the Svalastoga scale was computed. The range on the latter scale was from 3.5 to 7.9. The logarithm to the base 2 for each of 20 prestige scores thus computed, among which a few proved to be equal, constitutes the operational value of log Z introduced in equation 3. In order to obtain a measure of y = education we used answers to a question stating four possible levels of education

3. The author is indebted to Mrs. Kirsten Skau for careful programming.

4. The so-called international scale is a Danish adaptation of a scale of socio-economic states recommended by a conference of European statisticians (1958).

lasting respectively 7, 10, 12, and about 18 years. The logs of these figures to the base 2 constituted the measure used for log y.

Regarding log X, the measure of responsibility, we used the above equation (eq. 15)

$$\log_{\sqrt{10}} X = \frac{1}{3} \log_{\sqrt{10}} S + \frac{1}{5}(1 - \alpha)$$

$\log_{\sqrt{10}} S$ was directly given by proper coding of respondent's information regarding the number of persons employed at his place of work. Likewise α is the self-assignment of the person in his work organization with $\alpha = 1$ for top position.

The total regression equation thus becomes

$$\log_2 z = k + l \log_{\sqrt{10}} X + m \log_{\sqrt{2}} Y = 7.303 - .088 \log_{\sqrt{10}} X - .409 \log_{\sqrt{2}} Y$$

$$R_{\log_2 z;\, \log_{\sqrt{10}} x,\, \log_2 Y} = .768$$

$$r_{\log_2 z,\, \log_{\sqrt{10}} x} = -.487$$

$$r_{\log_2 z,\, \log_2 Y} = -.753$$

Note: high z value = low prestige.

If it may be assumed that the number of hierarchical levels in an organization increases with size according to the equation

$$L = \frac{1}{\log n} \log_{\sqrt{10}} S + \text{constant}\ (\textit{Cf.}\ \text{eq. 7 above})\ \text{and}\ \frac{1}{\log n} = 2\ \text{and constant} = 0$$

Then we have

$$L = \log_{\sqrt{10}} S$$

We shall tentatively use this equation to test the validity of the self-placement given by the sample for all sizes of business between S = 3 and S = 10 000 employees by assuming the bottom stratum in an organization with S employees has the number $\log_{\sqrt{10}} S$. Thus, for an enterprise with 100 employees we expect L = number of layers to be 4 and all higher numbers to be suspect.

This analysis gave 172 unsuspect self-placements and 122 suspect self-placements in a group of 294 employees.

Converting the regression coefficients into β coefficients gives essentially the same result. The prediction of prestige depends more strongly on education than on responsibility [5].

5. For a group of employers or self-employed (N = 56), likewise fathers of 15 year-old boys in the Copenhagen area, the following results were obtained :

In combination, the two factors introduced here accounted for about 60 % of the observed prestige variation.

In order to analyze in more detail the contribution of the responsibility component a multiple regression analysis was undertaken in which $\log_{\sqrt{10}} S$ and α appear as two independent variables in addition to the educational variable. We then obtained

$$\log_2 z = 6.948 - .016 \log_{\sqrt{10}} S + .047\,\alpha - .352 \log_2 Y$$

The multiple correlation coefficient was now

$R = .802$

Although the rank order of the regression coefficients are preserved even if they are converted into β coefficients, the difference becomes smaller since the standard deviation of $\log_{\sqrt{10}} S$ and of α is much larger than that of $\log_2 Y$.

Both models analyzed thus suggest education as a more powerful factor than responsibility. Since this very finding runs counter to commonly accepted theory suggesting the superior importance of job responsibility, it seems necessary to conclude that the present operationalization of responsibility was somewhat less than successful.

One other possible interpretation is that education, as measured here, already accounts for so much of the variation, not only in job difficulty but also in job responsibility, that there is little left to explain.

It should also be mentioned that our independent variable is a somewhat circumstantial measure of occupational prestige. A more direct measure could have given more satisfactory results.

Still more important may be the circumstance that our estimate of organizational rank is based on self-ratings and hence (*cf.* footnote 4) only partly valid measures of rank.

$$\log_2 z = 6.556 - .051 \log_{\sqrt{10}} S - .222 \log_2 Y$$

$r_{\log z \log S} = -.401$

$r_{\log z \log Y} = -.511$

$R_{\log z.\ \log S,\ \log Y} = .547$

$\sigma_{\log S} = 1.127$

$\sigma_{\log Y} = .496$

Hence, in this case too, education stands out as more predictive of prestige than does our measure of responsibility.

REFERENCES

Guttman, L.
1964 "Job evaluation: How it works", *Jerusalem Post* 31, January.

Hill, J.M.M.
1956 "The time span of discretion in job analysis", *Human relations* 9: 295-323.

Jaques, E.
1956 *Measurement of responsibility.* London, Tavistock.
1961 *Equitable payment: A general theory of work, differential payment and individual progress.* New York, Wiley.
1964 *Time-span handbook.* London, Heinemann.

Klöcker-Larsen, F.
1959 *Aflenning paa grundlag af arbejdsvurdering.* Copenhagen, Gyldendal.

Lanham, E.
1955 *Job-analysis.* New York, McGraw-Hill.

Lytle, C.W.
1954 *Job-evaluation methods.* New York, Ronald. (Cited from Lanham, *op. cit.*)

Machonin, P. *et al.*
1969 *Ceskolovenska spolecnost.* Bratislava, Private edition.

Mills, C.W.
1956 *The power elite.* New York, Oxford University Press.

Reiss, A.
1962 *Occupations and social status.* Glencoe, Ill., Free Press.

Simon, H.A.
1957 "The compensation of executives", *Sociometry* 20: 32-35.

Starbuck, W.H.
1965 "Organizational growth and development", pp. 451-533 in: J.C. March (ed.). *Handbook of organizations,* Chicago, Ill.

Svalastoga, K.
1959 *Prestige, class and mobility.* Copenhagen, Gyldendal.
1970 "Longitudinal research designs", *International journal of comparative sociology* 9: 283-291.

Slomczyń, K.
1970 "Socio-occupational differentiation". Warsaw. (Mimeo.) (Paper delivered at the Seventh World Congress of Sociology, Varna, 1970.)

Whisler, T.L.
1964 "Measuring centralization of control in business organizations" pp. 314-333 in: W.W. Cooper; H.J. Leavitt; M.W. Shelly (eds.). *New perspectives in organization research.* New York, Wiley.

REFERENCES

KARL ULRICH MAYER

Dimensions of mobility space : Some subjective aspects of career mobility

Introduction: assumptions of the concept of social mobility

In contrast to early or dissident contemporary writers on social mobility such as Schumpeter (1927) and Strauss (1971) in most of the current literature a concept of social mobility is being used which is not specified with respect to social groupings, historical or structural contexts, but is taken to be applicable to all segments and members of industrial societies. This concept of social mobility is defined as movements of individuals along a single hierarchical dimension, which has mostly been measured in terms of occupational prestige. Rose (1964) and Porter (1968), among others, have noted that the underlying rationale for this fairly dominant view of social mobility, which is both very individualistic and highly generalized, seems to be based on a set of specific assumptions:

1) Rising in the stratification system, *i.e.* upward social mobility, is a universal value-orientation. As Luckmann and Berger formulate : "...practically everybody feels committed to upward mobility as a central life goal...". "Through the mobility ethos a potential motivation of some or even many becomes a compulsory life-goal for all. Mobility is no longer a means to an end, but becomes an end in itself and thereby a yardstick for other values in the life of the individual" (1964, p. 340). And Merton (1957, p. 139) states as a cultural axiom: "All should strive for the same lofty goals since these are open for all."

2) The restriction of the concept of social mobility to vertical movements in the occupational structure suggests that the attainment of high occupational rank or of the rewards connected with it is a goal commonly shared and highly valued by the people in the societies under consideration.

3) Inasmuch as the prestige dimension of the occupational structure has been the object of measurement it seems to have been assumed that this particular aspect of occupational rank is the common value sought after in mobility processes or at least a good and convenient indicator for it [1].

These assumptions regarding the universality of mobility aspirations and the homogeneity of mobility goals derive in part from psychological postulates as in the theory of universal ego needs for improving favorable self-evaluations (Lipset/Bendix, 1959, p. 60 ff.) and from postulates concerning culturally prescribed societal values (Merton, 1957, p. 131 ff.).

The implications of these premises are manifold. If they hold true empirically, mobility, as measured in the dimension of occupational prestige, should not only be a powerful predictor of behavior and attitudes, but also those changes in life which appear subjectively as the most obvious and relevant should correspond to this type of social mobility. Likewise in the subjective perception of social structure (images of society) the occupational prestige dimension and its gradations should prove to be the most apparent and visible.

As Porter (1968, p. 13) states, it would further follow "that by providing certain opportunities where they previously did not exist, latent mobility aspirations and achievement motives will be triggered and the previously deprived will be brought in the mainstream of an upwardly mobile and achievement oriented society". Failure in the occupational career should result in low satisfaction, heightened frustration and deviant behavior, as Merton (1957) maintained in his *Social structure and anomie*. The level and development of aspirations during the course of an occupational career should conform to what Tauski and Dubin (1965, p. 725) called the "unlimited success theory": "The goal is to reach a position in or near the peak of an occupational structure, and self-esteem is lost if the goal is not reached."

Some contrary findings

Many research findings cast some doubt on the general applicability of the notion of social mobility described above. They suggest that mobility goals are emphasized differentially and cannot be subsumed under one common orientation.

Turner (1964), in a study of high school youth, found generally high occupational and educational aspirations moderately related to level of social

1. Logically, in this notion of social mobility, the structural arrangements in which individual movements occur, are defined in the same terms as the goals of these movements, *i.e.* occupational prestige is attained by changes within a structure of occupational prestige. For an attempt to define social mobility independently from the motivations and aspirations involved in terms of changes of the role- and status-set of individuals, *cf.* K.U. Mayer, W. Müller, "Progress in social mobility research?" *Quality and quantity* 5 (1), 1971, pp. 141-178.

background, a higher evaluation of acceptance of risk and secular success and more emphasis on education and occupational ambition for students of higher than for those of lower origin, the latter more often stressing security and material possessions.

Katz (1964), in a study of Australian adolescents, found marked variations in the definition of success held by children of different social background. "Wealth and possessions" was clearly the most important dimension for those with fathers in skilled and unskilled manual occupations, while for children with fathers in white collar occupations "status in educational and occupational hierarchies" appeared to have about equal weight.

Mizruchi (1964, pp. 72 and 80) reports, for an adult sample, that lower class respondents select mostly home ownership and job security as symbols of success, whereas middle class respondents favor educational attainment. Moreover, while middle class respondents tend to view education as an end, providing personal satisfaction, lower class people see it more often as a means.

In his well-known secondary analysis, Hyman (1966) concludes that lower class respondents generally place low emphasis on (college) education, favor security, job stability and material gains as the goals of their occupational careers and have more modest aspirations for occupational status and income increase than middle class respondents, who see congeniality to personal needs as the prime value in occupational activity. Hyman also reports differences between persons of high and low occupational position in the perceived opportunity for occupational advancement in the future and in the belief that hard work would benefit chances of promotion.

Svalastoga (1959, pp. 274 ff. and 375 ff.) concludes from questions on occupational aspirations in his Danish study that mobility aspirations are modest and decrease with social status, but that even among the lowest strata, 38 percent would like to have their own business.

In the volume on *The reluctant job changer*, Herman (1965, pp. 125-132) examines for the Norristown and Springfield survey whether aspirations among production workers tend to be lowered with advancing age, as the research by Chinoy (1955, p. 110 ff.) and Guest (1954, p. 158) has suggested. Only partial evidence was found. Occupational plans were higher at the time of entry in the labor market, but there were no differences between those above and those below the age of 35 who would not want to enter the same occupation again. Herman, like Goldthorpe and his coauthors (1970, pp. 130-143), indicates only limited interest in higher ranking jobs among workers (*ca.* 50 percent of the respondents in both studies). Concerning the concepts of success held by respondents Herman reports that apart from professionals all groups favor economic security above career advancement and non-economic goals.

Goldthorpe and his coauthors (1969, pp. 116-156; 1970, pp. 126-157), in their study of affluent workers, stress that collective economic advancement rather than individual occupational promotion are the typical expectations of the workers studied and that the wish to improve their living standards can be considered their key motivation in mobility and clearly not the wish to advance in social prestige. On the other hand, only slight differences appear between manual couples and white collar couples in regard to educational and occupational aspirations for children. But the authors refer to other British investigations where working class parents' aspirations for their children were considerably lower.

Other studies report variations in the level of aspiration (Kahl, 1953; Empey, 1956), achievement motivation (Rosen, 1956; Crockett, 1966), deferred need gratification (Strauss, 1962) and images of society (Bott, 1954; Willener, 1957; Goldthorpe, 1970).

This kind of results does not, of course, permit us to refute the assumptions regarding mobility orientations and the level of aspirations in any rigorous manner. The main reason is that the prerequisites of such a test are not at all clear. What percentage of a given population or group must agree or may disagree on which items in order to speak of "common" value orientations toward the achievement of occupational or monetary success (Turner, 1964, p. 76 ff.)? When do dominant values plus deviations end and subcultural heterogeneity start (Rodman, 1963/1964)? Can the degree of commitment to values be inferred from the relative percentages accepting them (Merton, 1957, p. 170 ff.)? How is one to evaluate relative in contrast to absolute levels of aspirations and how are ceiling effects to be taken into account (Turner, 1964, p. 46 ff.; Empey, 1956)?

But the findings of the studies reviewed, however fragmentary and inconsistent, do show that the premises of generally high commitments to upward mobility and a common frame of reference for its direction obliterate differences worth describing and explaining. Many reasons can be found as to why a highly generalized concept of social mobility based on a specific view of American society can hardly be expected to be fruitful. The reification of this concept tends to obscure historical changes in the institutional bases of mobility, the impact of differential opportunities for and experiences of occupational mobility, the existence of ethnic and age-related countercultures and intersocietal differences.

When success was based on the acquisition of independent property a generalized definition of mobility in terms of money and material possessions may have been an apt description (Mills, 1951). But when mobility processes are institutionalized in utterly different ways — entrepreneurship, trade-union backed improvements in income and working conditions in blue collar work, educational achievement and bureaucratic careers — a common perspective on mobility and its goals seems less likely. Orientations toward consumption, money or property and occupational satisfaction or prestige need not coincide. Even if initial aspirations are high and homogeneous, it should be expected that low educational and occupational opportunities or career ceilings will result in a reduced emphasis on advancement and in a reorientation of dominant concerns. The recent impact of the youth culture must suggest even to the superficial observer that, at least between age groups, level and dimensions of mobility aspirations will be at variance. If such considerations apply to the context of American society, it seems presumptuous to reify, without prior investigation, for other societies a concept of social mobility which is based on the idea of a value-consensus regarding lifegoals.

Two questions follow from this discussion. First, if motivations, aspirations, emphasis on mobility values and dimensions of the perception of stratification vary both in extent (or level) and direction within a given population, do these factors, in addition to structural changes, influence actual mobility in a specific dimension and, if so, to what extent? Second, if, in fact, social mobility is oriented toward a variety of ends, should it not be described and measured in accordance with its subjective intentions (*cf.* Gouldner, 1970, p. 56)?

Subjective factors of social mobility as independent variables

With regard to the first problem, Duncan (1969) has made an attempt to clarify the causal role of dispositions, *i.e.* attitudes and motives, in the occupational status attainment process. He distinguishes between four alternative types of hypotheses. Dispositions towards occupational achievement may be seen as exerting partial influence on attainment independent of background factors such as status of family of origin, as intervening variables between background factors and occupational status, as sources of spurious correlation between achievements at earlier or later stages of the career or, conversely, as a result of the level of occupational status achieved. Intricate methodological problems have to be solved before these alternatives can be settled. Dispositions have to be measured as properties of individuals and cannot be inferred from the national or group level. The presumed causal relationships between the selection of indicators measured and underlying theoretical variables must be made explicit in order to evaluate validity and strength of association with achieved occupational status. Measurement of the variables should take place at the time when they are assumed to operate according to the causal model or, otherwise, precautions must be taken to ensure that measures are not being contaminated by effects of the dependent variable. Duncan (1969) has shown that neglect of these standards leads to discrepant results and interpretations.

Data from cross-sectional studies suggest that strength of achievement motivation is a causal factor contributing to upward occupational mobility for men from the lower portion of the occupational hierarchy (Crockett, 1962), whereas the attitudinal variable "striving for occupational accomplishment" — being negatively related to occupational attainment — may probably best be interpreted as influenced by mobility experiences (Kahl, 1965; Duncan, 1969).

The relative weight of the effect of dispositions on occupational achievement can most reliably be judged from longitudinal studies. They indicate that occupational and educational aspirations are indeed causal factors influencing occupational attainment partially independent of background variables (Elder, 1968; Sewell *et al.*, 1970).

In terms of the assumptions stated above all these studies question the invariance of commitment to mobility and level of aspirations and examine the causal consequences of their variability, but they implicitly affirm the premise of a common dimension of mobility and mobility orientations. In the following part of this article we shall try to answer the second question posed above and ask whether the traditional one-dimensional concept of social mobility is a valid description of how people perceive their movements within the social structure.

Subjective definition of social mobility

A generalized one-dimensional concept of social mobility presupposes either common value-orientations in the population to which it is to be applied or a stratification system which is organized according to one specific dimension of social inequality and has such a great impact that people have no other choice than to define their life goals and concerns in terms of this structure.

In a preliminary way our review of research findings suggested that these conditions cannot be taken for granted. Thus it becomes necessary to describe differential subjective definitions of social mobility more extensively and to interpret them in terms of differential past experiences and expected future life chances.

Several proposals have been made for the conceptualization of diverse mobility orientations by Miller (1955), Lipset and Zetterberg (1966), Westoff *et al.* (1960) and Wilensky (1966). They are presented together in Table 1. Some of these authors have proposed the combination of measures of mobility in different dimensions or to add a measure of mobility orientation to indices of "objective" mobility. This shortcut between the theoretical recognition of diverse definitions of social mobility and index-building, which has only seldom been followed in actual research, certainly increases our information on mobility processes and may better enable us to account for their hypothesized effects. We maintain, however, that the study of subjective definitions of mobility does not only serve an auxiliary function, but is of interest in its own right, since it should provide direct access to the "reality constructs" which make up mobility experiences [2].

2. A short-hand rationale on the utility of "subjective definitions" for the assessment of orientations can be found in C.W. Mills' article "Situated actions and vocabularies of motives" (pp. 439-452, in his collection of essays *Power, politics and people*, edited by I.L. Horo-

Table 1. *Aspects of mobility orientation*

Dimension of desired rewards	Receiver of rewards	Space of movement	Time perspective	Level of aspiration Level of commitment
Occupation				
Skill, competence				
Personal satisfaction				High
Security			Retrospective	Moderate
Responsibility				Low
Social class	Self	Society	Last generation	
Prestige			Own career	
Life style				
Association	Family	Community		
Wealth			Present	Realistic
Income				Fantasy
Possessions	Children	Workplace		
Consumption			Future	
Leisure			Unstable	
			Stable bureaucratic	
Education			Own career	
Power			Next generation	
Independence				
Autonomy				
Influence				

Supplementing the elements of the subjective definition of social mobility presented in Table 1 by some contextual aspects, we obtain the following catalogue :

1. Perception of the structure and dimensions of stratification,
2. Perception of the dimensions, directions and major events (and their timing) of the mobility process,
3. Evaluation of past mobility and present situation,
4. Level and direction of mobility aspirations,
5. Perception of opportunities,
6. Expectations for the future,
7. Definition of success and failure,
8. Perception and evaluation of criteria of social selection.

witz, New York, Oxford University Press, 1963) where he presents a symbolic-interactionist view on the relation between verbalization and conduct: "The choice of lines of action is accompanied by representations and selection among them, of their situational termini. Men discern situations with particular vocabularies, and it is in terms of some delimited vocabulary that they anticipate consequences of conduct. Stable vocabularies of motives link anticipated consequences and specific actions. [...] Institutionally different situations have different vocabularies of motive appropriate to their respective behaviors."

Below, data concerning aspects two, four and six will be presented and analyzed [3]. Working hypotheses can be formulated according to the assumptions and their implications stated at the beginning. Thus we hypothesize that:

1) social mobility will be defined in terms of occupational advancement or related concepts,
2) the respondents agree widely in their definition of social mobility,
3) the level of aspirations will be generally high.

Sample and methods

The data to be analyzed is taken from a study of all accessible males of the cohort being 33-years old, living in the city of Konstanz, Germany, and having been registered on the electoral rolls at the time of interviewing (1969). This excludes all persons who did not have permanent residence or had not registered with the reporting office and all foreigners. Interviews could not be obtained from *ca.* 20 percent of the initial sample due to obsolete addresses, permanent absence or refusal to cooperate. Refusal to be interviewed was disproportionately higher among unskilled and semiskilled workers. All together, data is available on 398 respondents.

A cohort was selected, since for such a small sample size, age categories could not be differentiated containing enough persons in all of the major occupational and status sub-categories. The particular age group, that of 33-year old men, was chosen, since this group has already experienced considerable mobility, while not having been overly affected by the special conditions of the war and postwar period. The city of Konstanz, location of the study for reasons of economy, has about 60 000 inhabitants. Its occupational structure can be characterized as follows: an above average proportion of small proprietors and dependent employees in the service sector, an above average proportion of persons employed in public administration ("öffentlicher Dienst"), an electronics industry (mostly development) which has grown rapidly in the last ten years employing highly qualified technical, administrative and research personnel, and a relatively high proportion of young university staff. These conditions, to a large extent, explain the disproportionately high percentage of respondents in the higher status categories. The data on dimensions of social mobility to be analyzed in the section below are based on open questions. They were asked almost at the beginning of the interview in order to avoid the responses to these questions being influenced by the vocabulary

3. An analysis of empirical data on the perception of dimensions and structure of inequality from the same study is being published by the author under the title "Soziale Mobilität und die Wahrnehmung gesellschaftlicher Ungleichheit", *Zeitschrift für Soziologie* 1 (2), 1972.

and intentions of questions on specific movements such as educational attainment, occupational training and advancement or income changes.

The interviewers were instructed to follow the wording of the questions closely and to give no help whatsoever to respondents in formulating answers. Coding schemes were devised and revised on the basis of an inspection of all answers to particular questions. Working with a coding scheme common to the responses on past and future mobility as well as concerning aspirations has proved feasible. The categories used can be seen as labels for the institutional spheres within which an individual occupies and changes socially defined positions (family, education, occupation), carries on specific activities (leisure) and their spatial basis (residence), for dimensions of social rewards (income, property) and as labels for residuals which have another unit of change (personality, society). The type of responses subsumed under these headings will be illustrated in the course of the discussion of the data [4].

Measuring perception of mobility dimensions

Since the term "social mobility" or "mobility" is seldom used in colloquial German and since, as an academic concept, it has various connotations such as occupational fluctuation or frequency of residential mobility or capacity to be mobile, it could not be used to ask respondents what it means to them to be mobile and whether they have been mobile. In the decision on how to word questions in this area, we proceeded from the observation that in ordinary speech as well as in traditional concepts of social mobility, processes are expressed by means of particular events. Further, we took the least suggestive equivalent of what sociologists very generally mean by social mobility, that is *important changes in the life of individuals.* That sociologists consider changes between social classes or strata as *the* most important ones, was not our concern here, since their understanding was not the object of measurement.

Past and future changes in life, perceived as important, were accordingly taken as indicators of the subjective definition of social mobility and its dimensions. The respondents were asked :

Considering all the changes in your life since the time you were twenty, which were the important ones?
What do you believe will change in your life in the future?

Measuring dimensions of mobility aspirations

Insofar as they do not reflect perceived constraints, the answers relating to mobility expected in the future should indicate in which dimensions mobility is regarded as desirable. To tap aspirations, apart from such constraints,

4. *Cf.* the appendix for a shortened version of the coding rules.

two questions were asked. The first one aims at mobility aspirations which the respondents are able to verbalize, but which they judge unrealistic:

Assuming your greatest dreams would come true and nothing stood in your way, what would you be doing ten years from now?

The second question introduces the assumption that no economic constraints would hinder social mobility and aims at aspirations which are blocked due to scarcity of economic resources:

Suppose you would, by winning in a lottery for instance, get so much money that you could live well on it till the end of your life, what would you do?[5]

These four questions represent only a part of the efforts in this study to measure definitions of, and aspirations for social mobility, but combined, the answers should most directly describe in which terms actual and potential mobility is being conceptualized.

Distinguishing status groups

As an initial attempt to relate differences in the subjective definition of social mobility to particular social backgrounds, cross-tabulations by "status groups" are presented. What we shall call "status groups" in the following refers to categories of respondents with similar social and economic ranks as judged by their occupations. The hierarchy of these status groups has been determined by their place in the internal order of legally defined occupational categories and a scale of self-evaluated status developed by Kleining-Moore (1968) for West Germany.

Table 2. *Status groups and occupational categories*

	Occupational category			
Status groups	Manual workers	White collar employees	Civil servants	Self-employed
Upper middle UM	—	Professional managerial	Higher (Höherer Dienst)	With more than 20 employees
Middle middle MM	—	Higher sales or technical	High (Gehobener Dienst)	4-20 employees
Lower middle LM	Dependent artisan	Qualified clerical	Middle (Mittlerer Dienst)	Up to 3 employees
Upper lower UL	Skilled worker	Unskilled clerical	Lower (Einfacher Dienst)	—
Lower lower LL	Semiskilled Unskilled	—	—	—

5. Similar questions have been asked by Svalastoga (1959, pp. 441-445): "If by pushing a button you could get any occupation in life whatsoever, which would you choose?" (Ques-

Perception of past mobility

It must be kept in mind that the data presented relate to a particular point in time in the career of the respondents. They are 33 years old and have occupational histories varying in length from nearly twenty to only five years. Since the question on past life changes gives the age of twenty as a point of departure, the answers refer to about thirteen years of mobility experience.

Table 3. *Dimensions of mobility perceived in the past. Percentage distribution of respondents, by status groups**

Dimension of social mobility	All respondents	LL	UL	LM	MM	UM
(Totals = 100 %)	(398)**	(35)	(86)	(115)	(105)	(52)
Family	74	57	72	76	77	73
Education	23	6	6	17	35	48
Occupation						
Advancement	23	11	13	28	29	27
Other changes	34	29	19	42	34	46
Economic rewards	12	20	6	16	10	12
Residence	11	6	10	11	10	12
Leisure	2	—	1	3	3	2
Society	6	6	5	5	7	10
Own personality	11	17	15	6	9	19
Unspecified/DK	5	3	6	6	3	6
Average number of changes specified	2.0	1.5	1.5	2.0	2.1	2.5

*Percentages add to more than 100 due to multiple responses.
**Includes 5 respondents who cannot be classified by status groups.

As shown in Table 3, most answers fall into the "family" - category. More specifically these concern leaving the parental family, marrying or marrying and having children, which are perceived as the major changes in these years, mentioned by nearly three quarters of all respondents. Movements in the occupational sphere take second place, but references which clearly indicate occupational advancement, like promotion or becoming independent, are less frequent than changes which say nothing specific as to whether upward mobility is implied or not, *e.g.* entering first job, changing jobs or occupations. Mobility by way of school or university education or occupational training is mentioned by about a quarter of the respondents. Improvements in living standards or increase of income and a few cases of building a house — indicat-

tion No. 54); "If you won 10 000 Kroner in a lottery, what would you do with the money?" (Question No. 101).

ing changes in economic position — are mentioned only by a minority (12 percent). About as many perceive changes in residence, a third of which refer to migration from the GDR (the German Democratic Republic) and other eastern regions.

All these answers conform to the idea of social mobility as movements of individuals between positions in social structure or along dimensions of social inequality. 17 percent of the respondents, however, did not interpret the question in this way. 11 percent see their own personality and 6 percent particular aspects of society in transformation. The former refer, for instance to becoming self-reliant, autonomous or contented, the latter to automation, technological development or changes in politics or public morale.

Table 4. *Perception of social mobility and length of occupational and marriage life, by status groups*

	All respon-dents	LL	UL	LM	MM	UM
(Totals = 100 %)	(398)	(35)	(86)	(115)	(105)	(52)
Occupational changes perceived in the past	57	40	32	70	63	73
Occupational life longer than 15 years (since first job)	27	47	30	23	20	2
Familial changes perceived in the past	74	57	72	76	77	73
Percent married	84	71	85	88	90	80
Married longer than ten years	16	29	23	18	12	2
Married less than six years	18	6	14	13	21	34

There are a number of differences between status groups which deserve attention. The percentage of respondents mentioning changes or events in the area of education and occupational training increases with social status. The frequency of references to occupational advancement is, for all the three higher groups, more than double that for the two lower groups. There is also a clear break between the middle and the lower status groups, if one looks at the proportion of answers falling into both occupational categories, the three higher groups having nearly twice as many responses as the two lower ones. Improvements in the standard of living are mentioned most often in the group of unskilled and semiskilled workers and, relatively, also quite frequently in the lower middle group. Furthermore, the lowest group indicates marriage and other familial changes to a lesser extent than the other ones. Both in regard to familial and occupational changes these results point to differing biographical patterns influencing the responses as indicators of perceived mobility dimensions. This is clearly confirmed in the case of marriage as the major mobility step in the family dimension. In Table 4 it can be seen that perceptions in this respect are a function both of the fact of being married and of the length of married life. A similar relationship is shown with regard to occupational changes perceived in the past and length of occupational life since first job. That the relative fit between these two series of proportions is not as good should surprise no one. Length of occupational life is not the ideal indicator for occurrence of occupational changes. Thus, these perceptions appear to be unstable features, in part depending on the time distance between the mobility events mentioned and the moment of the interview.

Mobility expected in the future

In their expectations for the future (Table 5) our 33-year old respondents are not very articulate on the average, not more than one change is mentioned and the proportions of those who do not expect any specific change or just do not know is high. Among the respondents expecting to be mobile, occupation is the major dimension of movement. References to occupational advancement — promotion or becoming self-employed — are more frequent than those indicating other shifts in occupation. Some way behind, expectations of eco-

Table 5. *Dimensions of mobility expected in the future. Percentage distribution of respondents, by status groups**

Dimension of social mobility	All respondents	LL	UL	LM	MM	UM
(Totals = 100 %)	(398)**	(35)	(86)	(115)	(105)	(52)
Family	16	—	12	11	21	27
Education	3	3	7	1	1	6
Occupation						
Advancement	28	20	21	31	29	33
Other changes	15	14	15	13	12	19
Economic rewards	18	14	12	18	26	19
Residence	9	14	12	4	4	19
Leisure	3	3	3	1	5	2
Society	6	3	2	4	10	8
Own personality	4	9	1	1	5	8
Unspecified/DK	29	34	35	36	26	13
NA	2	6	1	2	1	—
Average number of changes specified	1.0	0.8	1.0	0.9	1.1	1.4

*Percentages do not add to 100 due to multiple responses.
**Includes 5 respondents, not classifiable by status group.

nomic improvements rank second in importance. In the family dimension there is some overlap with the previous question; those who have not yet married or had children look forward to doing so. As in the perception of past mobility, though to a lesser extent, personality and social developments are mentioned.

Differences between status groups are most pronounced with regard to marriage and having children reflecting delayed career beginnings in the higher status groups. The lowest and highest groups appear to expect residential mobility most often and seem most concerned with their own personality, but due to the small size of these groups one should be hesitant to attribute too much significance to these findings.

The consistency of the responses on movements expected for the future may be checked by a series of closed-ended questions which tap the same area.

Table 6. *Occupational career expectations, by status groups*

Do you believe that you have attained your highest occupational position already or do you expect this for the future?

Highest occupational position...	All respondents	LL	UL	LM	MM	UM
(Totals = 100 %)	(398)*	(35)	(86)	(115)	(105)	(52)
Attained already	22	29	34	22	19	6
Expected in the future	78	71	66	78	80	92
NA	1	—	—	—	1	2

*What do you expect for this better position?***

Expected improvement	All respondents	LL	UL	LM	MM	UM
(Totals = 100 %)	(309)	(25)	(57)	(90)	(84)	(48)
Other kind of work	22	40	30	20	18	21
Higher income	81	68	68	83	86	88
Position with higher prestige	27	28	16	20	30	42
More responsibility	53	40	44	53	56	63
More influence	34	20	21	28	45	50
More decision-making power	46	28	33	41	60	50
More autonomy	45	56	37	42	45	54

*Includes 5 respondents not classifiable by status group.

**Follow-up question directed only to those who expect a higher position in the future. Answer categories were given and any number of them could be chosen.

The additional information confirms that, for the respondents in this study, expectations of occupational advancement are emphasized more frequently the higher the occupational status (disregarding the inversion among the two lower categories). Here again one could argue that this may in part be due to the fact that length of education and training vary and careers are started at different age levels.

The more startling observation, however, is that in all status groups the proportion of those expecting at least some occupational advance is very high. Even among the unskilled and semiskilled workers, about two thirds do not consider themselves to be at the end of their occupational career.

Do these figures imply a firm expectation of upward occupational mobility? This question can be assessed by examining anticipated improvements in future positions. In doing so it must be borne in mind that the answer categories were given and no constraints were imposed with regard to the number of possible selections among the seven attributes.

A higher income than earned at present is by far the most important expectation being chosen by four out of five. About half the respondents anticipate more responsibility, more freedom in decision-making and more autonomy, *i.e.* less dependency. Less significant, or less realistic hopes, appear to be: getting more influence, higher prestige and another kind of work, in that order. With few exceptions we find a monotonic relationship between level of status and the frequency with which respondents expect particular items; in the cases of prestige, influence and decision-making power, the proportion in the highest group is almost, or more than, double that in the lower groups. The exceptions to be noted are an inverse relationship between level of status and expectation of another kind of work and higher frequencies in the lowest group in respect to prestige and autonomy. The overall impression then is that all value essentially the same improvements, but the higher the occupational status the greater the frequency of respondents who expect them to occur.

If one interprets "Other kind of work" as "intrinsic work satisfaction", all these attributes can be seen as vertical aspects of occupational position. As improvements anticipated, therefore, they indicate expectation of upward occupational mobility. Assuming, for a moment, that these expectations are realistic, the crucial question is the following: are such ascents expected as a result of general rises in the standard of living, as a result of normal developments in the occupational career or as genuine movements out of the present occupational position?

In another question with given answer categories we have asked whether the respondents expect in ten years time to have the same occupation, to work in the same organization and to live in the same city (*cf.* Table 7). Among unskilled and semiskilled workers only 23 percent and among skilled workers and unskilled white collar employees only 15 percent expect not to be in the same occupation in ten years time. About a quarter of both groups assume

Table 7. *Expectations for the future. Percentage distribution of respondents expecting occupational-, job- and residential mobility, by status groups*

Expect in ten years...	All respon-dents	LL	UL	LM	MM	UM
(Totals = 100 %)	(393)	(35)	(86)	(115)	(105)	(52)
To have the same occupation	77	49	70	83	86	80
Not to have the same occupation	14	23	15	11	10	18
DK and NA	9	27	15	6	5	2
To work in the same firm or organization	59	57	59	62	64	47
Not to work in the same firm or organization	24	23	25	21	21	39
DK and NA	16	20	16	17	15	14
Still to live in the same city	68	83	77	70	71	37
Not to live in the same city	17	9	7	16	17	39
DK and NA	15	9	16	15	12	24

that they will not work in the same firm. If one also considers the relatively high degree of uncertainty concerning the stability of current occupation in these groups as expressed by the size of the "DK" and "NA" category, it can be inferred that only few of them tend to think of their occupational advance in terms of upward mobility into the "middle class". The improvements they anticipate must then either be due to collective economic rises or minor ones due to some sort of career development.

For the higher status groups, the members of which to an even higher degree expect to remain in the same occupation, ascents in occupational status must be taken as almost entirely career-based, although they might be of a greater magnitude. It is in the highest status group, which comprises mostly academically trained respondents that a higher expected rate of change in work place and change of place of residence may lead to major career advances also with regard to non-economic aspects of occupational status, *e.g.* responsibility, influence, prestige and autonomy.

With respect to shifts between places of work and occupation the proportion of respondents answering "don't know" or giving no answer is of special significance. There is a high degree of definiteness in the responses of the higher groups, while the lower ones show a great deal of uncertainty. Without overstating the case it may be inferred from these data that respondents in higher occupations are themselves the agents of mobility, while the degree of uncertainty at the bottom of the hierarchy suggests that, there, many look to a future as objects rather than as agents of mobility.

Aspirations for the future

Asked what they would do in ten years time, if nothing stood in their way and their greatest dreams came true (*cf.* Table 8), more than half of the respondents think of their work. Among them, a small majority clearly indicates that they are hoping for steps up the occupational ladder. Second in importance appear to be changes in the economic dimension. The typical aspiration here does not refer to high income, but to the acquisition of property. Specifically, it is owning one's own house which as a single item is most frequent among all goals mentioned. The relatively high proportion (18 percent) favoring leisure activities, if they could realize what they want to do most, seems large, but is misleading. The persons in this category do not aspire to a leisure class lifestyle. More modestly, almost all of them would either like to do some traveling, take holidays or spend more time on their private interests and hobbies.

Table 8. *Dimensions of aspirations for the future, assuming no external restraints. Percentage distribution of respondents, by status groups**

Dimension of social mobility	All respondents	LL	UL	LM	MM	UM
(Totals = 100 %)	(398)**	(35)	(86)	(115)	(105)	(52)
Family	5	—	3	4	6	10
Education	5	—	3	4	10	4
Occupation						
Advancement	29	23	24	26	30	42
Other changes	27***	34	24	28	28	25
Economic rewards						
Income	6	6	7	9	4	2
Property	20	15	27	21	12	10
Residence	2	3	1	1	3	6
Leisure	18	11	13	22	19	17
Unspecified/DK	19	3	22	17	22	23
NA	1	3	1	1	—	—
Average number of changes specified	1.1	1.2	0.7	1.1	1.1	1.2

*Percentages do not add to 100 due to multiple responses.

**Includes 5 respondents not classifiable by status groups.

***About half of the answers in this category refer to "immobility": *e.g.* continue to work, doing occupationally the same as today.

The most noteworthy differences in aspirations between status groups are: an increase in family orientation with ascending status; a comparatively high proportion of respondents wishing for more education in the group just below the one whose members typically hold university degrees; an increase in the expressed desire for occupational advancement is found going up the hierarchy; more concern for property ownership in the three lower groups, most pronounced in the group of skilled workers and lowest ranking white collar employees; a somewhat higher preoccupation with leisure in the three higher groups.

Table 9. *Dimension of aspirations, assuming sudden affluence. Percentage distribution of respondents, by status groups**

Dimension of social mobility	All respondents	LL	UL	LM	MM	UM
(Totals = 100 %)	(398)**	(35)	(86)	(115)	(105)	(52)
Family	4	—	7	3	2	6
Education	6	3	3	4	7	10
Occupation						
Advancement	11	9	10	11	10	15
Other changes	47***	40	47	51	46	48
Economic rewards						
Income****	5	3	6	4	7	4
Property	58	74	63	57	55	46
Leisure	26	34	18	23	25	31
Unspecified	9	6	3	8	12	12
Average number of changes specified	1.6	1.6	1.6	1.6	1.5	1.6

*Percentages do not add to 100 due to multiple responses.

**Includes 5 respondents not classifiable by status groups.

***Over three fourths of the answers in this category refer to "immobility": *e.g.* continue to work, doing occupationally the same as today.

****Here this code refers to answers concerning standard of living, *e.g.* living free from care, etc.

The second question tapping aspirations does not, as does the first one, relate to projections into the future. It is designed, rather, to show which kind of immediate changes people have in mind assuming that they do not have to earn their livelihood. The wording of the question suggests two possibilities of interpretation: are economic resources converted into mobility of a non-economic kind and, if so, which kinds of changes are desired.

As can be seen even from the crude codes presented in Table 9 the majority of respondents do not seem to think of converting economic resources into changes, other than those which are little more than tautological, in their economic standing. This becomes even more obvious when we look at the answers in more detail. A few think of their family, though not with respect to changing its social status; most often they want to improve the chances of their children. Only about 10 percent would use the money to achieve a higher occupational position and about as many indicate they would make some other changes with regard to their occupation. A quarter of the respondents would want to engage in leisure activities, most often by traveling or taking a vacation. That the answers falling within the property dimension do not show any genuine mobility can be inferred from the fact that the great majority simply want to save or invest the money, whereas the rest consider buying a house or real estate.

Differences between status groups show most clearly in inclinations to property ownership and occupational advancement including education, the former decreasing and the latter increasing with level of social status.

Table 10. *Work attachment. Percentage distribution of respondents indicating occupational changes under the assumption of sudden affluence, by status groups*

In regard to occupation would...	All respondents	LL	UL	LM	MM	UM
(Totals = 100 %)	(391)*	(35)	(85)	(115)	(104)	(52)
Stop working	5	6	5	7	3	2
Change occupation	21	31	26	24	17	8
Stay in same occupation, but in other form	45	37	46	44	47	49
Do exactly the same	29	26	24	25	33	41
*(If changes were indicated, respondents were asked whether they would...**)*						
Work as much	26	40	42	41	32	29
Work less	29	29	30	26	31	28

*Table contains only cases classifiable by status groups and with answers to this question.

**The follow-up question was put to those checking categories "Stay in same occupation, but in different form" and "Change occupation"; the percentages are computed from the group totals above.

The finding that our respondents apparently cannot conceive of major changes in their life as a result of sudden affluence, can partially be checked against the answers to a question with given answer categories which was asked immediately following the one discussed above. Granted that the necessity to earn one's livelihood would cease, would they want to change the kind or amount of work? Merely one out of twenty would quit working and one out of five would like to take up another kind of occupational activity. Among those who neither want to stop working nor leave everything as it is, the majority desires no change in the amount of work.

Taking the answers shown in Table 10 as measures indicating job satisfaction and work attachment, an observation frequently reported in other studies can be confirmed. Job satisfaction increases with level of status (which has been measured here by occupational status!). But as both the answer category "Stop working" and the follow-up question indicate, lower job satisfaction does not imply lower work ethos. Quite the contrary, the three lower status groups want to work as much as they do now to a greater extent than the higher status groups, even if they would prefer to alter the character of their occupational activity [6].

Occupational value orientations

For the 33-year old male respondents in our sample we have found that the occupational sphere is the major dimension of mobility perceived in the past, expected or aspired to in the future and that over three quarters believe in attaining a still higher occupation as compared with the one they held at the time of the interview. On the other hand, most of them expect to have the same occupation and to work in the same organization when they are 43 years old. And even if relieved of the need to work, three quarters would stick to their current occupational activity.

Above, we have argued that this seeming contradiction between expected improvements in occupational status and a widespread tendency toward occupational immobility might be explained by general rises in the level of income or career-based ascents of various, but mostly minor magnitude. The counter-hypothesis would hold that the improvements anticipated are not quasi-automatic consequences of careers and economic growth, but advances decisively brought about by individual efforts. This latter contention would imply that our respondents are indeed to a great part oriented toward occupational advancement.

6. The finding that most respondents, and manual workers in particular, show a high degree of work attachment or, better, have internalized the social norm of work to such a high degree stands in contradiction to the dictum by Marx: "Der Arbeiter fühlt sich daher erst ausser der Arbeit bei sich und in der Arbeit ausser sich. Zu Hause ist er, wenn er nicht arbeitet, und wenn er arbeitet ist er nicht zu Hause. Seine Arbeit ist nicht freiwillig, sondern gezwungen, Zwangsarbeit. Sie ist daher nicht die Befriedigung eines Bedürfnisses, sondern sie ist nur ein Mittel Bedürfnisse zu befriedigen. Ihre Fremdheit tritt darin rein hervor, dass sobald kein physischer und sonstiger Zwang existiert, die Arbeit als eine Pest geflohen wird. " K. Marx, "Ökonomisch-philosophische Manuskripte", in: K. Marx, *Frühe Schriften* (H.J. Lieber; P. Furth, eds.). Stuttgart, Cotta, 1962. Vol. 1, p. 564.

Table 11. *Occupational values. Percentage distribution of respondents preferring particular aspects of occupations in choices between alternatives, by status groups**

Alternatives of occupational values	All respondents	LL	UL	LM	MM	UM
(Totals = 100 %)	(393)	(35)	(86)	(115)	(105)	(52)
No spare time, good chances of promotion	42	60	31	47	44	29
vs. spare time, no chances of promotion	58	40	69	52	56	71
Very good relations to workmates	80	77	87	75	79	86
vs. getting ahead by "pushing"**	19	23	13	22	21	12
Permanent acquisition of new skills and knowledge	55	51	43	53	59	75
vs. practical experience	45	49	57	47	41	25
Chances of getting much money	73	71	72	72	77	65
vs. high esteem by others	26	29	28	25	21	33
Individualistic advancement	60	60	52	66	62	53
vs. chances to help others	39	40	48	32	38	43
Undisturbed working at tasks	40	54	58	33	29	41
vs. exerting influence on others	59	46	42	65	71	55
Security for oneself and family	82	89	94	84	76	66
vs. promising position with risks	17	11	6	15	24	33

*In translation the question was worded: Assuming you wanted to make a change occupationally and you had the choice between two different possibilities, which of the two possibilities printed together would you prefer?

**In German: "Arbeit, bei der man mit Durchsetzungsvermögen vorankommt."

We have a means of assessing this alternative in the answers to a closed-ended question. The respondents were asked which attributes of an occupational position they would prefer (choice given between several pairs of attributes), assuming they were to change their occupation.

The answers indicate that "security", *i.e.* economic security and stable employment, "good relations with workmates" and "high income" are being preferred as against a promising, but risky job, ruthless striving and high prestige. To most respondents spare time seems more important than chances of promotion and only where advancement competes with the altruistic motive of helping others, does the disposition towards upward mobility predominate. Although, in general, occupational advancement does not appear to be a dominant concern, it should be noted that for the lower and middle status groups the lowest category in each (LL, LM) have the highest relative frequencies when advancement is one of the choices. Only in the alternative where a secure job is put against a promising, but risky one, does this observation not apply

Here, the disposition towards advancement with risks is most pronounced in the two highest groups, but even among these the security-minded are in the great majority.

Thus, it may be inferred that the criteria by which occupational improvements are principally evaluated can be met without a genuine change of position in the traditional sense of upward mobility. Further, with the exceptions noted, the improvements anticipated do not seem necessarily to be dependent on individual striving in contrast to general or career-inherent developments.

Summary and interpretation

We began this paper with a critique of the reification of a concept of social mobility which seemed to imply that *a*) upward mobility is a commonly shared value and a dominant life-concern, *b*) mobility is universally oriented toward high occupational rank or the rewards derived from it, and *c*) that mobility aspirations are generally high and persist even where their fulfilment is unlikely.

The data presented here, from a local survey on a cohort of 33-year old men, were selected primarily to test inferences concerning the dimensions of social mobility as subjectively defined. By means of this exploratory procedure an evaluation of the extent to which the subjective notion of mobility corresponds to the current sociological conception of this term was to be made. The information collected on perceived changes in the past and on expected future changes should indicate in which terms actual mobility is articulated. The questions concerning aspirations were intended to probe whether respondents also entertain mobility goals different from those that were within the limits of their current life situation.

If we take the amount of education received as an important prerequisite of occupational placement, even if it is also in part sought after as a source of satisfaction in itself, and consider income, standard of living and property as benefits largely derived from occupational activity, movements in such a broadly conceived occupational sphere account for the major portion of subjectively defined social mobility. Only a small part of these responses, however, refer specifically to upward mobility within educational and occupational hierarchies and an even smaller share manifest any status or prestige connotations.

While only few think of themselves predominantly as being mobile in physical space or in terms of kind or amount of leisure, the great number of responses in the dimension of family affairs deserves attention. Leaving the parental family, marrying and having children are ends to be achieved in a certain age-period and may conflict with educational and occupational goals. These rival orientations of social mobility may pose a real value-dilemma between economic and occupational success on the one hand and satisfactory social relations, emotional and sexual ties on the other which cannot easily be resolved by manipulating the personal time-budget. This point has been phrased succinctly by Wilensky (1960, pp. 549-550): "Apparently the United States (perhaps every industrial society) has so structured the timing and balance of obligations in the economic, kinship and other spheres that peak demands in economic life (launching a career, getting established in a job) coincide with peak demands in procreation and hence consumption — doubtless a source of strain for both person and social structure."

Since only about 10 percent of our respondents see aspects of society at large or their own personality as changing, it may be concluded that the sociological idea of social mobility as changes in social structure with the individual as a moving unit has an extensive counterpart in subjective definitions. Differences in the *perception* of mobility in the past and future clearly reflect differences in career patterns associated with various levels of occupational status. In the past, higher status groups more frequently perceive educational and occupational changes, in the future, they expect familial changes and occupational advancement more often than the lower groups. Longer training, delayed career beginnings and delayed marriage lead to a more frequent articulation of mobility concerns in these dimensions.

Although both questions on aspirations are slightly weighted in favour of the occupational *viz.* economic dimension, some respondents define their hopes and wishes with respect to the family, some in terms of education and quite a few in terms of leisure activities. Nonetheless, the bulk of aspirations are connected with the occupational and economic position of the individual. Regarding the latter area it is not so much level of income or consumption which manifestly define aspirations but property ownership. In particular, house-ownership appears to be a widespread symbol of achievement. There are certain indications of an inverse relationship between aspirations for occupational advancement and for property ownership. If one assumes this to be a reliable result, it would suggest the hypothesis that unfulfilled aspirations concerning rank and the intrinsic rewards of work roles are being diverted into the area of material possessions.

The questions on "fantasy" aspirations apparently do not reveal mobility orientations of a markedly different kind from those shown in expectations for the future which are framed within all the economic and other constraints of the present situation of the respondents. These questions merely reveal that the level of aspirations is somewhat higher if no restrictions are assumed to exist. This is indicated most clearly by the small proportion of respondents who would make major changes with regard to their current occupation, if relieved of the need to earn their livelihood.

Thus, on the basis of the empirical material scrutinized we have to concur with the assumption embedded in the traditional mobility concept that in the main mobility orientations are subjectively defined in relation to the occupational and economic position of the individual.

More specifically, however, which aspects of occupational and economic position are seen as criteria of improvement or ascent? On the economic side, we have already mentioned house-ownership as an important symbol of success. With regard to occupation, it is higher income, economic and employment security, good relations with workmates, responsibility and some degree of independence and autonomy which seem to be most desirable. And yet, advancement is either not expected or aspirations to it are unambitious, rarely going beyond present occupational position and its normal career developments. In other words, while work and occupational activity certainly is a dominant life-concern besides the family, upward occupational mobility does not appear to be so (at the age level of our respondents). Also, prestige and recognition by others do not seem to be primary and manifest mobility goals.

Finally, we have to answer the question whether mobility goals are essentially of the same kind or are emphasized differentially by respondents located at different levels of the occupational hierarchy. Furthermore, we will ask whether there are widely differing levels of aspirations or a lowering of aspirations in the face of contrary experiences.

From the various pieces of information presented one can point to several differences between occupational status groups. Income, security and property ownership seem subjectively more significant in the lower groups, whereas continuing education and acquisition of knowledge and the intrinsic aspects of work seem more so for the higher groups. What is emphasized more frequently by workers and unskilled white collar employees can probably be taken for granted by incumbents of higher occupational positions, most of whom have bureaucratic careers.

Going down the occupational hierarchy the desire for another kind of work increases notably as well as the aspiration to a change of occupation if no obstacles were in the way. This kind of dissatisfaction, not with labor, but with the kind of work one is constrained to carry out, may explain the tendency toward extrinsic economic rewards as more likely tokens of improvement. In the tables presented one can observe that the lowest group of unskilled and semiskilled workers in many instances deviates from monotonic relationships between level of status and relative frequency of responses. Among such items are "promising position with risks", "individualistic advancement", "good chances of promotion", expectation of "higher prestige" and "more autonomy". Disregarding the danger that the small number of respondents in this category easily plays tricks on the resulting percentage values, these observations, together with the high proportion of those expecting occupational improvements in the future, lead to the following conclusion: at the age of 33, those less successful in their occupational career seem neither to be resigned nor to have rechanneled their aspirations into other spheres of social activity.

From cross-sectional data on a cohort, of course, nothing definite can be inferred concerning the development of aspirations, and only the use of quantitative measures would permit safe conclusions on the level of aspirations.

But relative to the age of the respondents the material scrutinized neither points to very high aspirations in comparison with present occupational position and career expectations in general, nor to widely differing relative levels of aspirations. Nonetheless, going down the occupational hierarchy, and particularly in the group of unskilled and semiskilled workers, expectations for the future are closer to aspirations than to realistic appraisals of their likely futures.

Both the limitations of the body of data and the exploratory mode of its analysis preclude anything other than preliminary results which suggest rather than rigourously test hypotheses. With this caution in mind, it may be concluded that aspirations for some improvements in the future are widespread though relative to the position already attained. They are less centered on the individual person, as an agent of their realization, and more on the common properties of the position one holds or else on quite general advances. Aspirations persist even in the face of past contrary experiences and of the unlikelihood of fulfilment in the future.

At various levels of the occupational hierarchy, goals are differently emphasized, a result largely congruent with the findings reviewed in the beginning of this paper. These differences, however, accord much better with what Turner has called *the culture-variation hypothesis* in contrast to a subculture hypothesis of class values: "The subculture position depicts class differences in value as differences in kind rather than in degree.[...] The culture variation approach, by contrast, begins by assuming a generally uniform system of values throughout a society and treats class differences as variations on a society-wide theme. Culture takes priority in analysis over subculture. The observed differences [...] arise because the characteristic life situation in each class makes any given value relatively attainable or unattainable, or relatively comprehensible or incomprehensible" (Turner 1964, pp. 10-11).

Interpreted in this way our findings run counter to most of our initial expectations. This might in part be attributed to our rough measure of occupational status or to the non-industrial character of the place of the survey. If, however, these findings are valid for West German society, mobility measured in terms of generalized occupational rank does not stand in contradiction to its subjective definitions and perspectives. On the other hand, these findings also imply that a less voluntaristic view of social mobility, which examines the logic of given careers for ensuing attitudes, may be more adequate.

APPENDIX

Shortened version of codes for questions on perceived changes in the past, expected changes in the future, aspirations for the future and aspirations assuming affluence

Perceived changes in the past *Expected changes in future*	*Aspirations for the future* *Aspirations assuming affluence*
Family Changes with regard to family of origin, *e.g.* death of a parent; changing relations to family of origin, *e.g.* becoming independent from home. Marriage Children, *e.g.* birth, etc. Divorce.	Children, *e.g.* to have more children, taking care of education and future of children. Taking more time for wife and family.
Education School, education and related events. Occupational training and related events.	Studies : education as fulfilment, intellectual interests. Occupational training.
Occupational advancement Occupational improvements in the sense better conditions of work, *e.g.* good, secure job, independent, interesting work. Occupational advancement, clearly upward mobility. Independence = Self-employment.	Same as on left side.
Other occupational changes Entering or leaving an occupational position, retirement. Change of job. Change of occupation.	Occupationally doing the same as today = no occupational change. Change of job or occupation. Working less. Stop working.
Economic rewards Improvement of standard of living. Higher income. Acquisition of property, *e.g.* building a house.	*Economic rewards : income* Economically secure existence. Becoming affluent, living in luxury. *Economic rewards : property* Investing money. Saving. Own house, own apartment. Houses and real estate. Acquisition of shares, foundation or enlargement of own establishment.
Residence Change of residence. Change of place of residence. Emigration, immigration, long stays abroad. Resettlement from GDR or other eastern regions.	Same as on left side.

Leisure More spare time, less work, engaging in hobbies. Traveling, vacations.	*Idem*
Society Social changes which concern the role of the respondent as consumer or producer, *e.g.* technological development, automation, general rise of standard of living. Political changes, *e.g.* orientation of society toward the left, democratization, looser morals.	*Idem*
Personality Change of interests, adaptation, maturation, becoming contented, personal autonomy. Change of health.	*Idem*

REFERENCES

Bott, E.
1954 "The concept of class as a reference group", *Human relations* 7: 259-283.

Chinoy, E.
1955 *Automobile workers and the American Dream,* Garden City, NY, Doubleday.

Crockett, H.
1962 "The achievement motive and differential occupational mobility in the United States", *American sociological review* 27: 191-204.
1966 "Psychological origins of mobility", in: N.J. Smelser; S.M. Lipset (eds.). *Social structure and mobility in economic development.* Chicago, Ill., Aldine.

Duncan, O.D.
1969 "Contingencies in constructing causal models", in: E.F. Borgatta (ed.). *Sociological methodology.* San Francisco, Calif., Jossey-Bass.

Elder, G.H.
1968 "Achievement motivation and intelligence in occupational mobility: A longitudinal analysis", *Sociometry* 31 (4): 327-354.

Empey, L.T.
1956 "Social class and occupational aspiration : A comparison of absolute and relative measurement", *American sociological review* 21 : 703-709.

Goldthorpe, J.H.; Lockwood, D.; Bechhofer, F.; Platt, J.
1969 *The affluent worker in the class structure.* Cambridge, Cambridge University Press.
1970 *Der "wohlhabende" Arbeiter in England: Industrielles Verhalten und Gesellschaft.* Munich, Goldmann.

Guest, R.
1954 "Work careers and aspirations of automobile workers", *American sociological review* 21 : 155-163.

Gouldner, A.W.
1970 *The coming crisis of Western sociology.* New York, Avon

Herman, M.W.
1965 "Class concepts, aspirations and vertical mobility", in: G L. Palmer *et al.* (eds.). *The reluctant job changer.* Philadelphia, Pa., University of Philadelphia Press.

Hyman, H.
1966 "The value-systems of different classes: A socio-psychological contribution to the analysis of stratification", in: R. Bendix; S.M. Lipset (eds.). *Class, status and power.* New York, Free Press. (2nd ed.)

Kahl, J.A.
1953 "Educational and occupational aspirations of 'common man' boys", *Harvard educational review* 23: 186-203.
1965 "Some measurements of achievement orientation", *American journal of sociology* 70: 669-681.

Katz, F.M.
1964 "The meaning of success: Some differences in value systems of social classes", *Journal of social psychology* 64: 141-148.

Kleining, G.; Moore, H.
1968 "Soziale Selbsteinschätzung (SSE): Ein Instrument zur Messung sozialer Schichten," *Kölner Zeitschrift für Soziologie und Sozialpsychologie* 20: 502-552.

Lipset, S.M.; Zetterberg, H.
1966 "A theory of social mobility", in: R. Bendix; S.M. Lipset (eds.). *Class, status and power.* New York, Free Press. (2nd ed.)

Lipset, S.M.; Bendix, R.
1959 *Social mobility in industrial society.* Berkeley, Calif., University of California Press.

Luckman, Th.; Berger, P.L.
1964 "Social mobility and personal identity", *European journal of sociology* 5 (2): 331-344.

Merton, R.K.
1957 *Social theory and social structure.* Glencoe, Ill., Free Press.

Miller, S.M.
1955 "The concept of social mobility", *Social problems* 3: 65-72.

Mills, C.W.
1951 *White collar : The American middle classes.* New York, Oxford University Press.

Mizruchi, E.
1964 *Success and opportunity : A study of anomie.* New York, Free Press.

Porter, J.
1968 "The future of upward mobility", *American sociological review* 33 (1): 5-19.

Rodman, H.
1963- "The lower class value stretch", *Social forces* 42: 205-215.
1964

Rose, A.M.
1964 "Social mobility and social values", *European journal of sociology* 5: 324-330.

Rosen, B.
1956 "The achievement syndrome: A psycho-cultural dimension of social stratification", *American sociological review* 21: 203-211.

Schumpeter, J.A.
1927 "Die sozialen Klassen im ethnisch homogenen Milieu", *Archiv für Sozialwissenchaft* 57: 1-67.

Sewell, W.H.; Haller, A.O.; Ohlendorf, G.W.
1970 "The educational and early occupational status attainment process : Replication and revision", *American sociological review* 35: 1014-1027.

Strauss, A.L.
1971 *The contexts of social mobility: Ideology and theory.* Chicago, Ill., Aldinc.

Svalastoga, K.
1959 *Prestige, class and mobility.* Copenhagen, Gyldendal.

Tauski, C.; Dubin, R.
1965 "Career anchorage: Managerial mobility motivations", *American sociological review* 30: 725-735.

Turner, R.
1964 *The social context of ambition : A study of high school seniors in Los Angeles.* San Francisco, Calif., Chandler.

Westoff, C. F.; Bressler, M.; Sagi, P. C.
1960 "The concept of social mobility: An empirical inquiry", *American sociological review* 25: 375-385.

Wilensky, H.L.
1960 "Work, careers and social integration", *International social science journal* 12: 543-560.
1966 "Measures and effects of mobility", in: N.J. Smelser; S.M. Lipset (eds.). *Social structure and mobility in economic development.* Chicago, Ill., Aldine.

Willener, A.
1957 *Images de la société et classes sociales.* Bern, Stämpfli.

DANIEL BERTAUX

Two and a half models of social structure

"It is always in the immediate relationship between the masters of the means of production and the direct producers [...] that is to be found the intimate secret, the hidden foundation of the whole social structure."

Karl Marx

"You want to be a doctor for us miners? Then you must first go down to the pits; I mean, not once or twice, but 10 years, 15 years.

You must learn to know what it means to choke, what it means to have stones fall on your face. To see your kids dying, and have to wait for hours in an office to get a paper. Sometimes, to lack the money to buy drugs, or to eat. To walk to the mine with high fever, under the rain.

My father was a miner; he died from silicosis. I never got married; what is the use of bringing to the world unhappy children?" (Quoted from a conversation recorded in May 1968 in Northern France; this 48-year-old miner died since from silicosis.)

"Social inequality is thus an unconsciously evolved device by which societies insure that the most important positions are conscientiously filled by the most qualified persons."

Kingsley Davis and Wilbur Moore

Introduction

The rise of social consciousness

The seventies might witness a general, worldwide rise of social consciousness.

There had already been a strong revival of critical thought by the end of the sixties, in the wake of social movements in various parts of the world.

Now it seems that the long winter of bourgeois conservatism, fascism and stalinism is drawing to a close: if the political regimes under which we live are still of these types, more and more people cease to recognize them as legitimate. Many signs converge to announce the coming of a social springtime.

Why this sudden and unexpected greening[1] of the whole world? Most probably because the time for it is right. Humanity was, and still is, going straight to the abyss: the blind logic of the development of capitalism and the resulting struggles between empires push us towards total, definitive self-destruction. Besides the steadily growing threat of thermo-nuclear eradication of life on earth, it is also daily that the situation of human beings is growing worse. In Asia, Latin America and Africa, the perspectives offered by imperialism to the oppressed peoples — under the gentle names of "civilization" and "progress" — are total destruction of the local culture, hard labour for miserable salaries, and tons of bombs and napalm for those who dare to resist. At the same time, at the other end of the domination relationship, the people of the rich, *i.e.* exploiting countries, find that their daily life has become meaningless. There, the way to "the pursuit of happiness" seems mysteriously blocked; but as the causes of this situation, *i.e.* the social "structures " evolved by capitalism in its monopolist phase, remain hidden, people tend to put the blame on each other or on a vague, universal "pollution".

A feeling of powerlessness is growing in everyone. Nobody wants the thermonuclear holocaust — but nobody knows what to do to prevent it. Nobody wants the cruel killing of Vietnamese children nor the starvation of Indian or Brazilian babies, but a "system" which after all has engendered such events seems to have no way of preventing them. Nobody wants an increase in crime, pollution of nature and the loss of meaning of everyday life, but all feel helpless in face of these phenomena.

This brings us to the question of consciousness. Right actions cannot spring from false consciousness, and false consciousness is everywhere. We are all immersed in a giant sea of lies, and our images of reality are completely distorted. Any action, however good the will, is therefore bound to fail. Hence the feeling of powerlessness. And as consciousness cannot be gained save through action, the vicious circle seems interminable...

But the new generation is beginning to find the way out. The first actions of its most courageous members, who were fed up with lies, began revealing the truth to the others. Thus they grew stronger. Now the fight has begun and will go on, with its ups and downs; it will take a lot of courage — and some knowledge. But it will not stop until all the social relationships are transformed, and life has become meaningful again.

Consciousness dawns again at the right moment — when history needs it.

1. I borrow this expression from Charles Reich, whose book *The greening of America* (first published New York, Random House, 1970) constitutes by itself, and even more by its social success, one of these signs.

And it starts where it is easiest: with those in all social classes who are young enough not yet to be completely immersed in the sea of the ruling ideology. But consciousness will not be limited to youth — or to the exploited classes. It will grow in everyone, and the talkative lier, the "hidden persuader" who is constantly active in our heads — the ugly offspring of the ruling ideology — will be forced to loosen more and more its grip on our minds.

Each of us must find, where he happens to be, his own way to contribute to the general movement. For us, "social scientists", it seems that the main task would be to develop social theory in the direction of truth. This may mean a serious reorientation of our work, which will not be easy to actualize.

In this paper I will take up the question of social structure. It is probably the most important, and also the most difficult question of social theory: here I cannot hope to do more than gather and propose a few concepts and insights which should help to make sense of the contemporary social phenomena. We will start with the soundest part of present-day social theory, Marx' critical works on political economy, and proceed to the embryo of a theory of the middle classes and of their ideology [2].

1. The world class structure

Since the Second World War, class structure has to be understood in a worldwide sense. It is virtually meaningless, nowadays, to talk of the "class structure" of a town, or even of a country; for the social relationships which determine the lives and deaths of people are worldwide, be they military, economic,

2. This symposium is on career mobility. Considering the present state of social theory, I believe that the best way to develop the understanding of "mobility" phenomena — or for that matter of any other aspect of social reality — is to make advances in the field of social (class) structure. My first sociological research was on social mobility in France; from it I learned that it was impossible to do empirical research without a sound conceptual framework, and that the vagueness of the "concepts" used in current mobility studies does not come from a flaw in the "theory of mobility" but from the representation of social structure as a stratified pyramid which underlies all sociological thinking on mobility. This seems to be a typically middle class representation of society — as is the concept of career mobility, which only has meaning for the institutional middle classes.

To progress in the study of mobility phenomena, I found it necessary first to make a thorough study of social structure. Reading the literature, it took me two years to become convinced that Marx' works were not just another ideological system, but the most sincere and serious attempt to discover the fundamental logic of social reality. Having compared them with the rest of the sociological literature, I today consider them as the sound core of contemporary social theory.

This paper is my first attempt to summarize my current thinking concerning social structure. I beg the reader to excuse its numerous imperfections. (For earlier sociological studies, see especially "Sur l'analyse des tables de mobilité sociale", *Revue française de sociologie* 4, 1969, pp. 448-490, and "Nouvelles perspectives sur la mobilité sociale en France", *Quality and quantity* 1, 1971, pp. 87-129.)

political or ideological. Willingly or not, we are all located within a world class structure — the world class structure of the age of imperialism.

Weapons as the ideal output of capital-determined production

By imperialism, I mean the movement towards the spread of capitalist relationships of production (capitalism) throughout the world, and its consequences. The history of capitalism is the history of its development under the weight of the blind forces of its inner contradictions. It should be recalled, briefly, that production in a capitalist system does *not* mean the production of goods, as most social scientists believe — or pretend to believe — but the production of *money*, more precisely, the production of capital under the transitory form of goods, as capitalists very well know. (As a former President of General Motors once put it: "My predecessor thought he was here to make cars; but *I* know I am here to make money.") The recurrent problem facing capitalists has been how to sell these goods to people who at the same time, as salaried workers, are paid the lowest wages their employers can get away with. This permanent economic contradiction has repeatedly led to crises, along with attempts to avert them. Colonialism is one of these attempts; pre-capitalist areas are conquered in order to "export" internal contradictions. But when the whole world has been submitted to capitalism, the same old problem of overproduction rises again, only on a larger scale. Wars represent another means whereby crises have been averted, as history very clearly demonstrates. Most recently, the mass production of armaments is the latest and most dangerous trick developed by capitalism for its survival. Armaments are the only type of goods for which there is virtually no marketing problem, and whose actual consumption (in the Second World War, in the Korean or Vietnam wars) stimulates both their own reproduction and also, through the destruction caused, the reproduction of just about every other type of goods. Here, in the second half of the 20th century, humanity has reached the ultimate point of the inner logic whereby production for the sake of the enlarged reproduction of capital leads to the production of destructive "goods" (goods!), then to the destruction of productive goods — and of humanity, as a secondary, though inevitable consequence of the whole blind process [3].

3. Several important *empirical* studies have been made on imperialism. An excellent and highly readable synthesis has recently appeared: F. Greene, *The enemy*, New York, Vintage Books, 1971. See also H. Magdoff, *The age of imperialism*, New York, Monthly Review Press, 1969, which contains illuminating data on such phenomena as foreign aid, the world finance network, the importance of exportation of capital in dominated areas, etc. On the production of weapons, see especially M. Kidron, *Western capitalism since the war*, London, Weidenfeld and Nicholson, 1968, augm. ed. 1971; and P. Baran and P. Sweezy, *Monopoly capital*, New York, Monthly Review Press, 1966.

False ideas lead to tragic consequences

At the same time as we are being led to destruction, we are made to believe that we are on the road to an era of everlasting abundance and peace. And these false ideas cannot be easily swept aside: on the contrary, they are deep-rooted in the class position of the so-called middle classes. They are also reproduced and strongly reinforced daily by the concrete conditions in which we live our lives outside work (structure of the family, type of urbanization, etc.) and by the flood of false ideas that continually swamps us.

We are all located somewhere in the world class structure. To say this does not mean that we are "located" somewhere in the spatial sense of the term, *i.e.* as left free of our thoughts and actions, as the notion of "individual" seems to presuppose. Our location within this structure means we are literally constrained, and submitted to very strong fields of force determining our actions. Thought is imposed upon us, yet made to seem our own; our actions are conditioned but made to seem original; but our thoughts and actions are also conditioned *according to our location* within the world class structure [4].

The failure of the social "sciences"

The thoughts in our brain are not free, but socially constrained. But if daily life conditions us to think in a biased way, should not the social sciences at least provide us with an objective picture of the social world? The fact is that the only accepted form of social science, the academic one, has instead of developing in the direction of truth, come to play more and more a role opposed to cognition. That role is the very obscurantist one played in the past by religion: of producing and reproducing the key notions, representations of the world, and values of *dominant ideology*, that system of lies which prevents us from perceiving reality. This is the tragi-comic side of the situation: it is precisely when humanity, driven to self-destruction by the blind mechanisms developed from centuries of class structure, would most urgently need the insight afforded by social science, that the social "sciences" are the

---

On the specific problem of the relations between the world centres of capital and the "dominated periphery", interesting work has recently been done, *cf.* S. Amin, *L'accumulation à l'échelle mondiale*, Paris, Anthropos, 1971; C. Palloix, *L'économie mondiale capitaliste*, Paris, Maspero, 1972; A. Emmanuel, *L'échange inégal*, Paris, Maspero, 1970; P. Jalée, *L'impérialisme en 1970*, Paris, Maspero, 1969. See also the works of C. Furtado, A.G. Frank, and of other Marxist economists, especially from Latin America.

Recent advances can be found in such journals as *Monthly review*, and *Science and society*, New York; *New Left review* and *International socialism*, London; *Les temps modernes*, *L'homme et la société*, *Politique aujourd'hui*, Paris; *Quaderni Piacentini*, Piacenza; *Kursbuch*, Berlin, etc.

4. By far the best text on this question is still *The German ideology*, a long forgotten work of Marx and Engels. See especially its first part.

furthest away from the search for truth, and that the social scientists are the most confused.

How did this become possible? Basically, because social research is done not in a social void but in institutions, *i.e.* parts of the class structure. Therefore, it is not social scientists who dominate the class structure, but the class structure which dominates social science. As a consequence, social science explodes into dozens of "disciplines", which tolerate superficial statements of "truth" (to gain credibility) while avoiding making an approach at the fundamental level, *i.e.* the level of the world class structure. The key concepts and hypotheses that would have made this world understandable, were rejected, and an alternative, smooth image of social structure, the "stratification" model, was put forward.

Economists, sociologists, political "scientists", historians, etc., were and still are institutionally compelled to think in this direction (*away* from where the truth lies), and most of them for reasons of personal convenience have internalized this orientation [5].

Western anti-Marxism as a visceral, pre-intellectual reaction

In the recent history of social science, there had been one exception: the works of Marx and the best of his followers. But from the very beginning, they were strongly attacked by academic economists and sociologists, not to mention the many other professional ideologists. After one century of such an institutionally-legitimated attitude, reactions of Western, particularly of Northern American intellectuals to Marxism have become visceral, not intellectual; they belong to the realm of conditioned reflexes. It is true that Marx' ideas were greatly distorted sometimes by Marxists who were constrained by *their* own institutions; but the blame was put upon Marx himself, as if Christ was personally to blame for the action of the churches. It is also true that there are many questions that Marxian theory, in its present state, cannot answer: but the agressivity towards it is so great that any *particular* silence is immediately interpreted as proof of the falsity of the *whole* theory — an attitude which would destroy any attempt at explaining the world if it was systematically applied to all other theories, which is of course not the case...

5. The example of C. Wright Mills shows very clearly that the logic of the academic social sciences is *not* the logic of the quest for truth (adequation of description and theorization to reality) but the logic of the production of these ideas and bits of practical knowledge which are useful for the ruling class. Despite the fact that Mills clearly demonstrated what was the true nature of academic sociology, and that by his own empirical work he began to show the way towards sound social research, he remained completely isolated. Academic social research went on as if Mills had not existed — with the same methods, the same concepts, th same bureaucratic approach to reality, the same ignorance of history, etc. Even if some sociologists understood Mills' message, they did not have control over research funds: it was those who controlled (and still control) them who had the power to orient social research, and this they did in complete conformity with the goals of the class they represented.

Visceral anti-Marxism has prevented most of Western intellectuals from seriously considering and adopting what is probably, with all its silences, the most reliable body of social knowledge today: a body of knowledge which does not belong any more to Marx but to humanity and whose acceptance does not mean that one has become a Marxist (if this term is taken to mean uncritical adhesion to the "holy texts"), no more than to accept that the earth is revolving means becoming a Galileist [6].

The weaknesses of contemporary social theory

To develop social theory, the sound attitude seems to be to take as base Marx' critical approach to political economy, and work from there. It is this approach which has been used to deepen the understanding of international relations, *i.e.* the theory of imperialism, which is probably the best contribution made in recent years to social theory (see references in note 3). The empirical and historical evidence in favour of this theory is now so overwhelming that no serious attack against it is attempted any more: ignorance and sarcasm are the only weapons left to its opponents.

But in other areas, and particularly with regard to the construction of a theory of local (here, national) class structure, Marxism has been less successful. As sociology has also been unsuccessful, as could have been predicted, we are left with no clear understanding of the phenomena of social structure on a national scale [7].

In Marx' writings, there is no explicit theory of social classes to be found. But there is an excellent analysis of the laws of *capitalism* — undoubtedly the form of production of contemporary Western social formations (societies). Marx' analysis of the relationships between the working class and the capitalist class (the bourgeoisie) seems to correspond to empirical and historical reality. What is lacking is an understanding of the nature of the *new middle*

6. The understanding that class-based relationships between men must disappear, must be brought down, if we want to avoid our transformation into mindless robots, and the total and definitive destruction of humanity in the near future, does not necessarily mean that one has become a power-thirsty, bomb-throwing activist, as is thought in some circles. But it is not surprising that the best is taken for the worst and vice-versa in a world where lies are widely diffused as truth, and truth, if ever uttered, is first denounced as lie; where the most destructive and criminal activities are relabelled "peace-keeping", while the most productive, constructive project, *i.e.* social revolution, is understood by so-called common sense as a destructive, criminal idea. We are all immersed in the ocean of ideology that the "system", as an octopus, continuously secretes for its own protection.

7. Is it necessary to recall that the works of the founders of modern sociology, Weber and Durkheim, were explicitly conceived by their authors as "answers to Marx"? Most of the contemporary North-American sociological research is of the same orientation, although at a much lower level. See for instance the historical genesis of one of its key concepts, the concept of "status" as opposed to the concept of "class", as described by L. Reissman in his "Introduction" to *Class in American society*, Glencoe, Ill., Free Press, 1959,

classes; a theory of the *institutions* of capitalist social formations, and also an analysis of contemporary "*socialist*" *social formations*. These three "silences" in Marxist theory, together with the political silence of the working classes of developed capitalist countries, have constituted the basis for the refutation of Marxism as a theory able to explain the social world. In other words, Marxism has once more been attacked for what it did not analyze.

Middle class ideology versus the theory of the middle class

Here I shall try to develop the (critical) theory of class structure to include the new middle classes[8]. My fundamental hypothesis is that these classes are actually constituted by members or agents of "state apparati", *i.e.* institutions which, whether public or private are actually parts of the State as "Boards of Management of the common affairs of the (national) ruling class". Middle class people are therefore conceived as being in positions of *agents of the ruling class*. But these "institutional petty-bourgeois" (IPB), as I will rename them, protect themselves from discovery through an elaborate ideological system, part of the ruling ideology, which makes them appear as working for the people whereas they are actually working for the ruling class, *i.e. against* the people. The class structure produces an institutional middle class serving the interests of the ruling class, and this middle class elaborates an ideology which dissimulates the class structure; hence the difficulty of the analysis...

If developed and confirmed, such an hypothesis would serve to answer the three silences of social theory quoted above: the rise of the new middle class would be explicable by disclosing the true function of the institutions (repres-

8. The analysis of the "salaried middle classes" which this paper summarily develops, is based on the conception of institutions, whether public or private (churches, media, private schools, etc.) as "State apparati" (*appareils d'état*). This conception goes back at least to Marx (see his *Critique of the Gotha programme* for instance; *also* Engels, *The origin of family: private property and the state*, and *Anti-Duhring*; Lenin, *The State and revolution;* and Gramsci's works). Institutionalized Marxism, understandably, did little to develop this conception. New advances are currently being made; I refer especially to N. Poulantzas' work. See his two important books, *Pouvoir politique et classes sociales*, Paris, Maspero, 1968; *Fascisme et dictature*, Paris, Maspero, 1970 (especially section 7); also L. Althusser, "Note sur les appareils idéologiques d'état", *La pensée*, avril 1970; R. Miliband, *The state in capitalist society*, London, Weidenfeld and Nicholson, 1969; and the discussion between him and Poulantzas in the *New Left review*. This theoretical orientation is beginning to produce empirical studies; on "institutions", see for instance the excellent study of the French school system by C. Baudelot and R. Establet, *L'école capitaliste en France*, Paris, Maspero 1971. Miliband's and Poulantzas' works contain numerous references to the history of capitalist social formations (Great Britain, France, Italy, Germany, etc.), *i.e.* they are based on empirical evidence.

So far, these authors have studied institutions as such, and little attention has been paid to their "agents", as constituting a particular social group (see however section 7 of Poulantzas' second book). It is in this direction that I shall try here to pursue the analysis.

sion); a theory of the class content of the State as the system of repressive institutions could be developed; and a lucid analysis of the social formations where the State is predominant (developed capitalist countries; but also "socialist" societies) could be made [9].

2. Fundamentals of "national" class structure

The two fundamental relationships of class structure: exploitation as end, domination as means

First a common sense assertion: all social phenomena — and social structure to begin with — are rooted in the process of production, of material production, to be precise: after all, if the production of essential commodities ended, we would all pretty soon die [10].

In parallel to the recognition of the predominant role of production, it should be remembered that "societies" are not made up of unconnected individuals (as vulgar ideology would have us believe) but of *social relationships*, which constantly determine human thoughts and actions and constitute the forces that shape social life: this is the basic credo of social science, on which both Marx and his opponents, *i.e.* the founders of "bourgeois" sociology, Weber and Durkheim, are all agreed.

Putting together these two very basic observations, we realize that if production is the basis of social life, then the matrix of all social relationships has to be found in production: to find it is to find the key of the door to an understanding of societies and history.

In all historical societies, this basic matrix relationship has been the relation between those who "do the real work" and those who dominate and exploit them: a relation of exploitation and domination. Under the various *forms* that this relationship has taken in historical times (slavery, feudalism, capitalism) it has always had the same *content*: exploitation of those who work by those who rule — *exploitation* as the goal of the class structure, *domination* as the means to attain it.

Why exploitation?

That exploitation and domination are at the basis of every historical "society", can be logically understood as well as empirically verified. Empirically: all

9. After completing this paper I discovered that a different view of the "new middle class" had been developed by some North-American Marxists, who define it as a "new working class". See especially the interesting journal *Socialist revolution*, San Francisco. It seems that both views are compatible; but they emphasize different aspects of the same reality.

10. See for instance the famous text of K. Marx, "Introduction" to the *Grundrisse* (*Grundrisse der Kritik der politischen Ökonomie*, written in 1857), New York, Harper and Row, 1971.

social history is an obvious verification of this — and it is only in "defining", or rather creating *ex abstracto* its own intemporal, irreal "reality" that the academic social "sciences" achieve this tour de force of not seeing the most obvious feature of our societies. Logically: it is easy to show that the fundamental nature of the class relationship (exploitation and domination) can be quite directly and logically deduced from the simple fact that *there is only one useful thing that a dominant group can get from a dominated group, and that is its work — or rather, the products of its work.*

From people who are powerless, all can be taken: their life, their physical integrity, their health, their freedom, their time, their work, "their" children, and so on: all these things can be taken away, but only one can be *appropriated* by somebody else: the products of their work.

The comparison with animal species is instructive. It seems that the use of tools to work on matter, which constitutes the main difference between humanity and other species, is also the feature which permits class structures based on exploitation to develop among human beings. This would be unthinkable among, say, fish or herbivorous animals of the same species. And it seems that it is only through the full development of this other feature of human species, social consciousness, following the full but blinkered development of a tool-based process of production, that the class structure may be abolished — when the historical moment has come at last.

From basis to superstructures

Exploitation has so far been a permanent fact of human history, the history of its class societies [11] and of their class struggles. The awareness of this (not, of course, taught in schools...) allows us to understand the dynamic of the *basis* of social formations, *i.e.* the class-structured *process of production.* But what also require explanation are the *institutions* and *ideological systems* that have been created by the historical evolution of class-structured production.

To begin studying the logic of these "superstructures" as Marx called them, I propose to hold an imaginary interview with this master of social forms, this ever-active builder and destroyer of institutions and ideologies, the ruling class: for none can better explain such structures than the social entity which created them. So, let me for a while set you, the reader, in the position of the dominated classes, and have you listen to what the cynical ruling class would have to say about the way it intends to organize its relationships with you.

11. The first exception could be China after the recent "Cultural Revolution". However, we as yet lack the testimony of direct witnesses. See the very interesting book of M.A. Macciochi, *Della Cina*, New York, Monthly Review Press, in publication; and for the years preceding this second revolution (besides the well-known books of Edgar Snow and Han Suyin), *Fan Shen* by William Hinton, New York, Monthly Review Press, 1966.

An imaginary interview with the ruling class

So you are in my power, would it begin: what should I do with you? There would be no point in killing you, for it would not help me live a second longer. By destroying your health I would not feel any healthier. I could imprison you, but that would not set me free. The only thing I can take from you and appropriate for myself is the product of your labour: this alone is transferable and can be alienated from you. It is the result of your action on *matter*; and that I can certainly use!

Let me make this quite clear: it is no innate wickedness that makes me exploit you. But in order to survive we must all eat, be warm, and so forth. This has always required labour — hard labour, in fact [12]. So I would rather have you work for both of us, if this can be managed. This will be possible, for you seem to prefer to remain alive and exploited rather than dead and free. Therefore, if I can lay my hands on some weapon, the mere threat to your life will do the trick efficiently. This is slavery — the crudest form of class structure.

Thus a class society will arise. My descendants will become the masters, and yours will become slaves. The domination of "masters" over "slaves" will tend to appear natural, and all memory of a distant past, where the two classes were of the same breed, will be erased. An ideology will be elaborated to justify the situation, and if this were an ideology originally created by the slaves and subsequently turned against them, so much the better for they will submit to it more willingly (see the history of Christianity). The whole thing will be more smoothly run by ideology than by weapons: naturally I will retain violence as a standby. The politico-ideological structure of feudalism typifies these characteristics.

However, so long as agriculture is the main source of wealth, there is a weak point in my system: for working in the fields will constantly remind you that the products of your labour are the products of *your* labour — and that it is unjust to have them taken from you. But with the development of industry, this all changes: the "means of production" becomes increasingly *separated* from the actual labourers. You can no longer claim that the products of your labour belong to you since you have produced them with *my* tools and *my* knowledge. In the machine age, you are totally unable to produce anything without recourse to me. I will decide whether you shall work with my tools or not, and accordingly demand your gratitude. Think what you like, anyway, but be sure you respect "my" property. It is true that I acquired it through theft — but that is another story, which I choose not to remember, and which you would also best be advised to forget.

That you should labour for me does not, however, set me free. I am very active watching you, organizing your work and persuading you that everything is, and shall be, for the best. This is my part in the "division of labour". I shall enjoy it, for the exercise of power fulfills my desires, such as they have been implanted in me by my education in the context of a class society.

But I am few and you are many: I need support. I pay armed guards to watch over you, I pay ideologists to socialize you from the cradle to the grave, so thoroughly that you will play their role with respect to your own children. I pay administrators to organize your labour and ensure that everything that can be extracted from you is effectively so done (we may call this the "optimalization" of the production process).

All these people are paid with your labour, of course, which prompts me to follow the principle that the more they help me to extort from you, the greater should be their reward. This seems to me a fair enough principle.

As these groups develop, so the nature of my activities changes. I am no longer concerned

12. This is no longer entirely true, however, since in the second half of our century, productivity has increased to such an extent that it would be possible for all human beings to work only four to five hours a day in order to live comfortably — were production for the sake of consumption instead of for the profit of private capitalists and the power of their empires (see, for instance, the amount of labour expended on weapons...). Hence the obsolescence of capitalist forms of societies.

with the direct control of the labour force, but with its indirect control through the direct control of my agents. The latter I organize into *institutions*: it seems a powerful way to keep them powerless. Institutions are systems of hierarchically arranged *positions*, backed up by very strict *rules*, *i.e.* norms and sanctions which orient the activities of my agents solely towards the fulfilment of my interests. There should be no other horizontal relationship in the institutions save competitive relationships: this is necessary to divide the body of my agents into hostile atoms (if they united against me I would be totally powerless, needing to plead assistance from my neighbour who would no doubt take advantage of the situation).

All my institutions have a fundamental hierarchical principle. This states that every inferior should strictly obey his superior; and that every superior is responsible for the actions of his subordinates before *his* superior. With these two levers of *unquestioning obedience* (criticism of a superior is strictly forbidden) and *individual responsibility* (with the attached sanctions) I can easily manipulate millions of agents.

The supreme ruler, the superior above all superiors, is of course myself: the ruling class. However, being modest, I take care not to play this role too openly. My best ideologists are charged with finding the most adequate "supreme universal value" in whose name my authority can be exercized, and explaining this to the people as well as to my agents. According to the situation, the supreme value may be God, the Country, Order, the State, or Democracy, the Will of the People (I like this one), Freedom, Rationality, 5 % GNP growth, the Party, Socialism, or whatever else they may dream up: any idea will do, in fact, provided it convinces the masses.

My agents are always the most ardent believers in "supreme values": they seem to need them. It probably helps them accept a situation whereby they spend their lives in my totalitarian institutions. One must admit that this kind of bureaucratic existence, in which only the illusion of power remains, and which utterly excludes all possibility of friendship or rebellion, is highly unappetizing: at least the labouring classes can have solidarity and negativity. In compensation, I have devised a number of minor advantages which make life inside these institutions bearable, enjoyable even, provided people do not reflect too deeply on their social condition.

Firstly, I offer my agents full employment and a good pension (or, more importantly, the illusion of both). Unlike labourers, my agents are not compelled to present themselves on the labour market and sell themselves, for it is I who have bought them once and for all.

Next, I try to pay them adequately, but in a progressive way: I give them a *Career*. This is important, for labourers do not have "Careers": they just grow weary and worn out with age and labour. On the other hand, taking good care of my agents, I arrange for their gradual movement up the hierarchy of institutions. It gives them a pleasant impression of personal achievement and the rise to power. Their salary rises accordingly. This is rather artificial from the strict point of view of immediate efficiency, for the younger ones are often the most active. But it is absolutely necessary if I am to keep my agents faithful to me: career mobility gives them the impression that today is better than yesterday, and that tomorrow will be better than today. Consequently, their main expectation is that things will continue in this way indefinitely.

In fact, the longer my agents "live" in my institutions, the more they identify with my interests. This is one good reason why no power should be given to the young. Power must come as a reward for servility. The young often enter the institutions highly critical of the system of norms and sanctions which is their very foundation, the very essence of my power. These idealists must be socialized. I leave them to mature, powerless, for a year or two, having them carry out studies and "research" which are of little interest to me, but which help to establish a basis for their subsequent ideological switch. Then, I give them some small responsibility. There is nothing like practice to modify a person's ideas: as soon as they start *enacting* the institutional game (albeit often reluctantly at first), they begin to enjoy it and come round to a more reasonable point of view. Ultimately, of course, my aim is that my agents should enact their role *spontaneously*, having completely internalized the ideology which legitimizes my institutions, *i.e.* the service of my interests. This usually takes only a few years.

In order to help them feel they are working for the "general good" we have suppressed such crude labels as "agents" or "institutional petty-bourgeois". Instead, we discovered a more respectable name for them: the "middle classes". This has the precious advantage of allowing me, by virtue of their mere existence, and at the very same time as they are keeping my slaves enslaved, to demonstrate that classes, as such, no longer exist. One has simply to point to this stratified social group and ask: "Now, where are your two antagonistic classes? Can't you *see* they have disappeared? We now have nothing but a smoothly graduated prestige hierarchy (it would be inappropriate to speak of power in this context). Won't you awake from your 19th-century sleep? Everybody is middle class now."

My creative ideologists, those near the top of the ideological institutions, help me elaborate such useful images. I value these ideologists very highly, and treat them with special favour; for they are a sensitive breed. It is necessary to isolate them from the rest of the people, to keep them in ignorance of the treatment of my slaves. I pay them a good salary (feed your bird if you want it to sing) and give them honours (which cost nothing), and they twitter like canaries in the sunshine. In order to produce good ideology, ideologists have to be completely sincere: otherwise it shows.

What I want them to do is *sing*, to sing freely the songs I want to hear: about how good life really is; how everybody is exactly in the right place, how happy and contented they are; how the rulers and their agents, I beg your pardon, the representatives of the Will of the People and the qualified and loyal servants of the nation, are good and warm characters; how the labourers have all been given a chance to rise out of their own condition (if they remained there then it is their own fault); and how the villains who claim to disagree with the established social order are embittered power-hungry characters.

I always enjoy reading my journalists, whose task is to "inform" the people (to put into form, to deform and to chloroform would be closer to the truth), my writers and my art directors, who always write about love and adventures (and, have you noticed, rarely about work?), my teachers, those highly-trained manipulators and brainstuffers of children, and my social scientists, probably the dullest of the lot however: all of them the deserving successors of their great ancestors, the Jesuits, the most efficient group of ideologists who ever lived. I always rejoice, when listening to them praising in the most beautiful and imaginative forms, the rationality, the glory and the happiness of this brave new world.

The practice of production and class struggle as a permanent training for the ruling class

Were it ever to admit reality, thus might speak the ruling class. It is not too difficult to reconstruct its "instinctive" point of view [13]. The worst method would

13. It may be thought that this is a curious way of writing "science". As a former student and researcher in physical science and engineering, I do not share the fetishism for "scientificity" so common among sociologists trained in the humanities. It is common knowledge, in the physical sciences, that mathematical equations and "rigorous" demonstrations are of little importance as compared with the quality of adequation to reality of the concepts or "ideas" on which they are grounded. The rest is just like the gilt on a work of art, designed to make the finished product shine more brightly. Any good craftsman is capable of gilding, but the difficulty lies in the fashioning of the statue itself. I am afraid that, given the poverty of the principal ideas upon which the social sciences are at present based, the development of mathematical formulae or rigorous demonstrations is about as worthwhile as gilding heaps of rubble.

It is also worth noting that one of the few attempts to explicitly state the ruling class point

of course, be to look for this in its public speeches: for it will not be found there. One must pay attention instead to the literature and conferences that the rulers reserve for their internal use only (business journals, management textbooks, transcripts of committee meetings, etc.), and also the *practice* of the rulers, be they corporate heads or high administrative officials, political leaders or generals, newspaper directors or police chiefs: for their practice always betrays their true intentions. What emerges is very clear indeed.

Why is it worth reconstructing the rulers' point of view? Simply because they know many things about society — much more than any academic social scientist can ever hope to learn. Having the power, they have the practice, the best of all trainings; it is through it that their knowledge of social matters acquires an *experimental* quality.

The ruling class point of view projects a crude light on the whole social edifice. It affords a clearer view of its architecture and its inner logic. One understands also why it is never expressed publicly: this kind of thing is not for the masses to hear. The ignorant should remain ignorant; thus will they remain contented.

But the masses still need representations of the social formation in which they live. Ideologists are there to provide them. They will not produce them at random: the false images of class structure will be determined down to their very details by the class structure itself.

3. Class structure and its ideological representations

Before studying the various ideological representations of class structure, which is the main topic of this paper, we must examine the general features of ideological phenomena as such.

Particular class interests, overall class structure and biographical history as the three main determinations of concrete ideological patterns

In the particular ideological patterns which have their material existence in the minds of concrete humans, I shall tentatively distinguish the effects of three main determinations:

— The determination by *class position* (present and anticipated) through the

---

of view, Machiavelli's *The prince*, prompted an outraged response from a European prince who also happened to be a "philosopher". The ideologist in the future Frederick II of Prussia was unable to bear the cynicism with which Machiavelli described the objective role of a king — a role that the same Frederick was later to play to perfection. See his *Anti-Machiavelli*.

The ruling class itself may not be completely conscious of its role, since it, too, is a "victim" of the ruling ideology. It can be relied upon, nonetheless, to distinguish its true class interests in every concrete situation, and act accordingly.

mediation of so-called class interests. This would seem to constitute the core of ideological patterns — the "class instinct" — for it is reproduced daily in the concrete production practice of people in the course of their lives as class-situated agents; we shall call its results "class determined" ideology.
— The determination by the *ruling* ideology, as produced under various forms, though with a single content ("keep quiet, stay put, everything is just fine") by ideologists in the pay of the ruling class, and as diffused through the ideological "state apparati". It appears to cover class-determined ideas with a uniform layer of porridge, which penetrates more or less deeply beneath the surface. Answers to survey questionnaires usually originate at this level.
— The determination by the *personal life history*, which, in people of similar class positions, might induce a differential sensitivity to the effects of the ruling ideology and thus "explain" their different concrete ideological systems.

This somewhat crude hypothesis (in the absence of any theory relating ideology to class structure we are obliged to begin with crude hypotheses) can be expressed in the following diagram:

Schema 1.

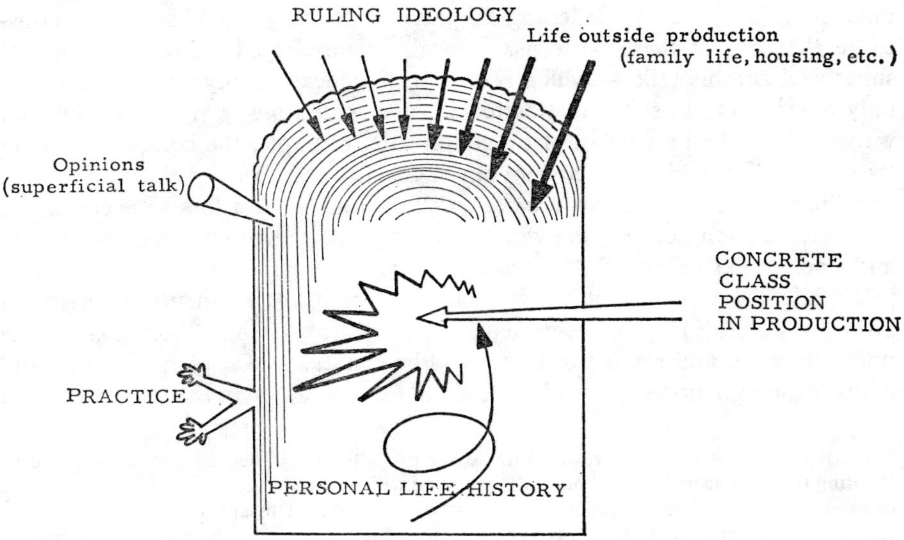

Let us now take a closer look at the three determinations. "Class instinct", or class-determined ideology is so powerful because it is a direct expression of *class interests*. The latter concept should not be misunderstood, however. It is not intended to refer to the supreme interests of people as human beings, which I take to be common to all of us, whatever our class position, sex, age or nationality and which consist in the establishment of world peace and fraternal relationships between us; all of these being things which, today more than ever before, will only be brought about by worldwide social revolution.

On the contrary, class interests refer to the particular interests of people *as situated in the world class structure*, in other words, as divided by social-structural relationships. It is not my aim, here, to review the contemporary world situation. If we limit ourselves to national class structures as described above, we will see that:

— the class interests of the members of the ruling class are to conserve the existing social "order";

— the class interests of the labouring classes lie in the rapid achievement of a social revolution;

— the class interests of the institutional petty bourgeoisie, agents of the ruling class, lie in the removal from power of the present rulers and the establishment of "petty-bourgeois" domination, probably under some form of state capitalism, with strongly nationalistic tendencies.

These class interests, it must be emphasized, pertain to people as *agents of their classes*, considering them from the somewhat narrow viewpoint of the existing social structure [14]. They are very important, however, to the understanding of concrete ideological patterns, for they would appear to constitute the core of these patterns, generally camouflaged behind a screen of superficial zombie talk — which is what ruling ideas usually amount to — and only re-emerging in sharp distinction in crisis situations. Without this core, we would not be in a position to explain, for example, the contradiction between the *liberal ideology* current among many members of the upper class and their very authoritarian *practice.* We would be at a loss to account for the contradiction between the working class conservative vote and the sudden and unexpected revolt of these same workers. Again, we would be unable to explain the rapid penetration, at certain historical moments of crisis, of powerfully anti-bourgeois sentiments and practices among the ranks of the normally quiet and respectful lower middle classes. To explain all these and many other phenomena would seem to require an hypothesis assuming a

14. It will be noted, however, that I make use of a "political" definition of class interests, ignoring the even narrower "economic" definition which would lead me to conclude that "the class interests of the workers consist in higher wages", etc. This approach, adopted by the majority of modern trade unions, is conservative in that it presupposes implicitly the perpetuation of the social structure as it is today. Still less am I prepared to accept the definition conservative ideology would have us use, namely that "the true psychological interests" of all "citizens" lie in contented acceptance of their fate. It is no mere chance if it is only for the ruling class that "economic" interests (to increase profits) coincide with political interests (to continue increasing profits). If, on the other hand, the overall interests of all human beings are the same (worldwide revolution leading to a fraternal world society), they only coincide with the class-determined interests of the working classes. This is what Marx meant when he wrote that "by liberating themselves, the workers will liberate all the classes above them".

constant struggle between a "spontaneous", *i.e.* class-determined ideology (set of values and representations) surging up from "below", from the practice of production and class struggle, and a socially hegemonic "ruling" ideology, weighing down from "above", through parents' behaviour towards their children, as agents (and prisoners) of a particular form of family [15], and later, through the convergent actions of all the apparati shaping our "cultural" environment.

As for social biography, I am referring here to "individual differences" as determined by the concrete passage of individuals through institutions, from their particular family to their particular school, their life experiences, etc., all of which have some importance in the differential structuring of the "characters" of people belonging to the same social class [16].

The three main determinations I have distinguished here provide us with the generative framework of concrete ideological patterns, whose internal structure we are now in a position to examine.

Ideological patterns as sets of values and representations

The positivist tradition distinguishes between value-judgments and judgments of fact ("representations" of the world). Although open to criticism, this seems to be a good distinction with which to begin.

The influence of the class structure being such as it is, it is virtually impossible to separate radically values from representations. Everything appears to be heavily value-loaded. It is very difficult, for instance, to persuade members of the bourgeoisie and the petty-bourgeoisie to accept certain facts about society, the nature of which is such as to be liable to provoke practice directed against their social class. They have a strong tendency to reject such facts and to stick to their more reassuring representation of reality. The true account of the crimes of their ancestors makes painful listening for the "citizens" of bourgeois nations; the crimes are best buried and forgotten. Men find difficulty in admitting women as their intellectual equals; they prefer to hypothesize "a particular form of intelligence", though they have never tried to observe it experimentally. There are many more examples, but they all add up to the same thing: *values* are the dominant force in the sets of values

15. See, on this point, the highly original books of Wilhelm Reich, especially *Mass psychology of fascism*, New York, Farrar and Strauss, 1971 (written 1932) and the empirical studies which have been carried out by the British anti-psychiatrists, R.D. Laing, David Cooper and D. Esterson. See also E. Mantell's *Americanism: A study in the formation of fascist and pacifist personalities*, 1972, in publication; G. Deleuze, and F. Guattari, *L'anti-Œdipe : Capitalisme et schizophrénie*, Paris, Éd. de Minuit, 1972.

16. I do not think it very relevant to speak *generally* of people's experiences concerning, for instance, love, leisure, sport, death, relationships with one's father and mother or with one's own children or whatever, since these have utterly different and sometimes even inversed *meanings* in different social classes. At least, this is the feeling of my colleagues and myself while studying people's life experiences in different social classes, through the use of the biographical technique.

and representations constituting ideological patterns. In the final analysis, truth and falsity are "only" intellectual patterns, while questions of value lead directly to practice and are consequently of burning relevance to concrete life.

We can therefore trace false representations of society back, not to ignorance, but, at least in part, to class interests (which tend to become the dominant, if not the only values of most people as they grow older) and again, in part, to the overall impact of the ruling ideology, which diffuses not only lies about social life, but also conservative values. There is a connection between these lies and class values, for in order to be able to say "keep calm, everything's just fine", convincingly, one has to be able to present a somewhat biased image of the state of things.

But these two components of ideology may yet be relatively independent of each other. Employers and workers, for example, may be able to agree entirely on the description of their situation, yet completely disagree in their evaluations of it. On the other hand, the grand bourgeoisie and most intellectuals both wish to keep the present system while entertaining utterly different representations thereof.

Two and a half models of social structure

The expression "two and a half models" of social structure is used here to express briefly the central idea of this paper, *i.e.* that there are two, and only two, fundamental, antagonistic representations of social structure. One is the class-structure model, as developed by Marx and Machiavelli, Bakunin and Guizot and many others; the second is the stratification model as developed by contemporary ruling ideology and social "science", very popular among the so-called new middle class, *i.e.* the institutional petty-bourgeoisie, which lives under the misapprehension that the whole of society is as hierarchically stratified as the institutions on which it depends for its livelihood.

The preceding developments may be summarized in Schema 2, below. This diagram summarizes our main hypothesis concerning class determined models of social structure:

a) Members of the ruling class and of the working class, through the *direct* experience which they have of class relationships of production, should develop a vision of social structure as based on a fundamental *class* relationship of exploitation (as a goal for the ruling class) and domination (as a means to attain it). They ought to agree in their *description* of the present state of the social order, and disagree only in their *evaluation* of it: the rulers finding it quite acceptable, and the labourers quite unbearable, the rulers wanting to preserve the statu quo, the labourers wanting to change it [17].

17. Representations of possibilities for the future are even more interwoven with *values* than representations of present (and past) social reality. In this last case there is a material reality against which ideas can be matched (provided one is willing to try); but the future is

Schema 2 *.

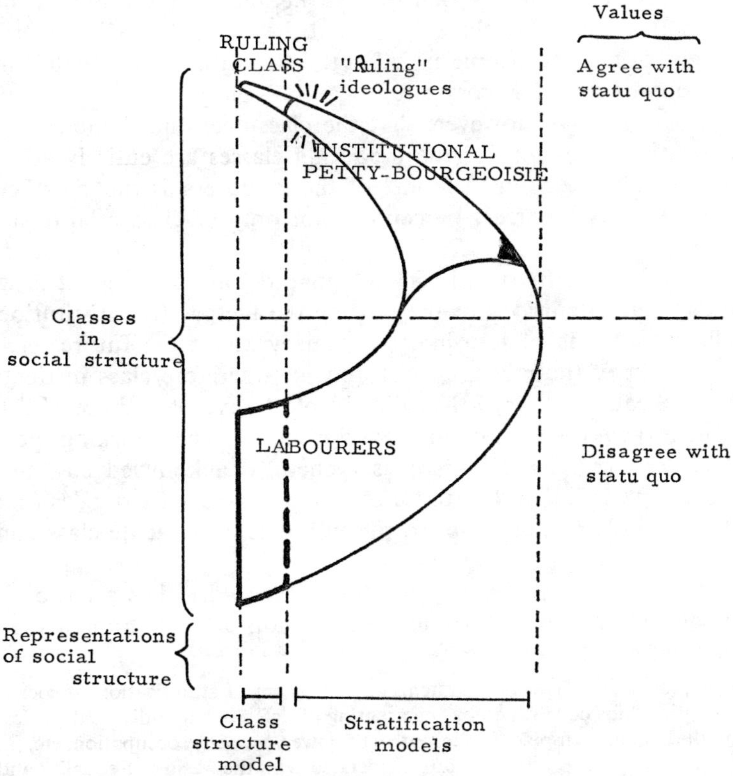

*The class-structure model, also called the dichotomous representation of society, I hold to be the correct one. As there is only one way to tell the things as they are but many ways to err, there are many false models of society; but according to my hypothesis, they are only different versions of the same stratification model. Thus we get one correct representation of society (to be found mostly among rulers and labourers) and a whole range of false representations of society (especially popular among the petty-bourgeois): hence the expression "two and a half models of social structure".

b) As for the institutional petty-bourgeoisie, ensconced within institutions as it is (the armed forces and police, the administration, the health and school systems, the churches, the mass media, etc. — and the non-productive people who fulfill various repressive tasks in the process of production) their life experience leads them to develop a vision of social structure as stratified, graded, devoid of any "exploitation" whatsoever or of any irreconcilable anta-

not material, only its determinations are, and they are much more difficult to see. The void of cognition is instantly filled in by values. Beneath its "scientific" mask, futurology describes nothing else than the perspectives of a particular class, the imperialist ruling class. The very concrete possibility of worldwide social revolution is "forgotten" by "scientific techniques of prediction" from the very outset.

gonism between social groups [18]. They value social peace and individual security. They dream of personal success (*i.e.* joining the ranks of the ruling class, maybe through their children). And they love "their" country, which for them means not the people in it but the "apparati of the State" in which they have found a relatively cosy refuge.

This does not mean, however, that the class-determined models of social structure of the ruling and of the labouring classes are entirely adequate to reality. The class-determined model of the labourers is the most complete one, for it includes a correct perception not only of class relationships, but also of the possibilities for their transformation. But it is towards this class that all the efforts of the ideological "apparati" are directed, it is within it that the concrete conditions of life outside the factory (the institution of the family, the conditions of housing, uncertainty about the future, etc.) make the development of thought the most difficult; therefore class instinct all but disappears beneath the fogs of the ruling ideology, except in those who through class struggle acquire a certain consciousness. The working people are much less "embourgeoisé" than is generally acknowledged; the class-instinct is always there, and in times of large scale social struggles (like today in Italy) it expands and develops to the full scale of an acute class-consciousness [19].

As for the ruling class, its vision of the social world has a basic vice, that we shall call "structuralicism", *i.e.* the reduction of every human creature to his or her structural components.

18. See for instance: "The class system, or the system of stratification of society, is [...] the set of relationships constituted by the granting of deference to individuals, roles and institutions in the light of their place in the system of power, property, occupation, etc. [...] Deference is an action of respect and honour, associated with the feeling of equality and inferiority". Further: "The class system is an imperfect equilibrium of innumerable acts of deference."

These remarkable quotations are extracted from the article on Social Class in the *Encyclopedia Britannica,* William Benton, 1969. It was written by Messrs. E.A. Shils and S.M. Lipset, and also contains statements such as "The human mind finds inferiority hard to accept in unadulterated doses, and some persons find it harder to take than others", or "Tensions and misunderstandings among classes..." Not a single reference to Marx's works is to be found in the article or in its bibliography; the only allusion is in one passage which deserves full quotation: "Thus what Marxists call 'class consciousness', which could be more precisely called 'aggressively alienated class identification', is a rather uncommon phenomenon, even in modern industrial societies. Normal class conflict is fully compatible with a high degree of citizenship and a considerable measure of social order."

The reader may be interested to compare this article, whic his written for the large middle class public of the *Encyclopedia Britannica,* with the article on Social Class (see under "social stratification") of the *International Encyclopedia for the Social Sciences,* MacMillan and Free Press, 1968, which addresses itself to a more sophisticated public. This second article contains a section in which some of the most important ideas of Marx on social classes are correctly if highly summarily presented. Interestingly enough, the author of this section is also S.M. Lipset.

19. All traces of this process seem to have been carefully wiped out of the "respectable" literature; hence no references can be given here.

The basic structuralicism of the ruling class

Ruling class discourse makes interesting listening, for it reveals how the forces shaping social formations from above actually work. This discourse describes very aptly the structures of class society: for they have been created and shaped by the very practice of the ruling class.

But this very aptness also produces a specific blindness — a blindness to all non-structural aspects of social life, especially to spontaneous individual or social rebellions against the structures. For to think in terms of structures is to think of people as *agents* located somewhere in the process of production and in "state apparati" (a worker, a salesgirl, a policeman, a doctor); it is to reduce them to their social *positions*, to consider them as mere *role-players* — as perfect zombies. This is the way the ruling class and its agents spontaneously see society: for the director of a factory, the term "worker" means not the man, but the *position* he occupies. The same holds true for the terms clerk, secretary, and even director. This reductionist point of view leads him to consider working class children as mere future labour-power, retired workers as useless nuisances, and even one's own children, especially the sons, as mere successors, *i.e.* agents of one's own capital and name. This systematic reduction of people to their structural positions derives from the basic reduction that the rulers themselves suffer when, leaving college or university to enter production (of capital), and leaving bachelorhood to enter the institution of the family, they are transformed from flesh-and-blood humans to mere *agents* of capital and of its institutions. The more they live for the system, the less they live for themselves; they too are alienated, and even more than any other social category, for while alienation is *imposed* on the others, in their case it is self-imposed.

This character of self-imposition may account for the fact that they, of all people, are the least able to imagine that one sometimes wants to escape from this "shirt of Nessus" of social position which prevents one from living one's own life as a human being. Individual rebellions make no sense to them; they cannot interpret such acts otherwise than by labelling them as "unsound behaviour" (unsound!). Having accepted to give up their lives by enacting the social game (*i.e.* here, class game), they are furious to see other people choosing to refuse this "solution". As for *collective* rebellion, it is outrageous and frightening to them: it constitutes an obvious threat to the "system" of which they have become a *part*. Another life, another way of arranging the relationships between people, belongs to the unknown — to the terrifying unknown.

Death they cannot understand or accept, for they do not understand life; they are afraid of death because they are afraid of life. They cannot perceive the biological time of life-death-and-reproduction, and the time of social history — or the time of change. On the contrary, their perception of time is reduced to the perception of the linear, quantified time of circulation of capital ("time is money"); it is a time in which things remain the same eternally, it is an abstract timeless time.

Seen from the position of the ruling class, society looks like a lifeless structural framework standing in the void of eternity, something like this:

Schema 3.

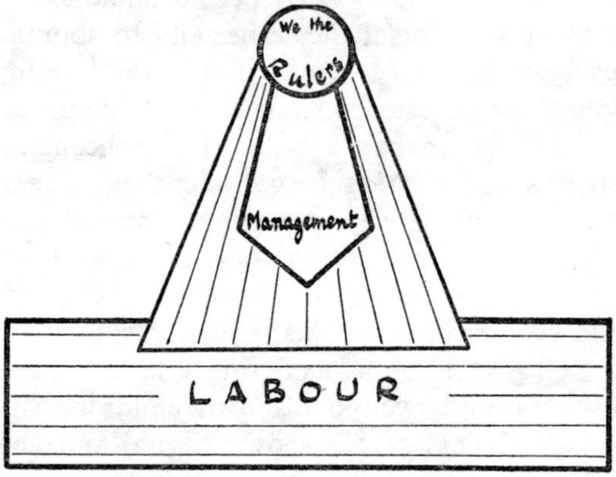

I believe this image corresponds indeed to the *skeleton* of class social formations, but as an image of reality, it lacks one thing: life.

The structuralicism of the ruling class is particularly well adapted to the monopolistic phase of capitalism (imperialism), *i.e.* to its national forms, the corporate states [20]. Its message is rigidification. "The system must not evolve, things should stay as they are." But there are more and more people who want to live. If the life of capitalism requires the disappearance of all traces of humanity, either though physical murder or through mental anesthesia, then the fight for human life requires the disappearance of capitalism. It is as simple as that — and millions of young people have already understood it all over the world.

Different "institutional petty-bourgeois" types

People in capitalist institutions do not constitute an homogeneous group. The heads of the institutions are always members of the ruling class. But the upper ranks are filled with people who by position and career are very close to the ruling class. They all aspire to join it, and the most complacent are indeed absorbed. Every conformist petty-bourgeois' aim in life is to penetrate the bourgeoisie, either through promotion or through marriage, either by himself or through his children. Hence an anticipatory identification with

20. On this point see H. Lefebvre, *Au-delà du structuralisme*, Paris, Anthropos, 1970, and also Baran and Sweezy, *op. cit.*

"bourgeois" ideology and culture, which is produced precisely by the creative ideologists among them: politicians, top journalists, professors and physicians, lawyers, architects, artists, writers, sociologists, economists, church authorities, etc. These people are the principal, even the only, producers of the legitimate (*i.e.* legitimated by the ruling class) discourse about society. They have earned the right to this monopoly because of their twisted perception or simply utter ignorance of social realities.

On the other hand, in the lower ranks of the institutions there are to be found people who, through identification with their superiors, strongly adhere to the ruling ideology, but who find it curious that their concrete life experience in no way corresponds to it. If they try to realize their dreams of social ascension they soon find out they cannot make it — but they continue to believe that "chances are equal" and put the blame on their close competitors. They have a hard time making ends meet, but they still believe in the message of advertising, that *everybody else* lives in a consumer society. Their frustrations remain at an individual level and express themselves in tensions inside the family, for instance in highly repressive educational practices. Having lived all their life looking upwards waiting for orders, they cannot move by themselves — they need a leader. Their aggressivity is in the first place directed against the rich, but no analysis is made of why the rich are rich, and their anger can easily be turned against the working class by the "right" kind of leader (*i.e.* fascist), especially if the labour movement is weak [21].

Right in the middle of the middle classes live the most middle of middle men. They like to believe themselves above all classes, while camping right between them; when the fighting starts again they find themselves kicked from both sides. Their opinions shift in time with the shifting of victory, they try to choose the winning side and join it just in time. Opportunism is their characteristic feature. They believe actually in conciliation, and conceive of society as a continuum of more or less "qualified" citizens between whom "inequalities should be reduced". As all middle groups, (*e.g.* the French bourgeoisie before 1789) they would like to have a share in "democracy, freedom and justice", which the ruling class reserve for the relations between its own members. To obtain political equality and justice, as well as a bigger share of total GNP, they are ready to make an alliance with the labourers against the ruling class — only to betray them as soon as they have got what they wanted: this process has been witnessed many times in history.

When the class struggles become fierce and spell the death of the conservative form of the ruling ideology, it is to the ideologists of the middle and lower

21. Wilhelm Reich had remarkable insight into the ideology of the lower institutional petty-bourgeoisie; see especially his *Mass psychology of fascism*, *op. cit.*, (and also *Americanism*, *op. cit.*). The influence of lower petty-bourgeoisie ideology on the upper working class is important; which explains why many attitudes and practices, whose origin can be traced back to the objective (class) situation of the lower petty-bourgeois, are to be found in the working class itself.

ranks of the IPB (Institutional petty-bourgeoisie) that the ruling class turns. For instance, since the beginning of the recent social movements (so-called social troubles — troubles for whom?) there has been a sudden blooming of "radical" literature. From radical sociology to radical man, from radical America to radical middle class, all radical combinations in the book have been tried. This radicalism however is probably no redder than the cheeks of a blushing Japanese girl: very charming, but superficial — and ephemeral. Ideologists who affect to look for the *roots* of the social phenomena do not even understand the roots of their own ideology. Underlying their writings there is an implicit vision of society as conveniently stratified (but most unfortunatcly "uncqual"). The notion of "inequality" is typical of such disguised versions of the stratification model. It is like speaking of the "inequality of incomes" of the slave of a plantation, of his master and of the overseer, while the first is based on work, the second and the third on violence: they are qualitatively different. The notion of inequality conveys the idea that there are only quantitative differences between things *of the same nature*. Such notions not only close the door to the real questions but do it so discreetly that one does not even notice there is a door. The indexes of such works conspicuously omit the names of Marx and Marxists, as also the concepts of class and class struggle are absent from their vocabulary, and the process of production from their field of interest[22]. Among the "radicals", a few may become even further radicalized, transforming their own lives and their ideology in consequence; but for most of them, the current goal is probably a position as a "liberal" $ 25,000 professional ideologist — following in the footsteps of the New Deal radicals.

The double nature of "state apparati" and enterprise bureaucracies

It would be inexact to *reduce* all the activities of the institutional petty-bourgeois to repressive tasks. Many of them actually fill *repressive-productive* positions: the tasks of engineers and managers, architects and physicians, school teachers and artists, are good examples of the ambiguous nature of middle class positions.

22. For instance, they will forcefully denounce pollution... in the rivers and streets, forgetting that pollution begins inside the factories, in the air that the workers have to breathe.

To understand what it really means to be an institutional petty-bourgeois, one must ask the key question: who works for whom? The IPB's are fed by the work of peasants, truck-drivers, salesgirls, etc.; they are clothed by the work of women in textile factories, and of the workers who made their machines; they are housed by the work of construction workers; they drive around thanks to the work of assembly line workers; they drink the coffee and tea gathered by the labour of Brazilian, African and Indian plantation labourers; they are kept warm by the work of miners and railroad workers, etc.

And what do they give to these people in exchange for all their labour? Repression, mostly. Their main activity — it is difficult to call it work, although it is certainly tiring — is to provide the ruling class with the hundreds of various *means of repression* that it needs to keep alive its cruel system.

If this is certainly not a sound basis for a happy life, neither is it a favourable one for the development of a critical consciousness.

This dual nature is only a consequence of the dual nature of the "state apparati" of which they are a part: undoubtedly used by the ruling class according to its own specific interests (which are most if not all of the time radically opposed to the interests of the people), in class societies they also fulfill *some* useful tasks without which the reproduction of social life would not be possible: education; health care, communications; defence, etc. The ambiguity results from the *appropriation by the ruling class of the means to fulfill collective functions.*

To further develop this idea, we must start from the observation that in every social formation, some of the people's needs cannot be met through individual or family action: they require community action. These needs range from road building to the management of relations with other communities (from trade to defence), the construction of collective means of production, the reproduction of a sentiment of community (communitarian ideology) which cements the group, etc. All these essentially collective functions could well be carried out by the *people themselves,* were they to be left free to organize appropriately: ethnography and history are full of local examples of this process. It is usually realized through the establishment of systems of norms, deciding everyone's responsibilities and whose observance is thereby controlled by everybody; no permanent specialized position is usually created as everyone contributes to defence, road-building, justice or collective decisions.

But as soon as a ruling class establishes its power (either by military domination or by seizure of the means of production — or by magic) it takes over all these collective institutions and reshapes them according to its own interests, keeping the external *shape* but completely transforming their *content.* The first step is to replace the people's control by the appointment of permanent "functionaries". The last one is to *invert* the proclaimed goal of the institutions in their concrete functioning: the first institution to switch over is usually the army, which begins to kill people on the pretext of "protecting" them. Next comes the judicial system which in the name of justice legalizes the social injustice of every class society — and so forth.

The inversion between proclaimed goal and actual functioning is, however, never complete, so that the agents of the institutions and the people may retain the illusion that they function "for the general good". And indeed, they do fulfill useful social functions — but in the same way that a prison fulfills the "need of housing" of the prisoner...

This process concerns "state apparati" outside production. For the middle categories in production, engineers, managers, research scientists, etc., the process is basically the same but takes very different forms. These categories are specific products of capitalism. A remarkable study of the development of forms of production under the logic of capitalism was made by Marx in *Capital* (fourth section of book 1). To read it is to understand how, when the process of production develops around a capital/labour relationship, the capital tends to appropriate for itself the intellectual parts of the labour: creating and inventing, planning, decision-making, controlling, etc. The once unified labour of the craftsman is divided into two parts: the intellectual and the manual, or rather into tasks of *decision* and tasks of *execution*. And the craftsman himself disappears and is replaced by a collective worker divided into two groups: unqualified labourers who do the material work with the machines, submitted to their rhythm, and managers, engineers, etc., who *prepare* and *control* their work. Especially in the control tasks, the managers are made to serve the particular interests of the capital; they become "agents of the despotism of capital" (Marx). Their work presents a dual aspect, for their positions result from the fusion of two types of tasks: production and repression. Although the productive side is always put forward, it is the repressive side which dominates. To make a career means for the engineeer progressively to free himself of all productive tasks and become more and more of a controller, a direct agent of capital opposed to labour and consequently better paid [23].

We may now summarize our hypothesis concerning the nature of the new middle classes. According to our analysis, it is composed of agents of the ruling class whose task, either in the units of production or in the global social formation, is to maintain the established social order. This is seldom their only task: on the contrary, they fulfill by the same token repressive tasks and also social functions which are objectively necessary to the reproduction of that particular form of social life, handed down to us by existing class structures. *"State apparati" and enterprise bureaucracies result from the appropriation by the ruling class of the means of organization of collective work and collective life;* they result from the *fusion* of these functions with the function of repression (domination) which is fundamental to all class structures.

Qualification as the keystone notion of institutional petty-bourgeois ideology

How do the people allocated into positions of institutional petty-bourgeois, agents of the ruling class, accept their roles? First of all, they feel rather comfortable: their salary is better than that of the labourers, and unlike them they are not constrained to an alien rhythm, that of capital made real, the rhythm of the machines. As we have tried to show, an important feature of their situation is that they are unaware of this, in that they believe they fulfill

23. This analysis also clarifies why the development of capitalism produces at the same time qualified and unskilled jobs. In older branches like the textile and automobile industries, the process described above has been pushed to its limits: the scission of the working class is completed, with, as a result, an increase in the proportion of unskilled jobs. But in newer branches such as space industry, capital has not yet been able to appropriate for itself and embody into machines and processes, all the knowledge which is still largely in the heads of the experienced workers (technicians, engineers and skilled workers): hence their large proportion of skilled people. But there is no doubt concerning the direction of the evolution.

socially useful tasks, and deserve their better salary because of their higher *qualification.*

This term is the keystone. It is certainly not by chance that in the theory of stratification currently accepted by academic sociology, it plays a central role: for it legitimates the social structure as (falsely) represented by a stratified pyramid. If society is a hierarchy of qualifications, it seems normal that the people at the top are better paid, for they are more qualified.

But *qualified for what*? For the production of useful products — or for repression of the people? This is the question that we may now ask. Let us not forget that to be educated means to be able to express oneself correctly and to write clearly, two features which are mandatory to be a good commander of men. The ability to write essays or to make exposés means also the ability to manipulate the ruling ideology and, consequently, the people who believe in it. It may for instance require a certain amount of education to find the appropriate label for illegal military attacks on a harmless enemy ("reactions of protection" or "preventive actions"). Years of training are necessary to be able to talk about things that everybody knows in terms that nobody will understand, as psychiatrists and sociologists will do. Certainly a very interesting study could be made of the "skills" that one learns at college and the university...

But if a critical analysis of the content of higher qualifications needs to be made, I do not intend to make it here. So far we only need to know that whatever it hides, the notion of qualification is used to convey the impression that well-paid and relatively powerful positions are more difficult to occupy than less well-paid and powerless ones, and at the same time that people in high positions are better paid because they are more useful to society.

Therefore with one single concept, the institutional petty-bourgeois legitimate both their social positions (which means that the existing division of labour is acknowledged) and their own occupation of them (which is the true meaning of the word "occupation"). For qualified *positions* can only be occupied by qualified *people*.

But who are these qualified people? Who are those who can *qualify* for a job as agent of the ruling class? The answer is: people who have been *educated, i.e.* transformed into the right type of products by the school system and secondarily by their passage through the structures of production. Examinations and screenings are nothing but controls of conformity. Success means that one is recognized as a good product. The deeper the transformation that the person must have undergone, the higher the qualification: thus works the logic of qualifying institutions.

The principle of rotation as revealing class structures

It is sometimes thought that a school reform could induce some transformation in society itself. But social formations are wholes; there is a consistency between base and superstructure, between, for instance, the class division of labour, the school system which reproduces it and the ruling ideology which justifies the whole. The relationships between these three social forms have recently been beautifully analyzed by Baudelot and Establet [24].

To illustrate this interdependency, let us suppose for a while that, keeping the class division of labour as it is, we modify not the school system, which is the main institution for allocating people into positions, but the principle according to which everybody should stay in "his" position for his lifetime. The abolition of this principle leads to the idea of *rotation*, according to which people exchange places in the process of production — not only horizontally but also vertically: men and women in positions of workers, peasants and in service activities becoming engineers, teachers, executives and journalists for a while; whereas the people already in these positions in turn replace them for significant spans of their lifetime.

This perspective is a real nightmare for our petty-bourgeois, who are so proud of having "non-manual" jobs. This nightmarish idea will automatically be dismissed as "utopian" and a "scientific" judgment of utter impossibility, sociologically speaking, will be quickly passed. And it is true that it would be impossible to implement such a process *while keeping the rest of society unchanged.* For a start, if everybody was to spend some time in the most unpleasant jobs, such as furnace worker, miner, assembly line worker, garbage collector, sewerman, etc., where some human beings spend their whole life and energies for "our greatest material benefit", these positions themselves would be quickly transformed *and the people passing through them would also be transformed*, being freed from the contempt towards some of their fellowmen that they carry with them at present [25].

Then, if the positions of engineers and managers, teachers and journalists were open to everybody, they too would be greatly transformed, and not, I believe, for the worst. The teacher would become just another one of us, humbly but knowingly speaking of his own life experience and what it taught him — but contrary to today's situation teachers would have lived a real life. It would be the same for journalists. As for the positions commanding great power, they would progressively be abolished, as the fundamental principles of democracy in which everyone concerned by a decision should directly take part in it, would tend to be implemented. Collective decision-making, which is practically impossible to implement *in a class society* (always leading to the reconstitution of elites), would become the rule, while the case of a person wanting to decide for others what *they* should do would become a preposterous and ridiculous aberration.

24. *L'école capitaliste en France, op. cit.*

25. See in Macciochi's book, already quoted, the extraordinary chapter on the "schools for Party executives", which are actually farms in rather poor land where Party executives are said to go and live for months and years as simple peasants.

Through this parable, we see that a change in the process of allocation of people to positions would induce a change in the positions themselves, *i.e.* in the class division of labour — and thus a change in the class structure itself. But as everything is interconnected, the strongest arrows of determination point in the opposite direction: it is only through a change in class structure that the social division of labour and the process of allocation could be transformed.

4. Class structure and its dynamics : class struggles

The relationship between class structure and the social "division of labour"

Class structure is not grounded in the social division of labour, as many radicals and Marxists appear to believe, but in class relationships: exploitation and domination. The social division of labour, primarily separating those who labour from those who do not, is the *consequence* of these relationships and not their cause, nor even their historical origin. Though this division of labour serves the interests of the ruling class, it did not create these classes.

It is true, however, that by being embodied in the material environment (technology generated by capitalism, capitalist urbanization, etc.), in the social environment (capitalist State institutions, bourgeois law, bourgeois and petty-bourgeois norms), and in human beings themselves (as products of the patriarchal family, of a school system controlled by the ruling class, of the constant invasion of people's minds by the ruling ideology), the existing "class division of labour" reproduces, in everyday life, social-structural relationships between positions and roles which determine people, forced to live in these structures, to reproduce among themselves dependent, defiant, rival, hierarchical, egotistical, money-, power- and status-orientated social relationships. If it is the class structure which produces the social division of labour, it is the latter which produces the kind of people who are going to reproduce class relationships.

For this reason, class relationships cannot be erased by government decrees. Quite the reverse, for it is the people themselves who must constantly battle against them, firstly in their relationships among themselves and secondly, against the socio-structural matrices of these relationships; first in the production process, but also in law and culture, in politics and in the army, in technology and urbanism and architecture, in schools and in the communications media — until all are completely remodelled and begin reproducing free and autonomous relationships, in which equality and personal differentiation, brotherhood and constructive mutual criticism are the prevailing forces. It is only in this case that the process deserves the name of *social revolution*; otherwise it is no more than the replacement of the group in power by another soon resembling the previous one, for nothing has changed the class structure itself.

Political revolution versus social revolution

A political revolution occurs when the ruling class is replaced in power by another class — or rather, by the "representatives" of another class. Should this new class happen to be the working class (the labourers), the number one priority facing their "representatives" on reaching power should be the mobilization of the masses for an all-out assault on the old relationships, with the firm goal of establishing new *social* relationships in factories, on farms, in institutions, insofar as these survive, and, above all, in politics. It would at last become clear to all what the word democracy really means.

The group wielding power should be aided in this task by its "proletarian ideology". However, from the outset, the new ruling group is confronted with the existing, class-determined division of labour. This means that the concrete conditions of existence of the new rulers (as non-labouring, power-wielding people) will tend objectively to foster in them an anti-proletarian ideology, a strong tendency to *preserve* the structures as they found them.

The condition of millions of people depends on the issue of this pathetic struggle in which two conflicting ideologies attempt to seize the minds of the new men in power. The conservative forces are undoubtedly greatly strengthened if there is a scarcity of resources, enhancing the differences between labourers and rulers. They are also greatly strengthened by the pressure of foreign ruling classes, who will feel their own position to be indirectly threatened. Nor should we underestimate the power of the remnants of feudal ideology or the absence of a prior bourgeois revolution. Also thrown into the balance, in favour of the forces of conservative ideology, is the low level of consciousness of the masses, unable to catch the drift of their leaders' policies until it is too late, and the organization of the revolutionary group *before* the revolution, resembling strongly the hierarchical structure of the society in whose womb it develops. This explains why no *social* revolution can emerge from a highly centralized organization. It is this type of revolutionary party that is invariably reconstructed by the impatient, ultra-radical petty-bourgeoisie, in conformity with the Leninist formula but lacking the genius of Lenin himself. These parties are excellent as instruments for seizing power, but catastrophic once they are in control: the history of Russia affords a cruel example of this. The first principle of the Statutes of the First International stated: "The emancipation of the workers must be conquered by the workers themselves." [26]

Conversely, the superiority of the new ideology lies in the fact that, *wherever it is put into practice*, the people immediately perceive how closely it corresponds to their real needs. In consequence, the triumph of the new ideology depends not only on the "ideological struggle", but also, and principally,

26. See C. Lefort, *Éléments d'une critique de la bureaucratie*, Geneva, Droz, 1971.

on the concrete existence of a growing number of liberated sectors of social life. These permit the development of relationships of solidarity and brotherhood, and liberate the creative energies and potentialities of the people, thus winning them round to new ideas and revealing to the others, through real-life practice and not only through distant scholarly demonstrations, the superiority of socialist life. The new ideology must seize the masses, and the masses must seize the new ideology. Once begun, the process is cumulative; as it develops, it cannot avoid questioning the very existence of positions of leadership. Hence, perhaps, the lack of enthusiasm among leaders to encourage this kind of process.

There is an important contradiction here. It seems that the dissolution of the Workers' Soviets by the Bolshevik leaders, soon after the October Revolution, spelled the death of a genuine, embryonic social revolution, at the hands of the leaders of the political revolution. Things may have been different in China; a fraction of the political leadership seems to have actively encouraged the mass movements of 1966-1967. Whatever its true nature and final outcome, this is a sign that the Cultural Revolution was an historically highly significant process. Perhaps for the first time in human history, with the exception of the Paris Commune of 1871, the first years of the Russian revolution of 1917 and a few other, brief experiments, it has become possible to imagine the real meaning of the expression "social revolution": it means, not a change in top-level personnel — the political rulers — but a process of mobilization and struggle of the masses for their *own* liberation.

Why is social revolution relevant to the Western world?

Considering the totality of historical determinations, Marx concluded that social revolutions were most likely to appear first in the most developed capitalist countries. So far, however, we have witnessed nothing of the kind. Again and again, we are told that the working class of the industrial countries is becoming increasingly conservative, while revolutions appear in pre-capitalist countries (Russia, China, Cuba — and many more, were it not for the "vigilance" of the CIA). Heaving a sigh of relief, conservative observers conclude that socialism may be appropriate for poor countries, but capitalism suits the rich nations better.

Perhaps we should take another look at 20th century world events. Firstly, we are now at a stage of worldwide imperialism; the capitalist relationships of production extend all over the world. While the capital is mainly North American, Japanese and Western European (insofar as the nationality of capital still has relevance), the labour force working for this capital is situated not only in these areas of the world, but also in Asia, Africa, and in Latin America. Social movements are constantly being born in these parts of the world, though they are generally not recognized as working class revolutionary movements but as petty-bourgeois nationalist "revolutions" (Egypt, Libya,

Syria, Peru, Burma, etc.) attempting to prevent their country's riches from escaping on imperialist ships. It is probably wrong to interpret Marx's conclusion as announcing first a proletarian revolution in the USA, then in Canada, then in Sweden, then in Germany, etc., for these are no longer independent entities. It must be interpreted in the context of a worldwide capitalist system.

Secondly, the ideas and new social forms arising out of the Cultural Revolution have deeply influenced Western European intellectual circles which, thanks to the existence of a strong workers' movement, have been able to retain some power of autonomous thought. Numerous books, articles and lectures have been produced on the subject, very often by non-Marxists. But the most interesting factor is that these people talk of the Cultural Revolution, not as some curious, remote accident of history, but as something very important and *very relevant to all of us*. It is not easy to unearth the roots of this Western "sinophilia"; but considering that the obstacles in the passage from a political revolution to a social revolution, as described above, are far less awesome in Western Europe than they were in China (scarcity, for example, could be eradicated tomorrow, were it not maintained artificially as a result of capitalist organization of production), it may be that the instant success of the ideas of the Cultural Revolution means that, in fact, they very closely correspond to our historical situation. By a strange quirk of history, a very distant people have formulated and put into practice ideas that we have all been nurturing subconsciously, without daring to express them on the conscious level.

Thirdly, again it is in those countries where capitalism is now ultra-ripe (USA, Canada, Sweden) that the conduct of dropping out of the system (*i.e.* the capitalist system), of living in communities, of trying to develop free and fraternal relationships among people, have developed and met with a huge response among the young. The reactionary aspects of these movements, the religious forms in which many express their search for "something else", for example, or the return to outmoded forms of production such as non-mechanized agriculture, cannot hide the fact that these people are actively looking for an alternative to the stupid and cruel "system" within which they have been born.

Of course, hippies living in Goa live off the money their fathers have earned as agents of imperialism, *i.e.* from the desperate overwork of the "wretched of the earth": this, in my opinion, would account for the "reactionary" aspects of their thought. As long as the question of *production*, of the relationships of production (and distribution) between people is not posed, nothing will radically change. And let us not delude ourselves: unfortunately nothing will change in the sphere of production so long as the problem of power is not posed — and solved. But we can already observe a certain convergence between all these, and certain other, phenomena, such as the recent increase in the number of mass strikes in all industrial countries, the chronic social fever in Italy and France, the crisis in imperialist finance and economy, the diminished legitimacy of bourgeois political institutions and so on. Like the navigator approaching land, we are now able to make sense of all these myriad signs and to join with Charles Reich in saying "There's a revolution coming."

Towards liberation

A good society would be one which would give to all its members the means for "the pursuit of happiness". The quality of a society is the quality of its social structure, from which all social relationships derive. To change society — to "change life" — it is not enough to change men's ideas, or to reform the institutions (the reformists have hardly ever reformed anything anyhow): what must be changed are the *social relationships of production*, and the social relationships in all the *institutions*. Only then will it be possible to have peace and prosperity — and consciousness to the fullest degree, which is what makes humanity human.

For the moment, the basic social relationship between men is exploitation: this determines all their other relationships, even those between man and woman or between parent and child. Marx would not have denied that exploitation was active throughout history because it was historically necessary for the development of productive forces. But now that those productive forces are fully developed, this relationship, under its modern form of capital/labour, has become the principal danger for humanity. Consequently, it is responsible for the absurdity of the world in which we are trying to survive, and for the risk of its thermo-nuclear destruction: it must, by all means, be suppressed.

Already it has begun producing the very people who shall happily bring it down. Not only workers, as Marx thought, but also peoples of the dominated areas of the world, and youths of all social classes. Consciousness is now spreading and transforming people, who more and more understand that the "choice" between working for somebody else's profit or living off the back of somebody else's labour is the only choice open to them, and that it is an absurd one. Above all, they realize that things could some day be different.

I believe it is part of the work of an honest sociologist to study the potentialities of transformation of social formations. For the "science" of society includes not only the fair description of its present reality but also the description of the forces ("determinations") which are at work behind its surface phenomena, and therefore its future possibilities. In every epoch, the ruling class tries to convince itself that history will stop, that after centuries of class struggles that have carried it into power, the established order will suddenly freeze. But this is not so: the movement of social history cannot be resisted, it can only be oriented. Our present choice is probably between social revolution now, or a long period of very strong "1984-like" totalitarianism ending in revolution anyway; or in thermo-nuclear war, bringing with it, like previous World Wars, revolutions — if there are any people left to make them. The days of bourgeois democratic conservatism may be regretted by some of the more nostalgic middle classes, but they are already leaving the stage of history. It is not socialism which has killed them but the movement of capital itself, in its forceful passage from competitive to monopoly and State capitalism. Today's world is the world of imperialism and of the struggle to have it down and breathe.

It may seem paradoxical to say these things to the public of a sociological journal: for this public is socially determined, and composed of precisely those among the upper middle classes whose responsibility it is to elaborate the ruling ideology. Still, it may not be useless to remind them that they have a certain power *of their own*, that they can gain some control over their production, *provided they make the distinction between the position they institutionally occupy and their "own self"*. This distinction, I am afraid, cannot be made realistic without some struggle, some *negation* of the institutions of which they are agents. Thus it takes a little courage to make a start, but this is a cheap price for what one obtains in return: consciousness. It is the right course to take, for in the seventies, sincerity leading to consciousness will not only be a matter of personal pleasure and dignity, a choice of living with one's eyes open; it will also be, for humanity, a question of survival.

Post-scriptum: a short note on objectivity versus neutrality

The manner in which I have chosen to present my argument may appear circular to some readers — especially if their present "values" do not coincide with those expressed in this paper. I have tried, here, to demonstrate that the ideological content of a number of models of social structure is the product of class structure, a demonstration which itself is entirely based on a particular model of social structure. In view of this fact, some readers may see no reason why one might not try to raise the inverse argument.

Such a view, however, remains within the bounds of academic discussion. The value-judgement I have made on the class structure model derives from the adequation which I, together with many others, perceive between it and the social reality of the contemporary world. I am now firmly convinced that, much more than the methodology-oriented approach which I employed in my first academic works, it is this approach that is likely to open the doors to the comprehension of such phenomena as imperialism, wars, political revolutions, social rebellions, etc.; all those phenomena that academic sociology carefully excludes from its field of enquiry. Even in the field of academic sociology (*i.e.* the study of the reproductive aspects of social life), the class structure approach, recurrently posing the question of the class content of every social phenomenon, proves far more efficient — despite the fact that it is still at an embryonic stage — than the far more refined and "consistent" stratificationist approach.

In this paper I have tried to remain objective, which is not the same as remaining neutral.

The confusion between objectivity and neutrality is very common, and not by chance : for it can be used very effectively to block the way towards objective descriptions of reality. In the historical situation of which everyone of us is now a part, it so happens that social reality is characterized by the cruel, forceful exploitation, oppression, and murder of the peoples of the world by the system of social relationships in which they live; furthermore, all of humanity is sitting on the powderkeg of thermo-nuclear war and the fuse is sizzling. To remain at the same time objective *and neutral* in face of the first aspect of the situation, one would have to be an extremely dehumanized cynic. And in face of the second aspect one would have to be simply a frightened fool. The only attitude that honest members of the human race can take today is precisely to combine objectivity and *involvement*, not neutrality.

Objectivity is not antagonistic to involvement, as the ruling ideology would have us believe; it is, on the contrary, the only way to become knowingly and usefully involved.

REINHARD KRECKEL

Toward a theoretical re-orientation of the sociological analysis of vertical mobility

During the last two or three decades the empirical investigation of vertical mobility on the societal level has enjoyed a veritable boom, particularly among "Western" sociologists. Numerous national studies [1] and international comparisons [2] have been presented during this time. Nevertheless, the culminating point of this period seems to have been reached with the detailed empirical study by Peter M. Blau and Otis D. Duncan (1967), which was carried out in 1962. During the last few years quite a considerable number of sociologists have begun to show a certain uneasiness about the prevalently atheoretical research practice of the preceding period (*e.g.* Ammassari, 1967; Bolte and Kreckel, 1968; Cutright, 1968; Goldthorpe, 1966; Mayer and Müller, 1971; Porter, 1968; Rose, 1964). It seems to be a consequence of increasing disillusionment that lately there have only been very few publications about vertical mobility at the societal level [3]. Instead, we today find a great number of limited case studies and treatises, focussed on special questions of research technique and data analysis or on particular aspects of the mobility problem. Thus, a visible theoretical re-orientation of the sociology of vertical mobility hardly took place but there was, rather, a "*retreat into detail*". This development can be illustrated by comparing the far-reaching thematical homogeneity of the contributions on vertical mobility, which were presented in the fifties at the Second and Third World Congress of the International Sociological Association (ISA), with the obvious disparity of the papers presented at the Seventh World Congress in Varna in 1970.

It is the aim of this paper to make a theoretical contribution to help over-

1. Recent bibliographical reviews of mobility studies are given by Goldhamer (1968) and Bolte (1970).

2. For a critical survey of comparative mobility studies see Bolte and Kreckel (1968).

3. Obviously, this assertion is only valid for vertical mobility research. There seems to be no comparable stagnation in the field of horizontal mobility research.

come this conspicuous stagnation of mobility research. As a first step in this direction we shall try to recall the conditions which have supported the "rise and fall" of scientific interest in the investigation of vertical mobility processes at the societal level. It is my thesis that these conditions, which have not allowed any important theoretical progress in the area of mobility research during the last few years, can only be counteracted if the sociology of vertical mobility is ready for a sincere confrontation with the self-critical question of Robert S. Lynd: *Knowledge for what?* (*cf.* Lynd, 1948).

1.

Ever since Pitirim A. Sorokin (1959, pp. 133-163) coined the concept of vertical mobility it has been inseparably connected with the idea that the social structure can be conceived by analogy with a spatial framework whose component parts — be it social positions, roles, strata or classes — are arranged in a hierarchical manner: whenever individuals or groups (or categories of individuals) move from one social position, role, etc., into another, which from the standpoint of those concerned and/or of the sociologist passes for "higher" or "lower", the phenomenon of *vertical mobility* is present.

However, the idea of a hierarchical societal structure, within which alone vertical mobility can take place, is not a mere product of the nominalistic discretion of the researcher. For it is preceded by a highly realistic — though never unambiguous — *experience of social inequality* grounded in the language, thought and behaviour of everyday life. In other words, the sociologist must have a scientific concept of social inequality which is oriented towards the empirical reality *before* he can use the logically inferior concept of vertical mobility in a clear and distinct way.

In the construction of the concept of inequality then, the sociologist is bound by the experience of everyday life in which this concept is made. But such basic experience does not determine the process of scientific concept building in a definite way. For no sociological concept, even if it has been derived from the same socio-cultural reality which it is to describe, can represent this reality completely. In the transition from the hermeneutical identification to the conceptual denomination of socio-cultural phenomena there always remains a margin which is open for terminological decisions. Thus the most basic theoretical alternatives are already decided *before* the very process of formulation and empirical testing of sociological hypotheses or theories has even started (*cf.* Kreckel, 1972).

We can conclude from these basic epistemological principles that the possibility of the coexistence of a plurality of concurring scientific concepts of social inequality, which are nevertheless equally applicable for empirical research, can never be excluded. Thus we can formulate the following three questions of which we must not lose sight during our further discussion:

a) What are the concepts of social inequality which are — or could be used in sociology?

b) How is the decision made as to which one of these concepts is chosen and applied by the sociologist?

c) Is the term of vertical mobility compatible with all, with some, or with only one of these concepts of inequality?

2.

As a first step, we shall try to stake out the field within which the sociologist can move freely when he develops his concept of social inequality. We shall begin with the limitations of this range of conceptual discretion: there is one limitation which follows from the special (but usually implicit) decision of the sociologist to carry out the task of concept formation in connection with the real (though pre-scientific) experience of social inequality, and to analyse the social structure by analogy with a hierarchically constructed framework. Another limitation follows from the general decision of the researcher to strive — according to the most general conventions of "sociology" as a scientific discipline — for an empirically founded and theoretically orientated description, explanation and/or criticism of socio-cultural reality. Sociologists who accept these premises — and presumably all researchers who work on subjects like "social class", "social stratification", "vertical mobility", etc., do so — might come to the following *minimum consensus* about some general characteristics of the sociological concept of social inequality:

Not all social characteristics by means of which individuals (respectively social roles, positions, groups or other units of analysis) can be distinguished are useful for the definition of social inequality, but only those which *a*) are in some way or other accessible to *empirical* investigation, which *b*) permit the classification of the unit of analysis in question as to its *rank* within a hierarchical model of societal structure, which *c*) are so *generalized* that they are applicable to all empirically existing units of analysis within the society in question, which *d*) are relatively *stable*, because they are legitimized and supported by certain values, norms, institutions and sanctions, and to which *e*) a *strategical* importance for the sociological analysis of a societal structure can be attributed.

This minimum consensus about a phenomenon which has rightly been called "structured social inequality" (Heller, 1969) leaves a considerable *margin for some inevitable theoretical decisions*. For our problem, three theoretical decisions to be made on the basis of the following three questions seem to be especially important:

a) Which characteristic or which combination of characteristics is chosen to define social inequality — *e.g.* power, wealth, social prestige, relation to the means of production, autonomy of behaviour, income, life style, education, occupation, etc.?

b) Does the sociologist apply only those characteristics and rank differentiations of which the subjects are conscious themselves, or does he also use, or exclusively use, such criteria as can be theoretically expected to determine the thinking and acting of people without their being conscious of them?

c) What is the formal composition of the hierarchical model of societal structure which is the basis for the classification of ranks? Does it contain two ranks (or "classes") only, does it contain a greater amount of gradations (or "strata"), or is it an entirely fluid continuum?

It is obvious that these questions are closely interrelated. Nevertheless, we shall first turn our attention to the last question, which is visibly influenced by Stanislaw Ossowski. Ossowski (1962) has shown that the decision to use a concept of social inequality which is based on a two-class or dichotomous image of society implies the hypothesis that the structure of the society in question is strongly determined by the antagonism of these two classes. If, on the other hand, an image of society is used which is characterized by three or more gradations, the idea disappears that structured social inequality is based upon a fundamental cleavage of the society into two antagonistic groups (*e.g.* the "rich" and the "poor", the "dominators" and the "dominated" or the "exploiters" and the "exploited"). This consideration is even more valid if one chooses an image of society which represents the distribution of social inequality within a society by means of a fluid continuum: the more the sociologist orientates his terminological decisions towards the "empiricist" demand for a highly "differentiated" description and analysis of social inequality, the more he departs from the idea of a class conflict as a determining element of the societal structure.

After this, it seems to be rather self-evident that the concept of "vertical mobility" has not been coined with respect to a dichotomous model of social inequality. For it would be rather unlikely that a sociologist who considers the existence of an insurmountable class antagonism to be an "essential" characteristic of the structure of a certain society would take the process of vertical mobility — which is, in fact, a way of surmounting this antagonism — for equally "essential". Thus the investigation of individual or collective transitions between two antagonistic parts of a society is only of secondary importance, if a dichotomous frame of reference is used (*cf.* Fürstenberg, 1961, pp. 1-3; van Heek, 1956, p. 131). For the same reason, it is not very astonishing that Pitirim A. Sorokin, the father of the concept of vertical mobility, as well as later mobility researchers have always been inclined to study highly differentiated processes of mobility by means of a scheme of multiple gradations, if possible [4].

On the basis of this formal reasoning it is obvious that it has not been on

4. That is also true for those mobility studies which have been forced by technical or practical reasons to use a two-level-scale of social inequality which permits only a discrimination between "manual" and "nonmanual" occupations or similar simple characteristics (*cf.* Lipset and Bendix, 1959, pp. 14-17).

the basis of an interest in the "class struggle" that the concept of vertical mobility has been formed. On the contrary: whoever thinks the concept of vertical mobility to be a promising instrument for the analysis of a certain societal structure seems to be forced to impute at the same time that no class antagonism is decisive for the structure of the society in question. Paradoxically, a strong support for this argument is given by certain Marxist sociologists of Eastern Europe, who take it for granted that the problem of class antagonism has been overcome in principle in their own societies. On this basis they take up vertical mobility research with the same candour as their anti-Marxist colleagues in Western countries (*e.g.* Armelin, 1970; Milic, 1966; Sarapata, 1966).

We can now retain as a provisional result that serious difficulties seem to arise if one tries to analyse a certain societal structure both by means of a dichotomous class theory and by means of the concept of vertical mobility which is oriented towards a gradation model of social inequality. It is to this state of affairs that the well-known reproach that the sociological analysis of vertical mobility in capitalist societies always fulfills ideological functions refers, because it conceals the basic class antagonism which determines the societal structure. Therefore the "bourgeois" sociological analysis of vertical mobility cannot but become an expression of the interests of the dominating and privileged parts of capitalist society (*cf.* Ossipow, 1969, pp. 135-137; Steiner, 1967, pp. 202-240). However, most Western mobility researchers will probably not be bothered by this reproach, as the critical conception of "ideology" which is employed against them is based on just the same dichotomous model of society that they have already rejected by the mere decision to use the concept of vertical mobility (*cf.* Brock, 1970, pp. 7-10). However, another criticism can be brought forward which cannot be put aside as easily, because *it tries to measure the sociological analysis of vertical mobility against its own scientific intentions.* The thesis can be formulated that the sociology of vertical mobility is not able to replace the rejected dichotomous class theory by its own theory, which permits the establishment of a stringent scientific connection between societal structure and vertical mobility. This reproach of theoretical deficiency cannot be avoided, and it must be discussed.

3.

Apart from the approach of Seymour M. Lipset and Hans L. Zetterberg (1956), which is primarily a social psychological one, no explicit essay on a deductive sociological "theory of vertical mobility" is available. Nevertheless, there can be no doubt that contemporary sociological analysis of vertical mobility disposes of a fairly homogeneous "theoretical orientation" which we will discuss below.

A clear convergence of perspectives can already be found in the field of problem formulation and terminological decision:

a) In the national and international studies to hand, a concentration on the specific problem of *occupational* mobility is predominant. Furthermore, we notice a preference for the investigation of processes of *inter-generational* mobility, especially among *men*.

b) Most often the criterion of occupational *prestige* is used for the identification of upward and downward movements. That is, no theoretically deduced standards are employed for the hierarchical classification of ranks of occupations; instead the empirically discovered evaluations, towards which people's behaviour in everyday life is orientated, are used as a basis.

c) Since the prestige aspect of social inequality has been the primary concern of the sociology of vertical mobility, stratification models containing several gradations or fluid continua of occupational prestige have been preferred.

Thus it is my thesis that the great theoretical complexity of the phenomenon of vertical mobility has been largely reduced during the period of the "boom" of mobility research to the very special question of *vertical intergenerational occupational mobility among men, evaluated by means of a model of prestige stratification* (*cf.* Fürstenberg, 1962, pp. 35-42; Goldthorpe, 1966, pp. 649-655; Heller, 1969, p. 312; Mack *et al.*, 1957, pp. 1-2; Mayer and Müller, 1971, pp. 2-3; Wilenski, 1966, pp. 129-133; Westoff *et al.*, 1966, pp. 376-380). Furthermore, there has been great interest in the measurement of the *amount* of vertical mobility within societies. This rather astonishing unanimity of problem formulation and terminology can only be understood because it is based on some common "theoretical orientation" [5].

By "theoretical orientation" we mean a set of propositions which can be used to give "plausible interpretations" of the most general dynamic processes and stabilizing mechanisms taking place within a specific societal structure. In this sense, the so-called "functional theory of stratification", as well as the "Marxist class theory" have the logical status of theoretical orientations. Our conception of theoretical orientation must not be confounded with "the" great sociological theory in the sense of a natural science, which is desired by many sociologists. The terminology of a theoretical orientation in sociology is bound to certain "extra-scientific" values and interests, and it contains tautological elements which exclude its precise empirical testability. Its heuristical function is to guide concrete empirical research into a "meaningful" direction and to stimulate the formulation of fruitful and testable hypotheses. But as soon as the values and interests upon which a theoretical orientation is based are no longer accepted as legitimate, the results of empirical research, guided by this theoretical orientation, risk becoming equally illegitimate and "meaningless". In such a case, the somewhat disconcerting question "Knowledge for what" assumes immediate importance.

---

5. The concept of "theoretical orientation" is an attempt to combine Merton's concept of "general sociological orientation" and Dahrendorf's concept of "para-theory", which both originate in the neopositivistic tradition of sociology, with Habermas' idea of an empirically falsifiable "critical theory of society" (*cf.* Merton, 1957, pp. 87-89; Dahrendorf, 1967, pp. 343-345; Habermas, 1967, pp. 192-195; Habermas, 1968, chap. 12).

It will be our next task to inquire into the nature of that theoretical orientation which has favoured the reduction of mobility research to the specific problem of "vertical intergenerational occupational prestige mobility among men". This question may appear rather crude, as it is obvious that there has never been one "monolithic" theoretical orientation of vertical mobility research. However, I think it is justified, within the context of this critical location of the sociological analysis of vertical mobility, to work out certain general characteristics which are more or less explicitly included in the theoretical arguments of most mobility researchers [6].

1) The question of the amount of vertical mobility in a society can only have a genuinely sociological meaning if the empirically ascertained "more " or "less" of mobility can be related to, and explained by, specific conditions of the social structure. Usually, this theoretical connection between mobility and social structure is established by means of a general historical-sociological thesis [7], which says that it is a characteristic of the so-called "pre-industrial" and less differentiated societies that social positions are mostly transmitted by heredity from generation to generation, whereas in differentiated and industrializing societies social positions are increasingly "achieved" by means of the individuals' own activity, and not "ascribed" [8].

On the basis of this thesis the *amount* of mobility in a society — and primarily the amount of *inter-generational mobility* — can be considered as a meaningful indicator for its degree of differentiation, industrialization, or even modernization [9], measurable and usable in historical or international comparisons.

Thus, we come to the *first conclusion*, that societal mobility research is closely bound to a historical-comparative frame of reference, if it wants to give theoretically meaningful interpretations of empirical mobility rates : contemporary societies are measured against the past. Whenever the analysis of vertical mobility tries to depart from this historical basis of comparison and instead mobility rates are measured against the ideally constructed

6. An analogous proceeding has been justified by Lipset and Bendix (1959, pp. 284 ff.) in the following way: "Because the bulk of modern research is published without any explicit statement of its intellectual rationale, our statement of this rationale is the result of inferences and impressions."

7. The thesis of the direct interrelation between industrialization and mobility is the core of the publications of Lipset and Bendix (1959) and Lipset and Smelser (1966). For a critical discussion of this thesis see Ammassari, 1967, pp. 30-41; Goldthorpe, 1966, pp. 649-655; Lancaster Jones, 1969, pp. 292-306.

8. In this connection, a typological scale is often used which goes from relatively closed "caste-societies" to modern "open-class-systems". The so-called "estate-societies" of pre-industrial Europe take an intermediary position on this scale (*cf.* Barber, 1957, pp. 335-350).

9. *Cf.* the concept of "social mobilization" which has been introduced by Deutsch (1961, pp. 493-514).

type of a "completely open society", serious theoretical difficulties will arise. This question will be discussed later on.

2) It would be rather astonishing if the only cause of the temporary rise of mobility research had been its apparent utility for the measurement of the degree of differentiation, industrialization or modernization of a society, for there are more direct methods available for this purpose. If the boom of research on vertical mobility has occurred in spite of this, there must be additional causes which are primarily of a political or ideological kind : the genesis of an "open class system" within parliamentary and capitalistic industrial societies is not only considered as an empirically testable regularity of societal development, it is also a highly valued aim within the dominating political creed of these societies. According to this aim, each individual should have the same right and the same opportunity to determine his place in society freely, and without any hindrance, by means of his own abilities. Thus, the more the ideal of freedom and equal opportunity is realized, the more individuals must be mobile. This idea of freedom and mobility clearly derives from the philosophy of the enlightenment and liberalism (*cf.* Habermas, 1969, pp. 86-91; Mannheim, 1930, pp. 200-212) which gained political and social importance in Europe and North America in the 18th and 19th century. The rise of enlightened and liberal ideas in this period is largely due to the fact that they were congenial to the economic and political interests of the aspiring industrial bourgeoisie which could make use of them in its struggle against "feudal" hindrances, and against absolutist or colonialist regimentation. Karl Mannheim says:

"The idea of 'freedom' [...] was the utopia of the aspiring bourgeoisie. It was partly a real utopia, *i.e.* it contained elements which broke up the preceding structure of reality in the direction of a new ontological order, and which were partly realized after the establishment of this idea. Freedom in the sense of the break-up of the restrictions of the guild and estate systems, freedom in the sense of the freedom of thought and opinion, freedom in the sense of political freedom, in the sense of a full living of the consciousness of personality, became a vastly realizable [...] possibility. Nonetheless these utopias having been realized, today we know exactly to what degree the idea of freedom of that time contained not only utopian, but also ideological elements.

Wherever this idea of freedom was forced to halt in front of the complementary idea of equality, it speculated about possibilities which were not realizable in principle within the order of life which it had postulated and later carried out. An aspiring new social stratum had to come up, which separated the ideological elements of the preceding "bourgeois" consciousness from those apt for future realization, *i.e.* from the truly utopian elements" (Mannheim, 1930, pp. 180-182).

In the first place, this quotation shows how the liberal idea of freedom and mobility is linked to the problem of equality and inequality: originally, liberalism is directed against the extremely hierarchical order of estate societies, and it strives for a society which can do without rigid mobility barriers, but not without social inequality. Accordingly, the sociological interest in the question of mobility, which is derived from the liberal model of an "open society", must aim primarily at the investigation of *vertical* mobility processes. Furthermore, the quotation from Mannheim already alludes to the problem that the possibilities for a complete realization of the "bourgeois" principle of freedom are restricted by certain structural limitations which, in turn, influence the scientific content of the concept of a perfectly "open" and mobile society. We shall investigate this question below.

For the time being we want to retain as a *second conclusion* that the idea of the "open society" is clearly connected with the formative period of industrial capitalism. However, the struggle against estate systems and "pre-industrial" conditions is no longer a central structural problem of advanced industrial societies. Thus, the question arises as to what might be the special significance of vertical mobility today, social conditions having considerably changed in comparison to the period of transition from "pre-industrial" to "industrial" time.

3) In order to approach a solution to this question, we may now return to our above statement that the concept of vertical mobility is necessarily bound to the logically superior concept of social inequality — which in practice is usually a *non-dichotomous concept of inequality*, derived from the liberal tradition. To develop this the following point will be of importance: on the basis of the preliminary decision for a non-dichotomous and liberal concept of social inequality, it is perfectly legitimate to take any empirically existing system of social inequality as given and to investigate rates of vertical mobility *within* this structural frame of reference. If the inequality structure in question is sufficiently permeable, it may be classified as an "open class system" [10]. That is, there is no logical hindrance at all to considering a society with an extremely hierarchical structure as a nonetheless "open society" — and it is just this which has repeatedly occurred, when certain mobility researchers have emphasized the great "openness" of the society of the USA for example (*cf.* Lipset and Bendix, 1959, pp. 27-28; Blau and Duncan, 1967, p. 426). Thus we find a further parallel between traditional liberalism and the accepted sociology of mobility: liberal social policy is not directed primarily against the unequal (even unjust) distribution of power, privileges and prestige in society as such, and it is also not directly aimed at reducing those inequalities. Its primary interest *lies far more in creating equal opportunities of access to social positions of unequal social value.* The sociologists proceed analogously, formulating empirical statements about rates of vertical mobility with the aid of association indices or similar means, while at the same time leaving unquestioned the fact that these very processes of mobility take place within specific conditions of social inequality. For this reason *it is not social inequality but "equality of opportunity"* that represents the primary concern

10. This paradox has already been seen by Lipset and Bendix (1959, pp. 27 and 260) — but without their drawing any visible consequences for their own research work.

for liberally-oriented mobility researchers. To be sure, where social inequality is perpetuated by impermeable caste or class barriers, as for example in 18th or 19th century Europe, the notion of equal opportunity is of necessity directed against the prevailing conditions of social inequality. However, if the concept of equal opportunity is not explicitly connected with the problem of social inequality, the meaning can easily be perverted into its opposite, as is evident in such "industrially advanced achievement-oriented" societies as the USA, USSR, GDR and FRG. The permeability of social barriers in these societies is more or less guaranteed, without reducing social inequalities to a minimum. That is, vertical mobility and equality of opportunity can under certain conditions, as we shall see, function to preserve privileges and inequalities.

Therefore, the sociologist who investigates the extent of vertical mobility in advanced industrial societies without regard to the relationship between mobility and inequality is open to criticism. The notions of "equality of opportunity" and "open society", which seemed progressive 100-150 years ago, have in the meantime lent themselves to misuse as factors of ideological stabilization for conditions of social inequality. This represents the author's *third conclusion*, which should however be understood as a preliminary statement of orientation requiring further specification and elaboration.

4) Until now, not a word has been said about the question *why* vertical mobility research has shown such a preference for investigating *occupational prestige* mobility, especially among *men*. It is my opinion that this limitation of scientific perspective is a symptom of the problematical implications of vertical mobility research: if the reduction of interest from social to occupational mobility is explicitly justified at all, there is usually a combination of theoretical and technical arguments. The theoretical line of argument is generally based on the assumption that the structure of advanced industrial societies is shaped by the predominance of the economic sub-system, which is characterized by the "universalistic/achievement pattern". That is why occupation — as the "economic" aspect of the individual — is said to determine the social status in a decisive way[11]. The empirical objection that industrial societies are usually characterized by a high degree of status-inconsistency can be refuted by means of the technical argument that occupational status is more easily accessible to empirical research methods than other characteristics of social status, and that it is also the most feasible and the most precise indicator of social status (*cf.* Blau and Duncan, 1967, pp. 5-10; Bolte, 1959, pp. 25-30; Carlsson, 1958, pp. 42-57; Moser and Hall, 1954, pp. 29-50; Lipset and Bendix, 1958, pp. 269-276; Svalastoga, 1959, pp. 15-21). The technical accessibility of occupational status is often furthered by the

11. For the "classical" presentation of this conception *cf.* Parsons, 1964, pp. 182-191.

— mostly tacit — decision to concentrate on the vertical occupational mobility of *men*. This decision seems to be based on the rather "patriarchal" and questionable empirical generalization that the occupational activity of women is either no determinant of their status, or that it can be neglected as "atypical" (*cf.* Lenski, 1966, pp. 416-417). Nevertheless, the concentration on the occupational mobility of men would not be very alarming as such [12] if it were not combined with the further limitation of research interest in the dimension of *prestige*. This problem is thoroughly discussed in the paper by Helga Recker (1971). Here, we shall only emphasize the following point : the "subjective" phenomenon of prestige is treated as the only relevant criterion of social inequality and vertical mobility, whereas "objective" characteristics — like the unequal distribution of income, education, power, social security, autonomy of behaviour, life chances, etc. — are reduced to mere epiphenomena, or to simple indicators for the investigation of prestige [13]. With that, a complete *conversion of perspective* is realized. For there can be no doubt that, originally, it was not the "subjective" aspect of prestige, but the unequal distribution of "objective" conditions and chances of life in society which — as a permanent "social problem" — initiated the political discussion and the scientific investigation of the conditions of social inequality (*cf.* Lipset and Bendix, 1959). Within the so-called "modern industrial societies" relatively stable orders of inequality and privilege still exist, which are certainly not given by nature nor unchangeable in form. Obviously, they are a central part of the "objective" structure of these societies. Sociological analysis of vertical mobility which uses only the innocuous image of prestige stratification as an immediate frame of reference for empirical research threatens therefore gradually to move away from the central, politically and economically conditioned problems of sociological analysis of societal structures. At the same time, all politicians, ideologists or scientists can utilize such an analysis of vertical mobility as a comfortable moral alibi, if they want to maintain the existing order of inequality and privileges in their society or if they want to justify it as a "functional necessity". A quotation from Tumin (1970, p. 294) illustrates this reasoning — probably unintentionally:

"Mobility may be seen as the other "moral" side of stratification, for insofar as inequality is considered to be "unfair", at least to some degree, mobility — or the chance to improve one's position (and disimprove it as well) — is seen as the counterbalancing moral weight."

From this a *fourth conclusion* can be derived, which will again be a heuristic thesis: whenever the sociological analysis of vertical mobility drifts too far

12. Thus, Carlsson (1958, p. 46) has pointed out, "that occupational data are relevant to all contemporary theories of stratification. For sociologists who define 'class' in terms of prestige hierarchies, as well as for those who think of it as a class-conscious group, occupation is both an index and a determinant of class. In the Marxian class theory, occupation helps to delimit groups with different relations to the means of production. Likewise, those who follow Max Weber will find occupation a useful index of life chances."

13. The distinction between "subjective" and "objective" criteria of social inequality is taken from Carlsson (1958, pp. 38-39).

into the sphere of prestige research, it not only risks becoming an instrument of appeasement and self-appeasement for society and sociology, it also contravenes its own requirements as an empirical science. For in losing contact with the problem of the analysis of societal structure, the sociological analysis of vertical mobility necessarily loses a part of its ability for theoretical explanation, too [14].

4.

If this rough outline of the prevailing theoretical orientation of the sociological analysis of vertical mobility is approximately correct, the suspicion of an ideologically influenced limitation of perspective must not be excluded. But the criticism of ideologies is not the aim of this paper. Its primary concern is rather the idea that every reduction of sociological perspective which is not legitimized in terms of a theoretical conception of societal structure must lead to *shortcomings which can be proved by means of empirical science.*

One can find a first indication of this by commenting on the immediate circumstances which have favoured the rise of research in social mobility during the past decades. At first sight it appears to be rather surprising that the liberal idea of an "open socicty" has not been able to incite any systematic investigation of vertical mobility at the societal level before the middle of the 20th century. The interpretation given by Karl M. Bolte (1969, p. 30) and F. van Heek (1956, pp. 130-131) is rather plausible. According to them, the first rise of mobility research in the USA was brought about by the Great Depression and the closure of America's Western "frontier". These experiences raised doubts as to whether the deeply-rooted creed that America is the "land of unlimited opportunities" was still valid. As a consequence the empirical investigation of this question became a politically and ideologically interesting task. Also, on the basis of this contesting of the "American creed" there arose the complementary question, repeatedly discussed during the last decades as to whether American society is really more "open" than European societies, which are still handicapped by their "feudal" past (*cf.* Bolte and Kreckel, 1968, pp. 43-44). It seems obvious that no immediate necessity was felt to discuss the "objective" systems of inequality and privilege in this context; for attention was focussed on the question of their formal permeability, which could indeed be operationalized quite satisfactorily by means of the "subjective" indicator of occupational prestige.

This sketchy attempt at a historical interpretation is certainly fragmentary. But it will be sufficient for the purpose of the present argument, as its only function is to illustrate that the rise of societal mobility research has not been

14. A similar point has been made by Goldthorpe (1966, pp. 655-659) in his criticism of the thesis of the "logic of industrialism".

accompanied by very sophisticated theoretical reasoning about the structure of society. For the question of the "openness" of a society has grown, rather, out of a prescientific political interest in knowledge, and not so much out of a genuinely sociological one. Without this historical background, it would be hard to see why there has been such a considerable number of sociologists who have candidly constructed and applied formal indices for the measurement of the "openness" of a society without caring much about the theoretical and empirical clarification of the logically prior problem as to whether the ideal type of the perfectly "open" society is applicable at all to the "real types" of social structure as they are found in the contemporary systems of inequality and privilege — be it in capitalist or socialist societies. Therefore it is not surprising that a rather large number of sophisticated indices for the quantitative measurement of societal rates of mobility is now available. Furthermore, several sociological arguments have been accumulated, and empirically corroborated, by means of which the *relative* differences between mobility rates which are seen through historical or intercultural comparison can be causally interpreted. But there is nowhere any systematic approach which would allow the sociological explanation of *absolute* mobility rates.

Those authors who are conscious of this difficulty therefore abstain from explicitly evaluating empirical mobility rates as "high" or "low", and they arrive only at historical-comparative results (*e.g.* Bolte, 1959, pp. 213-226; Carlsson, 1958, pp. 107-113; Hall and Ziegler, 1954, pp. 260-265; Svalastoga, 1959, pp. 345-349). On the other hand, Seymour M. Lipset and Reinhard Bendix (1959, pp. 25-26), for example, assert frankly that the amount of vertical mobility in all industrial societies studied by them is "high", as "from one generation to another, a quarter to a third of the non-farm population moves from working class to middle class or vice versa". There is no explicit justification, as to why they decide to classify a society as "highly mobile" — in spite of the fact that they themselves have identified between two thirds and three quarters of the population as immobile! Similarly unjustified evaluations are found, for example, in the publications of Morris Janowitz (1958, p. 12), Bernard Barber, (1957, p. 468), Peter M. Blau and Otis D. Duncan (1967, p. 426) or, with some supplementary differentiations, Seymour M. Miller (1969, pp. 330-331).

It is obvious that the absolute numerical value of empirical rates of mobility (or immobility) depends on the index chosen and on the number of strata of occupational prestige premised; the rate of mobility is dependent on how fine the scale of gradations is (*cf.* Carlsson, 1958, pp. 115-116; Goldhamer, 1968, p. 431). But this technical aspect of the analysis of vertical mobility may be neglected in the present discussion. It is more important to see that in one respect there is no difference between those sociologists who, without further ado, classify their own (mostly "Western") industrial societies as "open societies", and those who prefer a more prudent attitude. *Neither of them gives a thorough theoretical examination of the question as to whether the structure of highly industrialized, especially Western, societies is at all compatible with the principle of an "open society".*

I think that the reasons for this deficiency can be traced back to the liberal concept of freedom of the 18th and 19th centuries to which the sociology of vertical mobility, explicitly or implicitly, has been oriented up to now. However, this concept can only be a promoter of social emancipation *and* an instrument of fruitful sociological analysis insofar as it is applied to a societal structure which is characterized by nearly insurmountable and institutionally stabilized barriers of caste, estate or class. But the liberal concept of freedom must fall into a vacuum and lose its primary meaning as soon as a societal structure is no longer determined by these barriers.

It can hardly be contested that the structures of advanced industrial societies are still characterized by the existence of institutionalized systems of inequality and privilege, but they do not contain impermeable barriers. Thus, the liberal concept of freedom seems to be outdated as a basis for the sociological analysis of advanced industrial societies, because it becomes unusable for the problem of structured social inequality as soon as the structural and institutional conditions of "permeability" are given.

However, my criticism is not directed against the liberal tradition and its concept of freedom as such, but against its formal and non-historical *use* in the modern sociological analysis of vertical mobility. Therefore, I do not agree with those sociologists who seem to consider that the customary forms of mobility research and the liberal conception of freedom have become equally outdated, and who try to replace them, for example, by so-called "manpower research" [15] or by a retreat into micro-sociology [16]. On the contrary, it is my opinion that the concept of the "open society" can be freed from its historical burden, and thus be transformed into a useful terminological tool for a revised sociological analysis of vertical mobility which will be able to include in its analysis the institutionalized systems of inequality and privilege which survive in advanced industrial societies.

5.

The above quoted passage from Karl Mannheim may serve as a point of departure for this theoretical re-orientation of the analysis of vertical mobility. Mannheim (1930, p. 182) alludes to the fact that the complete realization of the liberal idea of freedom — and thus of the ideal type of "open society" — contradicts the "order of life" in bourgeois society. The following argument is inspired by this reasoning. It is an attempt to advance some

15. A representative of this "solution" is John Porter (1968, pp. 5-19).
16. This tendency is favoured by Mayer and Müller (1971, pp. 11-16).

theoretical points of view which might serve as guide lines for a critically revised sociological analysis of vertical mobility which is adapted to the structural problems of contemporary industrial societies:

1) The extent of social inequality, *i.e.* of the hierarchical distribution of power, privilege and prestige, which is institutionalized in advanced capitalist and socialist societies, must by no means be considered as "a priori" necessary. For it is always a product of human history, and it can therefore be analysed, in principle, from the point of view of its *transformability.*

2) We proceed from the assumption — until shown to be false — that the degree of social inequality that can be established empirically as existing in contemporary industrial societies is *too high* compared with the extent of possible equality, given the available technical, economic and social means. These social inequalities should therefore be analysed with regard to their *reducibility.*

3) As long as the opposite has not been convincingly demonstrated, the heuristic usefulness of posing the following sociological problem remains valid: what are the social mechanisms that permit the maintenance of an excessive degree of social inequality in the so-called advanced industrial societies, though one would expect that reduction of this excess is in the interest of the population set at a disadvantage by these conditions of inequality? How are these strata brought to accept such conditions? Obviously, the answer to these questions is of strategic importance not only for the empirical investigation of given social structures, but also in the interest of social emancipation and the reduction of structural inequality. Therefore it seems heuristically justified to interpret modern capitalist and socialist industrial societies within the framework of a "critical functionalism" as *inequality-and-privilege-preserving-systems.* This perspective focuses sociological research on the empirical investigation of those functions and capacities of specific social phenomena which make for the stabilization, reproduction (or reduction) of social inequalities. With regard to the specific phenomenon of "vertical mobility", then, we proceed from the basis of the following theoretical orientation: *the extent of vertical mobility (and immobility) as found for example in the American, Soviet and German societies should by no means be seen as "functionally necessary" for the survival of "the" social system, but it can be justifiably interpreted as "functionally necessary" for the maintenance of the respective concrete historical systems of inequality and privilege.* Seen in this critical way, functionalism can indeed offer a heuristically fruitful approach for the structural analysis of advanced industrial societies if, in addition to formulating ahistorical statements about the survival ability of the social order in general, it attempts to investigate empirically the concrete social mechanisms whereby historical systems of inequality and privileges are main-

tained. The concept of an inequality-and-privilege-preserving-system, employed here as a principal idea (a *tertium comparationis*), enables us to subsume and compare socialist as well as capitalist systems with respect to their functions and capacities to preserve (or to reduce) structural inequality and privileges.

4) The preservation of inequality and privileges in advanced industrial societies seems to require as a necessary condition a certain *minimum amount of vertical mobility*, especially upward mobility, for the following reasons:

a) The idea of equal opportunity has important *legitimizing and integrating functions* for the support of capitalist and socialist systems of inequality and privileges (*cf.* Luckmann and Berger, 1964, pp. 331-344; Ossowski, 1962, pp. 127-149). The effectiveness of these functions could be shaken if the underprivileged part of the population had no "realistic" opportunity for upward mobility.

b) It has often been pointed out that people identified as either upwardly or downwardly mobile are more inclined to be politically inactive and conformist, or indeed evince conservative voting behavior, than immobile persons (*cf.* Lipset and Bendix, 1959, pp. 64-72; Lopreato, 1967, pp. 586-592; Zloczower, 1971). Furthermore, high rates of mobility are frequently referred to as a *means of combating political radicalization* among underprivileged groups, although this generalization has never been subjected to strict empirical testing (*cf.* Dahrendorf, 1968, pp. 70-79; Germani, 1966, pp. 376-384; Lipset and Bendix, 1959, pp. 260-265).

c) Socialist and capitalist industrial societies exist equally under the self-imposed pressure to *increase economic productivity and technical innovation.* This requires an enormous and ever-growing labor force of highly qualified and achievement-oriented people (*cf.* Porter 1968, pp. 5-19). The availability of material and social rewards — in the form of opportunities for upward mobility — seems one of the most effective methods of recruiting and motivating such manpower.

5) Undoubtedly, additional arguments could be advanced to show that the inequality-and-privilege-preserving-systems in East and West require a certain minimum of vertical mobility. We are, however, more interested in stressing the complementary thesis: that the rate of mobility in these societies cannot exceed a *limited maximum degree of vertical mobility* without endangering the existing order of inequality and privilege. (That this diverges from the ideal of an "open society", need hardly be restated.) For even if we reject, as some conservative sociologists do, the image of a pyramidal distribution of power, privilege and prestige in Western (and Eastern) industrial societies and accept instead the picture of a rhomboid distribution, the overwhelming majority of people in all contemporary industrial societies belong to the less powerful, less privileged and less esteemed population strata. Since, moreover, the relative proportion of these "large" groups in the total population has not undergone any far-reaching changes over a long period of time (*cf.* Kreckel *et al.*, 1971, pp. 42-75) the principle of statistical probability alone tells us that *most of the members of this underprivileged part of the population have no opportunity to bring about decisive changes in their life conditions or to influence crucially the social status of their children:* even in the most favour-

able circumstances only a small percentage of these strata can make the ascent into the numerically much smaller powerful and privileged social group. Obviously these restrictive conditions, this *systemic pressure toward immobility*, operating in all inequality-and-privilege-preserving-systems, affect primarily the lower income brackets, usually the less qualified wage earners and their relatives [17]. The statements above call for further comment:

a) The concept of an inequality-and-privilege-preserving-system can *ex definitione* be applied only to societies in which a minority of the population has at its disposal the greater part of all power, privilege and prestige. For example, assuming that the privileged minority represents — according to whatever criteria — 20 % of the total population, the remaining 80 % thus constitute the socially disadvantaged.

b) Obviously the social asymmetry expressed in the proportion 20 : 80 need not have the slightest influence on the number of individuals within the society who can become vertically mobile by achieving a social status either above or below their previous social position. It is even conceivable that all the members of such a society regardless of their point of departure within the social hierarchy, achieve during their lifetime or between generations a change in status, for example in prestige status or income status. In this case, despite the 20 : 80 distribution, one could speak of "perfect mobility" or, as this condition will be called hereafter, perfect *micro-mobility*.

c) Traditional mobility research is concerned almost exclusively with micro-mobility, though not of course in the form described above. Empirical mobility studies can never encompass all existing status changes and register them as processes of mobility; they embrace only movements across boundaries which have been fixed in advance in order to permit the distinction of a limited number of status groups in society (*e.g.* strata, classes, social categories, etc.). Individuals who change social status solely within such status groups appear to be immobile according to this line of thought. It follows therefore (*ceteris paribus*) that the resulting micro-mobility rate, first, depends on the size of the social groups as defined and, second, grows as the number of defined status groups increase. For this reason the usefulness of micro-mobility rates for the structural analysis of total societies is strictly limited.

d) If however the mobility rate of total societies does not presume numerous status groups but only, as in the example above, two, one of which includes 20 %, the other 80 % of the population, even in conditions of perfect "circulation of elites" at most a quarter of the lower group have a chance to ascend intergenerationally into the upper group and become *macro-mobile*. Thus the distribution of inequality remains basically stable, as the notion of an inequality-and-privilege-preserving-system implies. The remaining three quarters may be micro-mobile, but not macro-mobile. Hence we are dealing — to state the case more precisely — with *systemic pressure towards macro-immobility*.

6) One may view this bipartition of the societal structure as unjustifiable, as the division of society into two status groups seems to be arbitrary and as its advantage for structural analysis is not altogether clear. This objection is wholly admissible at this stage of the argument, though only partially correct. Up to this point, our intention has only been to contrast the formal indices applied in traditional mobility studies to quantify social mobi-

17. These hypothetical conclusions have been corroborated in the meantime by Kreckel *et al.* (1971) who have carried out a detailed secondary analysis of the empirical data available about vertical occupational mobility and immobility in West Germany. Similar results are reported by Ortmann (1971) and Weltz and Schmidt (1971).

lity rates with another, equally formal, index whose advantage is to apprehend relations of absolute inequality. To advance the discussion a further step, we propose to dichotomize the status hierarchy in a manner by no means arbitrary theoretically:

Income distribution is one important "objective" dimension of structured social inequality in advanced industrial societies (*cf.* Carlsson, 1961, pp. 189-199; Hamilton, 1968, pp. 250-257). Income distribution, unlike power or prestige, is itself quantifiable[18]. Thus, at least in principle, it is possible to ascertain the total amount of individual net earnings and net property income for every industrialized society at any point in time. If income distribution were completely egalitarian, each earner would draw an equal share of this total amount. In fact, the situation in systems of social inequality is such that half of the "income pie" is distributed among a minority, whose share is disproportionate, while the numerically larger group has to split the other half. Stated formally, disregarding all specific social structural conditions, the proposition is that all who divide the "upper half" of total income belong to the "overprivileged" minority; the rest represent the "underprivileged" majority. According to the calculations of Gabriel Kolko (1962, pp. 14 and 34), in the USA in 1959 between 70 and 80 % of all earners divided 50 % of total income. On the basis of Goesecke's and Foehl's data for the FRG, we compute that in 1959, 77.7 % of all private households disposed of only 53.4 % of total net income [19].

Assuming that such a dichotomization of the social structure is theoretically justifiable (and assuming that the official income statistics can provide the necessary data) an index measuring the societal rate of vertical intergenerational mobility ean easily be developed: to derive such an index, we find the number of those who have made an intergenerational transition from the lower to the upper half of the income distribution within society. This figure is divided by the absolute numerical membership of the lower "half" and multiplied by a hundred. The result is a percentage index, which measures *the degree of intergenerational macro-mobility* in the society. Analogously, relating the number of upwardly mobile individuals to the total membership of the "upper half" provides an index for *the degree of intergenerational macro-permeability* within a society. With the aid of both indices, it is not only possible to express relative, but also sociologically meaningful *absolute* statements concerning the actual degree of "openness" in advanced industrial societies possessing an asymmetrical structure of inequality and privilege.

The advantage of this method of measuring income macro-mobility is that it can be employed for historical and international comparison; for the income dividing line offers not only an analytical basis for comparison, but can also be determined empirically in all its variability. The measure is a rough one, however, taking into account neither the dispersion nor range of the distribution of inequality. But any attempt to refine the mobility index would probably be useless: it shares too many of the shortcomings of traditional mobility measures, to which it is related polemically. As a purely *synthetic* measure, it is unable to encompass any precise theoretical considerations about the particular structural conditions acting within concrete historical societies. The index as such cannot analyse or explain conditions of stability and change of given systems of inequality and privilege. It is, as all social

18. Thus, the "Lorenz curve" is a generally recognized instrument which is used to illustrate the quantitative distribution of socio-economic inequality.

19. The calculations were made by the author on the basis of figures contained in Föhl (1964, p. 53). See also Kreckel *et al.* (1971, pp. 48-55).

indicators are, a rather crude simplification; but at least, it is a simplification which is consciously directed by a theoretical orientation that can be sociologically justified. Since the present author has argued that it was a heuristically fruitful enterprise to analyse advanced industrial societies as "inequality-and-privilege-preserving-systems", he is interested in illuminating those facts which reveal the character of inequality. From this aspect the index shows at least the direction for further mobility research. Whenever empirical investigation into processes of vertical micro-mobility loses sight of the restrictive conditions created by the "systemic pressure towards macro-immobility" acting in industrial societies of different types, the analysis risks to become sociologically meaningless and even ideological. The task of the indices of macro-mobility and macro-permeability is to counteract this nocuous tendency which is rather common in the sociological analysis of vertical mobility, as we have seen above.

7) While the income-based macro-mobility index has the advantage of permitting the formulation of quantitatively direct statements which clarify the relationship between inequality distribution and vertical mobility, the procedure conceals a defect which can be illustrated by the following quotation from Marx (1920, pp. 466-467):

"The boorish human mind transforms class differences into a difference in the size of the money-bag! [...] the size of the purse is a purely quantitative difference, capable of inciting two individuals of the same class against each other."

Though we are aware by now that the empirical assigning of individuals to various classes is no simple task, Marx's quotation should alert us that the ranking of a population by income reveals neither the social grouping to which the individual earner belongs, nor his "occupational" position within the process of production, nor the interests typically associated with different positions. Isolated empirical statements about income mobility as such contribute as little to the precise understanding of structural relationships as does all atheoretical research into prestige mobility. That is, little is learned about the concrete social mechanisms which act on different social groups as either obstacles or encouragements to mobility. It is these mechanisms which define the real opportunities for mobility.

At this point of the discussion, Gerhard Kleining's concept of "structural mobility", developed to counterbalance the notion of prestige mobility, seems to lead a step further: Kleining (1971, pp. 1-33) distinguishes for West German society ten "occupational circles". Each "occupational circle" occupies a specific position within the asymmetrical system of social production and division of labour, and it is characterized by a particular style of work, by distinct forms of" access regulation and exit hindrance", and by specific forms of "controlling the profit of labour". He distinguishes the following "occupational circles" :

1. Professions
2. Civil servants employed in offices
3. Civil servants with other activities
4. Employees in offices
5. Employees with other activities (agents, salesmen)
6. Self-employed
7. Peasants, farmers (with own farm)
8. Craftsmen (employed)
9. Skilled laborers
10. Other laborers, rural workers

Kleining formulates empirical statements about the changing size of these "occupational circles" in history and about the mobility processes between them. Kleining's claim to have contributed to the class analysis of the FGR with his procedure is only half fulfilled. He writes:

"Despite the occupational turnover that has taken place since industrialization, the rate of mobility has *not improved* during the last fifty years. It increased during the early stages of industrialization but has remained stable since. The opportunities for upward and downward mobility, the chances of either achieving entrance into socially privileged positions or remaining in the underprivileged status categories, and the distribution of status positions in general as a form of social reward, have all remained unchanged since about the middle of the last century" (Kleining, 1971, p. 20).

Kleining however reaches these conclusions solely on the basis of an investigation of micro-structure and micro-prestige mobility. He does not however link up with the problem of "systemic pressure toward macro-immobility". To do this the following supplementary steps are necessary:

a) It seems practical and sensible to follow Kleining's example and distinguish between "occupational-circles" whose members have similar sources of revenue, *i.e.* occupy similar positions within the production process.

b) Within each "occupational circle" differences emerge in the distribution of power, privilege and prestige; they are in themselves socially stratified. Of course, certain "occupational circles" (*e.g.* workers) are located mainly in the lower parts of the system of social inequality and privilege ; others (*e.g.* the professions) have their centre of gravity at a higher level in the social hierarchy; still others (*e.g.* the self-employed) can be found at almost all levels of the social scale.

c) The sum of these different "occupational circles" forms the concrete content of the distribution of inequality and privilege for the whole of society, which has remained nearly unchanged in the FRG over a period of decades. That is, the relative size of different "occupational circles" has increased or decreased and their specific location within the distribution of social inequality and privilege has shifted to a large extent during the last century, but the overall distribution of social inequality has remained almost untouched. Now as before, the structure of social stratification narrows towards the top, and the number of social positions becomes fewer, the more power, privilege and prestige they possess.

d) Obviously, the members of different "occupational circles" do not start equally in the competition for the top social positions. Membership in some "occupational circles" (*e.g.* the professions) implies a high probability of success because certain top positions are already reserved for groups having a strategic starting place in the social production process. The members of other "occupational circles" (*e.g.* workers) only obtain a realistic opportunity to move upward through the "bottleneck" of structured social inequality by first making the move into some strategically favourable circle.

e) This picture, in which different "occupational circles" have different centres of gravity in a system of power, privilege and prestige that narrows like a bottleneck near the top, is difficult to represent in empirically convincing terms. To operationalize the differentiated distribution of power in society seems quite impossible at present. Most valuable is the distribution of property, at least for the capitalist societies. Apart from this, income and prestige distribution are useful indirect indicators. But they are useful only as long as they are interpreted with the necessary theoretical prudence.

f) The operation of the "systemic pressure toward macro-immobility" can be shown by means of prestige stratification. Lothar Schuster (1969, pp. 118-119) concluded, on the basis of a representative inquiry into intra-generational occupational mobility in the FRG in 1967, that:

> "The higher the social stratum, the lower the quota of those who change their occupation and the lower the frequency of occupational changes [...] In the upper social strata the percentage of those individuals who climb socially as a result of occupational change is higher than in the lower strata."

Stated differently: despite increased micro-mobility within the lower (prestige-) strata, the opportunities for upward mobility are small because the more favourable social positions are fewer in number and are usually occupied already by individuals who had a better start. "The air becomes thinner the higher you go."

g) In this example, the pressure toward macro-immobility is revealed indirectly through its consequences. Its actual operation is not yet grasped but must be different in different "occupational circles."

8) Consequently, an important task for a theoretically reoriented mobility research is the precise identification and internal differentiation of "occupational circles" whose members occupy comparable positions in the social production process. Taking into account their location within the social distribution of inequality and privilege, the inter- and intra-generational mobility rates within these circles, as well as the conditions tending to encou-

rage or discourage mobility between them should be investigated. Linking the micro- and macro-perspective in this way should enable sociology to overcome the theoretical sterility of purely synthetic mobility measures or mere detail analyses.

9) From what has been said, it is clear that the study of vertical mobility can no longer be based upon the concepts of the "open society" and "equal opportunity" in their old liberal form. Research cannot restrict itself to such questions as the degree to which mobility opportunities for underprivileged "occupational circles", such as the workers, are legally and factually "equal". More credible is the proposition that their chances, even in the best of circumstances, are *equally small* as long as the systems of inequality and privilege and the situation of the worker remain unchanged. The ideas of an "open society" and of "equal opportunity", taken over from the liberal tradition, should be interpreted literally and thus stripped of their neutrality vis-à-vis the prevailing distribution of inequality and privilege. No longer restricted to the aim of creating equal opportunities of access to the structure of unequal distribution of wealth, power, privilege, and prestige (which are in any case heterogeneous in different "occupational circles"), these ideas are directed against inequality as such.

10) The analysis of the structural, institutional, and motivational conditions, operating either to restrict or enlarge mobility chances in various "occupational circles", must be regarded as a contribution which sociology can make to the investigation — and therefore the reduction — of the inequality-and-privilege-preserving-mechanisms at work in advanced industrial societies.

REFERENCES

Ammassari, P.

1967 "Occupational opportunity structure in advanced societies", in: *Proceedings of the first Italo-Hungarian meeting of Sociology.* Milan/Rome.

Armélin, P.

1970 "Einige Fragen des Zusammenhangs von sozialer Struktur und sozialer Mobilität", in: *Soziologie im Sozialismus.* Berlin, Dietz.

Barber, B.

1957 *Social stratification.* New York, Harcourt and Brace.

Bergmann, J. *et al.*

1969 "Herrschaft, Klassenverhältnis und Schichtung", in: T.W. Adorno (ed.). *Spätkapitalismus oder Industriegesellschaft?* Stuttgart, Enke.

Blau, P.; Duncan, O.D.

1967 *The American occupational structure.* New York/London/Sidney, Wiley.

Bolte, K.M.

1959 *Sozialer Aufstieg und Abstieg.* Stuttgart, Enke.

1969 "Vertikale Mobilität", pp. 1-42 in: R. König (ed.). *Handbuch der empirischen Sozialforschung.* Stuttgart, Enke. Vol. 2.

Bolte, K.M.; Kreckel, R.

1968 "Internationale Mobilitätsvergleiche im Bereich der Soziologie", pp. 38-63 in: U. Gruber *et al.* (eds.). *Soziale Mobilität heute.* Herford, Maximilian.

Brock, D.

1970 *Ideologiekritische Anmerkungen zum Mobilitätsbegriff.* Munich. (Unpublished paper.)

Carlsson, G.

1958 *Social mobility and class structure.* Lund, Gleerup.

1961 "Ökonomische Ungleichheit und Lebenschancen", pp. 189-199 in: D.V. Glass; R. König (eds.). *Soziale Schichtung und soziale Mobilität.* Köln, Opladen, Westdeutscher Verlag.

Cutright, P.

1968 "Studying cross-national mobility rates", *Acta sociologica* 11: 170-176.

Dahrendorf, R.

1967 *Pfade aus Utopia.* Munich, Piper.

1968 *Die angewandte Aufklärung.* Frankfurt/Hamburg, Fischer.

Deutsch, K.W.

1961 "Social mobilization and political development", *American political science review* 55: 493-514.

Föhl, C.

1964 *Kreislaufanalytische Untersuchung der Vermögensbildung in der Bundesrepublik und die Beeinflussbarkeit ihrer Verteilung.* Tübingen, Mohr/Siebeck.

Fürstenberg, F.

1962 *Das Aufstiegsproblem in der modernen Gesellschaft.* Stuttgart, Enke.

Germani, G.

1966 "Social and political consequences of mobility", pp. 364-394 in: Smelser, N.J.; S.M. Lipset (eds.). *Social structure and mobility in economic development.* Chicago, Ill., Aldine.

Goldthorpe, J.H.

1966 "Social stratification in industrial society", pp. 648-660 in: R. Bendix; S.M. Lipset (eds.). *Class, status and power.* New York, Free Press of Glencoe. (2nd ed.)

Goldthorpe, J.H.; Hope, K.

1972 "Occupational grading and occupational prestige", *Social science information* 11 (5). (Paper presented at the International Workshop on Career Mobility, Konstanz, 1971.)

Habermas, J.

1967 *Zur Logik der Sozialwissenschaften.* Tübingen, Mohr/Siebeck.

1968 *Erkenntnis und Interesse.* Frankfurt, Suhrkamp.

1969 *Strukturwandel der Öffentlichkeit.* Neuwied/Berlin, Luchterhand. (4th ed.).

Hall, J.R.; Ziegel, W.
1954 "A comparison of social mobility data for England and Wales, Italy, France and the USA", in: D.V. Glass (ed.). *Social mobility in Britain.* London, Routledge and Kegan Paul.

Hamilton, R.F.
1968 "Einkommen und Klassenstruktur: Der Fall der Bundesrepublik", *Kölner Zeitschrift für Soziologie und Sozialpsychologie* 20: 250-287.

Heek, F. van
1956 "Some introductory remarks on social mobility and class structure", pp. 129-143 in: *Transactions of the Third World Congress of Sociology.* London, Hereford Times. Vol. 3.

Heller, C.S. (ed.).
1969 *Structured social inequality.* New York/London, Collier/Macmillan.

Janowitz, M.
1958 "Soziale Schichtung und Mobilität in Westdeutschland", *Kölner Zeitschrift für Soziologie und Sozialpsychologie* 10: 1-39.

Kleining, G.
1971 "Struktur und Prestigemobilität in der Bundersrepublik Deutschland", *Kölner Zeitschrift für Soziologie und Sozialpsychologie* 23: 1-33.

Kolko, G.
1962 *Wealth and power in America: An analysis of social class and income distribution.* New York, Praeger.

Kreckel, R.
1972 *Soziologische Erkenntnis und Geschichte.* Köln/Opladen, Westdeutscher Verlag.

Kreckel, R. *et al.*
1971 *Ursachen und Folgen vertikaler Mobilität.* Munich. (Unpublished document.)

Lancaster Jones, F.
1969 "Social mobility and industrial society: A thesis re-examined", *Sociological quarterly,* 10 (2): 292-306.

Lenski, G.
1966 *Power and privilege: A theory of social stratification.* New York, McGraw-Hill.

Lipset, S.M.; Bendix, R.
1959 *Social mobility in industrial society.* Berkeley, Calif., University of California Press.

Lipset, S.M.; Zetterberg, H.L.
1956 "A theory of social mobility", pp. 155-177 in: *Transactions of the Third World Congress of Sociology.* London, Hereford Times. Vol. 3.

Lopreato, J.
1967 "Upward social mobility and political orientation", *American sociological review* 32: 586-592.

Luckmann, T.; Berger, P.
1964 "Social mobility and personal identity", *Archives Européennes de Sociologie* 5: 331-344.

Lynd, R.S.
1948 *Knowledge for what?* Princeton, NJ, Princeton University Press. (6th ed.)

Mack, R.W. *et al.*
1957 *Social mobility. Thirty years of theory and research: An annotated bibliography.* Syracuse, NY, Syracuse University Press.

Mannheim, K.
1930 *Ideologie und Utopie.* Bonn, Cohen. (2nd ed.)

Marx, K.
1920 "Die moralisierende Kritik und die kritische Moral", in: F. Mehring (ed.). *Aus dem literarischen Nachlass von Karl Marx und Friedrich Engels.* Stuttgart, Dietz. Vol. 2. (3d ed.)

Mayer, K.U.; Müller, W.
1971 "Progress in social mobility research? Some comments on mobility analysis and new data on intergenerational mobility in West Germany", *Quality and quantity* 5 (1): 141-178.

Merton, R.K.
1957 *Social theory and social structure.* New York/London, Macmillan. (2nd ed.)

Milic, V.
1966 "General trends in social mobility in Yugoslavia", *Acta sociologica* 9: 116-136.

Miller, S.M.
1956 "The concept and measurement of mobility", pp. 144-164 in: *Transactions of the Third World Congress of Sociology.* London, Hereford Times. Vol. 3.
1969 "Comparative social mobility", pp. 325-340 in: C.S. Heller (ed.). *Structured social inequality.* New York/London, Macmillan.

Moser, C.A.; Hall, J.R.
1954 "The social grading of occupations", in: D.V. Glass (ed.). *Social mobility in Britain.* London, Routledge and Kegan Paul.

Ortmann, H.
1971 *Arbeiterfamilie und sozialer Aufstieg.* Munich, Juventa.

Ossipov, G.P.
1969 "The class character of the theory of social mobility", pp. 135-137, in: P. Hollander (ed.). *American and Soviet society.* Englewood Cliffs, NJ, Prentice-Hall.

Ossowski, S.
1962 *Die Klassenstruktur im sozialen Bewusstsein.* Neuwied/Berlin, Luchterhand.

Parsons, T.
1964 *The social system.* New York, Free Press of Glencoe.

Porter, J.
1968 "The future of upward mobility", *American sociological review* 33: 5-19.

Recker, H.
1971 "Ideological implications of social mobility research", *Working paper presented at the International Workshop on Career Mobility, Konstanz, 1971.*

Rose, A.M.
1964 "Social mobility and social values", *Archives Européennes de Sociologie* 5: 324-330.

Sarapata, A.
1966 "Distance et mobilité sociale dans la société polonaise contemporaine", *Sociologie du travail* 8: 4-19.

Schelsky, H.
1965 "Die Bedeutung des Schichtungsbegriffes für die Analyse der gegenwärtigen deutschen Gesellschaft", in: *Auf der Suche nach Wirklichkeit.* Düsseldorf/Köln, Diederichs.

Schuster, L.
1969 "Die Mobilität der Arbeitnehmer", *Beiträge zur Arbeitsmarkt- und Berufsforschung* 1: 111-127.

Smelser, N.J.; Lipset, S.M. (eds.).
1966 *Social structure and mobility in economic development.* Chicago, Ill., Aldine.

Sorokin, P.A.
1959 *Social and cultural mobility.* Glencoe, Ill., Free Press.

Steiner, H.
1967 "Grundzüge und Entwicklungstendenzen der westdeutschen Soziologie", in: H. Meissner (ed.). *Bürgerliche Ökonomie im modernen Kapitalismus.* Berlin, Dietz.

Svalastoga, K.
1959 *Prestige, class and mobility.* Copenhagen, Gyldendal.

Tumin, M.A. (ed.).
1970 *Readings on social stratification.* Englewood Cliffs, NJ, Prentice-Hall.

Weltz, F.; Schmidt, G.
1971 *Arbeiter und beruflicher Aufstieg.* Munich, Institut für sozialwissenschaftliche Forschung. (Mimeo.)

Westoff, *et al.*
1960 "The concept of social mobility: An empirical inquiry", *American sociological review* 25: 375-385.

Wiehn, E.
1968 *Theorien der sozialen Schichtung.* Munich, Piper.

Wilenski, H.L.
1966 "Measures and effects of mobility", pp. 98-140 in: N.J. Smelser, S.M. Lipset (eds.). *Social structure and mobility in economic development.* Chicago, Ill., Aldine.

Zloczower, A.
1972 "Occupation, mobility and social class", *Social science information* 11 (5). (Paper presented at the International Workshop on Career Mobility, Konstanz, 1971.)

RAYMOND BOUDON

Note on a model for the analysis of mobility tables

A basic problem in intergenerational mobility analysis is the circular relationship between mobility and stratification: it is meaningless to compute mobility rates unless a valid set of stratification categories is previously defined, which cannot themselves be defined independently of mobility.

In the present paper, a model will be presented which may be considered as an attempt to solve this problem. This model is a generalization of the intergenerational versions of the mover-stayer model. Thus, we shall present briefly, first, the original mover-stayer model, then the intergenerational adaptations which were proposed by Leo Goodman and Harrison White, before going on to the generalization of these latter models.

The original mover-stayer model

Blumen's original model deals with labor turnover, *i.e.* with intragenerational mobility[1]. The model is derived basically from the empirical finding that job mobility appears always to be weaker than would be expected under the assumption of a Markov chain. Assume, in other words that an observed transition matrix R describes the ways, a population of workers move from one occupational category to another from the beginning to the end of, say, a quarter. Then we may try to predict the turnover between the initial quarter, say 0, and quarter t, while

$$p_{(0)} R^{t} = p_{(t)} \tag{1}$$

1. I. Blumen, M. Kogan and P.J. McCarthy, *The industrial mobility of labor as a probability process*, Ithaca, NY, New York State School of industrial and labor relations, 1955 (Cornell studies in industrial and labor relations, vol. 6), and "Probability models for mobility", pp. 318-334 in: P. Lazarsfeld and N. Henry (eds.), *Readings in mathematical social science*, Chicago, Ill., Science Research Associates, 1966.

(where $p_{(0)}$ and $p_{(t)}$ are the distributions respectively at time 0 and at time t) predicts the occupational structure at the t-th quarter. However, the diagonal elements of R^t will generally be much smaller than the diagonal elements of the empirical matrix, say $R^{(t)}$, which gives the observed transition rates between quarter 0 and quarter t.

In order to account for this general empirical observation, Blumen and his colleagues proposed to consider the population as composed of two latent categories of people: the stayers and the movers. The movers are supposed to move according to a Markov chain. The stayers simply stay. In other words, they are supposed to stay with a probability equal to 1. Let us for instance consider r_{ii}, *i.e.* the proportion of people located in occupational category i at the beginning of quarter 0 who are still in category i at the beginning of quarter 1. This proportion will be considered as the sum of two latent components: s_i, the proportion of the stayers in category i, and $(1-s_i)m_{ii}$, where the proportion of movers is $(1-s_i)$ and these movers have a probability m_{ii} of moving from i to i, *i.e.* of staying, though they are movers. Then,

$$r_{ii} = s_i + (1 - s_i)m_{ii} \quad (2)$$

or, in matrix form,

$$R = S + (I - S)M, \quad (3)$$

where $R = [r_{ij}]$ is the observed transition matrix, S the diagonal matrix $[s_i]$, I the identity matrix and $M = [m_{ij}]$ the transition matrix of the movers.

White's intergenerational mover-stayer model

We shall then present briefly some adaptations of this model to intergenerational mobility. Obviously, this adaptation is possible: we may in the intergenerational case as in the intragenerational, introduce the latent distinction between stayers and movers. If this distinction leads to consistent models, it may be used to solve the problem of measuring social mobility. Nonetheless, there is an important difference between intergenerational and intragenerational mobility: the size of the time unit. As a consequence, in the intragenerational case it may be possible, as in Blumen's example, to observe a sequence of mobility matrices. In the intergenerational case, a single or at most a very small number of matrices will be available. Thus, the model (3) clearly cannot be directly applied to intergenerational mobility. With a single matrix, the equations of this model cannot be solved. The models to be presented below are derived from the original mover-stayer model in the sense that, as with this latter model, they introduce a distinction between two latent subpopulations. However, their mathematical structure is very distinct from that of the original model.

One of the interesting applications of the mover-stayer idea to intergenerational mobility is provided by Harrison White [2]. In fact, White proposed two models more or less directly inspired by the mover-stayer distinction. In this section, we shall present the most recent of these contributions.

The "modified inheritance model", as White himself calls it, assumes, like Blumen's model, that each social category i includes an unknown proportion of movers. Let us call s_i the number of stayers in i and m_{ii} the number of movers who happen to stay in i. (Note that to avoid the proliferation of symbols, these symbols have a slightly different meaning here and in the previous section.) For the rest, n_{ij} be the number of sons with father i who are themselves j; $n_{(0)i}$ the number of fathers in stratum i; $n_{(1)j}$ the number of sons in stratum j, etc. On the other hand, let us call m_{ij} the number of movers going from i to j, $m_{(0)i}$ the number of movers whose father belongs to category i and $m_{(1)j}$ the number of movers among the sons currently belonging to social category j.

The first equation of the model is:

$$n_{ii} = m_{ii} + (n_{(0)i} - m_{(0)i}). \tag{4}$$

This equation states that the total observed number of families staying in i from one generation to the next is the sum of the number of movers who stay in i and of the number of stayers. Note that the intergenerational case, the attributes "mover" and "stayer" apply to families and not to individuals.

A second equation states that all the families who moved from i to j belong to the class of the movers:

$$n_{ij} = m_{ij} \tag{5}$$

Of course, the equations cannot be solved without further assumptions. In the case of Blumen's original model, the estimation of S, the diagonal matrix describing the proportions of stayers, was made possible because of the assumption that M generates a Markov chain. Blumen and his colleagues used then M*, the equilibrium matrix, for this estimation. Here, since we have at our disposal only one matrix, a functional substitute, so to speak, must be found. White derives this substitute by using the traditional assumption of perfect mobility. This assumption is, of course, only applied to the movers. Then,

$$m_{ij} = m_{(0)i} \cdot m_{(1)j}/M \tag{6}$$

where M is the total number of movers.

We will not examine the problem of solving this model. This is a merely technical problem and we prefer to refer the reader to White's original text on this point. The logical and substantive interest of the model proposed by White is more important for our purpose.

In one of the applications presented, White used his model for analyzing British and Danish trichotomous mobility tables. He found that the

2. H. White, "Stayers and movers", *American jounal of sociology* 76 (2), September 1970, pp. 307-324.

model applied in neither of the two cases: it was impossible to fit acceptable values for $m_{(0)1}$, $m_{(0)2}$ and $m_{(0)3}$ simultaneously. This negative result shows that the data to which the model was applied are incompatible with the assumptions described by (4) to (6) according to which the population could be divided into two latent subpopulations, *i.e.* a subpopulation of stayers and one of movers submitted to the rule of perfect mobility.

White then proceeded with further assumptions. He found a good fit for $m_{(0)1}$ and $m_{(0)3}$ when the supplementary assumption

$$m_{(0)2} = n_{(0)2} \tag{7}$$

is introduced, *i.e.* when everybody is supposed to be a mover in social category 2. In another application, White used Blau and Duncan's data and found a good fit. He then computed what he calls the "inheritance fraction". Let us call this index I_w defined by:

$$I_{w(i)} = 1 - (m_{(0)i}/n_{(0)i}) \tag{8}$$

The inheritance fraction is, in other words, the proportion of stayers in a given social category. In applying this index to Blau and Duncan's data, White found the rather small average value of .092. The index reaches a moderately large value only for the professionals (professional, self-employed: .156; professional, salaried: .240 and for the farmers: .153). However, the fit of the off-diagonal elements of the mobility matrix is, according to the author himself, rather poor.

A particular version of the White's model : Goodman's model

L. Goodman has proposed in one of his papers, a model which may be considered as a particular version of the White model, though the former predates the latter [3].

In White's model, while the stayers have a probability zero of moving, the movers have a non-zero probability of staying. In Goodman's model, the assumptions for the two latent subpopulations are symmetric: the stayers are not allowed to move and the movers are not allowed to stay.
With this assumption, (4) reduces to

$$n_{ii} = n_{(0)i} - m_{(0)i} \tag{9}$$

since

$$m_{ii} = 0 \tag{10}$$

The other assumptions of White's model, (5) and (6) are kept: the movers are, in other words, supposed to move according to the rule of perfect mobility.

The Goodman model, by contrast to White's, is very simple. While in White's

3. L. Goodman, "On the statistical analysis of mobility tables", *American journal of sociology* 70 (2), September 1965, pp. 564-585.

model, the estimation of the number of stayers in each category is complicated, it becomes very simple in Goodman's model, since the stayers are those who are located in the main diagonal of a mobility matrix. Thus, the procedure for testing the adequateness of the model is very simple:

The first step consists in subtracting the diagonal figures from the corresponding row and column marginals and to blank out these diagonal figures. This will give the numbers $m_{(0)i}$ of movers in each row and the numbers $m_{(1)j}$ of movers in each column.

The next and final step is to verify that

$$m_{ij} = m_{(0)i} \cdot m_{(1)} \cdot_j / M \quad (i \neq j) \tag{11}$$

where, as in White's model,

$$m_{ij} = n_{ij} \quad (i \neq j) \tag{12}$$

Goodman has proposed several variations of this simple model. Let us suppose, for instance, a trichotomous mobility table. In the version of the model which has just been described, the families located in the main diagonal are all considered as stayers: an inheritance phenomenon is assumed in each social category, and the degree of this inheritance is simply measured by the proportion of families belonging to the i-th row that are located in the i-th column.

An alternative assumption supposes that an inheritance phenomenon is at work in some social categories, say, categories 1 and 3, but not in the other, category 2. Then, n_{11} and n_{33} are, as previously, considered to describe the numbers of stayers respectively in categories 1 and 3. The quantity n_{22} is considered to describe a subpopulation of, so to speak, apparent stayers, *i.e.* of families that are movers but happen to stay. With this assumption, the test of the model would include the following steps:

1) Subtract the diagonal figures from the corresponding row and column totals for the categories where a social inheritance is assumed, *i.e.* in our example categories 1 and 3 and blank out these diagonal cells;

2) Keep the original row and column totals for the social categories where no social inheritance is assumed (in our example, for category 2); and

3) Verify that $m_{ij} = m_{(0)i} \, . \, m_{(1)j}/M$ (for all cells not blanked out). (13)

Thus, in our example, where social inheritance applies only to categories 1 and 3, we have to check that (13) holds for all cells except the blanked out diagonal cell corresponding to these categories.

Goodman's model has a great advantage in its simplicity. On the other hand, this advantage is the consequence of the rigidity of the assumptions. Either we assume the action of a social inheritance effect in a given social category, say i, and the families of row i located in column i are *all* considered as *stayers*. Or we do not assume this action and the same families are *all* considered as *movers*, even if they happen to stay. Even with a good fit, it is hard to accept, from a sociological point of view, that the effect of social inheritance could be zero in some social categories. White's assumption that the families located in the diagonal cells are of two kinds, *i.e.* a latent subpopulation of movers and a latent subpopulation of stayers, is undoubtedly more appealing for a sociologist, even if it leads to greater mathematical complications.

Three types of mover-stayer models applied to intergenerational mobility

Goodman's model is characterized by the assumption that the stayers are not allowed to move and the movers are not allowed to stay. More exactly, the stayers are never allowed to move and the movers are only allowed to stay when there are no stayers already in a given social category.

By contrast, White's model assumes that the movers are allowed to stay. In other words, the diagonal cells of a mobility matrix will generally include stayers *and* movers, while in Goodman's model they include stayers *or* movers, but not both. On the other hand, White's model makes the same assumption as Goodman's for the stayers: they are never allowed to move.

Let us ignore for a moment the variations that Goodman has proposed of his model and consider its basic version described by the equations (9) to (11). Then, we can summarize the fundamental difference between White's and Goodman's models as in Table 1. There, we have called Goodman's model a type 1 model. White's model is called a type 2 model.

Table 1. *Three types of mover-stayer models with their assumptions*

Type 1 model (Goodman's model)	Stayers not allowed to move Movers not allowed to stay
Type 2 model (White's model)	Stayers not allowed to move Movers allowed to stay
Type 3 model	Stayers allowed to move Movers allowed to stay

This presentation suggests a third type of model given at the bottom of the table. In this model, the stayers are allowed to move, exactly as the movers are allowed to stay in White's model.

We shall develop it in the next section. A general point is worth mentioning: while Table 1 shows that the type 3 model appears, at the mathematical level, as a natural extension of the type 2 model, it does raise a semantic problem. Indeed, in Goodman's or in White's model, it is very easy to follow the stayers, since, by the assumptions of these models, they are always located in the diagonal. With the type 3 model, the symmetry of the assumptions with regard to the latent subpopulations has the consequence that the semantic interpretation of these subpopulations as stayers and movers will become questionable. Thus, the model we shall present belongs on the one hand to the mover-stayer family of models; but it has, on the other hand, a different interpretation and other uses.

A general model for the analysis of mobility tables

In the exposition of this model, we shall substitute a distinction between latent class 1 (LC 1) people and latent class 2 (LC 2) people to the distinction between movers and stayers. On the other hand, we shall retain the symbols m and s. The meaning of these classes will be examined later.

We shall suppose, as previously, that n_{ij} is the observed number of families in cell (i,j) of the mobility matrix. For all i and all j, n_{ij} will be the sum of m_{ij}, the number of LC 1 people, and of s_{ij}, the number of LC 2 people located in the cell (i,j):

$$n_{ij} = m_{ij} + s_{ij} \tag{14}$$

It is readily checked that if we suppose $s_{ij} = 0$ for $i \neq j$, we return to White's equations (4) and (5).

The second equation of the model is the same as equation (6) of White's model:

$$m_{ij} = m_{(0)i} \cdot m_{(1)j}/M \tag{15}$$

This equation states that the LC 1 people move according to the rule of perfect mobility. M is the total number of these people.

An equivalent assumption will be made for the LC 2 people:

$$s_{ij} = s_{(0)i} \cdot s_{(1)j}/S \tag{16}$$

where S is the total number of LC 2 people. Thus, s_{ij}, the number of stayers moving from i to j, is the product of the number of stayers who come from i times the proportion of stayers who go to j. In other words, within the latent subpopulation of stayers, the destination of the moves is supposed to be independent of their origin. The same is true for the movers.

Equations (15) and (16) reveal why it is impossible to keep the semantic interpretation of the two classes that was used in the previous models: these two subpopulations must behave symmetrically and thus are interchangeable.

Let us, as an illustration, consider the fictitious matrix reproduced in Table 2. Applying the present model to this matrix, we find the following values for the parameters:

$m_{(0)1} = 1\,800$, $m_{(0)2} = 3\,600$, $m_{(0)3} = 300$, $m_{(0)4} = 300$
$m_{(1)1} = 3\,600$, $m_{(1)2} = 1\,800$, $m_{(1)3} = 300$, $m_{(1)4} = 300$
$m_{(0)1} = 200$, $s_{(0)2} = 200$, $s_{(0)3} = 1\,600$, $s_{(0)4} = 2\,000$
$s_{(1)1} = 200$, $s_{(1)2} = 200$, $s_{(1)3} = 1\,600$, $s_{(1)4} = 2\,000$
$M = 6\,000$ $S = 4\,000$

The interpretation of this solution is that behind the four manifest social categories, we have two latent classes. The first one (LC 1) is characterized by the fact that its members are likely to come from social categories 1 and 2 or to go to categories 1 and 2. They are much less likely to come from categories 3 and 4 or to go to these categories. Reciprocally, the LC 2 people circulate between social categories 3 and 4, with few of them coming from or going to social categories 1 and 2.

Table 2. *A fictitious intergenerational mobility matrix*

Father's social category	Son's social category 1	2	3	4	Total
1	1 090	550	170	190	2 000
2	2 170	1 090	260	280	3 800
3	260	170	655	815	1 900
4	280	190	815	1 015	2 300
Total	3 800	2 000	1 900	2 300	10 000

This example illustrates the kind of uses the type 3 model may have. It also shows that the semantic distinction between stayers and movers has to be dropped.

While this model is an extension of White's model, the introduction of the possibility of any of the subpopulations moving or staying changes the interpretation of these subpopulations. In Goodman's model, the observed mobility matrix is split into a sum of two components. The first component is a diagonal matrix, the elements of which are either the corresponding elements of the observed mobility matrix or zero (for the categories where no inheritance effect is postulated). The second component is the difference matrix between the observed matrix and this diagonal matrix.

In White's model, the observed matrix is again split into two components: the diagonal matrix of stayers and the difference matrix corresponding to the movers.

Here, in the type 3 model, the observed matrix is again a sum of two components, both being non-diagonal matrices following the same rule as the second component of Goodman's or White's model, *i.e.* perfect mobility. Thus, finally, the rationale for this model is *to decompose the circulation system described by a mobility matrix into a sum of sub-systems characterized by freedom of circulation*, in the sense that according to the concept of perfect mobility, the arrival category is independent of the departure category. Of course, the sum of two perfect mobility matrices will not generally be a perfect mobility matrix.

Thus, in some cases, the model will make possible to isolate subsets of occupational categories *within* which a high amount of free circulation may be observed, while the amount of free circulation *between* these subsets is limited. These subsets will in this case represent much more meaningful stratification categories than the original occupational categories. In fact, they will be a step towards the transformation of these rough occupational categories into the more valid stratification categories to which the concept of "social class" is often associated.

Of course, in some other cases, the application of the model will not lead to this simple interpretation. More complicated patterns may appear when the parameters are solved for: the subsystems characterized by a free circulation may not lead to a clearcut partition of the occupational categories into stratification categories. Only repeated applications of the model to mobility tables could show which types of structures are likely to occur empirically.

Extension of the model to g components

Since the semantic distinction stayers-movers has to be abandoned, nothing prevents us from supposing that an observed non perfect mobility matrix may be decomposable into more than just 2 perfect mobility components. We may for instance wish to reproduce an observed matrix as the sum of 3 perfect mobility matrices. In this case, we speak of a three-components model.

Of course, the number of components which may be introduced is dependent on the number of social categories which appear in the observed mobility matrix. Let us suppose for instance that the number of latent components, 2 in the previous exposition of the model, is now g. This situation will introduce $2\sigma - 1$ independent parameters for each component except one or, for the g components, $(2\sigma - 1)(g - 1)$ independent parameters, giving the numbers of families going to and coming from the σ social categories in each latent component.

Then, the number of independent empirical quantities is equal to $(\sigma - 1)^2$. Thus, for the model to be determinate, g must be chosen small enough so that the inequality

$$(2\sigma - 1)(g - 1) \leqslant (\sigma - 1)^2 \Rightarrow g \leqslant \sigma^2/(2\sigma - 1)$$

holds. With $\sigma = 4$ or 5, g cannot be greater than 2. With $\sigma = 6$, g cannot be greater than 3, etc. This means that if a mobility matrix with 6 social categories cannot be decomposed into a sum of g = 2 latent perfect mobility matrices, we may try g = 3.

The problem raised by the solution of this generalized "mover-stayer" model will not be dealt with here. As the inequality (17) shows, the number of parameters will generally be smaller than the number of degrees of freedom of the observed matrix. Thus, there will generally be a unique algebraic solution of the model. In the exploration of the model and in the experimental application to actual data we are now conducting, we use a maximum likelihood solution [4].

4. A detailed presentation of this solution is contained in our forthcoming monograph on *Mathematical structures of social mobility*, Amsterdam-New York, Elsevier, to appear end of 1972.

Our hope is that the present model could be useful in the analysis of intergenerational mobility tables and that it could contribute to solving the problem raised by the circle between stratification and mobility. However, much further theoretical research and empirical application could be needed before a definite evaluation of the model may be reached.

PAUL DUNCAN-JONES

Preparing social stratification data for path analysis *

Introduction

Students of social stratification may disagree as to the value of path analysis in explicating social mobility. They certainly disagree about the details of how it should be done. What can scarcely be denied is that at least since the publication of *The American occupational structure* (Blau and Duncan, 1967) path analysis has become the most widely used single tool for data analysis in this area. Consequently, proposals for improving its application require no general apologia, and we shall not offer one.

Social mobility data, like most survey data, consists largely of classifications into categories. Sometimes the categories are ordered, sometimes not, but they seldom have any natural, inbuilt metric. So path analysis (or any form of correlational analysis) requires some preliminary decision about the treatment of the data. If one wishes to enter (say) "father's occupation" into a correlation matrix, three tactics are available:

— To dichotomise (say, into manual and non-manual),
— To treat each occupational category as a separate dummy variable, or
— To develop a scoring system, or set of weights, for the occupational categories.

This paper explores a particular class of scoring systems, fitted by canonical methods. The methods are quite generally applicable to survey data, and provide a basis for any form of correlational analysis. It is shown that they

* The work reported in this paper was undertaken as part of a programme of methodological exploration and secondary analysis of survey data, in connection with the planning phase of the Nuffield College (Oxford) Social Mobility Project. The project is funded by the Social Science Research Council. An earlier version of this paper was presented at the Annual Conference of the Market Research Society in Brighton, February, 1971. I am grateful to members of the Nuffield project for general discussions and to Roy Carr-Hill for comments on an early draft of the paper.

work well for social stratification data, at least in the British context. The objects of the paper are

— To exemplify the methods
— To explore the range of their applicability
— To show that they allow more effective use of social stratification data, and
— To indicate some pitfalls.

The main focus is the preparation of stratification data for path analysis, and other uses of the methods are only briefly mentioned. However problems of scoring, calibrating or quantifying classificatory variables are a pervasive feature of sociological research. If canonical scoring methods give satisfactory results for social stratification data, it is natural to ask if they will work in other contexts. We offer some hints on this later in the paper, in a discussion of dimensionality.

The need for quantification

The drawbacks of dichotomisation are well-known. Correlations and regressions are typically under-estimated, both because information is discarded and because different variables will almost inevitably be split in different proportions. Some correlations will be biased more than others and the results obtained are quite sensitive to the cutting points chosen.

One way of exploiting classificatory data more fully is by definition of dummy variables corresponding to the different categories of a classification. Boyle (1970) has provided a clear and persuasive exposition of this, and a most interesting example. But Boyle only advocates his method where the categories of a variable are ranked unambiguously *a priori*, and this is not always the case. And the method soon becomes unmanageable. Suppose one wishes to include half-a-dozen variables in a path analysis, with half-a-dozen categories each, and every variable presents problems in "quantification" or calibration. Virtually all variables do present such problems [1]. Already what might have seemed quite a small straightforward problem now involves thirty dummy variables. Computationally, this is manageable, but interpretatively it is a nightmare. One sets out to manipulate just six variables. But now each is split into component parts, which may be weighted differently in relation to each other at different points in the analysis. So it is no longer very easy to look on the dummies derived from one variable as a realisation of a single unitary concept. In Boyle's example he proposed to represent the three-cate-

1. Variables quite clearly measured on an interval scale, such as years of schooling, or even income, may only be indicators of the underlying concept in which one is interested. It is not too plausible to believe that "quality of schooling" or "educational advantage" increase an equal amount for each year in school, or that utility increases linearly with gross income. Hence there may be much to be said for re-calibrating interval variables, if one has satisfactory criteria for doing so.

gory variable "alienation" by two dummies, and saw this as a possible step towards reconstituting a single "alienation" variable, with appropriate calibration. But this kind of re-constitution founders, precisely because the regressions of the two dummies on other variables are not always in the same ratio. No single, definitive re-calibration emerges. The problem is further discussed by Lyons and Carter (1971).

It appears, then, that path analysis of survey data must rest on some means of calibrating or scoring the data. One may consider the calibration of each variate separately (as Lyons and Carter have suggested), and one or two key sociological variates (notably occupation) have been very extensively studied from this point of view. But there is much to be said for seeking scores that will be "optimal" for the task in hand, and for using a general method, applicable to all the variables under study. Let us consider an example of how this may be done.

Example 1 : the basic occupational mobility model

To make the discussion more concrete, we will look at a very simple model of intergenerational occupational mobility. Blau and Duncan (1967) give a path model based on the correlations amongst five variables:

Father's occupation
Father's education
Respondent's education
Respondent's first job
Respondent's current job.

To estimate these correlations, scores had to be developed for occupations and for education. Duncan proposed his well-known socio-economic score (SES) for occupations (Reiss *et al.*, 1961), using United States census tabulations of education and income by occupation. In the North American context, education could apparently be scored satisfactorily in terms of school grades or years of college achieved.

Suppose one wished to set up a similar model of social mobility in Britain. Two difficulties arise. First, we have no census tabulations of income, so we have to find an alternative basis for scoring occupations. Here, we take as our starting point the census classification of occupations into socio-economic groups [2]. Secondly, the quality of a child's education in Britain can-

2. For details, see General Register Office, 1960. I have discussed this classification in Duncan-Jones, 1970. Interestingly, it turns out that in the Butler-Stokes data, if one fits scores to a set of class-related variables including occupation, it makes no difference to the correlations whether one uses the Registrar-General's socio-economic groups or the "social grade" classification customarily employed in market research in Britain. The two classifications correlate highly, and the correlation may be exploited to estimate reliability (Duncan-Jones, in preparation). The writer's former colleagues J. Goldthorpe and K. Hope are currently doing very interesting work on the ranking of occupations, as part of the Nuffield project.

not be very fully captured in a single figure for age on leaving school. We have a variety of types of school, such that education to sixteen (say) in one type of school may be much more advantageous socially and economically, than education to the same age in another type of school. So to represent schooling simply by age of leaving is unsatisfactory, because it only tells part of the story, and also because the variable has a much more skew distribution in this country than in the United States. Anticipating results to be given below, school-leaving age only correlates about .6 with type of school.

Canonical scoring methods provide a direct and easy way through these difficulties. Scores can be fitted *simultaneously* to *all* the categories of *each* variable involved. This has now been done with several sets of data, and we use for illustration data for men from the first wave of David Butler and Donald Stokes' enquiry into political attitudes, reported in *Political change in Britain* (Butler and Stokes, 1969) [3]. We will focus attention on:

Father's occupation (when respondent was a child)
Respondent's school-leaving age
Respondent's type of school
Respondent's present occupation.

Table 1 gives category scores for these variables [4], and Table 2 gives the correlations, based on the 900 men in Butler and Stokes' sample.

The scores have considerable face validity. First note that the scores for educational categories increase monotonically, though not linearly. Obviously, one would have serious doubts about the method if this were not so. Next, the scores for most socio-economic groups seem very plausible. Professional workers come out on top, and the three grades of industrial manual workers come out in the right order. These are about the only gradings one could predict with complete confidence, and the positioning of the other groups may be regarded as a finding of the analysis. Similarly, with school types one could predict that the "Public schools" should come at one end of the scale and "elementary or secondary modern" at the other end, but the relative placing of the other categories tells us something new. Obviously the scores for some categories are based on tiny numbers, and are not very reliable. The small categories have been kept separate for purposes of illustration. We investigate the stability of such scores in our next example [5].

3. The writer would like to acknowledge very gratefully Butler and Stokes' permission to re-work their data in connection with the Nuffield Social Mobility project. Their original data did not include father's education.

4. The scores quoted were in fact fitted using a set of variables that also included income, further education, tenure of home, respondent's class self-rating, his rating of his family's class when he was young, and the type of daily paper he reads.

5. Clearly scoring can only be applied once a set of categories has been established. With all but the very largest samples, the number of categories in a classification will be limited by the problem of fitting valid scores to small categories. With "type of school", this is not too severe a constraint. Much of the variety in the British educational system can be captured in a handful of fairly homogeneous categories such as those used here. There main-

Table 1. *Example 1 : category scores*

Socio-economic group	*Respondent* (N)	*Respondent* Score	*Father* (N)	*Father* Score
Employers and managers	(115)	1.23	(68)	2.03
Professional workers	(36)	2.84	(16)	2.68
Intermediate non-manual	(46)	1.35	(20)	.95
Junior non-manual	(101)	.45	(50)	.66
Personal service	(9)	- .79	(5)	2.42
Foremen and supervisors, manual	(72)	- .30	(34)	.06
Skilled manual	(269)	- .56	(258)	- .32
Semi-skilled manual	(114)	- .96	(165)	- .86
Unskilled manual	(52)	- 1.09	(79)	- .91
Own account (non-professional)	(6)	.33	(50)	.58
Farmers (employers and managers)	(15)	1.12	(14)	2.26
Farmers (own account)	(4)	1.56	(31)	.73
Agricultural workers	(19)	- 1.13	(51)	- 1.33
Armed forces	(13)	.60	(20)	.05
NI	(30)	- .54	(40)	.85

Age left school	(N)	Score
- 13	(128)	- .88
- 14	(437)	- .46
- 15	(182)	.13
- 16	(82)	1.43
- 17	(29)	1.57
- 18	(25)	3.49
- 19 +	(12)	3.67
NI	(6)	.36

Type of school	(N)	Score
"Public" school (*i.e.* fee paying)	(18)	2.88
Grammar	(125)	1.59
Technical college	(14)	3.19
Elementary, Sec. Mod.	(719)	- .48
Private commercial schools	(11)	1.99
Other and NI	(14)	1.93

Next we use the scores to estimate the correlations amongst the variables. For each individual we substitute scores for category codes. Thus if a particular respondent is in semi-skilled manual worker and his father was an agricultural worker he is scored -0.96 and -1.33 on present occupation and father's occupation respectively. Assigning scores in this way, we calculate the correlations shown in Table 2.

ing heterogeneity principally concerns more elusive qualities of schools that could not be too readily elicited in a survey interview. Grouping occupations is a much more severe problem, and inevitably involves some loss of information. The appropriate criteria for grouping are not generally agreed, and practical problems abound. The writer's preferred solution would be *a)* for several independent groups of scholars to devote themselves to the problem of classifying occupations into 10-20 classes, *b)* to apply each of these "independent" classifications to surveys that required rigorous measurement of occupational status, *c)* to fit scores to each classification, and *d)* to use the classifications as multiple indicators of a single underlying concept. Something along these lines is attempted in Duncan-Jones (in preparation).

Table 2. *Example 1 : correlations*

	1	2	3	4
1. Socio-economic group, respondent	1.000	.416	.483	.481
2. Socio-economic group, father	.416	1.000	.334	.354
3. Age left school	.483	.334	1.000	.637
4. Type of school	.481	.354	.637	1.000

Before estimating the path model we combine the two "school" variables into a single index [6]. The correlations of the other two variables with the *average* of the two school variables is

Present occupation .532
Father's occupation .378

The path diagram is shown in Figure 1. Father's occupation and "schooling" together account for 34 % of the variance in present occupation. This compares with 31% explained variance if only the conventional educational measure had been used.

Figure 1. *Path diagram for example 1*

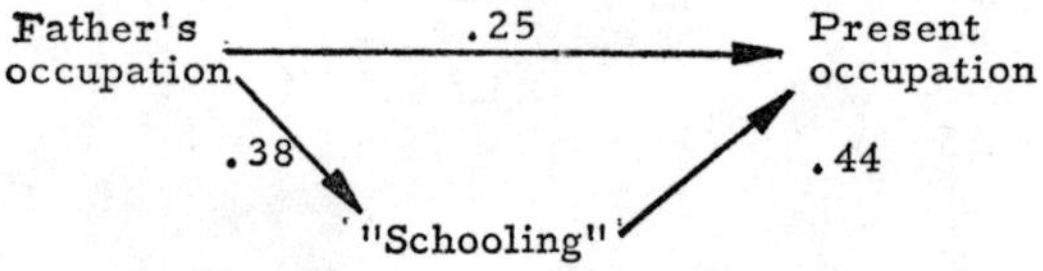

It is not our purpose to argue that this small exercise provides a valid comparison with Blau and Duncan. To do so would involve a great deal of special pleading about comparability of procedures and the like. Nor do we wish to argue that this is the optimal way of measuring occupation (though we *do* believe it is a reasonable way to exploit the available classification). Our aims with this example have been to introduce the notion of "optimal" scoring, to demonstrate it in action and to make the specific point about measurement of schooling.

6. This is a rather crude method of exploiting the two indicators. Elsewhere (Duncan-Jones, in preparation) we combine this information with data on the reliability of the other variables involved to estimate a path model for the underlying constructs. The immediate purpose is simply to show there is something to be gained from the extra information on type of school.

Scoring data

By now some readers may be bewildered, and others will be up in arms. Before explaining where the scores come from, it seems appropriate to say something about the principle of scoring categorical data. At first sight there is something bizarre about assigning scores to categories such as "Public school" or "Technical college" and to categories such as "Professional worker" or "Foreman", calculating a correlation coefficient between the two sets of scores, and calling this "the" correlation between type of school and occupation. What one is actually doing is extracting from each classification a single dimension of meaning, rather as in factor analysis, and focussing on this. When a survey analyst looks at a table showing type of school by occupation, he is (we believe) either looking out for specific associations between particular occupations and particular types of school, or else he is trying to form an overall impression of the strength of relationship between "school" and "occupation". In this paper, we are concerned with assessing such overall relationships.

Usually, to make such assessments one must, explicitly or implicitly,
— Abstract a single dimension from one set of categories (for instance, mentally rank the types of school)
— Similarly, abstract a single dimension from the other set of categories, and,
— Assess the relationship between the dimensions.

Typically one uses some rough scoring or rank order of the categories, and one finishes by characterizing the relationship as "strong" or "slight" or "quite substantial". In our example, the rank ordering would be intended to reflect the social class or economic advantage of the categories. But such vague conclusions clearly do not offer a basis for path analysis. This paper offers a way of formalising and automating the assessment of correlations between categorical variables.

The next section of the paper attempts to provide a simple informal account of the method. But readers who abhor all mathematics (if they have read thus far) may well prefer to skip it. To them, we would simply say that (put very loosely) the method used maximises the overall level of correlations amongst the variables, and scores are assigned to each category on this basis.

Fitting the scores: the original solution

We consider three methods of fitting scores. The fundamental method was given by Louis Guttman in an important and little-known paper (Guttman, 1941). This method is elegant and powerful, with a satisfactory mathematical justification, but is not computationally feasible for very large problems. The other methods may be regarded as approximations to it, though they have their own advantages.

The problem that Guttman posed was the optimal scoring of a set of attitude statements to form a scale. It was Lingoes (*e.g.* Lingoes, 1965) who pointed out that the method had wider uses, for instance as a basis for multiple regression. Lingoes named the method MAC1 (Multivariate Analysis of Contingencies, method 1). His terminology is adopted here. Guttman solved three related problems, and showed that the solutions were identical. He conceptualised the data set out as in Figure 1. This figure may be read as showing that respondent 1 fell into category 2 of classification 1, category 1 of classification 2, category 4 of classification 3 and so on. Clearly the column totals of this data layout are the total numbers of respondents in each category, and the row totals are the same for each respondent — simply the number of different classifications used in the analysis.

Figure 2. *Data layout*

Classification:	1	2	3	4
Category:	1 2 3 4	1 2 3	1 2 3 4 5	1 2 3 4 5 6
Respondent 1	0 1 0 0	1 0 0	0 0 0 1 0	0 0 1 0 0 0
Respondent 2	0 0 1 0	1 0 0	0 1 0 0 0	0 0 0 0 0 1
Respondent 3	1 0 0 0	0 1 0	1 0 0 0 0	0 0 0 1 0 0
Respondent 4	0 0 1 0	0 0 1	0 0 1 0 0	1 0 0 0 0 0

Respondents are classified on 4 classifications, each classification consisting of mutually-exclusive categories. Thus each respondent is scored 1 for each category into which he falls and 0 for every other category.

Let us look at the basis for calculating the optimal scores. Imagine that each of the 1s in the layout is replaced by a weight. These weights are specific to the columns of the layout — that is, to the categories of the classifications. Each column has its own weight, and we replacc cvery 1 in each column by the weight for that column. The 0s remain unchanged. Now each respondent will have exactly m weights, where m is the number of classifications included in the analysis. By adding up the row for each respondent we can calculate a *total score* for the individual, which is just the sum of the category weights.

The first criterion for fitting the weights is that the *total score* for each respondent should discriminate as well as possible. More precisely, one solves for weights that will maximise the between-person variance, relative to the overall variance. Thus one has a problem of a kind familiar to statisticians — the maximisation of a correlation ratio. One might ask how this technical formulation of the problem relates to one's original intention. Put loosely, one's aim might be described as finding category weights that will maximise the general level of correlations amongst the variables. For every pair of variables, one would like the correlation between them to embody as much of their inter-relationship as can be expressed in a linear form — subject to scoring any given variable in the same way throughout.

This general aim is too loose as it stands to provide a mathematical objective. The actual task set — to maximise the between-person variance — is related to the more general intention in the following way. To solve the maximisation problem we want respondents to be spread out as far as possible in terms of their total score. To do this the scores should be unidimensional — they should all relate to one common factor. If they relate to anything else they are not helping the maximisation. So the scores for each classification will, so far as possible, all be measuring the same thing. If each classification is scored to measure the same dimension, then, *to the extent that a single dimension underlies the set of classifications*, the level of correlations will be maximised. But if most classifications in the analysis have something in common which is not shared by the other classifications, the correlations amongst these other classifications will in general be low, since the scores cannot reflect something that is not there. In a multidimensional situation, one set of scores can only reflect one dimension, and this may turn out to be a conflation of two more meaningful dimensions.

Let us look briefly at Guttman's second approach to the problem. Refer back to Figure 1, recall the *total* scores for each respondent that we defined earlier, and now substitute these *total* scores, rather than the category scores, for each "1" in the data layout. Now each column of the layout (that is, each category) will have a mean (of the total scores), and a variance. One can now define another maximisation problem, which is the dual of the previous one. This is the maximisation of the between-*category* variance (of the total scores), relative to the overall variance.

Again, it may not be easy to grasp straightaway the relevance of this to one's objectives. Let us look more closely at what is proposed. For any given classification (say, type of school) we want the respondents in different categories of school to have overall scores as different as possible and respondents from any one category of school to have overall scores as similar as possible. The (total) scores are therefore to be assigned so that, if they are substituted into Figure 2, they will minimise the variance within all the columns of the data layout — that is, within each classification. It turns out that the solution to this problem is the same (apart from scaling factors) as the solution to the previous formulation — the maximisation of between-respondent variance. Guttman also proposed a third model, leading to the same solution. This model seems to have less practical interest.

Guttman's original paper (1941) provides a very clear exposition of the rationale and proofs of the method, and McDonald (1968) gives a summary as a special case of his "unified treatment of the weighting problem". The computations for this and the following methods are summarised in an appendix to this paper.

Fitting the scores : other solutions

The difficulties with Guttman's original solution (MAC1) are, that it is unmanageable computationally above a certain size of problem (and problems near the limit are expensive in computer time), that the results are sometimes unstable (in ways that we discuss further below) and that where data is definitely multidimensional one does not always obtain a clear solution. So it is worth looking at alternatives. The first of these, MAC3, was developed by Lingoes from a suggestion by Guttman (Lingoes, 1965). Scores are fitted to each classification in turn, by using the cross-tabulation of that classification by every other classification used in the analysis. Thus the same data — a complete set of cross-tabulations — is used in MAC3 and MAC1, but in MAC3 the solution for each classification is calculated separately, using only part of the data. Instead of one large latent root calculation there are a number of small ones. This could allow multidimensionality to come out in the scores where the MAC1 solution constrains all the classifications to contribute to the same dimension. Thus MAC3 will sometimes give a more reasonable solution.

Another method (developed by the writer) is closely related to MAC3, but is designed specifically for predictive studies. The MAC methods treat all variables equally but the predictive method first seeks scores for a criterion classification, and then derives scores for all the predictors. The criterion scores are derived from the cross-tabulations of the criterion classification by all the predictor classifications, and these are the only cross-tabulations needed. Scores for the predictors are calculated so as to maximise the correlation of each predictor with the criterion. The scores given in Example 1 were in fact derived by this method using informant's socio-economic group as the criterion. They are very similar (apart from scaling factors) to the scores from a MAC1 solution. The correlations are also similar, though the predictive method gives slightly higher values for the correlations with the criterion, and slightly lower values for the other correlations, than the MAC1 solution [7].

Example 2 : social class identification

The next example compares two solutions and examines their stability. The data is rather similar to the previous example, but comes from a different source. It is taken from a political survey conducted by Marplan Ltd. for *The Times* in 1963 [8]. This data is used here because the straightforward sample design facilitated calculation of standard errors. To give reasonable homogeneity, the analysis was restricted to male heads of households, aged 35-64, giving a base of 542.

The problem posed in the example is the "explanation" of people's identification with different social classes, as measured by such a question as "what social class would you say you were a member of". It is proposed to examine this in a path model, using

7. The method could be viewed as a short-cut form of multiple discriminant analysis.

8. The permission of the Thomson Organisation to use the data is gratefully acknowledged. The same survey was used by Morgan and Purnell (1969).

A. Father's occupation
B. Age respondent completed full-time education
C. Respondent's current occupation, and
D. Subjective social class, as defined above.

Hodge and Treiman (1967-1968) have given a similar model, based on a sample of 923, interviewed by the National Opinion Research Center in 1964. They scored "class identification" as follows:

Lower	1
Working	2
Middle	3
Upper middle	4
Upper	5

remarking that "such an arbitrary scoring is not wholly justified". Certainly it would be quite a long way from the optimal scoring in British data, as we have found it (see below; similar results have been obtained in other samples). They regressed these class identification scores on years of school, family income and occupation of the main earner in the household (scored by Duncan's SES). We cannot make an exact comparison with this study, since the Marplan data did not include income. And we have chosen to confine our analysis to "heads of households", to avoid the interpretative ambiguities associated with "occupation of main earner" and the like [9].

The model proposed is a simple, just-identified recursive one [10].
It states:

B depends on A (plus a residual, X)
C depends on A and B (plus a residual, Y)
D depends on A, B and C (plus a residual, Z).

This example is used to assess the stability of the scoring methods, and path analyses based on them. First scores are fitted. Most of them are shown in Table 3. Father's occupation is similar for this purpose to respondent's occupation, so is not shown. Solutions using MAC1 and MAC3 are compared. The MAC3 scores have been re-scaled to the same variance as the MAC1 scores (the mean for each classification is always zero, using either method). The two solutions are quite remarkably similar.

Tukey's jack-knife was used to calculate confidence intervals for all the scores [11]. The confidence intervals for the scores are fairly reassuring. It

9. To know of someone that he lives in a household that has a telephone, or owns rather than rents its accommodation is much weaker information than to know that he personally rents the telephone or owns the accommodation.

10. Obviously, this example (like the last) is only a toy, used to illustrate the method. A serious examination of this problem would require more data. The proposed causal ordering is not uncontroversial, but we need not defend it here.

11. For a clear exposition of the jack-knife see Mosteller and Tukey (1968). The sample was based on ninety constituencies, stratified by region and Conservative/Labour vote. For this jack-knife the constituencies were grouped in nine sets of ten each. So far as possible

Table 3. *Example 2 : category scores, with alternative solutions and confidence intervals*

Informant's occupation	(N)	MAC1 scores	MAC3 scores	Absolute difference	Jack-knife (with 90 % limits) MAC1	MAC3
AB	(63)	1.28	1.27	.01	1.24 ± .15	1.25 ± .08
C1	(106)	0.27	.29	.02	.26 ± .17	.32 ± .10
C2	(237)	- .23	- .22	.01	- .27 ± .06	- .23 ± .03
D	(129)	- .42	- .44	.02	- .40 ± .05	- .43 ± .04
E	(1)	- .29	- .37	.08	*	*
NI	(6)	- .30	.33	.03	- .30 ± .23	- .35 ± .10
Mean		.00	.00	.02		
Terminal education age						
- 15	(455)	- .17	- .17	—	- .14 ± .04	- .17 ± .01
- 18	(57)	.80	.80	—	.82 ± .21	.80 ± .11
- 23	(23)	1.20	1.19	.01	1.16 ± .22	1.17 ± .15
- 24 +	(3)	1.79	1.83	.04	1.66 ± .78	1.64 ± .49
Still at college	(1)	.32	.34	.02	*	*
NI	(3)	- .06	- .10	.04	- .22 ± .32	- .15 ± .31
Mean		.00	.00	.00		
Subjective social class						
Upper	(4)	1.17	1.12	.05	.94 ± 1.60	.77 ± 1.53
Upper middle	(3)	1.24	1.29	.05	.68 ± 2.63	.67 ± 2.30
Lower middle	(33)	.37	.40	.03	.38 ± .35	.39 ± 34
Middle	(140)	.39	.40	.01	.40 ± .11	.39 ± .10
Working	(287)	- .28	- .28	.00	- .29 ± .05	- .26 ± .05
Lower	(7)	- .39	- .35	.04	- .40 ± .12	- .34 ± .14
Don't know	(27)	- .02	- .04	.02	- .02 ± .37	- .06 ± .29
NI	(41)	.20	.13	.07	.20 ± .47	.11 ± .39
Mean		.00	.00	.01		

* No satisfactory estimate can be formed from a single case.

the constituencies from each region were spread evenly over the nine sets. It was not feasible to take explicit account of the other stratification (*cf.* Brillinger, 1966). The MAC solutions, correlations and regressions were then calculated ten times, once from all the data, once dropping out each of the nine sets in turn, giving nine estimates each based on eight-ninths of the data. Every confidence interval was then calculated as follows. Suppose we wish to calculate the confidence interval for x, where x may be a category score, a correlation or a regression coefficient. Form nine "pseudo-values" 9Xt-8Xi where Xt is the estimate from the total sample and Xi the ith estimate from eight-ninths of the data. The mean of the pseudo-values provides the jack-knifed estimate which often has less bias than the simple estimate, and the variance of the pseudo-values, divided by nine, can be treated as the square of the standard error. The confidence intervals are then calculated from these standard errors, using the t distribution with eight degrees of freedom. Being based on so few degrees of freedom, the confidence intervals will in turn have wide confidence intervals.

was to be expected that scores for the smallest categories would be unstable. On the whole the scores are very plausible. The small group who claim to be upper class score lower than the even smaller group who say they are upper middle. One would take this for sampling error, but the same effect has been noted in two other samples.

The MAC3 solution seems even more stable, in sampling terms, than the MAC1 solution. In almost every case the MAC3 scores have a narrower confidence interval. It should be emphasized that this data is quite exceptionally well fitted by the MAC model. Later, we discuss the situations in which one could hope to find this degree of agreement betwen the two solutions.

Table 4. *Example 2 : stability of correlations and regressions*

Correlations	MAC1 scores	MAC3 scores	Absolute difference	Jack-knife (MAC1) with 90 % limits
Informant's occupation:				
Father's occupation	.5146	.5148	.0002	.508 ± .091
Subjective social class	.4041	.4035	.0006	.373 ± .050
Age left school	.5215	.5217	.0002	.520 ± .112
Father's occupation:				
Subjective social class	.3130	.3115	.0015	.289 ± .073
Age left school	.4608	.4610	.0002	.451 ± .103
Subjective social class:				
Age left school	.3391	.3379	.0012	.325 ± .055
Regressions				
Informant's occupation:				
Father's occupation	.3483			.360 ± .076
Age left school	.3610			.366 ± .114
Squared multiple R	.3675			.360 ± .117
Subjective social class:				
Informant's occupation	.2729			.246 ± .077
Father's occupation	.1039			.091 ± .072
Age left school	.1489			.156 ± .061
Squared multiple R	.1933			.165 ± .044

Table 4 shows the correlation coefficients and regression coefficients. In this model the partial regression coefficients are the estimators of the path coefficients. The MAC1 and MAC3 correlations are almost indistinguishable so it did not seem necessary to calculate regressions from the MAC3 solution.

Figure 3 gives the path diagram corresponding to the MAC1 analysis. It is worth comparing this with the Hodge and Treiman analysis, even though such comparisons cannot be at all exact.

Figure 3. *Path diagram for example 2*

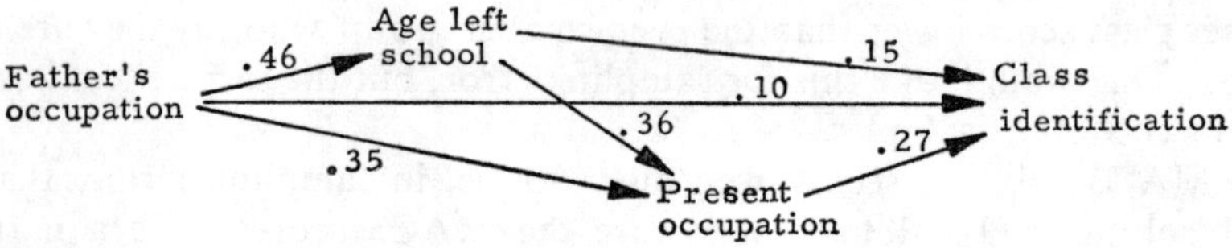

Hodge and Treiman's equation, in education, income and occupation, explained 19.6 % of the variance in class identification, compared with 19.4 % in our data. Their partial regression coefficients for education (.115) and occupation (.274) are also similar in magnitude to ours. Hodge and Treiman comment on the small proportion of variance in class identification explained by their equation and go on to remark that "education, income and occupation do not cumulate in a manner conducive to the formation of a well-defined, objective class structure around which class identifications can be unambiguously formed", leading to a "failure of class consciousness to crystallize uniquely around objective measures of socio-economic status".

In the British situation, at least, this explanation of the low multiple correlation does not seem wholly satisfactory. The key variables "cumulate" a little more strongly in this country than in the United States. Thus other studies in Britain suggest that income correlates .5 with school leaving age and .5 - .6 with occupation, whereas in the United States the corresponding correlations seem to be of the order of .3 - .4 (Duncan, Featherman and Duncan, 1968). We would suggest at least three other reasons for the low percentage of explained variance. First, we believe class identifications are usually formed fairly early in life and may be quite resistant to change. For this reason we included father's occupation in our equation, but we do not believe this satisfactorily captures all relevant aspects of the parental home. Second, any path model of this kind virtually always understates the true strength of the relationships involved (Duncan-Jones, in preparation).

Possibly the most important reason for the meagre results found is that advanced by Goldthorpe and Lockwood (1963). They argued that the usual type of class identification question in surveys (*e.g.* "Which of the following social classes do you belong to?") imposes a particular conception of class structure on respondents who may differ considerably in their "images of society" (Willener, 1957; Popitz *et al.*, 1957; Goldthorpe, 1970). Consequently, the same recorded answer may have the most diverse meanings for different informants. This conclusion is based on inference from the variety of "images of class" that may be elicited from different members of the same society, using a fairly non-directive style of questioning. So far as the writer knows, there is much less *direct* evidence on the way in which the traditional type of question is interpreted. It may well be construed in quite different ways by different informants. But on the other hand there might be a good deal of uniformity in its interpretation [12].

The analysis of class identification is used here only as an example, and we must return to more technical matters. It is time to look at the jack-knife estimates of the correlation and regression coefficients. These are rather disturbing. In the worst case, we can only say (with 90 % confidence) that age on completing full-time education explains between 17 % and 40 % of the variance in current occupational level. But this is not all the fault of the scoring system. Correlation coefficients from simple random samples have quite wide confidence intervals. So it seems useful to look at the problem in terms of "design factors". The "design factor" or "design effect" for a survey estimate is the ratio of the standard error calculated in accordance with the sample design, to the standard error from a simple random sample of the same size. In this case, we look at the ratio of the jack-knife confidence interval to a confidence interval calculated using Fisher's z transform.

Over the six correlation and five partial regression coefficients, the mean of the "design effects' is 1.14 (calculated from standard errors, not variances); this is similar to Kish's results (Kish and Frankel, 1970). The range of the design effects is large — from .7 to 2.0 — no doubt because rather few groups were used for the jack-knife. Coefficients involving age on completing education seem particularly variable.

It seems from this small example, that regressions based on canonical scores are about as stable as regressions from more ordinary variables. But the stability of regressions from multi-stage samples has not been very widely investigated; one would need much more evidence before reaching any definite conclusion. Certainly one cannot rule out canonical scoring on grounds of sampling instability [13].

Factor analysis, dimensionality and goodness of fit

Guttman first proposed the canonical method for scoring attitude scales. It seems that it will work well with a unidimensional set of items that are quite

12. In an analysis of the Butler-Stokes data the writer found that class identifications were somewhat less stable over three years than some more "objective" status indices; this does not necessarily militate against the theory of early formation of identifications, but it may reflect indecision in fitting one's private map of the class structure to the alternatives offered. In a third survey a factor analysis of twenty status-related variables suggested that housewives' class identifications loaded most strongly on a factor otherwise mainly weighted by their father's and mother's occupations, though it does also have quite a substantial loading on a factor mainly weighted by current income and husband's occupation.

13. However, the results *do* suggest caution in interpreting some published analyses. Admittedly the sub-sample of 542 used here is not very large. But it is also not very clustered — it averages just over six per constituency. There are some apparently quite dramatic differences between corresponding correlation coefficients in tables two and four. Using the jack-knife standard errors, and assuming the same standard errors apply to the coefficients from the Butler/Stokes data, one can show that none of the differences are significant.

strongly associated with each other. In less favourable cases peculiarities may arise. An analysis of 21 attitude statements (from the same Marplan survey) provides an example. These statements were of the familiar five-point agree/disagree type. An earlier analysis based on scoring the categories 1 to 5 had shown the overall level of correlation amongst the statements was pretty low. A MAC1 analysis gave a perfect U-shaped scoring system for every statement. The "optimum" scoring was one that contrasted *strong* agreement *or* disagreement with more moderate opinions; the major common factor was "intensity" — or response set.

The MAC1 method was discovered independently by Sir Cyril Burt (Burt, 1950). His motivation for it was quite different from Guttman's. He was seeking a method of factor analysis for qualitative data. His main focus was on the *interpretation* of the scores (or loadings) rather than their use *as* scores; and he was interested in extracting more than one factor. If there are m classifications in the analysis, with a total of n categories amongst them, one can extract n-m orthogonal factors or scoring systems. An alternative common factor model for this type of data has been proposed by McDonald (1969).

Our main concern in this paper has been the development of a *single* scoring system for a set of categorical variables, and for this purpose multi-factor solutions are of little direct interest. In other contexts, they may provide a valuable tool. We have made an analysis of husband's and wife's leisure interests which provides some interesting comparisons. The study will be reported elsewhere in due course, and we use it here simply to make a couple of methodological points. It was found that the canonical scoring analysis produced several interpretable factors, and some of these involved U-shaped relationships. As an example, interest in church-going tended to be *lukewarm* among those who were interested in gambling, going to the pub and so forth. Those who rejected gambling were *either* strong church-goers *or* very definitely *not* interested in church-going. There is nothing very striking or surprising about this finding. What is perhaps more striking is that it was elicited from a factor analysis.

Multi-factor solutions have other possible uses. They can be used, like any principal component analysis, to summarize data. Each respondent may be given a single score for each of the first few dimensions from a MAC1 analysis, by adding together his category scores. These summary scores would provide an excellent basis for taxonomic analysis. A taxonomic analysis on such a basis might well produce clusters with quite different relationships amongst the variables[14].

14. Adding scores together (or subtracting them to form difference scores) assumes that they are appropriately scaled relative to each other. With MAC1 scores there are grounds for believing this to be so. One may calculate a standard deviation for each variable, from the scores for its categories. One may also calculate a correlation matrix among the variables and find its principal components. It turns out the elements of the first principal com-

For our main purpose, fitting path models, the existence of multi-factor, possibly non-linear, solutions is a matter for some concern. As we suggested earlier, canonical scores will provide a solid basis for path analysis if the data is quite strongly dominated by one dimension. But if this is not so, interpretation may be confused. One may not be clear just what facet of each variable has been captured in the scoring system one has used. So we need to consider how one may recognise appropriate and inappropriate situations for canonical scoring.

Criteria for the use of canonical scores are of two kinds, statistical measures of "goodness of fit", and substantive knowledge. One would be rash to attempt a canonical scoring solution unless theory, background knowledge and previous research give good grounds for supposing the variables involved "hang together" — that they all have something in common [15]. Beyond that, one looks at statistical measures. Table 5 compares the squared correlation ratios found in four MAC1 analyses.

1. An analysis of eleven variables from the Marplan study (listed in Table 6).
2. An analysis of 16 variables from the 1949 British social mobility study (Glass, 1954) [16].
3. and 4. The analyses of leisure interests referred to above.

Table 5. *Some correlation ratios from MAC1 solutions*

Dimension	Marplan study	1949 Mobility study	Leisure interests Wife	Leisure interests Husband
1	.379	.394	.160	.171
2	.175	.188	.128	.149
3	.167	.173	.110	.116
4	.154	.162	.090	.087
5	.151	.146	.080	.085

It is evident that the social stratification data is much more firmly structured. The correlation ratio for the predominant factor is twice the size of the second one. In the leisure interests data the correlation ratios are much more evenly

ponent are identical with the corresponding standard deviations. The MAC3 results have no such natural scaling, but it seems reasonable to scale them to conform to the first principal component, in the same way.

15. Hope (1971) has suggested rather similar criteria for path analysis. One might suppose that the method of fitting scores would produce data that was virtually uni-dimensional, but this is not in fact the case. If one forms a correlation matrix of variables, canonically scored, which include measures on husband and wife and on their parents, then almost any factorisation of this matrix (*e.g.* by principal components or canonical correlations) provides a general factor (naturally) but also factors which contrast husband with wife and parents with children.

16. The original data cards of the 1949 study were made available to the Nuffield College social mobility project by the Government Social Survey by permission of Professor D.V. Glass. A number of new analyses of this data will appear in Ridge (1972).

spread. Thus, the correlation ratios from a MAC1 solution provide some overall indication of fit. One would hesitate to use the scores for path analysis if the first squared correlation ratio was much below .4 (in Example 2 above it was .6). Another test might be the agreement between the MAC1 and MAC3 scoring systems. We have already seen how close this *can* be, and Table 6 presents further evidence in a different form. Here we have compared principal components, not from the original scoring solutions but from correlation matrices derived from them. The Table also gives the correlation ratios (not squared) that are associated with each *variable* in the MAC3 solution. Once again, MAC1 and MAC3 results are very close. The mean of the absolute differences is .0019. The loading of each variable on the first principal component is an index of how well that variable fits into the overall picture. In this instance, one might be a bit dubious about including the TV variable, but the pattern of scores for it seems reasonable enough.

Table 6. *Measures of fit for some variables in the Marplan study*

	Loadings on first principal component			MAC3 Correlation ratios
	MAC1	MAC3	Abs. difference	
Parents' political party	.5016	.4998	.0018	.256
Voting intention	.6471	.6455	.0016	.332
Home ownership	.4899	.4899	.0000	.241
Car ownership	.4701	.4619	.0082	.242
Respondent's occupation	.7775	.7779	.0004	.393
Father's occupation	.6478	.6503	.0025	.324
Class identification	.5641	.5624	.0017	.276
School-leaving age	.6964	.6962	.0002	.350
Daily paper index	.4974	.4981	.0007	.260
Sunday paper index	.6472	.6485	.0013	.330
Television channel preference	.4014	.3991	.0023	.202

Considerations of this kind provide some basis for judging the goodness of fit of a MAC1 solution. Where problems are too large for the full solution one is driven back on using MAC3, and other criteria are needed. Two have been developed. One is the correlation between the principal component loadings and the MAC3 correlation ratios. In the example in Table 6, the Spearman rank correlation is .990. It seemed desirable to test MAC3 more stringently, since the fitting process ignores much of the information. In most survey data one finds correlations of the order of .2 to .5 but an example was taken which included a scattering of correlations of the order of .8 (essentially, reliability coefficients). In this example with 15 "stratification" variables, the mean of the differences between the MAC1 and MAC3 component loadings was .0009 and the rank correlations between the component loadings and the MAC3 correlation ratios were over .99. Graphic plots suggested an essentially linear relationship between the component loadings and the correlation ratios.

Contrast this with the analysis of husband's leisure interests. Here the rank correlations over 20 variables were:

MAC1 and MAC 3 component loadings	.75
MAC1 loadings and MAC3 correlation ratios	.92
MAC3 loadings and MAC3 correlation ratios	.90

Evidently one should require *very* high agreement between the MAC3 correlation ratios and the first principal component from the derived correlation matrix.

The other criterion we have found for assessing goodness of fit is the variability of the component loadings. In the Marplan example (Table 6) the MAC3 loadings give a coefficient of variation (standard deviation over mean) of .19. In the "high correlation" example the coefficient is .17. For husband's leisure interest it is .58. Thus one has another clear indication of the homogeneity of the variables, though more work is needed to determine exactly what counts as good, fair or poor fit.

Strategy, tactics and pitfalls in canonical scoring

In conclusion, some recommendations, based on the writer's experience of working with canonical scores. A rather attractive feature of the method is that it provides scores for Don't Know/No Information (DK/NI) categories. Trading on this can lead to disaster. One striking example occurred when fitting scores for the 900 men in the Butler/Stokes data. Most runs fitted scores simultaneously to between eight and twelve classifications. In this particular run, scores were fitted to five only:

Respondent's occupation
Father's occupation
School-leaving age
Type of school
Whether respondent had any post-school education.

Just five men (out of 900) had "No information" on all three education variables, and they accounted for the bulk of no information cases in each educational classification. The result was a scoring system that contrasted the NI categories of the education variables with all the other categories. If these five variables had been analysed in conjunction with a further five that could broadly be termed social class indicators, this freak effect would have been swamped and sensible results obtained — as they were in other runs. However, it is clearly prudent to eliminate from the analysis all respondents who are in the "No information" category on more than one or two variables.

We have suggested that canonical scoring should be applied to groups of variables that are homogeneous, where one wants the scoring to reflect what is common to all of them. If one's data includes (say) a set of social stratification variables and another set concerned with political involvement it will be sensible to fit scores separately to the two clusters of variables. One can then calculate correlations between as well as within the clusters.

In the examples above, we have given scores for some categories that are numerically very small. We have also shown that such scores are unstable. So long as the scores are not very extreme, this instability seems not to matter too much, precisely because the categories are small. However, it is better to play safe and, so far as possible, combine very small categories with other categories of similar meaning, prior to the analysis.

One may have to combine categories on other grounds. Where the categories of a classification have a clear ordering, it is usually unsatisfactory to work with scores that do not reflect this ordering monotonically. If the first solution produces irregular scoring patterns, one may have to merge categories and repeat the analysis.

In summary, work done so far suggests strongly that canonical scoring is useful in the study of social mobility. It will surely prove useful in other areas. But (like any multivariate method) it requires careful application and painstaking scrutiny of all the results.

APPENDIX

Notes on computation

MAC1

First form all possible 2-way frequency tables between the classifications included in the analysis. These are arranged in a symmetric matrix, with the marginal totals along the diagonal. (In other words, treating the layout in Figure 2 as a matrix, one pre-multiplies this matrix by its transpose.) Next, the elements of this matrix are adjusted, by subtracting the expected value (in the familiar "chi-square" sense) and dividing by the geometric mean of the corresponding marginals (that is, each element is replaced by the square root of its contribution to an overall chi-squared statistic, divided by the total number of respondents). Next, one finds the latent roots and vectors (or principal components) of the adjusted matrix. The first component provides the category scores. They are scaled to have sum of squares equal to the first latent root.

MAC3

A separate solution is obtained for each variable, treating each variable in turn as the "criterion". The solution can be described most conveniently in matrix notation.

Let F be a matrix of frequencies formed by cross-tabulating the criterion variable by each of the other variables.

$F = f_{ij} \quad i = 1, n, \quad j = 1, k$

where

k is the number of categories in the criterion variable
n is the *total* number of categories in *all* the other variables taken together.

Define

G (k, k) — a diagonal matrix containing the marginal total frequencies for the categories of the criterion variable
M (n, n) — a diagonal matrix of the marginal totals for the other variables.

Let

$A\ (n, k) = G^{-1/2}\, F\, M^{-1/2}$

A is simply a segment of the matrix analysed in MAC1 except that the expectations have not been subtracted out.
Now form
$C = A'A$

The latent roots of C (apart from the first) are squared correlation ratios and the corresponding vectors, after scaling, provide the weights or scores. The first latent root and vector represent a "size" effect that could have been removed by subtracting out the expectations.

So far as the writer knows, no formal justification of the MAC3 procedure has been published. He owes the details of the computation to a personal communication from J. Lingoes (1969). Two derivations seem reasonable. Both involve treating the categories of all the variables other than the criterion variable as if they were the mutually exclusive categories of a single classification. Then the solution could be seen as an instance of the fairly well-known canonical analysis of bivariate frequency tables (Duncan-Jones, 1970). Alternatively, it could be motivated by a discriminant strategy. The procedure will in fact find scores for the criterion variable which will maximise discrimination between all categories of all the other variables, treated as before as if they were mutually exclusive. This can be seen most easily by substituting for *A* in the formula for *C* (Duncan-Jones, 1972, Appendix A). Thus both derivations ignore all correlations apart from those with the criterion variable, when fitting scores for that variable. We would expect this to work well enough if the correlations are low. In fact we have seen above that the solution *may* agree very well with the full MAC1 solution even in the presence of high correlations.

The predictive solution

This simply performs the MAC3 solution once, for a single criterion variable, rather than for each variable in turn. The "predictor" categories (*i.e.* the categories of all the other variables) are scored straightforwardly by the procedure used in bivariate canonical analysis (Duncan-Jones, 1970). That is, for each predictor category, one calcultates the mean criterion score for the category and treats this mean as the score for the category. It can easily be shown that, given the fitted scores for the criterion variable, this maximizes the correlation of each predictor variable with the criterion.

REFERENCES

Blau, P.M.; Duncan, O.D.
1967 *The American occupational structure.* New York, Wiley.

Boyle, R.P.
1970 "Path analysis and ordinal data", *American journal of sociology* 75: 461-480.

Brillinger, D.R.
1966 "Application of the jack-knife to the analysis of consumer surveys", *Journal of the market research society* 8(2): 74-80.

Burt, C.
1950 "Factorial analysis of qualitative data", *British journal of psychology, Statistical section* 3: 166-185.

Butler, D.E.; Stokes, D.E.
1969 *Political change in Britain.* London, Macmillan.

Duncan, O.D.; Featherman, D.L.; Duncan, B.
1968 *Socioeconomic background and occupational achievement.* Washington, DC, US Department of Health, Education and Welfare.

Duncan-Jones, P.
1972 "Social mobility, canonical scoring and occupational classification", in: *Oxford studies in social mobility.* Oxford, Oxford University press. (Paper read to the 7th World Congress of Sociology, Varna, 1970.)
1972 *Social grading and social distance: A discriminant approach.* (Mimeo.)
In preparation: *Estimating the constraints on social mobility.*

General Register Office
1960 *Classification of occupations.* London, HMSO.

Goldthorpe, J.H.
1970 "L'image des classes chezl es travailleurs manuels aisés", *Revue française de sociologie* 11: 311-338.

Goldthorpe, J.H.; Lockwood, D.
1963 "Affluence and the British class structure", *Sociological review* 11: pp. 133-163

Glass, D.V.
1954 *Social mobility in Britain.* London, Routledge.

Guttman, L.
1941 "Quantification of a class of attributes", in: P. Horst (ed.). *The prediction of personal adjustment.* New York, Social Science Research Council.

Hodge, R.W.; Treiman, D.J.
1968 "Class identification in the United States", *American journal of sociology* 73: 535-547.

Hope, K.
1971 "Path analysis: Supplementary procedures", *Sociology* 5: 225-242.

Kish, L.; Frankel, M.R.
1970 "Balanced repeated repiications for standard errors", *Journal of the American Statistical Association* 65: 331; 1077-1094.

Lingoes, J.
1966 "New computer developments in pattern analysis and non-metric techniques", in: *Proceedings of the IBM symposium: Computers in psychological research,* Paris, Gauthier-Villars.

Lyons, M.; Carter, T.M.

1971 "Further comments on Boyle's 'Path analysis and ordinal data' ", *American journal of sociology* 75: 1112-1132.

McDonald, R.P.

1968 "A unified treatment of the weighting problem", *Psychometrika* 33: 351-381.

1969 "The common factor analysis of multicategory data", *British journal of mathematical and statistical psychology* 22: 165-175.

Morgan, N.; Purnell, J.M.

1969 "Isolating openings for new products in a multi-dimensional space", *Journal of the market research society* 11(3): 245-266.

Mosteller, F.; Tukey, J.W.

1968 "Data analysis, including statistics", in: J. Lindzey; E. Aronson (eds.). *Handbook of social psychology*. Vol. 2. London, Addison-Wesley.

Popitz, H.; Bahrdt, H.P.; Jueres, E.A.; Kesting, A.

1957 "The worker's image of society", in: T. Burns (ed.). *Industrial man*. London, Penguin, 1969.

Reiss, A.J. *et al.*

1961 *Occupations and social status*. Glencoe, Ill., Free Press.

Ridge, J.M. (ed.)

1972 *Oxford studies in social mobility*. Vol 2. Oxford, Oxford University Press.

Willener, A.

1957 *Images de la société et classes sociales*. Berne, Stämpfli.

SUGIYAMA IUTAKA • E. WILBUR BOCK

Determinants of occupational status in Brazil*

Numerous studies have been made on social stratification, primarily in industrial societies. Some of the well-known investigations are those of Rogoff (1953), Glass (1954), Carlsson (1958), and Svalastoga (1959). These studies were concerned with the profiles of social stratification regarding two generations, comparing the profile of fathers with that of sons. The purposes of these comparisons were to determine the chances that sons, given their social origins, would have in achieving certain social levels in the various societies. Since mobility has been the major preoccupation of these investigations, the profiles have been analyzed as self-sustaining entities by means of transition matrices. The number of factors has been limited, in general, to two or three taken simultaneously. Multivariate procedures taking a greater number of independent variables have not been applied to the study of stratification until recently.

A major breakthrough in the study of stratification was made by Blau and Duncan (1967) who used path models to ascertain the determinants of occupational status. The variables considered by these two researchers appeared in previous investigations but these factors were not systematically analyzed in terms of closed systems. The use of path models has permitted ascertaining the effects of each independent variable when all other factors are neutralized. Rather than noting the existence of a simple relationship between two variables, such models have helped describe the complexity of relationship and hierarchy of importance of factors implicated in stratification.

The studies carried out in the decade of the 1950's in industrial societies allowed certain comparisons to be made, but the types and amount of such comparisons were limited by the data. Most of the comparisons were in terms of 1) nonmanual-manual strata and, 2) inflow and outflow regarding

* The authors wish to express their thanks to George A. Watkins for his help during the computations, and to Felix M. Berardo, Benjamin L. Gorman and Irving L. Webber for their critical reviews of the manuscript.

these two strata (Lipset and Bendix, 1959; Fox and Miller, 1966; Broom and Jones, 1969). The comparisons made have enlarged sociological knowledge regarding occupational opportunities and have indicated that industrial societies, regardless of their historical formation, seem to present a high degree of social mobility. However, the results found have not been conclusive since limitations were imposed by the data available.

Investigations of non-industrial nations have been less frequently made and might be characterized generally as being simply descriptive (Pfautz, 1953). The same characterization can be made of the studies carried out in Latin American countries (Iutaka, 1965). Some exceptions are to be noted in the latter region of the world, and these investigations (Hutchinson, 1960; Balan *et al.*, 1967) have followed the model used in the Western industrial societies.

The lack of adequate data has prohibited comparisons between industrial and non-industrial societies and, therefore, has also limited the testing and refining of theories of social stratification. One exception appears to be a study by Miller (1969) which included three non-industrial countries. The objectives of the present research are 1) to ascertain the relative importance of the factors determining individuals' social statuses in one industrializing society, Brazil, and, 2) to compare the mechanisms of status achievement in such a society with those operating in an industrially mature nation.

The model the present investigators wished to test is that presented by Blau and Duncan. In *The American occupational structure* (1967, pp. 402-403), they concluded that education, first job, father's occupational status and father's education are the significant variables, in descending order of importance, regarding the determination of an individual's occupational status. The model indicates that education is the most effective avenue for reaching a given social status. The parental background is important in explaining the amount of education individuals acquire rather than being a direct influence on occupational achievement.

The present authors expected that the same mechanisms would be found in an industrializing society. However, certain differences were also anticipated due to the different stages of industrialization. In a society experiencing the earlier stages of industrialization, family background is more important for status achievement than it is in a more industrially mature nation. In the latter type of country, industrial structures demand skills that are generally attained through the formal educational system. Since industrialization is taking place in Brazil, education should be an important factor for status achievement in that country as well as in the United States. However, since Brazil is less industrialized than the United States, universal education is relatively less expected of the Brazilian population and the educational system of Brazil is just beginning to expand to meet the increasing demands for industrial and related skills. Thus, the investigators expected that parental background is more important for status achievement in Brazil than in the United States where educational attainment is of relatively greater significance.

Method

The data used in this investigation were gathered in Brazil in 1959-1960. The researchers obtained information on cards from the International Data Library of the University of California at Berkeley. The interviews were carried out in six Brazilian cities: 1 000 in São Paulo and in Rio de Janeiro; 750 in Belo-Horizonte; and 500 each in Juiz de Fora, Volta Redonda and Americana. Area sampling was used to select a representation of the adult population of those cities. The first stage of the sampling was to select blocks and then households. In each household, the sampling unit, an adult of 18 years of age or older, was chosen randomly, regardless of sex.

These cities in which the interviews were made are clustered in the southeastern part of Brazil, the most industrialized region of the society. São Paulo (population: 3 300 218) [1] is the largest urban center and also the largest industrial center in Latin America. Rio de Janeiro (3 223 408), the former capital of Brazil, was and still is the most important political and social center of the country. Belo-Horizonte (663 215) is the city planned to be the capital of the state. Juiz de Fora (128 364) was one of the first industrial centers in Brazil and, prior to the development of São Paulo, was called the "Manchester of Brazil". Volta Redonda (83 973) was created in the decade of 1940 and is centered around the steel plant which dominates the economic life of the city. Finally, Americana (32 000) in the State of São Paulo, was founded after the US Civil War by immigrants from the Southern United States.

Since the investigation concerns occupational achievement, females were removed from the sample because most of them were housewives. Individuals for whom data were incomplete were also removed. As a result, the sizes of the samples used are: São Paulo 456; Rio de Janeiro 432; Belo-Horizonte 349; Juiz de Fora 247; Volta Redonda 229; and Americana 246.

The measures used are: status of the respondent's first job, his present occupational status, his educational attainment, his father's last occupational status, and his father's educational attainment. The statuses of the respondents and of their fathers are measured in terms of their occupations, which are ranked according to a method employed by Glass (1954) and modified for Brazil by Hutchinson (1960). The occupations are classified into the following six categories: high administrative and professional, managerial, high white-collar, low white-collar, skilled, semiskilled and unskilled. Educational attainment of the respondents and of their fathers are measured in terms of completion of school levels; complete and incomplete college, complete and incomplete secondary, complete and incomplete primary, and no education are the categories used.

Two methods of analysis are utilized in the present investigation. Covariance is used to ascertain the relative importance of the independent vari-

1. All population figures are those of 1960.

ables when cities are controlled, and vice versa. The objective of this statistical analysis is to take into account the fact that occupational opportunities may vary from city to city (Lane, 1968). The second method uses the path model in which causality is assumed in a given system (Blalock, 1964; Duncan, 1966; Blau and Duncan, 1967).

Results

The determinants of individuals' social statuses in non-industrial societies are often perceived as being different from those factors considered important in industrializing nations. In industrial nations, the factors which are most commonly held to be important are education, first job, aspirations and family background. In contrast, it is often said that the mechanisms for achieving a given status in non-industrial societies are kin networks and friendships, while educational and occupational channels are of lesser importance.

When the factors suggested by Blau and Duncan are considered, Table 1 shows the importance of these four variables in the prediction of social status in urban Brazil. The ranking of these variables can be seen because a step-wise multiple correlation is used. The results indicate 1) that one-third (34 percent) of the variation in social status is explained by the four variables, and 2) that the relative importance of the factors is the same both for Brazil and the United States. The amount of education individuals have acquired is the most important determinant of the levels of status they achieve. This factor accounts for 28 percent of the variance in status. When education is taken into account, the first job the individual holds appears as the second significant variable for his achieving a given status level. These two factors, education and first job, together explain 32 percent of the variation in the social statuses of individuals. When these factors are taken into account, the social status and education of the father add little predictive power. When the total variance explained by these four factors is compared with the results found in the United States (Blau and Duncan, 1967, p. 174) the pre-

Table 1. *Relative importance of the four variables predicting social status*

	R's	R²'s	Significance
$R_{5 \cdot 1}$	.518	.278	.001
$R_{5 \cdot 12}$	.570	.325	.001
$R_{5 \cdot 123}$	.585	.342	.001
$R_{5 \cdot 1234}$	.585	.342	.001

1. Informant's education
2. Informant's first job
3. Father's social status
4. Father's education
5. Informant's social status

sent model appears adequate although it does not present a coefficient of determination as high as the one found for American society (.34 *vs* .43).

It is important to note that the populations under study are from six urban areas in Brazil. Occupational opportunities may vary from city to city, as suggested by Lane (1968). The authors decided, therefore, to investigate the influence of city differences in the determination of social status. The results can be seen in Tables 2 and 3.

Table 2. *Covariance analysis for testing importance of cities*

	Sum of squares	Degrees of freedom	Estimate of variance	F
	—	—	—	—
Unexplained by X_i	3 856	1 954		
Unexplained by X_i but explained by A	146	5	29.37	
				15.43
Error	3 709	1 949	1.90	

X_i = Independent variables: informant's education, informant's first job, father's social status, father's education.
A = Treatment: cities.

Table 2 indicates that urban differences should be considered in the study of social stratification. When the other factors are controlled, the findings show that the urban structure in which individuals live does have an effect on the social status they finally achieve ($F = 15.43$, significant at the .001 level). This finding confirms previous research (Lane, 1968; Blau and Duncan, 1967, pp. 244-250).

Although cities do influence status achievement, these urban structures do not alter the rank importance of the other factors being investigated. When the city variable is controlled, the relative importance of the other determinants remain unchanged. The results in Table 3 show that education is the most significant element followed by first job and father's status. Father's education remains the least important factor and is not statistically significant. The t-values in Table 3 indicate that the amount of education an individual has acquired and the status of his first job are approximately twice as important as is his father's social status.

Table 3. *Covariance analysis for testing relative importance of covariates with cities controlled*

Covariate	Coefficient	Standard error	t-value
	—	—	—
Education	.360	.025	14.390*
First job	.300	.026	11.765*
Father's social status	.138	.021	6.511*
Father's education	.008	.012	1.666

* Significant at .05 level.

Figure 1. *Coefficients in the path model of the process of status achievement**

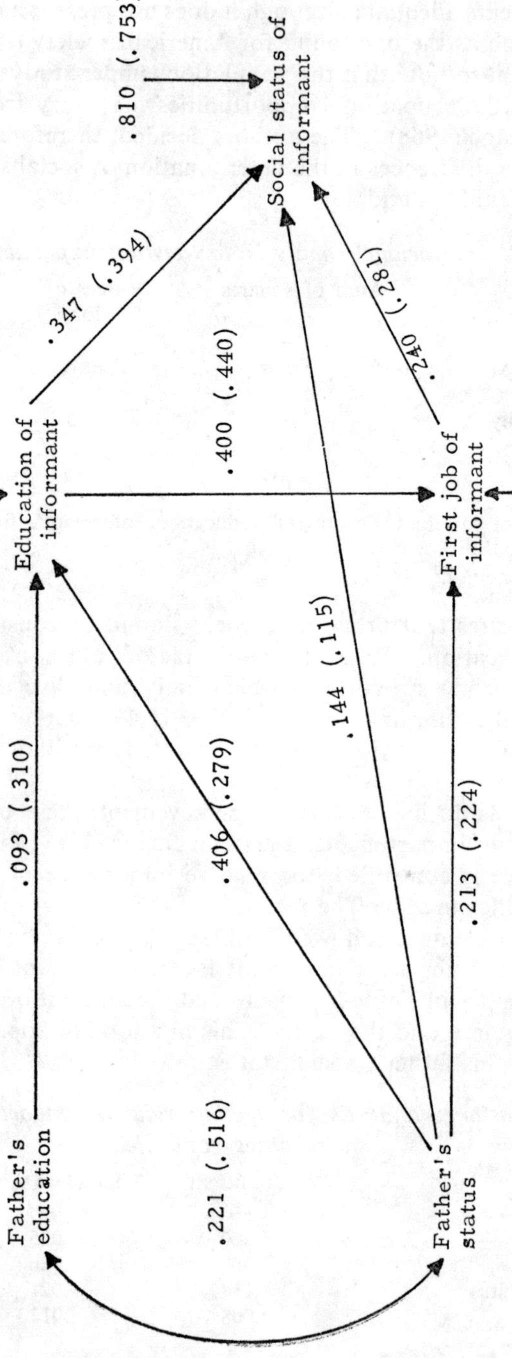

*The coefficients in parenthesis refer to the American data (*cf.* Blau and Duncan, 1967, p. 170.)

The preceding analysis has assumed, of course, that all factors have direct effects on the achievement of status levels. In other words, the analysis has assumed no temporal sequence. The authors decided to use the path analysis model in order 1) to ascertain the direct and indirect effects of the factors, and 2) to compare as closely as possible the patterns of status achievement in the United States with those in Brazil.

Figure 1 indicates the system of relationships among the five variables [2]. The different coefficients are presented for the Brazilian data; analogous coefficients for American data, taken from Blau and Duncan (1967, p. 170), are given in parenthesis to facilitate comparisons. For purposes of presentation, the authors will discuss initially results for Brazil and then compare the results of the model with that of the United States.

In the model for Brazil, Figure 1 shows that the residual of present occupational status is still large (.810) [3]. The amount of variation left unexplained for the education (.900) of the informant and that of his first job (.850) are greater than the amount of unexplained variation of his present status. In Figure 1, it can be noted that education is the single most important determinant of social status (.347), followed by first job (.240) and finally father's status (.144). Education, however, influences individual's first job more than it affects the last job he holds. The informant's education is largely determined by his father's status rather than by the level of education the father attains. Father's social status is more important in determining directly the son's education (.406) than it is in influencing the son's first job (.213). Finally, father's education is only slightly correlated with father's social status (.221), a relationship which is much lower than that between son's education and son's social status (.518) [4].

When the coefficients based on American data are compared with those for Brazil, as can be seen in Figure 1, certain salient features appear. Generally, the model predicts social status of the informant, his education and his first job better in the American than in the Brazilian society. Regarding the prediction of son's status, education and first job of the informant are more

2. Figure 1 is presented here to facilitate the interpretations involved in the path technique and to indicate explicitly the assumptions made regarding the temporal order of factors related to the dependent variable. Once these assumptions are made, this technique shows the indirect and direct effects of antecedent factors on social status. The path connecting two asymmetrically related variables is indicated by a one-way arrow and a path coefficient. A correlation coefficient and a curved two-way arrow represent a relationship between variables that is given and, therefore, is not to be explained by the system. A residual is given for each dependent factor to account for the variance of that factor that is not explained by the system (*cf.* Duncan, 1966).

3. It was seen previously in Table 1 that the independent variables explained 34 percent of the total variance in statuses. Therefore, 81 percent of the variance remained unexplained. Residual $= \sqrt{1-R^2}$.

4. The latter figure is taken from the matrix of zero order correlations which are not presented here.

important in the United States, while father's status is more significant in Brazil. Concerning son's education, father's education predicts far better in the United States than in Brazil, where, however, father's social status is a better predictor than in the American society. Finally, son's first job is more highly associated with his educational attainment in the United States than in Brazil, while there is almost no difference for the two countries regarding the relationship between father's social status and son's first job.

Discussion and conclusions

A major finding of the present investigation is that the model derived from a mature industrial society fits relatively well the data from an industrializing country. This result contradicts general expectations that the mechanisms determining social status in a developing nation are different from those operating in an industrialized society.

The regularity found may be due to differential sampling procedures. It is possible that if the Brazilian data represented a more national sample, the coefficients found would be lower than those found in the present investigation. Since the information used here refers to an industrial segment of the society, the model used applies relatively well. In the discussion which follows, it should be noted that the authors are not referring to the total society but only to this specific region of the country.

The differences encountered in the comparison between the United States and Brazil can be explained in two ways, 1) differential measurement and, 2) differential stages of industrialization. The authors contend that while small differences in the models may be due to measurement error, the large differences noted cannot be so easily explained.

The major differences found are in the educational mechanism. Father's education, as stated above, does not have the same importance in Brazil as in the United States. On the other hand, father's social status is more important in Brazil. Father's social status predicts son's educational attainment and his last social status better in Brazil than in the United States. This finding suggests that in an industrializing society, the father's social status plays a more important role than does his educational background. The expansion of the educational system is a recent phenomenon in the Latin American country. It is not surprising then, that father's social status is more important than is his education in determining the son's achievements. In a society where the general level of education is low, it could be expected that educational level of the parental generation would also be low. Thus, this variable does not play as important a role as it does in an industrial society. This finding tends to support the general expectation that in a developing society an individual's social position is more important than is his education.

The model suggests that while the mechanisms for achieving a given social status in an industrializing society are generally the same as those in a developed nation, differences can be noted. Industrialization involves an increasing emphasis on status achievement, primarily in terms of educational attainment, and a decreasing stress on ascribed status, as determined by parental characteristics. The authors contend that for the next generation of Brazilians, father's social status will be less important while his education will become more significant for his son's social status.

Taking into consideration the methodological differences between the Brazilian and American research, the present investigation demonstrates a remarkable similarity between an industrial society and an industrializing nation. This result suggests that the mechanisms determining an individual's social status are basically the same and that they will become more nearly identical as the processes of industrialization advance in Brazil. The close parallel between the Brazilian and American data perhaps points to a hierarchy of occupations that is said to be common to many nations and to be associated particularly with the process of industrialization (Inkeles and Rossi, 1956; Hodge *et al.*, 1966). Modernization may invariably produce not only similar hierarchies of occupational prestige but also similar avenues for the achievement of these occupational statuses. Future research can ascertain whether the more advanced stages of industrialization in Brazil result in an even stronger correspondence between that Latin American nation and the United States regarding the determinants of social status.

REFERENCES

Balan, E. Jelin de; Balan, J.; Browning, H.L.
1967 *Mobilidad social, migración y fecundidad en Monterrey Metropolitano.* Monterrey, Centro de investigaciones económicas de la Universidad de Nuevo León.

Blalock, H.M., Jr.
1964 *Causal inferences in nonexperimental research.* Chapel Hill, NC, University of North Carolina Press.

Blau, P.M.; Duncan, O.D.
1967 *The American occupational structure.* New York, John Wiley.

Broom, L.; Lancaster Jones, F.
1969 "Career mobility in three societies: Australia, Italy and the United States. "*American sociological review* 34, oct.: 650-658.

Carlsson, G.
1958 *Social mobility and class structure.* Lund, Gleerup.

Duncan, O.D.
1966 "Path analysis: Sociological examples", *American journal of sociology* 72, jul.: 1-16.

Fox, T.; Miller, S.M.
1966 "Occupational stratification and mobility", pp. 574-581 in: R. Bendix; S.M. Lipset (eds.). *Class, status and power* (2nd ed.). New York, Free Press.

Glass, D.
1954 *Social mobility in Britain.* London, Routledge and Kegan Paul.

Hodge, R.W.; Treiman, D.J.; Rossi, P.H.
1966 "A comparative study of occupational prestige", pp. 309-321 in: R. Bendix; S.M. Lipset (eds.). *Class, status and power.* New York, Free Press.

Hutchinson, B.
1960 *Mobilidad e trabalho.* Rio de Janeiro, Centro Brasileiro de Pesquisas Educacionais.

Inkeles, A.; Rossi, P.H.
1956 "National comparisons of occupational prestige", *American journal of sociology* 61, jan.: 329-339.

Iutaka, S.
1965 "Social stratification research in Latin America", *Latin American research review* 1 Fall: 7-34.

Lane, A.
1968 "Occupational mobility in six cities", *American sociological review* 33, oct.: 740-749.

Lipset, S.M.; Bendix, R.
1959 *Social mobility in industrial society.* Berkeley, Calif., University of California Press.

Miller, S.M.
1969 "Comparative social mobility", pp. 325-340 in: C.S. Heller (ed.). *Structured social inequality.* New York, Macmillan.

Pfautz, H.W.
1953 "The current literature on social stratification: Critique and bibliography", *American journal of sociology* 58, jan.: 391-418.

Rogoff, N.
1953 *Recent trends in occupational mobility.* New York, Free Press.

Svalastoga, K.
1959 *Prestige, class and mobility.* Copenhagen, Gyldendal.

WALTER MÜLLER

Family background, education and career mobility*

Studies in social mobility support almost universally the thesis that in intergenerational succession sons are most likely to attain positions of social status similar to those of their fathers. Differences in findings arise when the processes and mechanisms underlying the traditional intergenerational mobility tables are questioned more closely. One of the main problems here is to grasp the role of the school system in perpetuating inequalities of opportunities from one generation to the other. Not much has changed since Fox and Miller (1965, p. 80) described the situation : " Most sociologists engaged in mobility studies agree that education is an asset to the upwardly mobile, but there is no agreement on the relative importance of education." Allowing some rather broad categories we can divide this research area into two main approaches:

First, several studies use a two step model of more or less formalized matrix-transformations for studying the transitions from father's occupational status to son's education and from son's education to son's occupational status. The researcher is mainly interested in explaining different rates of mobility by differences in educational attainment or by differences in types of educational opportunities available in the school system. The main studies in this tradition are those of Carlsson (1958), Anderson (1961) and Boudon (1970, 1971).

The second approach, which is also our line of interest, is based on the multiple regression technique. It was introduced into this field by Duncan and Hodge (1963) and promoted particularly by path analytic models in Blau and Duncan's study of the American occupational structure (1967). Blau and Duncan refer to the ascription-achievement-typology of stratification systems and intend to submit "measurements and estimations of the strength of ascriptive forces and of the scope of opportunities in a large contemporary

* Part 1 of this article is a modified version of an article published in German: "Bildung und Mobilitätsprozess: Eine Anwendung der Pfadanalyse", *Zeitschrift für Soziologie* 1 (1), 1972, pp. 65-84. The author wishes to thank Richard Grathoff for his very helpful review of the English translation which considerably improved the text.

society'' (Blau and Duncan, 1967, pp. 163-164). The authors describe the governing conceptual scheme as follows:

''We think of the individual's life cycle as a sequence in time that can be described, however partially and crudely, by a set of classificatory or quantitative measurements taken at successive stages [...] Given this scheme, the questions we are continually raising in one form or another are: how and to what degree do the circumstances of birth condition subsequent status? and, how does status attained (whether by ascription or achievement) at one stage of the life cycle affect the prospects for a subsequent stage?'' (Blau and Duncan, 1967, p. 164).

Subsequently, the basic path model developed by Blau and Duncan has been applied to data gathered in several other countries. The coefficients estimated in the American study have already been compared with those based on Australian (Lancaster Jones, 1970), Czechoslovakian (Safar, 1970), and Brazilian data (Iutaka, 1972). For the German context a comparative study has not been made yet. This is, however not our primary goal, since several basic methodological questions concerning those previous studies have come to our attention.

In the first part of this study we analyse more specifically the impact of the education process on the occupational career. This will lead to several modifications of the original Blau and Duncan model. In part 2, we question the assumption that the influences of the familial origin on the attainments of sons can be satisfactorily accounted for by the socio-economic status variables of father's education and father's occupation. A summary estimate of additional familial influences will be presented in order to indicate the distorting effect of these influences on the coefficients of simple path models. It will be shown that a more complete account of the whole family background and its effects changes considerably the weight assigned to the independent influence of education on later occupational attainment.

The data used in this report were collected in 1969 by interviewing the age cohort of all male inhabitants of Konstanz [1], born in 1936 or in the first three months of 1937 (N = 398). The age cohort of 33-year old males has been chosen for two reasons: firstly, the subjects of the study were to have already reached an advanced stage in their occupational career at the time of the interview, and secondly, their earlier occupational career should be influenced as little as possible by the abnormal situation of the German labor market in the war- and immediate post-war-period [2]. Operationally, the variables

1. The town of Konstanz has 60 000 inhabitants. The occupational structure of Konstanz can be characterized as follows:

a. An above average percentage of employees and small proprietors in the service sector;
d. Above average proportion of people employed in public administration;
c. An electronic industry which has grown rapidly in the last ten years, employing highly qualified technical, administrative and research personnel;
b. A relatively high proportion of young university staff.

2. To what extent the pattern of intergenerational mobility in the particular population of our sample is comparable to the pattern of a more comprehensive sample of the West German society is shown in the article by Mayer and myself (1971). In the latter, we compare occupational status inheritance in the sample of Konstanz with occupational status

used in the following models are defined as follows: the occupational status of fathers is measured according to the five-point occupational prestige scale of Kleining and Moore (1968). In regard to father's status, the information used refers to his highest occupation held after the war or (if deceased during the war) the one held before the war started. The status of son's first occupation and of son's occupation at age 33 are likewise measured in terms of Kleining and Moore's scale. Father's education is defined by the number of years of schooling and formal occupational training. Various measurements of son's education will be described in the following exposition.

1. The structure of the education-occupation sequence

The model originally introduced by Blau and Duncan includes five variables: father's education, father's occupation, son's education, son's first occupation and son's occupation at the time of interview. It presupposes a temporal order within the sequence of these five variables. The authors point out, however, that for "an appreciable minority of respondents" (Blau and Duncan, 1967, p. 167) the sequence of son's education — son's occupation is reversed. In this case, people return to school after a shorter or longer period of occupational activity and only then do they reach their highest level of education, to which refers the operational definition of the variable. Obviously, this is inconsistent with the assumption of a non-recursive causal model. Blau and Duncan recognize this problem, but their data rule out its solution.

"Our assumption here is, in effect, that 'first job' has a uniform significance for all men in terms of its temporal relationship to educational preparation and subsequent work experience. If this assumption is not strictly correct, we doubt that it could be improved by substituting any other *single* measure of initial status" (Blau and Duncan, 1967, p. 168).

But is there no other way to solve this difficulty? We met with the same problem in our sample, where 61 % of the respondents received some kind of education after having worked for more than one year in some regular employment which they described as their first occupation. If the assumption of a non-recursive model is to be upheld, the simple order of son's education — son's first occupation can no longer be maintained under such conditions. We shall not follow the suggestion of Blau and Duncan who think to solve

inheritance found in a quota sample of Germany (GFR) by the Institut für Demoskopie Allensbach (1969). In more than twenty single comparisons of association between father's occupation and son's occupation no significant difference in the two setsof data was found. Sewell *et al.* (1970) compared path models including such variables as socio-economic origin, educational and occupational attainment for different sizes of community of residence, and in this study, too, only very small differences between various sizes of community could be found. These studies both support the assumption that in a path-analysis of variables such as social origin, educational and occupational attainment a sample of the West German society at large would probably produce results rather similar to those found in the data on Konstanz.

the problem by means of various measures of *initial occupational status* [3]. We propose to study instead changes of the model parameters which can be observed when the operational definition of *son's education* is varied. Hence, we shall first compare two models: the first one considers only the education attained before entering the labor market, the second includes also educational activities thereafter (adult education). We shall then compare the career of persons who had at least some adult education with those without such training. Finally, adult education will be introduced as an intervening variable into an enlarged model of the mobility process. In such a manner, we shall successively learn how different elements of the educational process are reflected in the coefficients of the model.

The "pre-employment education" model

As a first step, son's education is measured by the number of years of formal schooling and formal occupational training [4] completed before entering the first occupation. The scores range from 6 to 18. Educational efforts after the first occupation are excluded from consideration. As to the correlation coefficients in Table 1, the coefficients in row 3 and in column 3 relate to this

Table 1. *Zero order correlation coefficients between five status variables with two different operational definitions of son's education*

		X_1	X_2	X_3	X_3*	X_4
X_1	Father's education					
X_2	Father's occupation	.52				
X_3	Son's pre-employment education	.40	.47			
X_3*	Son's total education	.42	.50	.91		
X_4	Son's first occupation	.39	.42	*.86*	.76	
X_5	Son's occupation at age 33	.40	.48	.71	*.78*	.71

3. We define first occupation as the first occupation held after entry into the labor force. The point of entry into the labor force is that moment at which an individual leaves full-time education and enters the labor force for a period of more than one full year without re-entering full-time education during that period. Apprenticeships and the like are considered as part of the educational period. This definition is similar to the one used by Rossi and Ornstein and has been developed on the basis of criteria similar to those proposed by these authors (see p. 281 below).

4. Formal occupational training includes apprenticeships, vocational training courses and the like. In our sample, 60 % of the subjects have had such training. Since also systematic theoretical knowledge is obtained in an apprenticeship, we shall consider this stage of a career as part of the education. Additional reasons for including formal occupational training in the definition of education are given in the following footnote.

Figure 1. *The pre-employment education model : path coefficients in basic model of five variables**

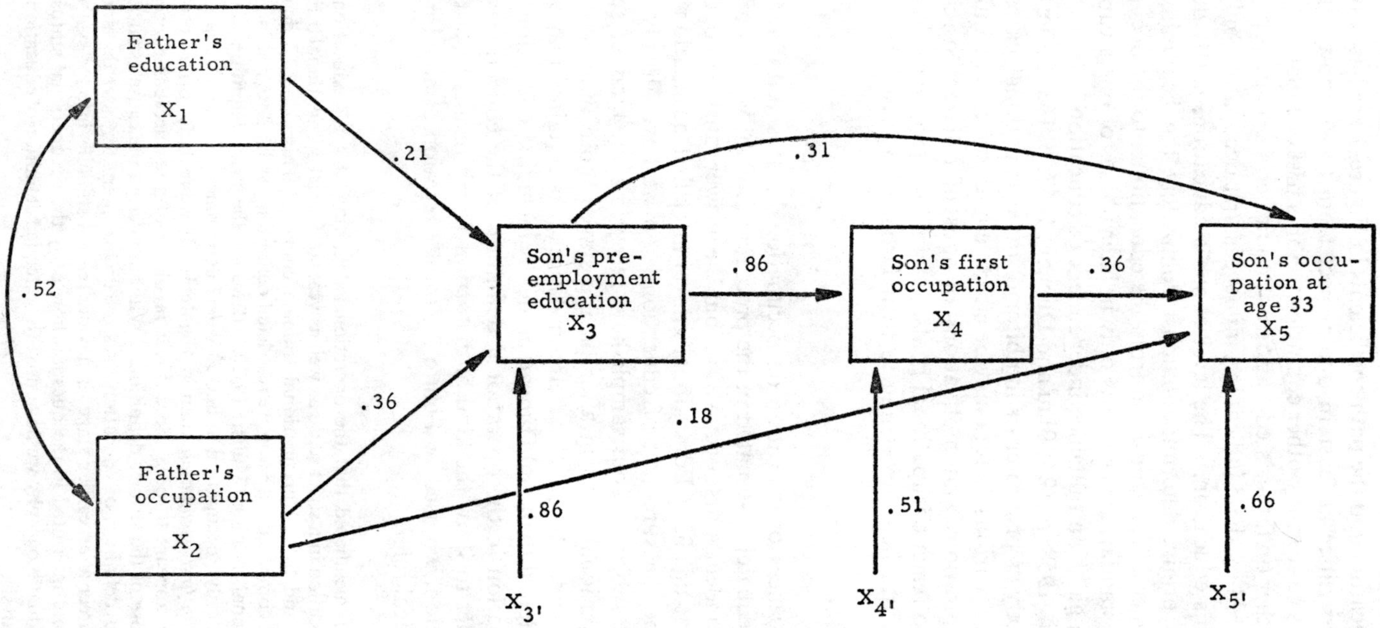

*The operational definition of education is: number of years of school and formal occupational training before first occupation.

definition of education and the path coefficients in Figure 1 are based on them. These coefficients differ at least in one respect from those known from the respective studies concerning other countries. Son's first occupation is directly dependent neither on father's education nor on father's occupation. Social origin (as measured by these indicators) influences first occupation only as it is mediated by son's education. The level of son's education, partly determined by his social origin, determines almost completely the beginning of the occupational career. The transition from the educational to the occupational system is highly standardized [5]. It is only in later phases of one's career that the social origin gains an influence independent of education. In a "delayed effect" (Carlsson, 1958, p. 127; Blau and Duncan, 1967, p. 168) father's occupation acts directly as promoter or inhibitor of the occupational career of his son ($p_{52} = .18$). Various factors may be effective in this respect: differential occupational aspirations and motivations of sons of different origin, their varying ability to reach occupational goals, paternal protection or, in the case of self-employment, their succeeding to their father's business.

The "total-education" model

But are the influences of education on occupational status at different stages of the career adequately estimated in the preceding model? We can affirm the case of the respondent's first occupation, but the answer must be no, concerning occupation at age 33. Educational efforts after first occupation are not considered in the measurement of education. As we have already pointed out, 61 % of the subjects in our sample have received some kind of schooling or formal occupational training after having stayed more than one year in regular employment. Under these circumstances it is certainly inappropriate to rely on the original Blau and Duncan model by including educational efforts after first occupation in the operational definition of the education variable. However, in order to show the kind of distortion which results from this definition of education, we used in Figure 2 "total education attained until age 33" as its empirical referent.

5. It should be remembered that the operational definition of son's education includes years of school education in a strict sense as well as years of formal occupational training such as apprenticeships and formal occupational training courses. This extended definition of education has been compared with a more restricted definition, which does not include years of formal occupational training (Müller, 1972). If we use the strict definition of education (years of schooling only), occupation at age 33 is *less* determined directly *by son's education* but depends *more on first occupation* than in Figure 1. If we include formal occupational training, education appears to be a more direct predictor of the succeeding occupational positions than in case of the stricter definition. Without altering the causal structure of the model the extended definition of education fixes the crucial point for later developments in the occupational career at an earlier stage: in a wider sense it still falls into the system of education. Since we are interested in the question how early the occupational status is determined in the individual biography we have used the extended definition of education throughout our present analysis.

Figure 2. *The total education model: path coefficients in model with five variables**

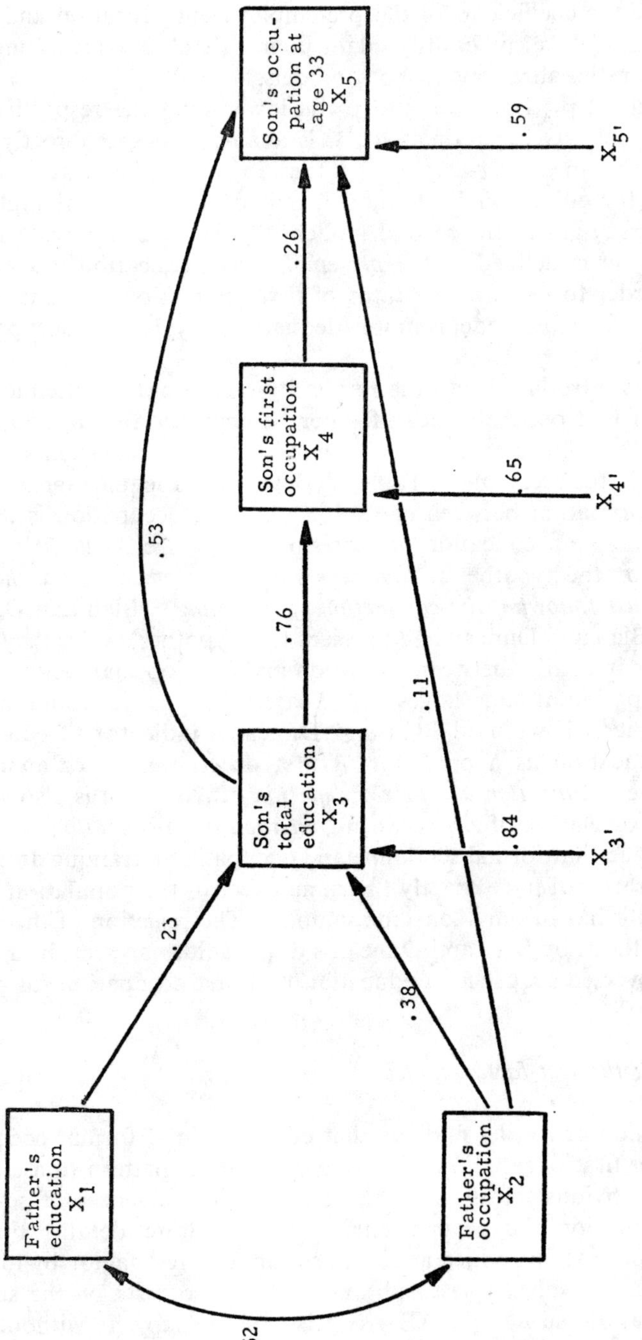

* The operational definition of education is: number of years of school and formal occupational training until age 33.

If we compare the coefficients of the pre-employment education and of the total education model we can easily explain their differences as resulting from the different operationalizations in both models.

In the first model p_{43} is higher and p_{53} is lower than the respective path in the second model. Occupation at age 33 is to a *lesser* degree directly determined by education in the *pre-employment* than in the *total* education model. But controlling for educational attainment, first occupation is of higher influence in the first than in the second model. These figures agree with the fact that education is defined in the *pre-employment* education model more adequately in order to explain the status of *first* occupation, while its definition in the *total education* model is more adequate for explaining occupational *status at age 33.*

The distortions introduced into the results by regarding "total education" as a predictor of first occupation can further be demonstrated by looking at the zero order correlation coefficients. The undistorted coefficients are the ones underlined in the rectangle of Table 1. Using the adequate measures for education the correlation between education and first occupation is .86 and the correlation between education and occupation at age 33 is .78. These coefficients support the hypothesis "*that education is most important at the stage of one's career just following the completion of schooling*" (Blau and Duncan, 1967, p. 180). Blau and Duncan had to reject this hypothesis since they found a slightly lower correlation between education and first job than between education and occupation at later stages of the career, just as we would have to reject the hypothesis if we used Blau and Duncan's indicator of education. Taking total education as a predictor of first occupation gives an overall correlation between *education and first occupation* of .76 which is also slightly lower than the correlation of .78 between *education and occupation* at age 33. We shall not argue that formal schooling and occupational training during the occupational career will have exactly the same effect in the population of the United States as it has in our Konstanz sample. The rejection of the abovementioned hypothesis by Blau and Duncan's data could, however, be a consequence of the reversed sequence of education and first occupation for part of their sample.

Adult education: the test-factor model

What should follow from the findings that education and formal occupational training after first occupation affect the correlation pattern to a considerable degree? Obviously it is advisable to study the influences of so-called "adult education" on the occupational career in more detail. For this purpose we propose to introduce adult education as a test factor by dividing our sample into two subsamples: subsample AE+ consists of the subjects with adult education, subsample AE— consists of the subjects without adult education.

Table 2. *Zero order correlation coefficients between five status variables. The sample is divided in two subsamples. 1st row : subjects without adult education (subsample AE—). 2nd row : subjects with adult education (subsample AE+).*

		X_1	X_2	X_3	X_4
X_1	Father's education	.56			
X_2	Father's occupation	.49			
X_3	Son's pre-employment education	.53 .29	.63 .34		
X_4	Son's first occupation	.58 .23	.65 .22	.91 .80	
X_5	Son's occupation at age 33	.53 .30	.65 .32	.84 .60	.89 .54

Table 2 shows the correlation matrices for both subsamples. In subsample AE— all correlations are higher than in subsample AE+. Thus we find a much stronger relationship between the individual stages of the mobility process (social origin, education, first occupation and occupation at age 33) for persons who do not participate in adult education than for those who had received such training.

The same holds true in a comparison of the corresponding coefficients in Figure 3. With the exception of the direct effect of son's education on occupation at age 33 the individual stages of the mobility process are generally determined *to a higher degree* by the specified variables for the subjects *without* than for the subjects *with* adult education. The career of non participants corresponds clearly to the pattern of direct determination of each successive step by the previous one. On the other hand, for subjects with adult education, especially their first occupation is of low predictive value for their occupation at age 33. It is between these occupational positions that the subjects in subsample AE+ had some form of adult education. This intervening variable explains why the coefficient between the two career stages in subsample AE+ is about 1/3 of the value in subsample AE—. But even before adult education intervenes, the career of the non-participants is more strongly determined than the career of the participants. As other data not presented here show and as we shall also see below, subjects beginning their career with high education and with a high first occupational status are less likely to take up adult education (*i.e.* they are prevalent in subsample AE—). These subjects starting from a high level also generally have high status parents who are particularly successful in transmitting their advantageous status to their sons. This conclusion is suggested by the higher coefficients from both origin status variables to son's

Figure 3. *Adult education, the test-factor model. Path coefficients in model with five variables*. The sample is divided into two sub-samples. AE—: subjects without adult education (underlined coefficients); AE+ : subjects with adult education***

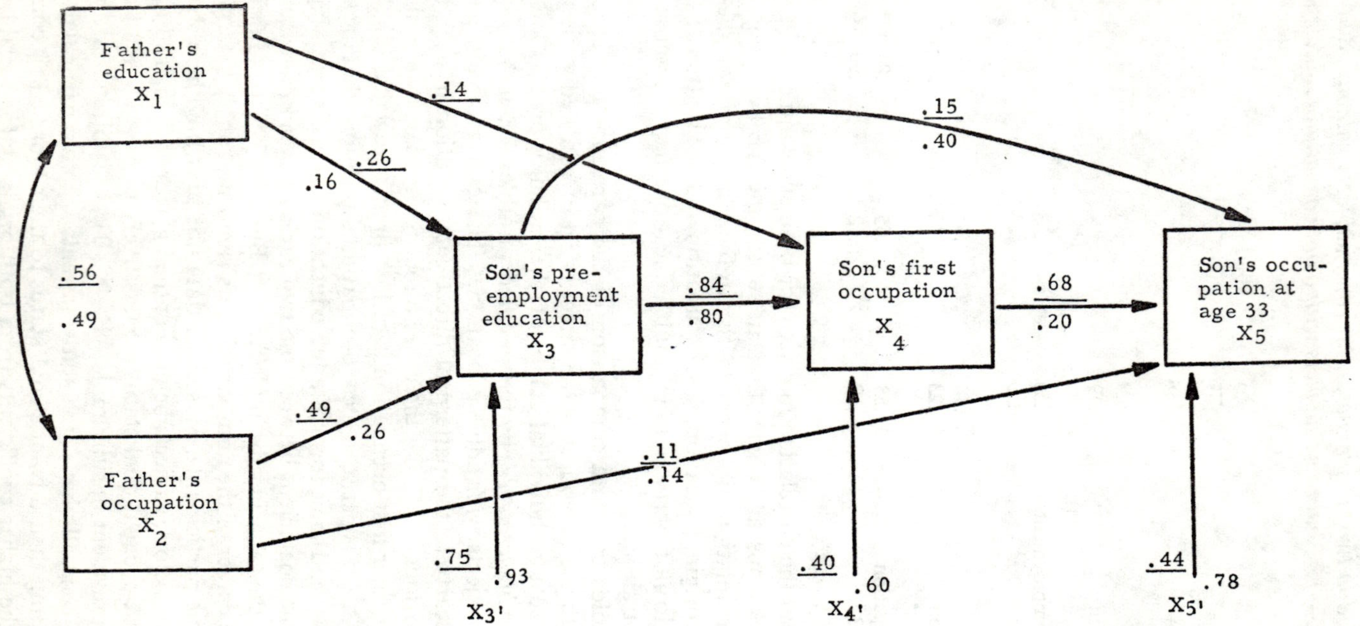

* The operational definition of education is: number of years of school and formal occupational training before first occupation.

** In sub-sample AE+, p_{41} is assumed zero, since its value lies below the limit of .10, which was set as a condition for a path to be considered in the model.

education and son's first occupation in the subsample AE—. Most subjects in subsample AE+ do not start under such favourable conditions. But a comparison of the residuals in both subsamples reveals that the careers of the latter are relatively open. *Adult education may help* these subjects *to improve their occupational status.*

The "two-phase education model" (the whole sample)

In an attempt to test this hypothesis we shall introduce adult education [6] as an intervening variable between first occupation and occupation at age 33. We shall consider the process of education as occurring in two phases: pre-employment education in the phase before first occupation and adult education in the phase thereafter. The assumed structure of dependency corresponds to the temporal sequence of the variables and is shown in Figure 4.

In commenting upon the different coefficients [7] let us first turn our attention to the determination of occupation at age 33. Controlling for the preceding variables we find as the highest direct effect the path from first occupation (p_{64} = .50). This value, however, may cause one to overestimate the total positive effect of the initial occupational status, since first occupation is in rather strong negative relation to adult education (p_{54} = —.45). Therefore the indirect effect from first occupation via adult education is also negative (—.45) (.30) = —.14. Adding this value to the corresponding direct effect gives .36 as numerical estimate for the influence of first occupation on occupation at age 33.

In comparison with this value, the direct effect of adult education on occupation at age 33 (p_{65} = .30) is only slightly lower and may therefore be considered relatively strong. Controlling for influences of origin status, preceding education and occupational status, adult education determines 9 % of the total variance of occupation at age 33 [8]. Hence the negative relationship between first occupation and adult education strongly emphasizes the function of adult

6. The operational definition of adult education is number of years of school education and/or vocational training courses followed and/or formal occupational training undergone by the respondent once he has entered his first occupation.

7. Figure 4 should especially be compared with Figure 1 since it differs concerning its structure and measurement of variables from Figure 1 only as to the additionally intervening variable of adult education. All paths in Figure 1 leading directly to occupation at age 33 are split up in Figure 5 into a changed direct effect to occupation at age 33 and an indirect effect mediated by adult education. For instance, the direct path from education, which is .31 in Figure 1, splits up in Figure 4 into a new direct effect (p_{63} = .22) and an indirect effect via adult education: (.30) (.30) = .09. The sum of both effects in Figure 4 corresponds to the direct effect in Figure 1.

8. The value of 9 % variance explained by adult education can be found by comparing the square of the residuals on occupation at age 33 in Figure 1 and in Figure 6. In Figure 1, which does not include adult education, 44 % of the variance of occupation at age 33 remains unexplained by the variable specified in the model, whereas in Figure 5 the unexplained variance is only 35 %.

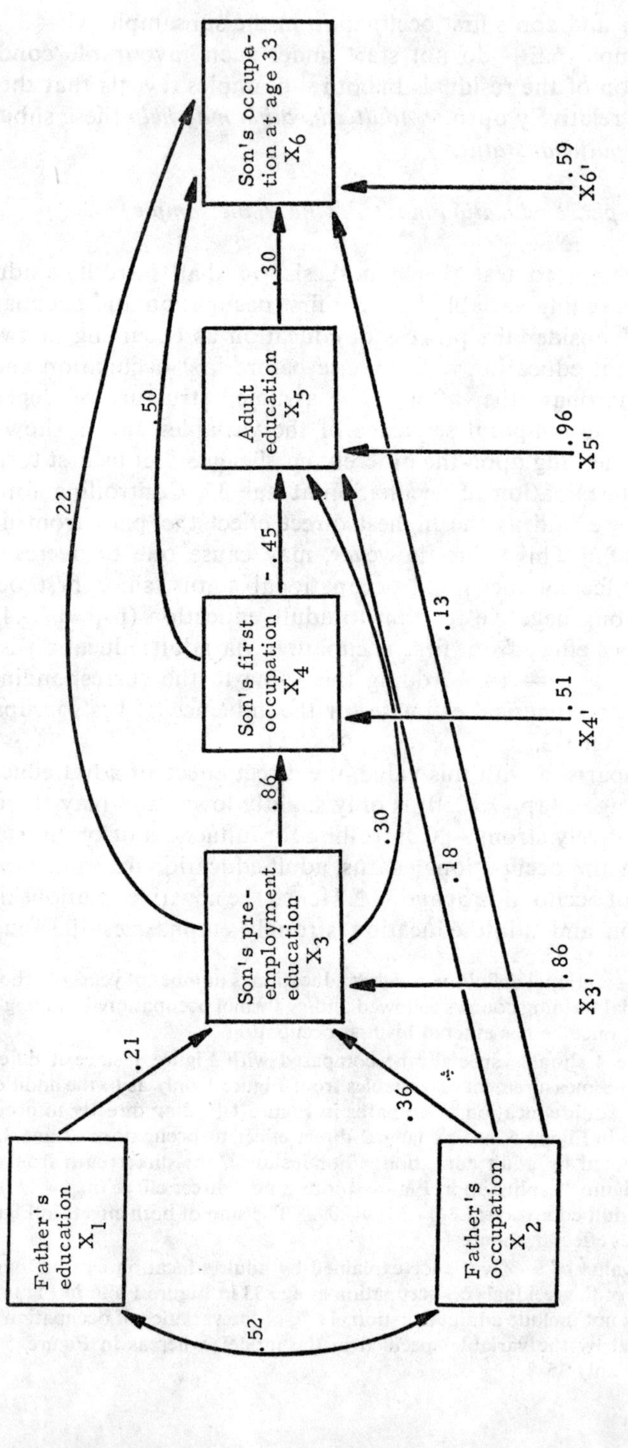

Figure 4. The two-phase education model (the whole sample). Path coefficients in model with six variables, all subjects included

education as a *counter*-acting mechanism. Persons starting worklife in occupational positions of lower status (mainly sons of lower status parents) are shown to improve their status by means of adult education in the course of their career.

A closer examination of Figure 4 reveals several additional findings which are of no less interest. In contrast to the negative path from son's first occupation we find positive coefficients for the paths from father's occupation and pre-employment education to adult education. Let me quote here from a letter from Keith Hope interpreting these figures :

"At a given level of first occupation, those with more education go in for more adult education whereas, at a given level of education, those who get a better job go in for less adult education [...] Leaving aside father's occupation for the moment, the diagram shows that the difference between, or balance of, initial occupational status and education determines take up of adult education opportunities. Those who get a relatively good job for their education do not undertake adult education, and those who get a not so good job go in for adult education. One may now interpret the direct path from father's occupation [...] to adult education as a compensatory mechanism which indicates that, at a given level of educational attainment and initial occupational status, father's status can intervene to promote adult education. It is clear, however, that intervention of father's status via adult education is less important than intervention which bypasses all intermediaries and acts directly on occupation at age 33."[9]

However, the influences of the temporally preceding variables on adult education should not be overstressed. Taken together the effect of social origin status, of education before first employment, and of initial occupational status explain only 10 % of the variance of adult education[10]. This very low determination clearly contrasts, for instance, with pre-employment education, where 26 % of the variance is explained by the indicators of social origin status. Thus it would be particularly interesting for further research to find the major determinants for participating in adult education which has been shown to have a strong influence on men's chances of advancement.

The "two-phase education model" (the reduced sample)

An important assumption in path analysis is the linear relationship between the variables. This presupposition has not been encountered in the last model studied above. Subjects who attained the highest status score in first occu-

9. It may be interesting to go back to the "pre-employment education" model (Figure 1) at this point. We had found there that father's education influences his son's career chiefly by providing differential access to educational opportunities and affects it to a smaller degree only in a more direct way. Now we find that the "delayed" effect in the pre-employment education model is also partly mediated through an "education variable". Its numerical value of .18 in Figure 1 is split up in Figure 4 in a reduced direct effect of .13 and an indirect effect via adult education of the size $(.18) \times (.30) = .05$.

10. The residual path $p_{55}' = 1 - R^2_{5\cdot 1234} = .96$. The proportion of variance of variable 5 explained by the variables 1 to 4 thus is .10.

pation are not in a position to improve their status through further educational efforts. At best they may maintain the highest score on the status scale. This ceiling effect introduces non-linearity into the relations between first occupation, adult education and occupation at age 33[11]. In order to eliminate this effect of non-linearity in the following, we shall exclude from consideration all subjects who reached with their first occupation the highest possible status (score 5). The correlations for the whole sample are contrasted in Table 3 with the correlations for the reduced sample which consists only of respondents whose first occupation was given score 1-4 on the status scale.

Table 3. *Zero order correlation coefficients between 6 variables.*
1st row: all subjects are included; 2nd row: only subjects included given score 1-4 on first occupation

		X_1	X_2	X_3	X_4	X_5
X_1	Father's education					
X_2	Father's occupation	.52 .46				
X_3	Son's pre-employment education	.40 .30	.47 .39			
X_4	Son's first occupation	.39 .28	.42 .30	.86 .72		
X_5	Son's adult education	.08 .17	.14 .21	.01 .18	-.11 .04	
X_6	Son's occupation at age 33	.40 .32	.48 .41	.71 .56	.71 .55	.27 .47

Except for the correlations with adult education all correlations in the reduced sample (second line of each panel) are smaller than the corresponding correlations in the whole sample (first line of each panel). Hence, excluding the respondents beginning their career at the highest occupational level, social origin and the single career stages are less interconnected than if all respondents are considered. Only adult education is in contrast with this general pattern. Disregarding the respondents scoring highest on first occupation, the correlations between adult education and all other variables are higher than for the whole sample.

11. Respondents given the highest status score for first occupation have generally graduated from university and given the conditions of our educational system have reached a ceiling implying rather low probability of attending later educational institutions.

Figure 5. *The two-phase education model (the reduced sample). Path coefficients in model with six variables. Only subjects given score 1-4 on first occupation included*

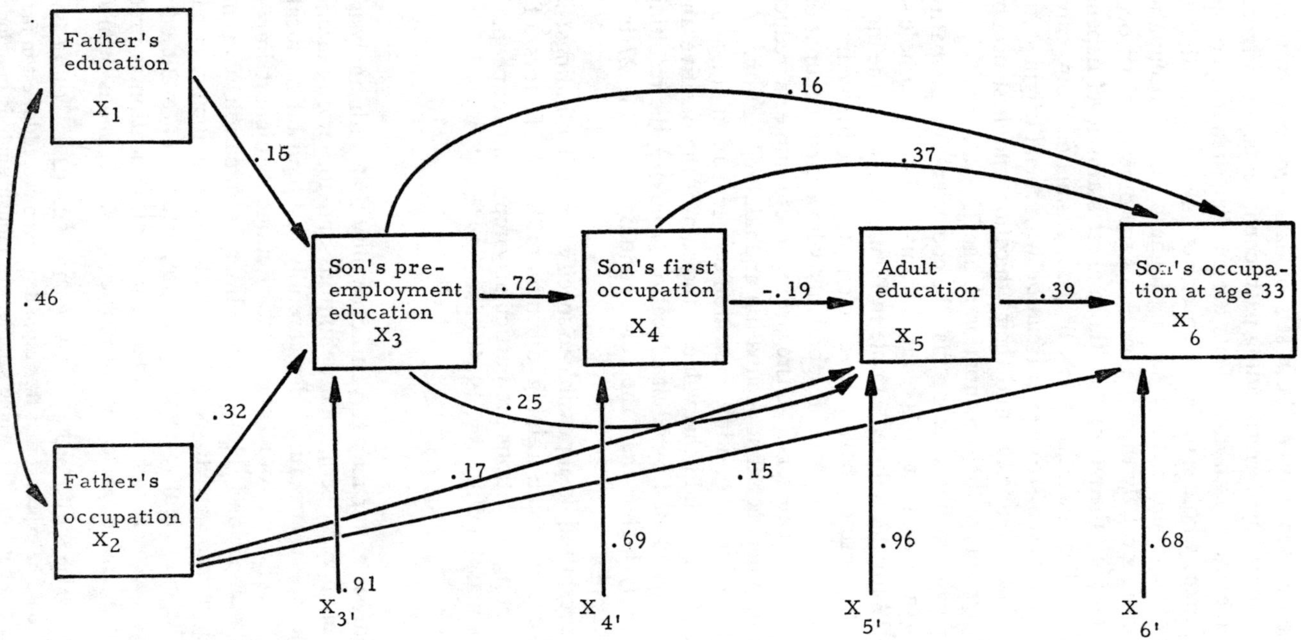

The difference between both sets of data becomes even more pronounced if we compare the corresponding path coefficients. In Figure 5 for the reduced sample most path coefficients are smaller than the corresponding coefficients for the whole sample. Hence, we may conclude that the career of the subjects excluded (*i.e.* those scoring highest on first occupation) is pre-determined more strongly than the career of the others. First occupation of subjects beginning their career at the highest status level depends in particular on their earlier education (most of them graduated from universities). Their education shows a stronger correlation with social origin status than the education of other subjects, and their education and first occupation determine to a higher degree their occupation at age 33.

It is particularly interesting that the coefficient for the path from first occupation to adult education is reduced from —.45 for the whole sample in Figure 4 to —.19 for the reduced sample in Figure 5. Thus, the high negative coefficient in the case of the whole sample results essentially from the low rate of adult education of those respondents whose first occupation falls into the highest status category. Disregarding these subjects reduces the negative relationship between first occupation and adult education. At the same time, the direct influence of adult education on occupation at age 33 increases from .30 to .39. If we add this value to the sum of the positive and negative indirect effects mediated by adult education (=.09) [12], the resulting score of .48 is considerably higher than the corresponding value of .27 in the case of the whole sample.

These results make it possible to specify our earlier findings: education and/or formal occupational training during worklife as factors of equalizing unequal starting conditions are particularly important for people belonging to the "middle mass" (Wilensky, 1964) of society [13].

Discussion

Our analysis so far may serve to exemplify that path analysis is rather sensitive to changing operational definitions and to varying assumptions concerning the causal structure. By carefully distinguishing education before and during worklife we found that education has its highest impact on the status of *first* occupation. However, a closer examination of a model, which at first glance appeared to be self-evident and convincing, produced a number of results consistently stressing the importance of adult education as well. The career of men not participating in adult education is predetermined to a higher degree than the career of participants. This has been shown to be the

12. This value is calculated as (—.19) (.39) + (.25) (.39) + (.17) (.39) = .09.

13. It could be expected that the respondents who scored lowest in first occupation differ also considerably from the whole sample. In tabular analysis one finds in fact that these respondents also are less engaged in adult education than people in higher status categories. Excluding them from the calculations in path analysis, however, brings only small differences in the correlation and path coefficients from calculations with the whole sample.

consequence of a rather complex network of causes. Sons of high status parents are found predominantly among the non-participants. These parents are particularly successful in providing their sons with higher education, allowing the latter to begin their occupational career in high status positions. Sons of less privileged parents find themselves in less favorable starting conditions. A considerable number of the latter try to improve their situation by adult education. In many cases this way is arduous, but not without rewards. Educational success during an occupational career depends less on the conditions of social origin than does success in the school system prior to entering first occupation. Since adults live at a greater distance from their family of orientation than children or adolescents, their success in education is less influenced by environmental factors of social origin.

It has further been shown clearly that adult education is rewarded in the later career by a better occupational position. Coleman *et al.* (1970, p. 40) report similar results in their Social Accounts Project. They examined a long series of events and activities between first job and the job held ten years later and found "that educational activity constitutes both for blacks and non-blacks the most important of these intervening events".

Our results may be compared with studies of an educational institution called "Zweiter Bildungsweg" in the German school system, which allows *adults* to reach the high school diploma of "Abitur" and hence to enter university. Students of working class origin are highly under-represented in these adult schools and are rather unsuccessful (*cf.* Zapf, 1971; Hamacher, 1968). The "Zweite Bildungsweg" serves mainly as a second chance for middle class students and has no effect on lessening educational discrimination. How can we explain this apparent contrast with our findings?

Most of our respondents participating in adult education attended institutions specializing in the improvement of occupational abilities (various courses in so-called "Fachschulen" and "Höhere Fachschulen"). These types of schools seem to be more adapted to level out inequalities of social origin than the "Zweite Bildungsweg". Lower class people seem to be particularly motivated to take part in such "occupation-related" education because of its immediate relevance for their daily activities.

As to the practical implications of these findings for mobility policies, they would appear to suggest that more possibilities for systematic, formal occupation-related training during the occupational career should be developed. Our conclusion is therefore in agreement with that of S.M. Miller *et al.* (1970):

> "And indeed that on-the-job-training and experience may prove a better way of developing many people than is the formal educational route [...] Three policy lines follow from this perspective. One is to reduce inappropriate educational requirements for jobs so that talented or developable persons with limited formal schooling would be able to obtain good jobs. The second is to develop routes to higher level jobs for those who have relatively little schooling. The third, connected with the second, is to build and expand a system of continuing education, connecting formal schooling with the education and development that takes place on the job."

2. The impact of the family background reconsidered

The models we have described in the preceding part of the paper yield a rather crude representation of the mobility process. One out of many objections may be stated as follows: if one of the objectives in mobility research is to estimate the total impact of the familial origin on later occupational status, then there is a distinct gap between the models used and the intentions of research. For instance the models consider family influence only in terms of father's educational and occupational status. Several studies, however, were able to improve considerably the theoretical explanation of the mobility process as well as the statistical estimation of the model parameters.

Duncan found that intelligence alone (16.4 %) accounts for at least as much variance in educational attainment as the number of siblings, father's education and father's occupation taken together (14.9 %), whereas intelligence and the three variables of family background jointly contribute 10.9 %.

Duncan *et al.* (1968) show a very high similarity between the determinants of own "ambition" and of peer's "ambition", the determinants of "ambition" being in both cases in decreasing importance: intelligence, own SES, (socio-economic status), parental aspiration and SES of peer. Furthermore, it has been found that the influence of own "ambition" on peer's "ambition" is the same as the influence in the opposite direction.

Besides tests of intelligence and grades in specific subjects the model of Hauser (1969) included school characteristics to interpret the influence of family background variables on educational and occupational aspirations.

Sewell *et al.* (1970) explain in terms of a path model how SES of origin and intelligence act on educational and occupational attainment through succeeding intervening variables such as academic performance, significant others, influence, level of educational aspiration and level of occupational aspiration.

How to measure all familial influences?

To the extent that variables such as family size, significant others' influence on aspiration and ambition, and even intelligence are correlated with the indicators of the family's status, their effects are taken into account in the models above. But surely not all familial influences are accounted for or mediated by the family's social status. As an example, we would take the intelligence factor, which influences later occupational status mainly by its effect on educational attainment. As Duncan (1968) has shown, one part of the variance of intelligence can indeed be accounted for by differences in the social status of the family. But another part will be determined by other familial traits as, for instance, by differences due to biological inheritance. Thus, controlling for the family's social status we should expect less variance in intelligence among siblings than among children of different families. But even controlling for social status and for all other familial influences, we shall find differences between single members of sibling groups. Only this remaining variance can be attributed to factors other than the specific conditions of birth and environment connected with living in a particular family.

We can paraphrase the problem in another way. Imagine two families A and B having the same scores on a social status scale. If in both families the family means of the scores in educational (or occupational) attainment of sons differ significantly, then this difference is to be attributed to the effect of family-specific influences, which are additional to the effect of factors already taken into account (social status of families). Take, for instance, educational attainment of sons as dependent variable. In this case, the additional family-specific influence could be given by the fact that the sons in family A receive a higher motivation than the sons in family B, or the sons in family A are more intelligent than the sons in family B. The differences between the two families may also be due to still other factors, single or combined, which influence equally the educational attainment of the sons of family A, but differently the sons of family B.

Let us return now to our data and consider not only two families but all families of the sample having at least two sons. We still keep the social status of the families constant. Assume that the family mean values, *e.g.* in educational attainment of the sons of each family, differ in such a way that the classification by families explains a significant amount of variance of all sons in all families. Then this part of the variance has to be taken as being the effect of all family-specific influences excluding the influence of the families' social status and all correlated effects of variables connected with social status. Assuming that the influence of the families' social status is the most important one, we control first for this effect. The effects of other family-specific factors represent then a kind of residual familial influence. We shall label it "family residual effect" (FR).

In the first part of the paper, our concern was with only one son in each family — the respondents of our sample. The perspective has shifted, meanwhile, to all sons of families in the sample having at least two sons. We want to find out whether by controlling for the family's social status the sons of a particular family tend to cluster around one family level, while the sons of other families cluster at other family levels. The more clustered the data, the higher is the FR-effect.

Since we also collected information on the educational and occupational attainment of all brothers of our respondents, we were able to calculate the contribution of FR to the total variance in educational and occupational attainment of all sons of the families considered. The statistical model applied is an analysis of variance of nested or hierarchical classifications with two classificatory levels: in the lowest level, the sons are classified according to the families they belong to. On the second level the families are classified according to the family's social status, indicated by father's education and father's occupational status (for a description of this model, *cf.* Snedecor and Cochran, 1968, pp. 291-294) [14].

As a result of this analysis we find the proportions of variance in sons' education [15] and sons' occupation which on the one hand are explained by father's education and his occupation and on the other by the FR-effect. The results are given in Table 4.

Table 4. *Proportions of variance explained by father's education and father's occupation and by the FR-effect in son's education and son's occupation*

Explaining variables		Explained variables: Son's education	Explained variables: Son's occupation
Proportion of total variance explained	Father's education and father's occupation (X_1X_2)	35 %	34 %
by	FR-variable ($FR.X_1X_2$)	23 %	25 %
Proportion of variance not explained		42 %	41 %

About a quarter of the total variance for both dependent variables, sons' education and sons' occupation, is explained by family differentiation in addition to influences due to the families' social status. Taking only father's education and father's occupation as indicators for an individual's familial origin, 35 % (respectively 34 %) of the total variance is explained. The total influence of the family on sons' education and sons' occupation, however, adds up to almost 60 %. Thus, family of origin determines the later educational and occupational status of sons to a considerably higher degree than one is led to believe, if possible influences of the family are seen only in terms of father's education and father's occupation.

How to interpret family residual effects?

A major shortcoming of the present analysis, however, is the fact that the FR-effect must be considered a black box. Without any further information

14. The status categories of families are the n × m combinations of n=3 scores of educational attainment of the father and m=5 prestige scores of father's occupation. Families classified together into one status category have thus simultaneously a common level of father's education and of father's occupation. Thus we control for father's education and father's occupation not in the same way as in the first part of the paper, but with a similar effect.

15. The operational definition of education corresponds to the definition of "total education" in the first part of the paper. Occupational attainment refers to the occupations of the respondents and their brothers at the time of interview. At this time the age of the brothers is above or below 33 years according to their sibling position.

we can merely state: FR is a residual effect including all those influences given by being part of a particular family and its environment, which are not accounted for by the indicators used to measure the family's social status. Dorrian A. Sweetser, to whom we are indebted for having been the first to apply the kind of analysis presented here, labels what we call FR "sibling group differentiation". The label is imaginative, since FR is a measure of influences upon educational or occupational attainments which bear equally on members of same sibling groups and differentially on different groups (families). We have avoided her label, since it could lead to the interpretation that the effect studied "is a group component, or group influence" (Sweetser, 1970, p. 195). This interpretation would be incorrect, if it means that the effect is exclusively due to some kind of reciprocal influences between siblings leading to similar attainments of the members of the same group. At best, part of the effect measured may be understood in terms of a levelling-out phenomenon brought about by reciprocal influences among siblings. We agree then with Sweetser (1970, p. 14): "It is certainly not due to a single influence but is rather the observable end result of a number of influences." But we would like to make Sweetser's main interpretation more explicit.

"The causal interpretation offered here for sibling group differentiation is that a force internal to the family is a major cause [...] The force internal to the family is conceived to be the effect of the family environment on aspirations, which then affect the occupations which sons choose [...]" (Sweetser, 1970, p. 195).

Several studies have shown that a family's social status influences the attainments of its children mainly through expectations of significant others and by influencing children's aspirations. "Social structural factors determine the expectations of an individual's significant others, which in turn exert causal influence over the person's attitudes. These attitudes themselves then exert directive forces over both academic performance and later educational and occupational attainments." (Woelfel and Haller, 1971, p. 85, *cf.* also Sewell, 1969.) Therefore, if we control for the family's social status we take into account already part of the "effect of the family environment on aspirations". Sibling group differentiation relates then only to a residual of this effect, *i.e.* to the influences of the family environment on aspirations not taken into account by controlling for the family's social status. However, since influence of the family environment on aspirations is not identical with (or completely determined by) the family's social status, it may well be a "major cause" of sibling group differentiation.

Searching for a substantive interpretation of the FR-effect the following point should also be noted: the FR-variable also includes direct effects of the family's social status on sons' attainment. This is the case insofar as effects of the family's social status are not isolated by controlling for father's education and father's occupation. This may happen because of measurement errors or if important aspects of the family's social status are not taken into account. In fact certain influences, *e.g.* from mother's education or occupation, from the family's economic situation or the social status of kin and friends of the family, are considered only as far as they correlate with the indicators for the family's social status [16].

Apart from speculations about reciprocal influences of siblings, influences of the family environment on aspirations, and unmeasured direct effects of the family's social status, one could mention numerous other factors to interpret the FR-effect. We could think of influences such as family size [17], family specific differences in intelligence or even familial differences in physiological conditions or still other factors. Without the support of further data, however, we will not be able to decide which one among the alternative explanations of this effect may be correct. This is particularly unfortunate since the effect in question is rather high.

Table 5. *Correlation coefficients between variables of familial origin and educational and occupational status of son*

	Explained variables			
	Education of son		Occupation of son	
Explaining variables	approximated from variance analysis 1	by Pearson Product-Moment Formula 2	approximated from variance analysis 3	by Pearson Product-Moment Formula 4
(X_1) Father's education	[.573]	(.583)	[.532]	(.573)
FR.X_1 *	.513		.557	
(X_2) Father's occupation	[.575]	(.553)	[.537]	(.512)
FR.X_2 *	.516		.556	
(X_1X_2) Father's education and occupation	.656** .592 (boxed)	.648**	.611** .579 (boxed)	.623**
FR.X_1X_2 *	.471 (boxed)		.498 (boxed)	

* Family residual effect if the variable(s) in the above row is (are) controlled.

** Values found by multiple correlation of X_1 and X_2 with sons' education resp. son's occupation, calculated from the corresponding zero-order correlations in the Panels 1 and 2.

□ Values found by controlling simultaneously X_1X_2 in variance analysis (see Table 4 and footnote 15).

16. In Sweetser's study this component will probably be more pronounced than in our case since Sweetser used only prestige of father's occupation for controlling the family's social status, whereas we control additionally for father's education.

17. In fact, it can be shown that educational and occupational attainment of sons depend on family size. Since family size, however, is correlated with father's occupational status the proportion of variance additionally explained by this variable is rather small.

Variance components and path model

We can throw an additional light on the interpretation of the family residual effect by discussing the respective findings within the models of the mobility process developed in Part 1. There is no exact mathematical equivalence between the correlation coefficients used in Part 1 of the paper and the variance components in this latter part, mainly because variance analysis does not assume linearity for the relationship between the variables [18]. However, correlation coefficients may be approximated from variance components. The zero-order correlation coefficient is the square root of explained variance. Therefore, we can transform the variance components into correlation coefficients by taking the square root of the explained variance.

In Table 5 comparisons are made between correlation coefficients found by the Pearson formula and coefficients approximated from variance components found by the model of hierarchical classification [19] (see first line of each of the three panels). The highest difference between the 6 pairs of coefficients in column 1 and 2 and in column 3 and 4 is as small as .04. The mean of the 6 differences is .02. The approximations can therefore be accepted as fairly good.

In general, path coefficients based on these differently calculated correlation coefficients similarly show only small deviations. Figure 6 gives the coefficients for a simple model with only two dependent variables: total education of sons and occupation of sons at the time of interview. One must carefully distinguish among the various coefficients shown in this Figure. The coefficients with no markings relate to the data used in the first part of the paper (*i.e.* educational and occupational attainment of the single informant son in all families studied). The coefficients in brackets or parentheses relate to the data used in Table 5 above (*i.e.* data also including the informants' brothers but referring only to families with at least two sons).

18. Even if in variance analysis, the independent variable would consist of the succeeding discrete scores of an interval scale we would not have to assume that the means of the dependent variable that correspond to the succeeding scores of the independent variable are linearly ascending (or descending). Such a linear relationship between the variables, however, is presupposed in the Pearson correlation statistics.

19. The explained scores of sons' education and sons' occupation are family mean scores. In case of the Pearson correlation coefficient between father's education and sons' education, for instance, each father's education score is correlated with the mean of the single education scores of his sons. Basically, the same is done in the analysis of variance. With the model of hierarchical classification used the variance to be explained for instance by father's education is the variance of family mean scores of son's education or of sons' occupation. It can be shown both empirically and theoretically that within a given sample the correlation coefficients remain the same if we correlate the family mean scores instead of the scores of one single son per family. In our case mean score correlations would only deviate from single score correlations if the correlations for the informant's brothers would be either stronger or weaker than the correlations for the informant himself. There is no reason why this should happen. For an empirical test of this hypothesis see Sweetser (1970, pp. 7-11).

Figure 6. *Path coefficients in model with four status variables, estimated from differently calculated correlation coefficients*

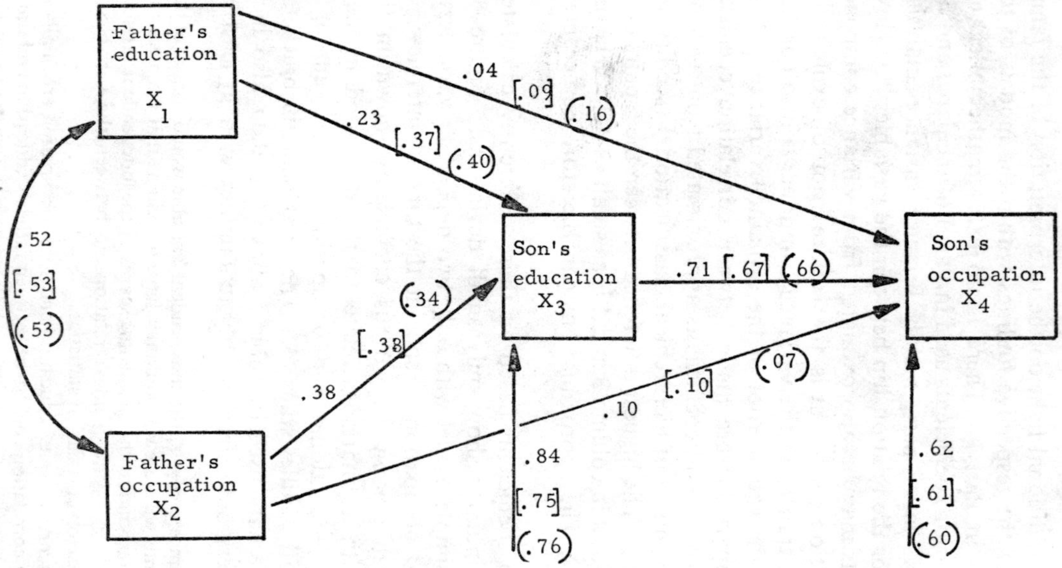

Legend: no parenthesis: Only respondents* in each family; correlation coefficients estimated by Pearson formula.
[ ] All sons of families with at least two sons; correlation coefficients approximated from variance analysis.
( ) All sons of families with at least two sons; correlation coefficients estimated by Pearson formula.
* Age of respondents is 33. Age of respondents' brothers is not controlled.

The values in brackets are based on the correlation coefficients approximated from variance analysis, the values in parentheses on those found by the Pearson formula.

It is worthwhile to comment on one difference between the various coefficients. Of the coefficients relating to the paths from father's education to son's education and to son's occupation, those not especially marked are lower than the corresponding coefficients in brackets or parentheses. In other terms: if we look only at families with at least two sons the coefficients indicate a higher impact of father's education on his sons' attainments than if the one-son-families are also taken into account. Independently of father's occupation, the influence of his education on the sons' attainments is stronger in families with a higher number of sons than in the one-son-families. Since with given resources, it is more difficult to secure a good education for several sons than for only one, it seems plausible that father's education has a greater impact on the sons getting ahead in large rather than in small families.

But the main purpose of Figure 6 is especially to point out similarities rather than dissimilarities. One can easily agree on an identical ranking of the coefficients: highest from sons' education to sons' occupation, medium from father's education and occupation to sons' education, lowest the coefficients of the "delayed effects" from father's education and occupation to sons' occupation. It should also be noticed that for all paths but one the coefficients approximated from variance analysis lie between the other two. Even though they are calculated from variance analysis in an unorthodox manner they are quite similar to those calculated from correlation coefficients.

Table 6. *Proportions of variance explained in son's occupation at age 33**

	FR-effect not controlled	FR-effect controlled
1) Total effect of father's education and occupation	26.2 %	26.2 %
2) Family residual effect, independent of 1)		24.9 %
3) Son's education, independent of 1) and 2)	35.8 %	18.7 %
4) All other factors, independent of 1), 2) and 3)	38.0 %	30.2 %

* Calculations are based on data used in Part 1 (*i.e.* only on respondents themselves).

This fact has encouraged us to a second unorthodox step. We have also transformed the variance explained by the FR-variable in Table 4 into correlation coefficients, even if the FR-effect is a measure of the combined effect of different (unknown) influences and is not a metric variable. But we need the correlation coefficients for introducing the FR-variable into a path model of the mobility process. The purpose of this procedure is merely to illustrate some pitfalls in the underlying assumptions of the various path-models we have discussed in the first part of the paper. The result will also point to the direction in which a distortion of the estimated coefficients may be assumed.

We propose the model given in Figure 7 as a very simplified attempt at formalization. Residual familial influences not taken into account by the indicators of the family's social status are assumed to act directly on sons' education and to influence sons' occupation both directly and in an indirect way via sons' education. Since FR acts on sons' education and education influences occupation, a part of the FR-effect on sons' occupation must be mediated by sons' education. The occupational status of brothers clusters around a family mean because their educational levels are clustered.

The correlations between the FR-variable and father's education and occupation must be assumed to be zero, since in measuring the FR-effect we have controlled for father's education and father's occupation [20].

Serious problems, however, arise by introducing the FR-variable into the path model as proposed in Figure 7. The FR-variable is not measured at one point in time as is the case, for instance, with father's education. A given family context may be favorable for educational attainment, but it may be unfavorable later for the sons' occupational attainment. If in both instances, however, the familial context acts similarly on each brother a positive amount of variance explained by FR will be found for sons' education as well as for sons' occupation. Imagine, for example, the following retroactive effect: under particular conditions the sons of a higher status family are rather unsuccessful in the school system. Reacting to this, the family will make all efforts to nevertheless ensure good occupational positions for their sons. Negative familial effects during schooling have changed into positive support during the occupational career. Cases like this would contradict the model in Figure 7 where we have made the implicit assumption that a familial context which is favorable to educational attainment is generally also favorable to occupational attainment. Only to the extent that familial influences at one point in time act in the same direction as influences at a later point in time does the model give a correct representation of real processes. Most of the evidence, however, would probably support this assumption.

With these restrictions in mind let us look at the coefficients of the model. In correspondence with the preceding figure they are estimated from differently calculated correlation coefficients [21]. The three coefficients for each

20. By controlling for father's education and father's occupation we have ensured that variance explained by the two indicators of father's status is not explained by FR. Therefore no correlation can exist between FR and the status indicators, because in terms of the model this would imply that FR and the status indicators explain partly the same variance in sons' education or sons' occupation.

21. The coefficients for the FR-effect are estimated from variance analysis (see Table 4 and the last line of Table 5). Since these coefficients are found by controlling simultaneously for X_1 and X_2 only the coefficients put together in the same rectangle of Table 5 correspond

Figure 7. *Path coefficients in model with four status variables and the family residual effect (FR)*

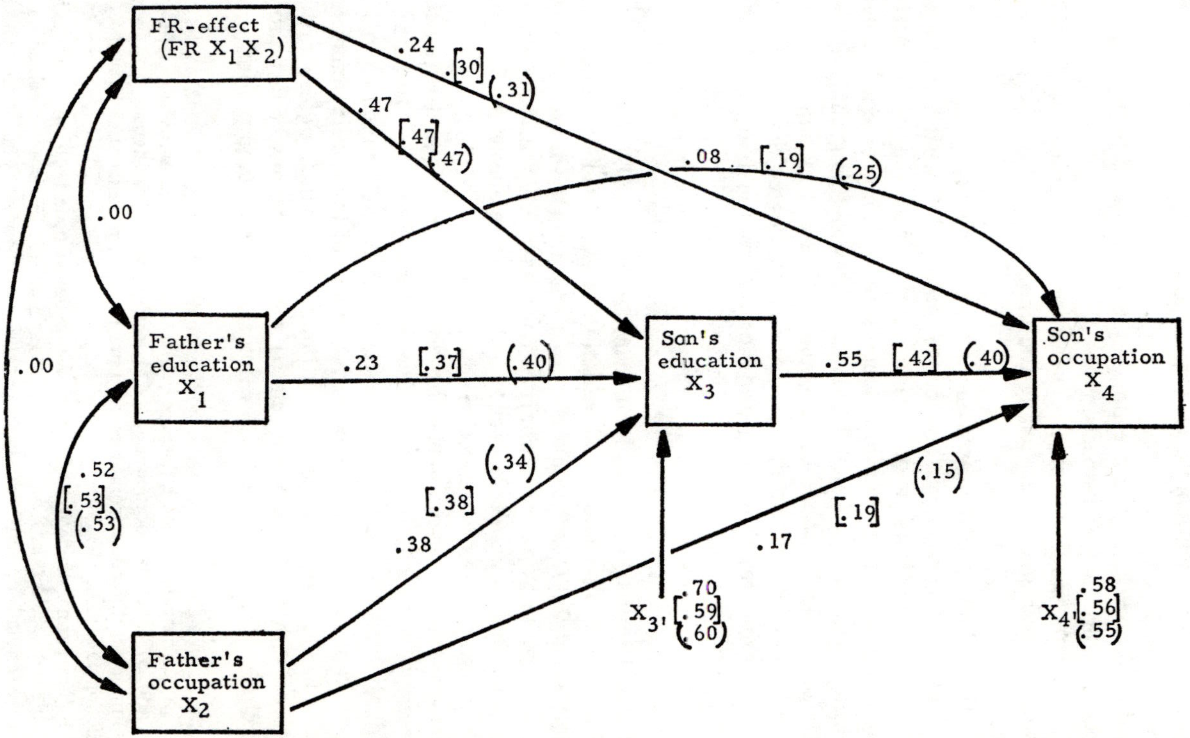

Legend: no parenthesis: Only respondents * in each family; correlation coefficients estimated by Pearson formula.
[ ] All sons of families with at least two sons; correlation coefficients approximated from variance analysis.
( ) All sons of families with at least two sons; correlation coefficients estimated by Pearson formula.
* Age of respondents is 33. Age of respondents' brothers is not controlled.

path do not differ much from each other and if they do the pattern of differences is similar to the one already found in Figure 6.

Comparing, however, the corresponding coefficients of both figures we find differences mainly in two respects.

First, since an additional part of variance is explained by the FR-effect, the values of *the residuals*, especially the one on sons' education, are *lower in Figure* 7 than in Figure 6.

The second difference concerns the *determination pattern of sons' occupation.* The path starting from sons' education is lower when the model includes the FR-variable than it is otherwise. On the other hand, the direct paths from the indicators of the families' social status get higher coefficients in the model which controls for FR. Thus, according to this model, the families' social status would influence the occupational status of sons by differences of success in educational attainment to a lesser degree than we were led to conclude from the preceding figure and the results of the first part of the paper.

Our major concern is not the fact that we succeeded in reducing the unexplained variance. We consider it a more important finding that education loses its potential "to induce variation in occupational status that is independent of initial status" (Blau and Duncan, 1967, p. 201). As Table 6 shows very clearly only little additional variation is explained by education, once the whole family context is taken into account. (It should be noted that for estimating the variance proportions we have chosen from among the different data sets available in Figures 6 and 7 that one which is most favorable to produce a high net effect of education.)

But how to explain the differences between path models and variance tables including resp. not including the family residual influences? In path analysis the residuals are assumed to be uncorrrelated. It can be seen from Figure 7 that apart from social status the other influences of the family determine both sons' educational and occupational attainments. Thus, Figure 6 does not justify the assumption of non-correlated residuals because FR is not specified therein [22]. Since Figure 6 does not control all common influences on

---

to each other. In a strict sense, only a model would be adequate which takes the *combined effect* of X_1X_2 as measure of the influences of the families' social status (*i.e.* .592 for sons' education and .579 for sons' occupation). Calculations with these figures, however, do not yield any important difference from the model presented here, which uses X_1 and X_2 as separate predicting variables.

22. In Figure 7 sons' education and sons' occupation depend both on the same independent variable not specified in Figure 6: the FR-variable. If FR is not specified its effect is implicit in the residuals on sons' education and sons' occupation. Thus in this case the residuals are correlated.

The specific differences between Figure 6 and Figure 7 can be understood in the following way: given the assumed causal relationship of Figure 6 the correlation between the variables 3 and 4 can be explained only by the variables 1 and 2. To this extent the path coefficient p_{43} (=.66) is lower than the correlation coefficient r_{43} (=.78). In Figure 7, the FR-variable additionally explains part of the correlation between variables 3 and 4. Therefore, the path coefficient p_{43} in Figure 7 becomes lower than in Figure 6. But in consequence of the lower

sons' education and sons' occupation, it gives higher path coefficients between these two variables than Figure 7, where we took account of at least all familial influences. Similarly, the lower "delayed" effects of father's education and occupation in those models, which do not acknowledge familial residual effects, follow also from correlating residuals.

Discussion and conclusions

Blau and Duncan (1967, p. 175) carefully point out the possibility of distortion induced by correlating residuals:

"It is all too easy to make a formidable list of unmeasured variables that someone has alleged to be crucial to the process under study. But the mere existence of such variables is already acknowledged by the very presence of the residual. It would be part of the task of the critic to show, if only hypothetically, but *specifically* how the modification of the causal scheme to include a new variable would disrupt or alter the relationships in the original diagram. His argument to this effect could then be examined for plausibility and his evidence, if any, studied in terms of the empirical possibilities it suggests."

Following this invitation we have especially examined one possible source of correlating residuals: influences of the family of origin on the status attainment process of the sons. It is actually not surprising to find that both the sons' education and the sons' occupation are dependent on familial influences not accounted for by the usually used indicators of the family's social status. If these influences are not controlled for, then several coefficients are seriously distorted estimations.

A more complete account of familial influences affects especially the weight assigned to the educational system as an institution counteracting inequalities of birth conditions. Educational attainment itself is influenced by the family background in such a determinant manner that it is almost impossible to act effectively as an equalizing force. The often upheld assumption that in modern societies the educational system has a distinctly independent effect on determining access to occupational opportunities has to be restricted at least in regard of our data. Once all familial background factors are held constant the additional variance of sons' occupation explained by educational attainment is rather small.

This does not contradict the high correlation between educational and occupational attainment. Still a large amount of familial background influences on the later occupational status is transmitted by educational attainment. But we find this to be more the case when a family's influences are considered

value of p_{43}, the direct path from father's education and father's occupation to sons' occupation must be higher in Figure 7 than in Figure 6. This follows from the fact that by controlling for the FR-effect the overall correlation between education and occupation of the father and the two dependent variables of sons' education and sons' occupation is not affected.

only in terms of its social status. Taking familial influences more into account the high correlation between education and occupation appears to be reducible to a greater extent to the fact that both variables are jointly dependent on prior familial background factors.

The distortions pointed out must be assumed to be present also in the figures used in Part 1 of this paper. Since the simpler models in Part 2 are merely abbreviated versions they allow us to indicate the line of corrections necessary to improve the estimations in the earlier more complex figures: the influences of the family of origin on the son's career are higher than we have found them to prevail in the models of Part 1; they are probably less mediated by education than the coefficients of the earlier models show. "Delayed" effects, which directly influence attainment in the occupational career, seem to be more pronounced than it appeared in these figures.

If it is argued that education loses a part of its independent function to determine a person's occupational status, once the whole impact of the family background is acknowledged, the following point should be noted: such an argument rests more on pre-employment education and less on adult education, since the latter has been shown to be influenced only slightly by the status of one's social origin. Thus, our earlier statement that adult education is an important mechanism in equalizing unequal starting conditions is also supported by the present consideration.

Do our findings have any implications for other studies of the mobility process? This question can be answered positively if the reported FR-effects of our study cannot completely be reduced to idiosyncrasies of our sample. The theoretical significance of this effect as well as its empirical evidence in other studies attest, we would argue, to its general occurrence. It should be remembered that Sweetser has found an FR-effect of similar size in her Finnish data. It is true, Sweetser's studies refer *only to the occupation of sons* but similar effects *on sons' education* may be expected. If it can be taken for granted that in other countries familial influences on children's attainment are measured only in part by father's education and father's occupation, then distorted estimations similar to those pointed to in this paper must be assumed.

The evidence presented would most likely support Anderson's (1961, p. 176) conclusion that "education is but one of many factors influencing mobility and it may be far from a dominant factor". It might prevent generalizations like "school influence is the most important influence on occupational attainment" (Himmelweit and Swift, 1969, p. 168), before more complete attempts to account for familial background characteristics have been made. Our findings also suggest some rather important specifications of theories of the modernization process for which Dahrendorf's description is an illuminating example:

"When Marx wrote his books, he assumed that the position an individual occupies in society is determined by his family origin and the position of his parents [...] At the time, this assumption was probably not far from truth [...] Today, the allocation of social positions is increasingly the task of the educational system [...] *the school has become 'the first and thereby decisive point of social placement* with respect to future social security, social rank and the extent of future consumption chances' (quoted from Schelsky, 1956, p. 3) [...] To be sure, there still are numerous obstacles and barriers *in the way of complete equality of educational opportunity*, but it is the stubborn tendency of modern societies to institutionalize intergeneration mobility by making a person's social position dependent on his educational achievement" (Dahrendorf, 1959, pp.58-59, my italics).

It is true that from the high education-occupation correlation one has to conclude that achievement in the school system is a prerequisite of a favourable later position in the occupational system of modern societies. On the other hand, only a small part of this correlation seems to be independent of the ascriptive forces of one's familial origin. Hence, the assumption of a distinct trend from stratification by ascription to stratification by achievement is at least ambiguous. There is a great deal of overlapping between both types. The position an individual occupies is still overwhelmingly determined by his familial origin and the position of his parents. The main difference between today and the past is that the determinative function of placing individuals into occupational positions has been widely taken over by the school as an intervening allocative institution. The educational system allocates on an achievement basis, but without altering effectively the structure of privileges. Besides, familial origin shapes men's advancement independently of achievement in school. Thus, in an apparently achievement-oriented system also the occupational future of men is still mainly determined ascriptively by birth.

Talcott Parsons (1970, p. 21) subtly describes a mechanism which might bring these results about.

"The children of high status parents derive special competitive advantages from their socialization, precisely in the form of capacities for more independent and more responsible action, so that their chances of maintaining or improving the parental level of status are actually improved, relative to children of less 'advantaged' homes [...] Hence the seeming paradox arises, that the ascription of children by birth to the families established by the parental marriage, accentuates the child's competitive advantage in the institutions governed by the value of equality of opportunity, rather than compensating for status disadvantages."

REFERENCES

Anderson, C. Arnold

1964 "A skeptical note on education and mobility", in: A.H. Halsey; J. Floud; C.A. Anderson (eds.). *Education, economy and society*. New York, Free Press.

Blau, P.M.; Duncan, O.D.

1967 *The American occupational structure.* New York, John Wiley.

Boudon, R.

1970 "Essai sur la mobilité sociale en utopie", *Quality and quantity* 4 (2): 213-241.

1971 "Éléments pour une théorie formelle de la mobilité sociale", *Quality and quantity* 5 (1): 39-85.

Carlsson, G.

1958 *Social mobility and class structure.* Lund, Gleerup.

Colemen, J.S.; Blum, Z.D.; Sorensen, A.B.

1970 *Occupational status changes for blacks and nonblacks during the first ten years of occupational experience.* Baltimore, Md., Johns Hopkins University, Center for the study of social organization of schools (Report No. 76).

Dahrendorf, R.

1959 *Class and class conflict in industrial society.* London, Routledge and Kegan Paul.

Duncan, O.D.; Hodge, R.W.

1963 "Education and occupational mobility: A regression analysis", *American journal of sociology* 68 (6): 629-644.

Duncan, O.D.

1968 "Ability and achievement", *Eugenics quarterly* 15 (1): 1-11.

Duncan, O.D.; Haller, A.O.; Portes, A.

1968 "Peer influences on aspirations: A reinterpretation", *American journal of sociology* 74 (1): 119-137.

Fox, T.G.; Miller, S.M.

1965 "Economic, political and social determinants of mobility : An international comparison", *Acta sociologica* 9 (1) : 76-93.

Hamacher, P.

1970 *Bildung und Beruf bei Studierenden des zweiten Bildungsweges.* Stuttgart, Klett.

Hauser, R.M.

1969 "Schools and the stratification process", *American journal of sociology* 74 (6): 587-611.

Himmelweit, H.T.; Swift, B.

1969 "A model for the understanding of school as a socialising agent", in: P. Mussen; J. Langer; M. Covington (eds.). *Trends and issues in developmental psychology.* New York, Holt, Rinehart and Winston.

Kleining, G.; Moore, H.

1968 "Soziale Selbsteinstufung (SSE): Ein Instrument zur Messung sozialer Schichten", *Kölner Zeitschrift für Soziologie und Sozialpsychologie* 20 (4): 502-552.

Lancaster Jones, F.

1970 *The process of stratification in Australia.* Paper presented at the Seventh World Congress of Sociology, Varna.

Mayer, K.U.; Müller, W.

1971 "Progress in social mobility research? Some comments on mobility analysis and new data on intergenerational mobility in West Germany", *Quality and quantity* 5 (1): 141-177.

Miller, S.M.; Roby, P.A
1970 *Strategies for social mobility : A policy framework.* Paper presented at the Seventh World Congress of Sociology, Varna.

Müller, W.
1972 "Bildung und Mobilitätsprozess: Eine Anwendung der Pfadanalyse", *Zeitschrift für Soziologie* 1 (1): 65-84.

Parsons, T.
1970 "Equality and inequality in modern society, or social stratification revisited", pp. 13-72 in: E.O. Laumann (ed.). *Social stratification : Research and theory for the 1970s.* New York, Bobbs Merill.

Safar, Z.
1971 "Different approaches for the measurement of social differentiation of the Czechoslovak socialist society", *Quality and quantity* 5 (1): 179-208.

Schelsky, H.
1956 *Soziologische Bemerkungen zur Rolle der Schule in unserer Gesellschaftsverfassung.* (Unpublished paper.)

Sewell, W.; Haller, A.O.; Ohlendorf, G.W.
1970 "The educational and early occupational status attainment process: Replication and revision", *American sociological review* 35, December: 1014-1027.

Snedecor, G.W.; Cochran, W.G.
1968 *Statistical methods.* Ames, Iowa, lowa State University Press.

Sweetser, D.A.
1970 *Social class and sibling mobility in Finland.* Paper presented at the Seventh World Congress of Sociology, Varna.
1970 "The occupational mobility of sibling groups", *Acta sociologica* 13 (3): 189-197.

Woelfel, J.; Haller, A.O.
1971 "Significant others, the self-reflexive act and the attitude formation process", *American sociological review* 36 (1): 74-87.

Zapf, W.
1971 "Der nachgeholte Aufstieg: Untersuchungen über Absolventen des zweiten Bildungsweges", *Neue Sammlung* 11 (3): 249-274.

ROGER GIROD • YVES FRICKER • ANDRAS KÖRFFY

Counter-mobility

Usually, studies of mobility consider only two points in the individual's trajectory. For example, in most intergenerational surveys only the social setting within which the child has been brought up (defined by the father's occupation when the son was a child) and the son's status (defined by his own occupation at the time of the interview) are considered. In most intergenerational surveys, only the social status at the beginning of one's career (occupational category at about twenty) and the social status later on are considered.

We shall leave aside all discussion of occupational categories as an index of social status and way of life. Obviously, it is necessary to consider this point differently at various stages of progress in a career. The occupation of a man who is still very young does not reflect his true standard of living, his social level and prestige as well as would do the occupation of an older man. In fact, at the beginning of their careers many persons have short-term or trainee positions which do not correspond either to their mode of living or to the type of employment they will eventually take up (except when further information is available).

Without discussing this any further, we shall accept these occupational categories, with all their imperfections, and consider another problem. We would like to show that only a sequential analysis, which considers at least three points in the individual's life, can lead to a faithful description of intra-career movements, and can, *a fortiori*, be used as a basis for accurate explanations.

Being very concise, the present article will limit itself to the changes between the two major occupational spheres which consist of blue-collar workers on one side and white-collar workers on the other (all middle and upper classes, including farmers, who are very rare in Geneva, and independent craftsmen).

Moreover, we will consider only two stages in the individual's life:
a) the formative years ending with the first genuine occupation [1];

1. Occasional activities performed while studying, etc., are discounted.

b) the adult career (from this first occupation to the occupation being exercised at the time of the interview) [2].

1. Magnitude of counter-mobility

This very simple device already allows us to point out that intra-career occupational mobility consists in great part of social counter-mobility movements. By this, we mean changes in occupation (Girod, 1971) which, far from moving the person considered away from his original milieu, on the contrary, draw him back into it or, more probably, cause him to be more deeply entrenched in it without him ever having left it [3]. Take for example two men starting in blue-collar occupations and subsequently obtaining white-collar occupations. If the former is the son of a manual worker, this job mobility is very likely to also represent a rather important change in his social situation. For the latter, if he is the son of a businessman, of a teacher, etc., this change will tend, apparently, to re-establish the temporarily reduced coherence which exists between the type of occupation being exercised and the social milieu in which he lives. From the sociological point of view, this works against mobility; it stabilizes the person considered in his original milieu.

These two very different kinds of movements can be considered together only within the framework of surveys limited to manpower problems: *e.g.* what are the activities usually acting as "channels" leading to certain other activities, what are the relations between career mobility and the long-term evolution of the relative size of the occupational groups? For the study of social mobility the distinction is to be made both as regards description and explanation.

From the descriptive point of view, that is to say with regard to the steps necessary to determine the actual types of cases and the basic problems to be examined about them, the above-mentioned distinction is necessary so as to avoid two mistakes.

The first one consists in identifying implicitly the first job with social origin. This leads to an exaggeration of the magnitude of intergenerational mobility due to career movements. In fact (see Diagram 1) *two thirds* of these changes are of a counter-mobility type, according to our sample. Conse-

2. The data come from a random sample of Swiss men, aged 24 and above, living in the canton of Geneva.

3. No nuance can appear on the basis of any binary division as, for example, the one used here (blue-collars, white-collars). More precise classifications should distinguish between: 1) partial counter-mobility (the first job creates an occupational distance between father and son and the changes occurring later lead the son closer to his father's level without him reaching it completely; 2) full counter-mobility (a return back to his father's level); 3) a "move backward in order to eventually jump higher" (starting below the father's level and then moving beyond it).

quently, they cause an increase in the proportion of intergenerational homosociality as measured at the end of the observation period, and thus, we stress again, they *reduce* intergenerational *social mobility.*

Diagram 1. *Counter mobility and other cases**

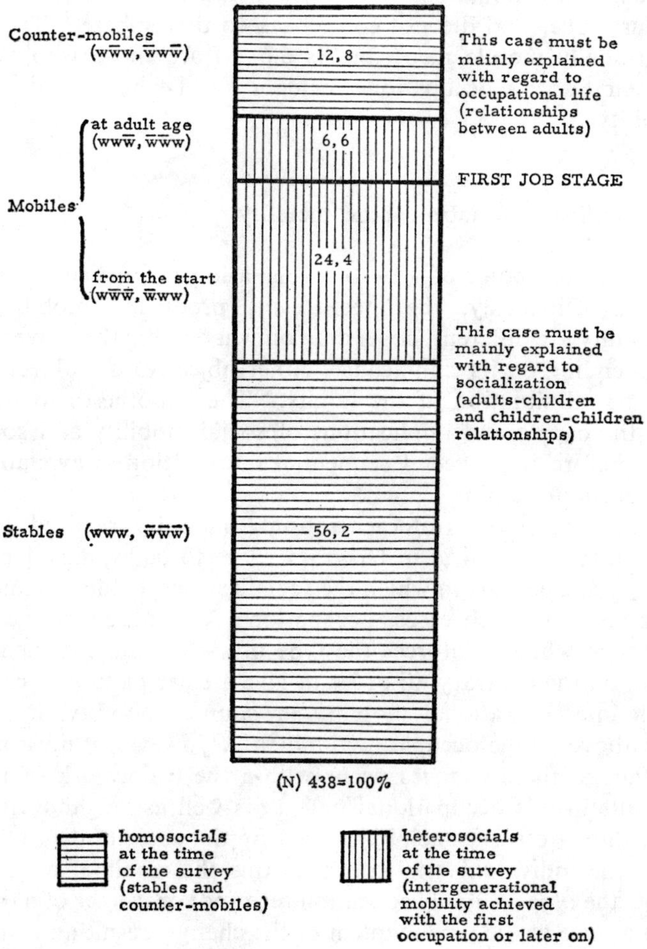

* According to the survey mentioned above (Geneva, 1969). Three points are considered: the father's occupation (when the son was about ten), the son's first occupation (at 20 or 25, exceptionally at 30 for individuals entering practical life after very long studies) and his occupation at the time of the survey. Our classification will be limited to two categories: w = blue-collar workers; $\bar{w}$ = all other occupations. Symbols between parentheses mean for example: www = the father is a blue-collar worker, the son began as a blue-collar worker, and was still a blue-collar worker in 1969; $\bar{w}w\bar{w}$ = the father is a white-collar, the son began as a blue-collar worker and was a white-collar at the time of the survey.

The second error in approach would be to consider as intergenerational mobiles only those individuals who leave their social status of origin by means of career movements. In fact, intergenerational mobility is more often a result of transfers occurring at the start of a career, that is, as early as the first job. According to our Diagram 1, in 1969 the number of intergenerationally mobile individuals in our sample constituted 31.0 % of which 24.4 % had left their occupational sphere of origin (father's sphere) when entering in the labour force, and did not come back to that sphere. The remaining intergenerationally mobile men (that is 6.6 %) are those who started their career in their father's occupational category and who moved out of it by career mobility.

2. Original milieu and intra-career mobility

Of course, from the point of view of explanation these distinctions are also indispensable. Obviously, the mechanisms producing mobility and the effect of mobility are different, depending on when in life the movement occurs and also depending on its significance, either objective or subjective, in relation to the social situation of the family. The hypotheses to be proposed concerning the causes and implications of social mobility and social immobility are therefore improved if sequential information is available, starting from the milieu of origin.

The "initial transfers" (intergenerational mobility realized definitively [4] since first job) that is, 24.4 % in Diagram 1, are to be explained principally [5] with respect to the context in which the socialization of children and teenagers is accomplished. In such cases, occupational life subsequently acts mostly as a mechanism which reinforces the type of status thus attained.

Of course, on the contrary, in order to give a clear picture of career movements, with intergenerational mobility or counter-mobility, it is necessary to consider above all the occupational milieu. However, it must be admitted that even though these changes occur within the framework of relationship between adults in this occupational milieu (as well as neighbouring relationships, etc.), they are very much influenced by the social milieu of the family from which the individual originates. Is this the result of a delayed effect (for example the type of family education received) or, rather of a direct action (help or hindrance at the very moment of the change, resulting from the reputation of the family, from its resources, from other similar factors)? Let us save this problem for the third section and only note here what is shown in Table 1.

4. At the time of the survey. Changes are of course still taking place, especially for the young.

5. It is also necessary to take into account personal characteristics, for example health, mere chance, and the labour-market situation at the stage of the first occupation.

Table 1. *Intra-career mobility according to social origin* *

First job and social origin	Job in 1969			
	Blue-collar	White-collar**	Total	
	%	%	%	(N)
First job: blue-collar worker				
Father blue-collar	78.0	22.0	100.0	(118)
Father white-collar**	52.8	47.2	100.0	(108)
Both	65.9	34.1	100.0	(226)
*First job: white-collar worker***				
Father blue-collar	9.1	89.9	100.0	(55)
Father white-collar**	1.9	98.1	100.0	(157)
Both	3.8	96.2	100.0	(212)

*Same data as Diagram 1.

** All non-working class occupations, including farmers (very few in Geneva) and independent craftsmen.

This table indicates to what extent the intra-career trajectory depends on the father's social situation, or more exactly, on what could be called the initial trajectory, that is from the original milieu to the first occupation.

One can see that with equivalent [6] first occupational situation, the possibilities within a career differ very systematically according to social origin. For example, in the case of the individuals who started as blue-collar workers, the average probability of integration into a white-collar occupation is about 1/3, while it is about 1/2 for those who are the sons of white-collars and less than 1/4 for those who are the sons of blue-collars. Conversely, for individuals coming from the same sphere of origin, the orientations are systematically different according to the first occupation held: the probability of the sons of white-collars still belonging to the middle and upper classes when they are middle-aged is 98.1 % if they started as white-collar workers, and 47.2 % if they started first as manual wage earners.

What has been mentioned before refers to an analysis in which mobility is the variable to be explained. However, this mobility is often treated as an explanatory factor. In this case, the common type of intrageneration data may lead to unfortunate confusions. We have had the opportunity to compare, for example, the percentage of voters among the people wc interviewed in 1969 according to the type of their three-points trajectory: from their original milieu to their first occupation, then to their occupation at the time of the survey. With identical intra-career trajectories (from the first job to the occupation in 1969) this percentage varies considerably according to the initial trajectory (from social origin to first job). Following are some examples expressed with the same symbols used in the above diagram:

		Percent voting regularly [7]
a)	Life-time white-collars ($\overline{w}\ \overline{w}\ \overline{w}$)	58.6
a')	Deproletarianized from the start ($w\ \overline{w}\ \overline{w}$)	49.0
b)	Life-time blue-collar workers ($w\ w\ w$)	54.0
b')	Proletarianized from the start ($\overline{w}\ w\ w$)	44.8
c)	Counter-mobiles of white-collar origin ($\overline{w}\ w\ \overline{w}$)	57.6
c')	Deproletarianized during career ($w\ w\ \overline{w}$)	54.2

As we just said, it can clearly be seen that in each of the above-mentioned pairs that fall into the same category with respect to classical criteria of intra-career mobility, the electoral behaviour is quite different.

Let us just note in passing that these facts are in agreement with the classic cross-pressures hypothesis: the persons who remained within their social milieu (including counter-mobiles) voted more often than those who moved

6. By reference to the very crude yardstick utilized here.

7. Voted three or four times in four elections and referendums chosen as points of observations. For two categories ($\overline{w}\ \overline{w}\ w$ and $w\ \overline{w}\ w$) the figures are too small to allow any measurement of percentage.

to a different milieu, a move which often produces hesitations and doubts which have a demobilizing effect. Furthermore, the middle and upper class milieu encourages electoral participation to a greater extent than the working class milieu does. The classification of groups corresponds very well in its main outline to what might be expected from the combination of the influences of these two types of mechanisms.

At the top are the groups (*a*, *c*) with both membership of the middle or the upper classes and intergenerational stability (including counter-mobility). At the bottom are individuals (*b′*) that are at the same time in a working class environment and under the cross-pressures resulting from a non-working class background. Life-time workers (*b*) are to be classified in between the two above categories but at a rather high level. The two other groups (*a′* and *c*'), that is worker background then deproletarianization, either from the start or during career) are also to be classified in the middle.

But it would be beyond the scope of our purposes to comment on these differences in detail: we simply want to draw attention to the necessity of dividing intra-career trajectories according to social origin.

3. Structure of sequential mobility

The method of "decomposition of proportions" (Boudon, 1967; 1971) gives a clearer picture of the interdependencies illustrated by Table 1. The algebraic equations used to effect this decomposition bring out, through a deductive process, unobserved connections in addition to those observed. Moreover, these equations give the possibility of defining the amount of influence exercised by each factor.

When the influence exerted by the original milieu on the first occupation and the influence of the latter on the social situation at the time of the survey are studied separately, that is in a non-sequential perspective, the number of connections considered is strongly reduced by comparison with all those that are really acting. Such a procedure, used by Blau and Duncan (Blau and Duncan, 1967) would limit in our case the network to three arrows (A, B, C) of the Diagrams 2 and 3, presented later. The diagram would be of the following type:

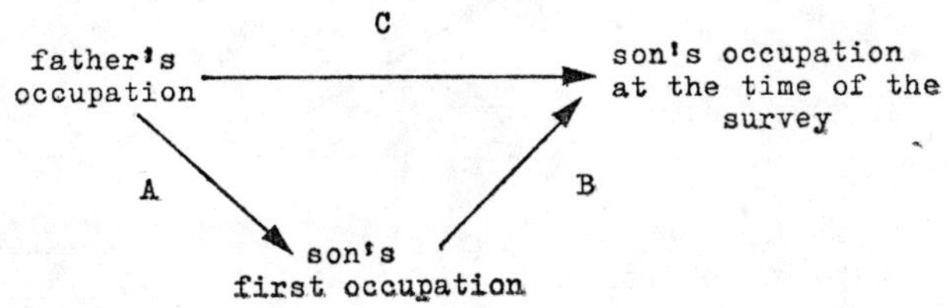

Let us examine now the Diagrams 2 and 3[8]. In addition to the direct relationship between the three points (father's occupation, son's first occupation, son's occupation in 1969), they include the effect of the initial trajectory and of all other influences presented globally as the residual effects of the factors which are supposed to be independent of the variables at hand: arrow E_1, the amount of influence exerted by those uncontrolled factors on the first occupation; arrow E_2, their influence on the rest of the career.

Diagram 2. *Effect of state w*

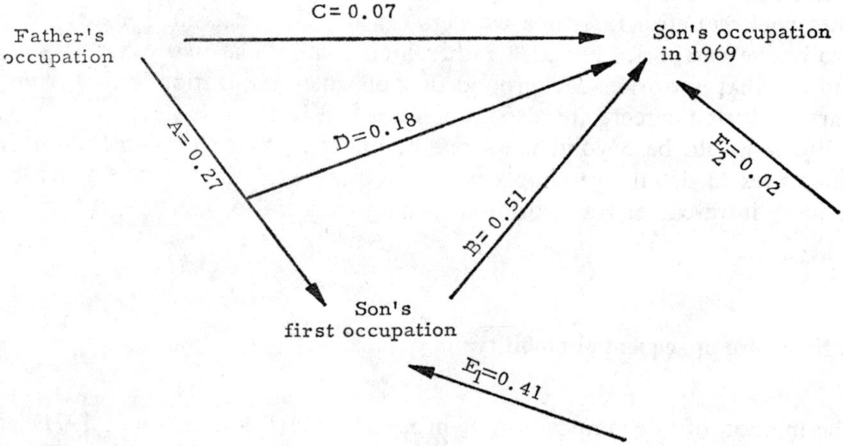

Diagram 3. *Effect of state* $\overline{w}$

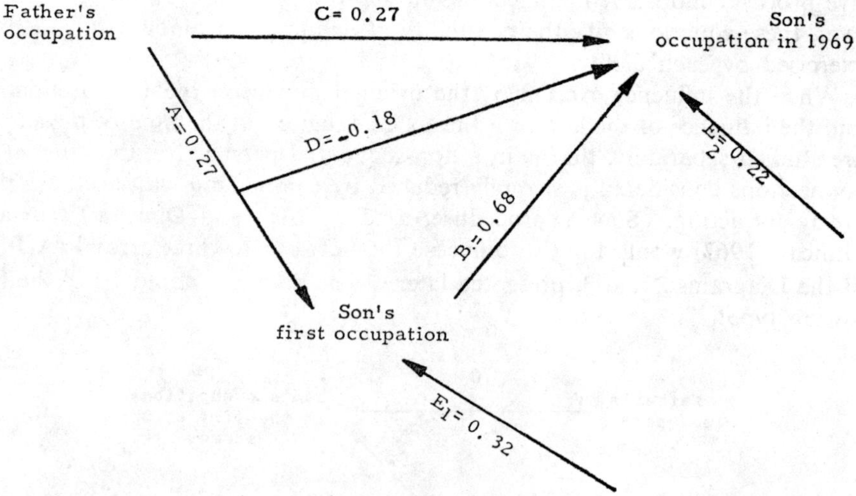

8. Calculated on the basis of Table 2.

In Diagrams 2 and 3, arrow A represents the fraction of all influences which are responsible for stability at the beginning of a career (the son belongs to the same occupational category as his father). Arrow B expresses the amount of influence which tended to make the first occupation and the one of 1969 coincide.

It is not difficult to obtain a picture of the concrete nature of these well-known influences: the social situation of the father makes it easier for the son to obtain a certain kind of education and vocational guidance; the son's first occupation places him within a career which has its own rules of promotion, etc.

In these diagrams, we have two more arrows. Arrow C corresponds to the amount of influence of the original milieu which is statistically independent of the first occupation. It corresponds to those advantages and hindrances linked to the family milieu which operate after socialization and which have no relationship with that socialization (for example, the influence of an inheritance, or any recommendation made by the father, etc.).

There remains arrow D which represents (after having subtracted all the other effects) the weight of the interaction of the father's occupation and the son's first occupation, on the son's occupation in 1969, that is to say the influence of the initial trajectory (from social origin to first job) on the son's occupation in 1969. In other words, this arrow reflects the share of influence of the interaction between father's job and son's first job on son's occupation in 1969. This interaction results from the differential effect of the first occupation on the occupation in 1969 according to the sub-population of origin, or reciprocally, it results from the differential effect of the father's occupation on the son's occupation in 1969 according to sub-population at first job stage.

In Diagram 2, we consider the effect of belonging to the working class as causing the relationships that come into play within the system. In the other one, the effect of belonging to the other occupational sphere is the basis of all calculations.

The interaction (arrow D) is positive in the first diagram and negative in the second one. This is an interesting fact, creating the possibility of a better understanding of the results given in Table 2, in pinpointing the significance of the interaction. In addition, the effect of this factor is rather important. It is of the same size in the two diagrams. That means that this interaction plays an opposite role but one which is equally influential with regard to the two original milieux. Dissymmetry in the effect of the initial trajectory on one's career gives us the explanation of this fact. For blue-collar workers' sons initial mobility ($w\ \bar{w}$) very rarely leads to intra-career mobility ($w\ \bar{w}\ w$). But for white-collars' sons, if they initially change ($\bar{w}\ w$), they often go back to their original milieu ($\bar{w}\ w\ \bar{w}$).

The retention capacity of the middle and upper classes is also reflected in two other ways: firstly by the relative importance of the coefficient of arrow

Table 2. *Father's occupation, son's first occupation, son's 1969 occupation (Absolute figures)**

Son's occupation in 1969	Social origin and first job: *Sons of blue-collar workers* — Son's first job: blue-collar	Son's first job: white-collar**	All sons of blue-collar	*Sons of white-collar workers* — Son's first job: blue-collar	Son's first job: white-collar	All sons of white-collar	Total (N)
	—	—	—	—	—	—	—
Blue-collar occupation	92	5	97	57	3	60	(157)
White-collar occupation**	26	50	76	51	154	205	(281)
Total	118	55	173	108	157	265	(438)

*From the Geneva survey (1969) mentioned in the paper.

** Same as in Table 1.

B in the second diagram, with regard to this coefficient in the first diagram; secondly, by the same kind of difference as regards the coefficients of arrow C in each of these diagrams. This results from the fact that if one starts in a white-collar occupation, one might very well stay there, whilst intra-career mobility from worker occupations to white-collar occupations is high. Moreover, in these cases, the direct influence (arrow C) of the original milieu is important, if it is a white-collar milieu, and negligible in the other case.

REFERENCES

Blau, P.M.; Duncan, O.D.
1967 *The American occupational structure.* New York, Wiley.

Boudon, R.
1967 *L'analyse mathématique des faits sociaux.* Paris, Plon.
1971 *Les mathématiques en sociologie.* Paris, PUF.

Girod, R.
1971 *Mobilité sociale.* Genève, Droz.

PETER H. ROSSI • MICHAEL D. ORNSTEIN

The impact of labor market entry factors: Illustrations from the Hopkins Social Accounts Project

Introduction

The main body of this paper is an outgrowth of the Johns Hopkins *Social Accounts Project*, a long range research program aimed at uncovering and understanding the social processes underlying changes in the social positions of major social groups within American society. The purpose of this paper is to provide an introduction to the main ideas involved in the conception of "social accounts" and to provide a concrete illustration of the kinds of substudies being undertaken as part of the general program. Part A of this paper will be concerned with an exposition of the general program, a description of some of the salient technical aspects of the major empirical research study that has been undertaken so far, and an overview of the topics covered in that research endeavour. Part B will present an illustration taken from one of the main themes of analysis of the project, centering around an analysis of the determinants and consequences of modes of entry into the labor force.

In addition to the authors of this paper, the Social Accounts Project staff consists of James S. Coleman, Zahava D. Blum and Aage Sorenson. The Social Accounts Project was initiated by James S. Coleman and Peter H. Rossi. It has been carried out under the aegis of the Center for the Study of the Social Organization of Schools, with financial support provided mainly by the US Office of Education, with supplementary support being provided by the US Department of Labor and the Office of Economic Opportunity.

Part B of this paper originally appeared as Report No. 75 of the Center for the Study of Social Organization of Schools under the title "Going to work: An analysis of the determinants and consequences of entry into the labor force" authored by Michael D. Ornstein and Peter H. Rossi.

Part A. The Hopkins Social Accounts Project

The central concern of the Hopkins Social Accounts Project is with understanding the sources of the considerable socio-economic differences between whites and blacks in the United States. This is a topic in which the interests of the policy oriented and the social science oriented intellectual coincide. Properly to construct social policy which would markedly reduce social inequality along racial lines requires a base of knowledge about the processes, personal and systemic, which produce and maintain the considerable differentials between the races.

The basic model underlying the project is a conceptual scheme developed by James S. Coleman (1967) for the purpose of assessing the progress (or lack of progress) of American blacks into a position of parity with whites. Although parity may be thought of as having many specific manifestations, the project has focussed primarily on parity in the areas of occupational status and income. In direct analogy to bookkeeping practices, Coleman suggested setting up "social accounts" for whites and blacks which could provide such an assessment. The social accounting scheme he proposed identified critical variables relating to the characteristics of American society, of major institutions, of American communities, and to the personal characteristics of blacks and whites in terms of which continuing inventories of "assets" and "deficits" may be maintained. A "deficit" in these terms is a condition of deprivation of the black population (or of any other identifiable subgroup) relative to the general population. An "asset" is a condition of at least parity with respect to some important resource. An inventory of such assets and deficits can provide a way of making an assessment of whether the social accounts for a particular group are close enough to a reasonable balance. But, most important, such a scheme naturally raises the crucial question of how assets and deficits in different areas are related to each other over time.

The advantages of such a scheme are several: firstly, it provides a means by which different subgroups of the population can be compared; secondly, it is the beginning of a theory of social change, since by isolating out various components in the "social wealth", so to speak, of a subgroup, one can begin to study how assets in one area of life may be converted into assets in another area; finally, it provides a means of highlighting those particular items in the description of a population subgroup to which it is worthwhile paying detailed attention.

An abbreviated version of Coleman's proposed inventory of assets and deficits as applied to American blacks follows:

1. *Freedom of action*

There can be little doubt that a major deficit of the American black population is the set of restrictions formal and informal placed on the actions of individual blacks and on blacks as a group that are consequences of skin color discriminatory practices. An exhaustive catalogue of such discriminatory practices could fill the remainder of this paper, but the important ones are very well-known — discrimination in employment and job promotion, payment for work, housing sales and rentals, differential treatment by police and the courts, exclusion from interaction with whites in formal and informal circumstances, etc.

It is important to note that this deficit is analytically distinct from those accruing to blacks by virtue of their poverty, for example, and represents the barriers to action which specially mark off blacks as compared with other persons of the same socio-economic rank.

2. *Economic power*

The deficit in economic power held by American blacks can be measured in a variety of ways — average income, rates of unemployment, property ownership, control over economic institutions such as manufacturing firms or retail stores, etc. However measured, it is quite clear that blacks have considerable deficits in economic power.

The importance of economic power is its versatility. It constitutes a deficit or asset in its own right, directly experienced through levels of consumption, and as a means of obtaining other assets, for example, political power.

3. *Political power*

The asset versus deficit aspect of political power is a little more difficult to assess in the case of the American black population. This is because there are three sources of political power — the franchise, the holding of political offices, and the wielding of political influence. Although in principle — especially in urban centers — the franchise is freely and openly available to blacks, in practice the importance of the franchise lies in its ability to affect who will hold political office, a connection which can be made extremely tenuous by the use of gerrymandering and the underrepresentation of urban areas in state and federal legislatures

The major way in which American blacks have been able to affect the outcome of political decisions has been through the organized direct action of civil rights groups which have, at times, wielded considerable influence on the national, state and local levels. This direct action has had considerable effects on the course of federal legislation on civil rights, an example of how one type of asset can be converted into another. Civil rights direct action has changed the legal rules concerning discriminatory practices in a wide variety of areas.

4. *Community cohesion*

A fourth deficit held by American blacks is the low level of social cohesion that characterizes urban black communities. Although American urban communities in general are reputed to have a low level of community cohesion — compared, for example, with England, Yugoslavia or the Soviet Union — this absence of cohesion is particularly pronounced in the urban black ghettos. Transiency, economic insolvency, and an absence of solidary institutions support the low community cohesion of ghetto slums, although these conditions do not entirely explain it.

Indeed, the black areas of our major metropolitan areas resemble to a disturbing degree the casbahs of North African urban centers in the days of colonialism, being "native quarters" dangerous for whites to enter and in which the enforcement of law and order is accomplished by the police forces acting almost as a military force occupying the territory of a hostile native population.

A higher level of community cohesion or solidarity would constitute a great asset in the drive towards the amelioration of the urban blacks' condition. It would give collective strength both in marking external demands (for example, on city government or landlords) and in inforcing internal constraints (for example, against delinquency and crime). It could also constitute a considerable asset as well in the existence of community institutions providing a variety of services and aids that may well compensate at least partially for the absence of individual economic resources.

5. *Primary group cohesion*

Whatever the causes may be, it is widely recognized that black families are more likely to be subject to disruption and breakdown than white families. Several observers furthermore have commented upon the fragility of friendship groupings in black communities. Although the importance of intact families in the socialization of children is somewhat in doubt, it is worthwhile to consider that this might be an important area of life in which to count assets and deficits. Similarly, whether solidary friendship groups are of any significance as far as social mobility is concerned is not clear, although this also appears to be worthwhile to study.

6. *Personal resources*

Under this heading we would place all those characteristics of the individual — values, skills, abilities, knowledge, physical strength, etc. — which are assets in social mobility in our society. There can be little doubt that the average black suffers serious deficits in these personal resources. Perhaps the most important deficit is the average black's relatively low level of educational attainment, narrowing the range of occupations into which he could enter.

7. *Systemic attributes of American society*

Some of the deficits of blacks stem from the characteristics of American society. Perhaps the most important in this respect is the widespread prejudice against blacks. This prejudice when either directly held by individual whites or indirectly held in the form of expectations held by whites about how other whites would react to blacks, constitutes an important source of the patterns of discrimination referred to earlier.

Although there is some evidence from sample surveys that some forms of prejudice against blacks are declining in the white population, there is still a popular perception that widespread prejudice on the part of the general population is still prevalent, leading in part to the personal reaction, "I'm not prejudiced myself, but my neighbors would not..." Of course, the concept of prejudice is not exhausted fully by the kinds of questions which can be asked on sample surveys so that there still remains a potentially considerable but as yet unknown amount of prejudice in the American white population.

The simple-minded view that it is necessary to eliminate prejudice before blacks can be brought much further into parity with whites overlooks two important items: firstly, at least the forms of prejudice which can be measured by items on sample surveys are quite sensitive to changes occurring in court decisions and in legislation. The 1954 Supreme Court decision on segregation in education did more to signal a change in the attitudes of the American population than the several decades of Brotherhood Weeks that preceded it. Attitudes themselves seem quite capable of changing in response to respecification of norms or their reinforcement in the form of specific legislation. Secondly, prejudice against blacks is in part sustained by some of the deficits enumerated above. The deficits in personal resources particularly support many of the popular negative stereotypes of blacks which in turn support approval of discriminatory practices against blacks.

Another attribute of the larger society which has important implications for blacks is changes occurring within the American occupational structure. Fewer and fewer unskilled and semi-skilled jobs requiring little education are being created. This means that employment opportunities for a great proportion of the urban blacks in their present condition are meager, making it all the more imperative that there be rapid shifts in the inventory of occupational skills available in the black population.

An attribute of the present society which could be considered an asset for American blacks has been the expanding wealth and resources of the society. With the Gross National Product increasing by a significant percentage each year, the society is creating sufficient additional income and wealth each year so that gains made by one subgroup need not necessarily come at the expense of another. For example, opening up employment opportunities for blacks does not mean necessarily that such employment opportunities are denied to whites.

There are other systemic characteristics of American society which could be listed as relevant to the social accounts of the black population. Perhaps the major one concerns major value themes in American society. As Gunnar Myrdal was so insightful to point out, there are strong egalitarian strains in American values to which blacks in their struggle for equality can point as justification for their aspirations, just as there are strong libertarian strains to which one can point for justification for extensions of civil rights. While there are inherent strains between the themes of liberty and equality, we have a long way yet to go before these strains in the case of blacks become evident. The main point is that an important part of our democratic tradition has a great many legitimating themes for the effort to bring blacks into full parity with whites.

This inventory of assets and deficits presents a total "balance" — in which deficits outweigh the assets. Clearly, the major assets available to the black population are their political potential, the expanding wealth of the society and the value themes in American ideology which support their aspirations. All three assets lead one to look to governmental actions as the prime movers for the amelioration of the conditions of blacks. Transfer payments, new legislation against discriminatory practices and increased efforts to intervene in the generation-to-generation socialization process can be expected to occur as our urban blacks learn how to use effectively their political power to affect federal, state and local legislation to remove those deficits which are systemic in character and to replace them with institutionalized practices which are assets.

The idea of "social accounts" as outlined above provides only a very general orienting framework for both understanding social change and guiding research. To go beyond this level of generality it is necessary to provide precise knowledge about the importance of each of the several kinds of assets and deficits in social mobility and about the relationship between different classes of assets and deficits. For example, we would need to know the relative advantages of electing black members to the national legislature as opposed to spending an equal amount of effort in some other direction, for example, building local mutual aid societies.

To provide the beginnings of such precise knowledge, the Social Accounts Project sets forth a program of research focussed upon the following problems:

a) On the level of individuals: longitudinal studies of career mobility which would focus on how individual blacks and whites used their assets (and/or deficits) in obtaining jobs and income.

b) On the level of community organization: studies of the organization of black and white communities indicating the ways in which community political solidarity, for example, can be used to facilitate social mobility.

c) On the level of institutional practices: studies of discriminatory practices in the sale and rental of housing, employment, delivery of educational services, and so on.

At the present time, most of the empirical work accomplished by the Social Accounts Project has been centered around a national study of career mobility, to be described in greater detail below. Some speculative work has been started on the level of community organization, primarily aimed at laying out the dimensions of the problem. It cannot be said that these efforts have been met with great success. It does not seem to be the case that this concern lends itself easily to empirical research. On the level of institutional practices, pilot studies have been conducted, aimed at studying such institutions as local police departments and employment practices of major firms. A large scale study has been designed to carry further the analysis of the discriminatory employment practices of business establishments, and funding for the study is now being sought.

The career mobility study consists of personal interviews with national samples of black and white men between the ages of thirty and thirty-nine. The study was conducted in the Winter of 1968-1969 and contains 850 white males and 737 black males.

The interviews cover the following major topics:

a) Family background: father's occupation at age fourteen, mother and father's educational attainment, number of siblings, etc.

b) Occupational life history: jobs held during the period from the point at which the respondent was fourteen until the time of interview, including wages earned, reasons for leaving the job, means by which jobs were obtained, etc.

c) Educational life history: educational experiences for each of the years from age fourteen until time of interview, including both formal educational experiences and vocational training in connection with jobs held.

d) Household and family composition: composition of the household for each of the years between fourteen and time of interview, including dates of marriage, divorce, birth of children, wife's labor market behavior, etc.

e) Migration history: place of birth, moves undertaken, type of housing lived in, etc.

f) Other information: short verbal ability test, salient life experiences, perceived happiness at various periods, etc.

The information was gathered using a unique interviewing device in which the respondent is encouraged by the interviewer to reconstruct in a longitudinal account the major changes which have occurred in his life starting with age fourteen.

The data obtained were transcribed onto magnetic tape using a system which made it easy to retrieve the status of the individual respondent month by month from age fourteen until the time of interview. Each type of status (for example, job changes, marital status changes, etc.) was stored in such a fashion that changes which were occurring in one domain of existence could be related to changes occurring in another.

The major dependent variables of the study consist of the prestige scores of jobs held and the wages derived therefrom. The major themes of analysis center around accounting for the sequence of jobs held and the end status of the respondent in terms of his social background and life experiences. Specifically, sections of the projected monograph to result from the study will be addressed to the following topics:

a) Assessing the impact of social background and educational attainment upon mode and level of entry into the labor force.

b) Assessing the impact of significant changes in life experiences, for example, migration, marriage, birth of children, military service, upon the prestige standings of jobs held and wages derived therefrom.

c) Assessing the impact of job changes upon subsequent job and wage history, involving the impact of unemployment, the meaning of job changes, mode of obtaining jobs, etc.

d) Development of a prototype of a social accounting model using occupational career outcomes as the dependent variable.

The analyses all concentrate on showing the differences between the experiences of whites and blacks.

At this writing approximately one-third of the contemplated analyses have been completed and are in draft form. Part B of this paper contains a good illustration of the forms of analysis used, relying heavily on multivariate analysis methods using prestige scores and wages as dependent variables.

Part B. An analysis of the determinants and consequences of entry into the labor force

1. *Introduction*

"The investigators in San José were left with the definite impression that chance has much to do with "landing" the first permanent job. For many a boy in the sample this first job had a decisive effect upon his subsequent occupational career, and the assignment of so dominating a role to mere chance presumably often has unfortunate results."

Percy E. Davidson and H. Dewey Anderson, *Occupational mobility in an American community* (1937, p. 39).

"[...] Most youngsters (and their parents) approach the choice of first job with no clear conception of where they were going; the great majority of first jobs were found in a very informal way, preponderantly through relatives and friends; the great majority of youngsters took the first jobs they found and did not make comparisons with any other job; their knowledge of the job before they took it was extremely meager and in most cases the job turned out to be a blind alley which did not lead to anything better."

Lloyd G. Reynolds, *The structure of labor markets* (1951, pp. 127-128).

"Three major generalizations sum up much of the research on factors affecting occupational careers. First, despite the net upward mobility which prevails in industrial societies, there is some tendency for men to inherit the occupational status levels of their fathers. Second, people are strongly influenced by the advice of significant others when they select jobs and choose occupational aspiration levels. Third, the general values which people hold are systematically related to their aspiration levels and to the kinds of occupations they choose."

Richard L. Simpson and Ida Harper, "Social origins, occupational advice, occupational values and work careers", *Social forces,* March (1962, p. 264).

For the cohort aged 26 to 35 the simple correlation between the occupational prestige of an individual's first job and the educational attainment of that person was .574, that between the occupational prestige of his first job and his occupational prestige at the time of interview was .584.

(Figures taken from Peter M. Blau and Otis Dudley Duncan, *The American occupational structure*, 1967).

Sooner or later, all American males enter the labor force. The exceptions to this generalization are so few that the statement is a truism. The significance of entry into the labor force lies in the variation among men in the points in their life cycles at which entry occurs, in the levels of the occupational system they enter, and in the modes through which their first jobs are obtained. These variations and their consequences for later occupational attainment are the central concerns of this paper.

Anticipating the findings to be presented, it will be made abundantly clear that the variations among men are systematically related to their race, social class origins, and educational attainments. It will also be shown that there are moderately strong consequences for subsequent occupational attainment. These are findings which have been asserted by previous research, as the excerpts in the epigraph of this report indicate. The contribution of this report lies not in the novelty of results, but in the degree of specificity in which the findings are given. Using modern methods of multivariate analysis, we will present quantitative estimates of the contributions that various background characteristics make to the entry period and estimates of how much difference is made to subsequent occupational careers.

In large part, previous analyses of the entry period have been handicapped by not having longitudinal data on occupational careers, which span the critical period ranging from early adolescence through to some point in the middle of the productive years. The data to be employed in this analysis, however, have this important feature, being detailed life histories collected from a national sample of males who were between the ages of thirty and thirty-nine in 1968. The life histories are retrospective, obtained from personal interviews in 1968, and contain data on family backgrounds as well as detailed accounts of jobs held and family status changes experienced from age fourteen up to the time they were interviewed. A more precise description of the techniques employed to gather these life histories and of the sample used is given elsewhere.

Throughout the paper we will pay special attention to class and race differences. The experiences of blacks and whites are so different and are conditioned so heavily by background factors such as parental social status and individual educational attainment that there cannot be said to be a single typical mode of entry into the labor force. Indeed, it was in anticipation of strong racial differences that the sample was designed to oversample blacks in order to provide sufficient case bases to make reliable comparisons between the two major racial groups in this country,

The first step in the analysis of entry is to develop a useful operational definition of the point at which an individual enters the labor market. We consider a set of alternatives and choose one that we think has decided advantages over the others.

With an entry point fixed for each individual, we can then provide descriptions of the experiences which precede and those which follow the point of entry. Special attention will be paid to shifts in marital status, previous work experience and the interruption of education.

Finally, an analysis will be presented bearing on the importance of modes of entry for subsequent occupational attainment. Here we will attempt to show how parental background, educational experience and mode of entry affect occupational attainment as of the end of the decade following entry point.

2. *Previous research on entry into the labor force*

The first three excerpts given at the beginning of this paper go a long way toward summarizing the results of research conducted on this problem up to 1967. Davidson and Anderson reporting in 1937 on one of the first large surveys concerned with the American occupational structure, characterized the entry period as one of "floundering". At the same time their results showed that there were strong systematic differences among individuals of different skill levels. Although there is no logical contradiction between the characterization of the period as "floundering" and the findings concerning systematic class and educational attainment differences, Davidson and Anderson, like the researchers who follow them, display an attitude approaching ambivalence in their discussions of the entry period. On the one hand, they describe the period as being one in which the individual connects with his first jobs by a process determined mainly by chance and luck. On the other hand, they document that the sons of the well-to-do enter the labor force at much higher levels than the sons of the poor.

The portrait of the entry period that emerges from Davidson and Anderson's study is one that subsequent studies over the next thirty years have done little to change. Entry is a process marked by a great deal of variation among individuals, yet social class, educational attainment and other factors exert unmistakably strong influences on modes of entry.

Perhaps the most important focus for research within the entry period itself has been on the ways in which new jobs are located. A number of studies (Simpson and Harper, 1962; Lipset, Bendix and Malm, 1955; Sheppard and Belistky, 1966) bearing on this topic have shown that workers seeking jobs do not spend much time on the job search. Informal contacts, relatives, friends and fellow workers, all relatively passive means, are found to be of great importance in finding new jobs.

Attempting to explain why workers do not invest more time in or make more systematic attempts to find good jobs but instead take one of the first few they find, Stigler (1962) provides a simple and compelling explanation that reveals an underlying rationality to this strategy. He shows that if the variance in the quality and salaries of the jobs available is not large for an individual with a given level of educational attainment and skill, then the marginal utility of finding additional job openings to consider, after the first three or four, is very small. The cost, however, of locating an additional opening remains uniform. The logical conclusion is that there is little to gain from an extensive job hunt.

Another consistent finding has been that persons with lower levels of skill and formal education have more difficulty in finding jobs and that when they do find them the jobs are likely to have both low occupational prestige and low income (Parnes *et al.*, 1969; Blau and Duncan, 1967). Studies show that less well educated persons receive less and lower quality vocational advice, partly a result of their coming from poorer social backgrounds — ones that are less able to provide the contacts to get good jobs (Simpson and Harper, 1962). In all of these studies the direct effects of parental social class and indirect effects on levels of formal education are the dominant variables, among the correlates of labor market behavior.

Work in the fields of stratification and occupational structure took a qualitative step forward with the publication of Blau and Duncan's *The American occupational structure* in 1967. The use of a very large sample, numbering over twenty thousand American men between the ages of twenty and sixty-four combined with their coding the occupational prestige scores of the respondents' first jobs on entering the labor market, their jobs at the time of the interview, and their fathers' occupations, made possible accurate calculations of the effects of different factors in determining an individual's place in the occupational structure. The development of an occupational prestige scale, that is known to have remained very stable over the past half century (Hodge, Siegel and Rossi, 1966; Rossi, Hodge and Siegel, 1970), made it possible to use powerful multiple regression techniques in the place of tabular methods. These occupational prestige scores have been shown to behave in a linear fashion, a further aid in most analysis.

For our purpose here, Blau and Duncan's most important finding was that the occupational prestige of the first job a respondent had on entering the labor force was an important determinant of the prestige scores of the jobs he had later in life, controlling both for the effect of the socio-economic status of his family of origin and his educational attainment. A combination of multiple regression techniques and a large national sample allow Blau and Duncan conclusively to establish this fact and hence the importance of the entry period in any analysis of occupational structure in the United States. Of course, these data do nothing to describe the processes of entry itself, beyond proving that it is important.

Career thresholds, by Parnes *et al.* (1969), also reports on data from a large national sample with detailed data on the entry period. This preliminary report goes little farther than the presentation of marginals for the data of the first year of a five year panel study of a national sample of males, aged initially fourteen to twenty-four. So far Parnes has not attempted either to present a theoretical framework for analysis or to use multivariate techniques to untangle the effects of different variables. Parnes provides many cross-tabulations showing the relationship between race, socio-economic status, educational attainment, and age run against occupation, aspirations, job satisfaction, and knowledge of the labor market. Predictably, the older, white, better educated individuals from higher status families have better jobs, experience less unemployment, know more about the job market, and have higher occupational and educational aspirations.

Taken together, all of these studies reveal that the entry period has an extremely important influence on the course of an individual's occupational career. This general finding shows through despite the variation from study to study in the populations being studied, in the time periods involved, and in the statistical techniques employed. Although much more sophisticated and detailed analyses can be expected to come from the Parnes study, so far very little is known about the process of entry. Indeed, from one study to the next, there is even some difficulty in squaring the varying definitions of the entry point itself. For example, Parnes defines entry as the first full-time job after completion of high school, while Blau and Duncan leave it up to the respondent to define what was his first full-time job.

The survey of previous literature points up several deficiencies in our knowledge concerning the entry point. First, there is need for a definition of this point which has face validity and can be easily applied in operational form. Secondly, the early studies suffer from employing samples which are not drawn from useful universes. Hence, to make progress it is necessary to move to universes that are at least free of regional and local variation. Thirdly, full advantage needs to be taken of modern data handling techniques and methods of statistical analysis. Fourthly, the analysis should be process oriented in the sense of investigating the impact of statuses at one point in time on statuses at a later point. We hope that this paper will start to fill in these gaps in our knowledge of entry into the labor force.

3. *The data*

The data consist of a set of 1589 interviews with American men between the ages of thirty and thirty-four at the time of the interview (the first months of 1969). The respondents were drawn using probability sampling techniques from the American population of these men [1]. In order to facilitate the

1. The sample target population was the total population of males 30-39 years of age residing in households in the United States. Individuals in the sample were selected by standard multi-stage area probability methods. The National Opinion Research Center drew the sample and conducted the interviews.

comparison of blacks and whites [2], blacks were over-sampled so that they occur about four times as frequently in the sample as they do in the population. Restricting the men to these in a comparatively narrow range of ages and the knowledge that these individuals entered the labor market during a period of quite uniform demand made it possible for us to ignore cohort effects, at least in this analysis. The instrument employed is of a unique design. Interviewers recorded, on the questionnaire, in a fashion so as to yield longitudinal data, all respondents' full and part-time educational and employment experience, including the wage, occupation, and industry of the jobs, how they were obtained and the reason for leaving them. In addition, the composition of the respondent's dwelling unit and hence his family, his geographical location, his feeling about the adequacy of his income, and a number of other variables were obtained. Important static variables, such as the respondent's father's educational attainment and occupation were collected. Wherever possible the race of the interviewer and the respondent were matched.

4. *Definition of entry point*

Although many persons have rather straightforward patterns of entry into the labor force, in which the first job is held only after the completion of a conventional unit of education (*e.g.* graduation from high school) there are significant proportions of individuals who have more complicated histories. Some of the complications include temporary summer employment while attending school during the regular academic year, part-time employment, and patterns of interruptions in schooling to participate in the labor force on a full-time basis. Some individuals who held full-time employment at the same time attended school on a full-time basis. Yet, sooner or later, almost all American males settle into a pattern of full-time participation in the labor force interrupted by periods of unemployment, bouts of illness, and the like.

We wished to develop a definition of the time point at which an individual makes a commitment to participation in the labor force. The definition had to satisfy the following criteria:

a) Short term entry into the labor market, followed by a return to full-time schooling (as occurs for each "summer job" while he is in school) was not to be treated as entry into the labor market;

b) Entry had to be marked by the individual's leaving school for a prolonged period of time;

c) The definition was not to be tied to chronological age, since entry into the

2. Throughout this paper, Mexican-Americans, Puerto Ricans, Chinese, Japanese, American Indians, etc., are classified in the "white" group. They constitute only 3.3 % of the total whites.

labor force can take place at any age beyond sixteen, the commonly defined legal limit of compulsory school attendance; and,

d) It had to be easily applied to our data.

The definition which satisfies the above conditions is as follows: the point of entry into the labor force is that point in time at which an individual leaves full-time education and enters the labor force for a period of more than sixteen months without re-entering full-time education during that period. Note that this definition exempts summer employment and dropping out of school for one academic year plus a summer and defines commitment to labor force participation as participation for a period longer than sixteen months.

Obviously, there is a degree of arbitrariness in this definition, as in almost all operational definitions. Perhaps its major drawback lies in its treatment of military service as full-time employment, so that a person's being interrupted in schooling by being drafted is interpreted as leading him to enter the labor force, even though he had intentions of resuming full-time education after completion of this military service. However, given the fact that educational exemptions were given out rather freely during the period in question, we feel that such cases are small in number.

5. *Educational attainment and age upon entry into the labor force*

A majority of the men interviewed entered the labor force upon the completion of a conventional unit of education, *i.e.* upon graduation from elementary, high school, college or the completion of an advanced degree, as shown in the first two columns of Table 1. Significant differences in this respect appear between the two racial groups; 62.7 % of the whites as compared to 39.8 % of the blacks enter the labor force upon the completion of a conventional unit. For both blacks and whites, the modal point of entry occurs upon graduation from high school; 42.2 % of the whites and 29.2 % of the blacks enter at that point. The median point of entry for whites is upon completion of high school with 42.2 % of the whites entering here; the mode point for blacks entering the labor force is after some high schooling when 35.4 % enter.

The most striking — and also the most expected — feature of the array of educational attainments shown in Table 1 is the strong difference between the two racial groups. Whites tend to enter the labor force after considerably greater amounts of educational attainments and to enter at the point of completion of an educational unit. Blacks enter with less education and most often break off before completing educational units.

Entering the labor force does not put an end to formal education, as the contrast between the last two columns of Table 1 with the first two columns indicates. By the time our respondents have entered upon their second jobs, some shifts in educational attainment have occurred. Between the start of the first and second jobs, the number without high school diplomas has dropped from 21.7 % to 15.2 % among whites and from 30.4 % to 25.9 % among

Table 1. *Educational attainment by race at entry into the labor force and at start of first and second jobs after entry into the labor force (Percentages)*

Educational attainment *	At entry		At start of first job		At start of second job	
	Whites	Blacks	Whites	Blacks	Whites	Blacks
Four years or less	1.6	4.8	6.0	10.2	1.5	4.7
Five to seven years	4.7	13.2	4.3	12.2	4.4	13.4
Completed elementary school	9.2	7.1	11.4	8.0	9.3	6.8
Total elementary or less	*15.5*	*25.1*	*21.7*	*30.4*	*15.2*	*25.9*
Some high school	21.1	35.4	19.1	33.4	18.4	33.2
High school graduate	42.2	29.2	39.4	6.9	42.3	30.5
High school graduation plus vocational training	0.7	0.4	1.0	0.5	2.5	1.2
Some college	9.8	6.7	8.7	5.7	10.1	6.5
College graduate	7.9	3.3	7.5	8.2	8.2	3.0
MA degree or equivalent	1.2	0.1	1.1	0.1	1.1	0.0
Some graduate training but no advanced degree	0.1	0.0	0.1	0.1	0.1	0.1
Ph.D or professional degree	1.5	0.0	1.0	0.0	1.3	0.1
(N)	(849)	(736)	(850)	(737)	(814)	(700)

* Note that our respondents have slightly more educational attainment at the point of entry into the labor force than at the start of the first job. This results from small numbers of respondents starting their first job, which lasts after entry, before leaving school, thus participating in both activities at the same time for a period.

blacks. The major sources of this change are part-time schooling, education obtained during military service and the fact that some individuals begin their first jobs lasting past the entry point before leaving full-time schooling, carrying on both the activities simultaneously for a time.

Because the educational attainment levels achieved by whites and blacks differ so strikingly, as shown in Table 1, and because educational level has so strong an impact upon occupational life, in tables to follow we will ordinarily show statistics for educational levels separately or hold education constant in multivariate analyses. The three educational levels we will ordinarily use are shown in Table 2. The categories correspond roughly to completion of major stages in the American educational system. Note particularly that the number of blacks who have completed college at time of entry into the labor force is quite small (24 cases out of 738) so that statistics shown for black college graduates will be less reliable than statistics shown for any of the other groups.

Looking within the three educational attainment categories in Table 2, we find that whites and blacks enter the labor force at very much the same ages. The exception is for those who graduate from college — on the average the whites in this category enter about a year later than the corresponding group

Table 2. *Age at time of entry into the labor force by educational attainment*

Educational attainment at entry into labor force	Average age for					
	Whites			Blacks		
	Yrs.	*Mos.*	(N)	*Yrs.*	*Mos.*	(N)
Did not complete high school	15	10	(311)	16	3	(444)
High school graduate or some college (no degree)	18	6	(447)	18	7	(267)
College graduate or graduate education	22	10	(89)	22	0	(27)
Average for total group	18	0		17	4	
Median for total group	18	4		17	4	

of blacks. This is no doubt due to the fact that more of the whites proceed to further study at the graduate and professional levels.

Typical entry into the labor force occurs within a year of one's eighteenth birthday. Those who receive more schooling obviously enter at later ages. For both races without high school diplomas, the average age at entry is approximately sixteen years; for high school graduates the average age is eighteen and a half years. The mean age on entry for white college graduates is twenty-two years and ten months; blacks in this category average just about twenty-two years of age when they enter.

The typical pattern of entry for white males is to complete a unit of education before going into the labor market for an extensive period of time. Since most typically finish high school and few go further, this means that the modal white male enters the labor force at the time of high school graduation. The pattern of entry for blacks shows much less modality. Fairly large proportions of blacks enter before the completion of either elementary school or high school. Although some do manage to obtain additional education, apparently through part-time education and while in military service, the proportion who finish high school remains still considerably lower than that of whites.

6. *Pre-entry work experience*

The definition of entry into the labor force which we have constructed does not preclude work experiences before entry. Indeed, three out of five (61 %) whites have had part-time employment and/or full-time employment before their entry points; the corresponding proportion for blacks is 34 %. Of course these proportions are highly affected by the age of entry into the labor force: the older he is at the time of labor force entry, the more opportunities a respondent has had to hold summer time or other short term commitment positions. The lower educational attainment of blacks and their correspondingly earlier age at entry means that they have had less opportunity to obtain short term employment before making a major commitment to the labor force.

Table 3. *Pre-entry full-time work experiences of blacks and whites by educational attainment at entry point*

Full-time jobs held before entry	Did not complete high school		High school graduate		College graduate	
	Whites	Blacks	Whites	Blacks	Whites	Blacks
	%	%	%	%	%	%
Held at least one full-time job	14.8	7.9	43.0	21.4	90.2	44.0
Average number of jobs	.31	.16	1.29	.64	4.65	1.68
Average time in jobs (months)	1.5	1.3	4.7	3.1	17.4	5.7
Average prestige scores of jobs	22.2	21.0	23.9	21.8	30.9	23.9
(N)	(311)	(444)	(447)	(267)	(91)	(25)

Data on the full-time jobs held by respondents before they entered the labor force are shown in Table 3. Because the major pre-entry activity of our respondents was full-time attendance at school, most of the full-time positions were held during summer vacations [3]. As we have intimated above, the longer an individual has postponed entry into the labor force the more likely he is to have had some full-time employment experience before entry. Thus, among whites, 14.8 % of those who have not graduated from high school, 43.0 % of those who have completed high school, and 90 % of those who have gone to college have held at least one full-time job before entry into the labor force. The same pattern obtains for blacks, except that at each level of educational attainment, blacks are only about half as likely to have held a full-time job before entry.

Not only are whites more likely to have held full-time jobs, they also get better jobs, as the last line in Table 3 indicates. Furthermore, the higher the educational level, the greater the gap between whites and blacks in the prestige scores [4] of the full-time jobs held before entry.

In order to interpret what these scores mean in terms of occupational levels,

3. The median duration time of pre-entry full-time jobs is 3.0 months for both whites and blacks, indicating that such jobs were most likely held during the typical three month school vacations.

4. Prestige scores are average ratings given the occupations by samples of the American population. The scores represent the consensus of American society concerning the social status of occupations. Such scores are used throughout this report because they provide a quantitative dimension for occupations which has been shown to be remarkably stable over time and over different groups within the American population.

it is useful to consider the scores obtained by a few occupations representative of different levels of the occupational system, as follows:

	Scores
1. Janitor	16.1
2. Unskilled laborer	18.4
3. Assemblers	27.1
4. Painter	29.8
5. Auto mechanic	36.7
6. Barber	37.0
7. Tailor	41.2
8. Bookkeeper	47.6
9. Skilled machinist	47.8
10. Medical technician	61.0
11. Physician	81.5

It can easily be seen that the full-time jobs held by our respondents tend to be on the lowest levels of the occupational structure, as one might expect from both the inexperience of the respondents at the time and the fact that the jobs are temporary. Even the temporary jobs of college students tend to be lower on the average in prestige than the position of skilled machinist.

Corresponding data for part-time employment during the pre-entry period are shown in Table 4. Part-time employment is much more compatible with going to school than full-time employment, and hence as we might anticipate the level of part-time employment during the pre-entry period is higher. Nearly half of the whites and one out of every four blacks had some part-time employment experience in the pre-entry period [5].

Table 4. *Pre-entry part-time experiences of blacks and whites by educational attainment at entry point*

Part-time jobs held before entry	Did not complete high school		High school graduate		College graduate	
	Whites	Blacks	Whites	Blacks	Whites	Blacks
	%	%	%	%	%	%
Held at least one part-time job	29.3	18.1	54.6	33.0	66.0	60.0
Average number of jobs	.46	.25	1.27	.77	2.74	1.12
Average time in jobs (months)	5.8	4.3	15.5	11.4	33.5	24.0
Average prestige scores of jobs	20.	20.5	23.1	19.8	29.1	27.1
(N)	(311)	(444)	(447)	(267)	(91)	(25)

5. Precise proportions for whites and blacks are as follows:

	Held at least one position during pre-entry	
	Whites	*Blacks*
Full-time positions	38 %	14 %
Part-time positions	46 %	25 %

The pattern of relationships displayed in Table 4 is very similar to that of Table 3, indicating that the more educational experience a respondent has had (and hence the greater opportunity), the more likely he was to have had some part-time employment before entering the labor force. Again, whites are much more likely to have held part-time positions than blacks, with the ratio of the average numbers of such jobs being of the order of two to one in favor of whites.

The average amount of time spent in part-time employment is, of course, considerably higher than in the case of full-time employment. For example, white college students have spent on the average nearly three years and black college graduates slightly more than two years at one or another part-time position.

The prestige positions of the part-time jobs held by respondents are about the same as in the full-time positions. In short, these are low level jobs involving low skill levels and undoubtedly low remuneration. Their average prestige scores are slightly below those of the full-time positions held, but even if those differences were statistically significant, they would not represent salient differences in prestige.

The pre-entry experiences of our sample indicate that a large proportion have had experience with holding a part-time or temporary full-time job before leaving full-time education to make a major commitment to work. The longer the educational experience, the more likely the respondent was to have had such pre-entry job experiences. Indeed, most college graduates have been into and out of the labor force several times by the time they receive their BA's. The jobs held are close to the bottom of the social status ladder, being the kinds of jobs that can be held by temporary help with miscellaneous skills and little experience. These are jobs which do not appear to be the sort that would lead to occupational careers, especially for those with at least a few years of normal schooling.

7. *Obtaining the first job after entry*

Once having left full-time education, our respondents found jobs rather quickly, as Table 5 indicates. Some, especially the poorly educated, apparently dropped out of school in order to retain the jobs they held prior to leaving school. The top row of Table 5 indicates that about one in five of males who did not complete high school continued jobs they had held prior to leaving full-tim eeducation on entry into the labor force. Much smaller proportions of high school and college graduates manifested this pattern, both among whites and blacks.

Around half of the respondents found jobs within a month after entering the labor force, with larger proportions of whites doing so than blacks. Especially disadvantaged in this respect were black college graduates,

Table 5. *Employment and unemployment after entry into the labor force by educational level and race (Percentages)*

How first job was found	Did not complete high school		High school graduate		College graduate	
	Whites	Blacks	Whites	Blacks	Whites	Blacks
Employed at job held prior to entry	7.0	9.0	11.2	11.2	13.1	8.0
Found new job within one month after entry	64.6	67.7	68.0	59.1	65.9	36.0
Unemployed one to six months	18.0	12.0	26.1	30.7	28.8	44.0
Unemployed six months or more*	18.4	20.3	5.9	10.2	5.5	20.0
Average number of months unemployed	4.5	4.6	1.4	2.3	1.5	3.3
(N)	(311)	(444)	(447)	(267)	(91)	(25)

* These percentages are included in the line above.

although it should be borne in mind that the number of cases on which this finding is based is very small.

Among those who were unemployed for more than a month, blacks were unemployed for longer periods of time and the length of unemployment for this racial group increased with the level of educational attainment.

For those who did not enter the labor force within a month after leaving school, the average length of unemployment is about six months for whites and ten months for blacks. The distributions are very skewed, the median times with no jobs are three and four months for whites and blacks respectively.

Not all were so fortunate, however. There are still significant proportions who experienced six or more months of unemployment, as the fourth row of Table 5 indicates. The incidence of such long term unemployment periods following entry is especially high among the least educated groups, among those who have completed less than high school education. 18 % of the whites and 20 % of the blacks have not found a job six months after leaving school. Blacks appear to be more likely to experience long periods of unemployment, with the college educated equally likely to do so. (Again, one must be wary of the small number of college educated blacks in our sample.)

The ways in which respondents found their first jobs are shown in Table 6. Note that friends and relatives are apparently the most commonly employed channels of information, although direct application to employers (the largest

Table 6. *How first jobs were found by race and educational attainment (excluding military service) (Percentages)*

How first job was found	Did not complete high school		High school graduate		College graduate	
	Whites	Blacks	Whites	Blacks	Whites	Blacks
Friends	24.8	31.9	23.8	26.2	16.4	6.3
Relatives	39.8	36.6	28.2	22.7	18.0	12.5
Public agencies	1.5	1.4	4.0	5.7	1.6	12.5
Private agencies	0.8	0.6	3.0	1.1	4.9	6.3
Advertisements	4.1	2.2	5.7	6.3	3.3	0.0
Other means *	28.9	27.4	34.2	37.5	55.7	62.5
No information	0.0	0.0	1.0	5.6	0.0	0.0
(N)	(266)	(361)	(298)	(176)	(61)	(16)

* "Other means" includes direct application either by mail or applying at business employment offices, being recommended by someone and consequently being solicited directly, and so on. It is our impression that the vast majority of the cases counted in this category involve direct application on the part of the respondent.

category [6] included in "other means") is also important. There are larger differences among the three educational levels in these respects than between the two racial groups. The lower educational levels tend to rely more on friends and relatives, and the higher educational groups use more active and impersonal means — *i.e.* direct application and to some extent private and public employment agencies.

The implications of the findings in Table 6 are rather important. If persons entering the labor market use their friends and relatives for job market information, it is not likely that they will become exposed to the full range of job opportunities available to them in the local labor market. Particularly handicapped in this respect would be blacks whose friendship and kinship networks are very likely to be restricted largely to their own racial group, thereby tending to perpetuate a dual labor market, one for each of the major racial groups.

8. *Characteristics of the first job after entry*

A few salient characteristics of the first jobs held by our respondents after their entry into the labor force are shown in Table 7. To begin with, the jobs held after entry, as one might expect, are a cut or two above those which the respondents held on either a part-time or full-time basis before they left school.

6. These data come from a check list which the interviewer used to probe after each new job was recorded. Unfortunately, "direct application" was not used as one of the categories and hence this very frequent means of finding jobs cannot be separated from this residual category, which contains other means as well.

The differences[7] are particularly striking for college graduates, but even for men who did not complete high school there are differences in average prestige scores between these first jobs and previously held positions, of the order of 3 points — equivalent to the difference in scores between assembly line workers and house painters. For those who have completed high school, the differences are of the order of 6 points, or about the difference between assembly line workers and auto mechanics. For college graduates, of course, the differences are much larger, averaging about 16 points for whites and 13 points for blacks.

Table 7. *Selected characteristics of first job by race and educational attainment at entry point*

Selected characteristics of first job	Did not complete high school		High school graduate		College graduate	
	Whites	Blacks	Whites	Blacks	Whites	Blacks
Average occupational prestige	24.9	22.8	29.0	26.8	45.8	38.5
(N)	(309)	(442)	(444)	(267)	(90)	(25)
Average duration of first job (months)	33.4	44.5	26.1	32.9	34.1	28.5
Median duration of first job (months)	19	28	15	24	19	22
(N)	(311)	(444)	(447)	(267)	(91)	(25)
Percent whose first jobs are military	15.7	12.7	17.4	20.9	16.4	28.0
(N)	(311)	(444)	(447)	(267)	(91)	(25)

Those who do not complete high school obtain first jobs after entry which have average prestige scores close to that of assembly line workers; those who finished high school do a little better but their jobs have average scores which are about 2 points above those accorded to operatives. College graduates,

7. The exact differences are as follows:

Differences in prestige scores between first job after entry and:	Educational attainment at entry point					
	Did not complete high school		High school graduates		College graduates	
	Whites	Blacks	Whites	Blacks	Whites	Blacks
Average score for previous full-time jobs	2.7	1.8	5.1	14.9	14.9	14.6
Average scores for previous part-time jobs	4.5	2.3	5.9	16.7	16.7	11.4

as might be expected, do considerably better, with whites averaging around the scores of bookkeepers and skilled machinists and blacks with scores a little lower than tailors, but higher than barbers. It should be borne in mind that these are first jobs, and although the scores appear to be low, especially for college graduates, promotions and job changes will bring the average scores for subsequent jobs more into line with common sense expectations.

At least part of the reason for the seemingly depressed prestige scores for college graduates can be seen in the last row of Table 7, where the proportions who enter military service as their first jobs after entry are shown. Blacks and whites are about equally likely to enter the military service immediately after entry, the overall proportions being 16.2 % for whites and 16.7 % for blacks. However, race differences appear if we examine the three educational attainment groups; the greater their educational attainment, the more likely blacks are to start their careers with a period of military service, while no clear pattern emerges for whites.

Considering the length of time spent in first jobs, it is difficult to characterize the period after entry as one of "floundering about". On the average, both whites and blacks hold their first jobs for more than two years, respondents with less educational attainment and blacks spending longer periods of time on these first jobs after entry. However, averages conceal the fact that there is a considerable amount of short term job holding. If we examine the median durations of first jobs, as in the third line of Table 7, we find that half of the whites hold their first jobs for less than two years, ranging from fifteen months for white high school graduates to nineteen months for those who do not complete high school to nineteen months for white college graduates. The median durations for blacks are higher, especially for those who do not complete high school.

Thus, it appears that the durations of first jobs are quite variable, with enough individuals holding them for long time periods to raise the average duration about a year above the median. Many of our respondents held their first jobs for short periods of time, showing that a certain amount of trial-and-error experimentation with jobs does occur during this early period. Table 8 contains a detailed breakdown of the durations of first jobs held by our respondents.

Should we assume that jobs held for short periods of time, say up to six months, include a large proportion of trials which either the respondent or the employer found unpromising, then at each of the white educational levels between 20 and 30 % of the first jobs are in this category. Blacks are less likely to hold their first jobs for short periods of time. Among the blacks who did not complete high school, only about one in ten held his first job for six months or less; the corresponding figures for high school graduates is one in five, and for college graduates, one in three.

We note that there are rather large proportions who hold their first jobs for long periods of time. The last two lines of Table 8 show the numbers who

Table 8. *Duration of first job after entry, by race and educational attainment (Percentages)*

Duration of first job after entry	Did not complete high school		High school graduate		College Graduate	
	Whites	Blacks	Whites	Blacks	Whites	Blacks
Three or less (months)	9.0	4.0	17.0	11.9	21.9	8.0
Four to six (months)	12.5	5.9	12.3	7.9	9.0	24.0
Seven to twelve (months)	16.7	13.9	17.2	14.2	11.0	8.0
One to two (years)	19.0	19.2	20.1	18.4	20.9	32.0
Two to three (years)	13.8	19.1	10.8	16.4	12.1	12.0
Three to five (years)	16.7	17.0	14.9	21.0	7.7	8.0
More than five (years)	12.3	20.7	7.7	10.2	15.4	8.0
(N)	(111)	(444)	(447)	(267)	(91)	(25)

held their first jobs for three to five years and for over five years, respectively. About one in three of the respondents who did not complete high school was in one of these long tenure groups, the proportions being slightly higher for blacks than for whites. Although the better educated are less likely to hold jobs for such long periods, the differences are not very great; thus, one in five white high school and college graduates have held their first jobs for more than three years. The corresponding proportions for blacks are higher for high school graduates (one in three) but lower for black college graduates (a little less than one in six, though once again the small number of black college graduates in our sample makes this last figure unreliable).

The durations of first jobs are so variable within each educational level and within each racial group that it is difficult to make a simple characterization of the first jobs held. Many of those in our sample hold their first jobs for three or more years. Obviously some find their first jobs not to their liking and shift, with whites more likely to shift than blacks, and the better educated respondents more likely to shift than the less well educated. This is hardly the picture of "floundering" that previous researchers have attempted to draw. Rather, the process appears to be one in which those who have more advantages on the labor market through their race and educational experience "shop around" for jobs while those who are not in such advantageous positions tend to persist longer in their first jobs.

9. *An explanatory note on method*

Up to this point in this report we have been concerned primarily with presenting a description of the ways in which white and black men of different levels of educational attainment enter the labor force. The remainder of this report will have a more analytic focus, attempting to explain both the variations in the characteristic modes of entry and the consequences for subsequent occupational attainment. The techniques to be employed may be somewhat unfamiliar to the reader and hence we will digress in this section of the report to present a rather detailed description of the type of multiple regression analysis to be employed. We will also use this opportunity to describe more fully the main variables to be used, especially those which will be introduced for the first time.

The main variables to be used in the analysis are as follows:

Social class background. This is a cluster of variables all pertaining to the parental family of the respondent, consisting of the prestige score of the occupation held by the respondent's father (or whoever was head of household), his father's educational attainment, and his mother's educational attainment. Educational attainment has been transformed in this analysis into a continuous variable taking on the values from zero through ten; *e.g.* a high school graduate is scored 4 and a college graduate is scored 7 [8].

Pre-entry employment experience. This is a cluster of four variables pertaining to the part-time and full-time employment experiences of the respondent prior to entry into the labor force. Two dummy variables are used to represent respectively the holding of any full-time or part-time employment before entry. The other two variables are the prestige scores for the jobs held on a part-time and a full-time basis.

Respondent's educational attainment at entry. This variable is a quantitative score ranging from zero to 10, using the same scoring procedure as employed in the case of mother's and father's educational attainment.

Job prestige scores. The prestige scores and their derivation have been discussed earlier. Such scores have been computed for each and every job held by respondent throughout his occupational career. These scores will be the main dependent variable in the analysis which follows.

We will present several measures of the effects of clusters of variables and of the single variables used in the analysis. The variance explained by a cluster or a single variable will be partitioned into the amount of variance which it shares with other independent variables and combinations of other variables and the unique variance (Wisler, 1969; Mayeske, 1969). The unique variance of an independent variable is the amount of the variance in the dependent variable which that independent variable contributes over and above its joint contributions with the other independent variables used in that particular analysis. Thus the unique variance for social class background in explaining, say, occupational prestige of the respondent's first job, would be the amount of additional explanatory power that social class background contributes over and above the other independent variables used in the analysis.

"Social class background" and "pre-entry employment experience" will be treated in the analysis as clusters of variables whose combined effects on occupational prestige will be calculated. There are two clear advantages to treating these variables as clusters rather than working with their individual components. The components of the clusters, for example the occupational prestige of the respondent's father and the educational attainment of both

8. The scale is essentially similar to the one used in P.M. Blau and O.D. Duncan, *The American occupational structure*, New York, John Wiley, pp. 165-166, which ranges from 0 to 8.

his parents, are in fact measures of the underlying social class of the individual's family of origin and their separate effects cannot, in substance, be separated. This is known as multicollinearity. The principal advantage, and the reason why we do not use a single variable in place of the cluster, is that by combining three or more measures of single effect, like social class, we can get a much better estimate of the importance of that effect than can be obtained from a single variable.

The task of the multiple regression technique presented here is to yield quantitative measures of the importance of different factors in predicting some outcome (like the occupational prestige score of the respondent's first job). We will present several measures of the effects of clusters of variables and of single variables in each of the multiple regressions described. If we consider multiple regressions in which there are two independent variables, the variance they account for when regressed against some dependent variable can be split into three parts: the variance uniquely associated with the first variable, the variance uniquely associated with the second variable, and a third part which cannot be uniquely assigned to either of the two variables and is the effect they share. In a similar fashion, if there are three variables, the variance can be uniquely split into seven such unique effects, one for each possible combination of the presence or absence of each of the variables (excluding, of course, the eighth combination, that where each of the variables is absent). If there are four independent variables, fifteen such parts exist.

These unique measures show the importance of a given variable or combination of variables, after removing the effect of *all* other combinations of variables — it is the absolute minimum measure of the importance of the variable or cluster: hence the term ''unique.'' The other measure we will present is the ''zero order'' effect. This value, or rather percentage of the total variance, is a measure of the maximum possible effect of the variable or cluster. It is obtained by entering only the variable or cluster in question into the regression equation; there is thus no control for the effects of other variables. There is often a wide discrepancy between the unique and ''first order'' effect of a variable or cluster, the latter often being several times larger than the latter.

An example of the general form of the regression technique is given in Table 9, where we present an analysis of the relative importance of three factors influencing the respondent's educational attainment at his first job after entry. The three social background variables — the prestige of father's occupation, father's educational attainment and mother's educational attainment — are the variables whose effects we evaluate. Each row in Table 9 represents a combination of the three variables used as independent variables in this analysis. Thus, the first row pertains to the combination in which only father's occupational prestige is present. The first two entries in the row contain the amount of the variance, for whites and blacks respectively, explained by this variable when it is correlated alone with educational attainment. The last two entries in that row contain the unique contribution of this variable when all the other variables and combinations of variables in the analysis are taken into account. Thus we may note that for whites, the zero order effect of father's occupational prestige explains 10.4 % of the variance in respondent's educational attainment; however, when the other effects are taken into account, the unique contribution of father's occupational prestige is only to explain 2.6 % of the variance.

Table 9. *Educational attainment at entry, by social class background variables, and by race*

Combinations of independent variables *			Variance in educational attainment explained (Percentages)			
			Zero-order variance		Unique variance	
Father's occupational prestige	Father's education	Mother's education	Whites	Blacks	Whites	Blacks
+	0	0	10.4	2.6	2.6	0.6
0	+	0	17.7	11.9	3.5	1.0
0	0	+	15.6	15.5	2.2	2.3
+	+	0	20.1	12.4	2.2	0.6
+	0	+	20.4	16.7	0.4	-0.1
0	+	+	21.3	17.1	7.8	8.8
+	+	+	23.9	17.7	5.3	1.5

* "+" signifies the presence of an independent variable in a combination, and "0" signifies its absence.

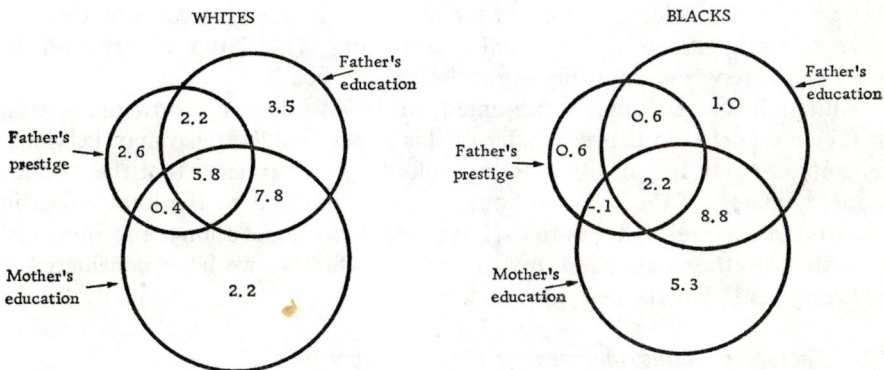

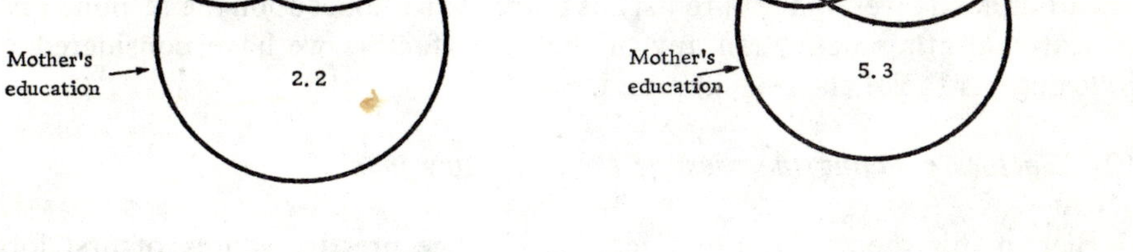

The last row of Table 9 contains the combinations in which all three variables are present. We find that the three variables together explain 23.9 % of the total variance for whites and 17.7 % for blacks. However, as the last two entries in the last row indicate, the three variables taken together have unique contributions of 8.3 % and 6.9 % respectively, indicating that the unique contributions of the overlap combinations of the variables are making up the difference. These figures reveal the common effect that cannot be distinguished as belonging to one of the three variables or pairwise combination of them. It thus represents a measure of the effect of social class, taken holistically, on the educational attainment of the individual growing up in the household.

The last two columns of Table 9 contain the most important data resulting from this form of analysis. The unique contributions are a concise way of assessing the relative importance of the variables designated as independent. Thus, the last two columns indicate that father's occupational prestige accounts for 2.6 % of the variance for whites and 0.6 % of the variance for blacks, father's educational attainment accounts for 3.5 % for whites and 1.0 % of the variance for blacks, while mother's educational attainment accounts for 2.2 % for whites and 5.3 % of the variance for blacks. It is clear that the educational experience of the respondent's parents is more important than the occupational prestige of whoever was the major breadwinner in the respondent's parental family.

For both races there is a large part of the variance that is common to the father's and mother's educational attainment and cannot be separated out as belonging to one of them: 7.8 % of the variance for whites and 8.8 % of a total of 17.7 % for blacks. There is more common variance associated with the father's occupational prestige and his educational attainment for whites than there is for blacks. Taken together, these figures show blacks to be much more strongly influenced by their mothers than their fathers, while for whites the opposite is the case. This finding has ample precedent in the literature. Furthermore, we see that there is an important variable that might be termed "educational climate of the family" that results from a factor common to both parents' educational attainment. This latter observation can only be made when a partitioning technique is used.

Although we have mainly presented Table 9 to illustrate how the analysis will be conducted in the remainder of this paper, Table 9 also may be viewed as containing an important substantive finding. It appears that the "educational climate" of the parental households, as indexed by the joint educational attainment levels of the parents, has more of an impact upon the respondent's educational attainment than any of the other factors we have considered as indexing his social class background.

10. *Factors affecting the prestige level of entry jobs*

Earlier in this report, we presented the average prestige scores of first jobs after entry and were able to show that typically our respondents entered the occupational system at fairly low prestige levels. However, these averages conceal considerable variation among individuals within each of the two racial groups. Within each educational attainment level, there was considerable variation from individual to individual in the social status level at which he entered the occupational system. For example, among college graduates, some entered as physicians, whose prestige score is among the highest of all occupations, and some entered as bookkeepers. Similarly, among those who did not complete high school, some entered as unskilled laborers and some as auto mechanics, a span of approximately 20 points in prestige scores.

What accounts for the level at which a respondent enters the occupational system? Table 10 presents part of the answer to this question, regressing social class background, pre-entry employment experience and educational attainment on the occupational prestige scores of the respondents' first jobs. Compared to the usual run-of-the-mill social science analyses, a rather impressive amount of the variance is explained: 37.9 % for the whites and 23.1 % for the blacks. For whites, jobs before entry account uniquely for 12.7 % of the variance in prestige of first job; for blacks 7.7 %. Note that pre-entry job experience has the largest of all unique contributions for both whites and blacks. This may indicate that being an experienced worker helps in placement after completion of education, or it may indicate that pre-entry jobs provide an *entrée* into the business involved, or it may mean that those who have the initiative to find full-time and part-time work while they are still going to school show an extra amount of initiative in looking for their first jobs after they leave school. Given our data, it is not possible to sort out these alternative explanations, although it should be clear that this finding indicates another way in which blacks are disadvantaged as they approach the labor force. Fewer blacks have had pre-entry labor force experience, as our earlier analysis indicated, and the proportion of the variance explained for blacks by this fact is considerably less, showing that blacks are less able to cash in on their pre-entry work experience when they do enter the labor force.

Class background, as measured by a three-variable cluster consisting of the father's occupational prestige and the educational attainment of both the parents, accounts for 3.6 % of the variance for blacks, only 0.6 % for whites. Educational attainment at the start of the first job uniquely explains about the same amount of total variance for whites and blacks, 5.2 % and 3.9 % respectively.

Among the more interesting findings are those related to the unique contributions of combinations of variables. For example, the overlapping effects of previous work experience and educational attainment for whites is 11.9 %, the second largest unique contribution, while the corresponding figure for blacks is not significantly different from zero. The actual figure is negative, - 0.3 %. A negative unique contribution can result from random error or from the inclusion of two variables strongly negatively correlated in the regression. In this case, the negative contribution is not significantly different from zero and is just a random error. Apparently, whites are better able to capitalize on their previous work experience if they have high educational attainment than are blacks.

Table 10. *Prestige of first job. Social class background, pre-entry employment, and educational attainment, by race*

Combinations of independent variables *			Variance in prestige of first job explained (Percentages)			
			Zero-order variance		Unique variance	
Class background	Pre-entry jobs	Educational attainment	Whites	Blacks	Whites	Black
+	0	0	7.9	10.1	0.6	3.2
0	+	0	31.1	11.0	12.7	7.7
0	0	+	24.4	11.1	5.4	5.6
+	+	0	32.5	17.5	0.2	1.1
+	0	+	25.2	15.4	0.8	3.2
0	+	+	37.3	19.9	11.9	-0.3
+	+	+	37.9	23.1	6.3	2.6

* "+" signifies that the variable in question is present in a combination and "0" signifies that it has been left out of that combination.

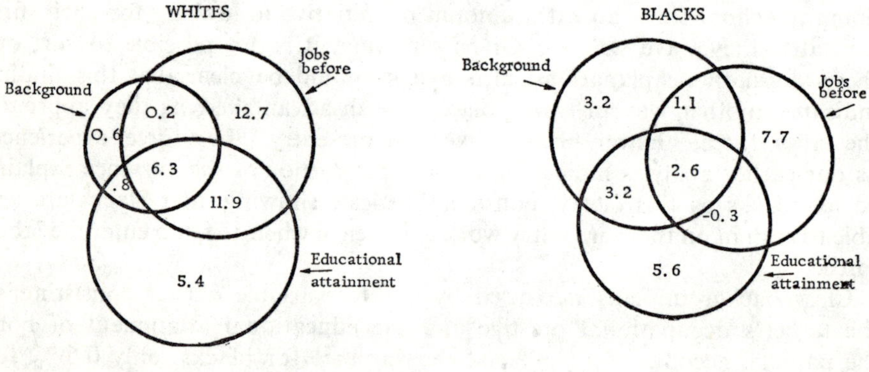

The general picture that emerges from the findings of Table 11 is that the prestige level at which whites enter the labor market can be better predicted than that of blacks. From one point of view, this can be viewed as disadvantageous to blacks and from another point of view, it can be viewed as having the opposite connotation. A finding is that those blacks with more education and who have some work experience before entry are not able to employ these characteristics in seeking for a job to the same extent as whites. In short, you get less credit for your work experience and attainment if you are black. From this viewpoint, the findings are consistent with the interpretation that blacks are being discriminated against on the labor market.

However, since blacks tend to be disadvantaged with respect to pre-entry jobs held and educational attainment, the lack of a close fit between these factors and prestige level of first jobs means that these handicaps are not too restrictive on subsequent occupational attainment, since poorer educated blacks are able to do better *relatively*. Hence, these findings have an interpretation which looks as if the occupational system is more easily penetrated by blacks without job experience. However, we should bear in mind that the term "relatively" pertains to blacks as a group and not to the total labor force.

Once again, we can define the effect of overlapping of the three sets of variables in the model (class background, pre-entry work experience, and educational attainment) at the beginning of the first job. For the whites, this common variance is 6.3 %; for the blacks it is only 2.6 %. As in our previous attempt to separate the factors influencing educational attainment, it appears that a broad social class measure, as measured by this overlap variance, is a source of better first jobs for whites but much less so for blacks.

The factors considered up to this point have been ones lying in the respondent's family background or his experiences preceding entry into the labor force. There are, of course, other factors which we have not taken into account, as is evidenced by our finding that the major portion of the variance in the occupational prestige of first jobs cannot be accounted for by the variables we used. We cannot hope ever to explain all the variance, but attempts can be made to see how some additional items of information about the process of entry itself affect occupational outcomes.

As we noted in an earlier section, although the majority of the men in our sample entered the labor force after finishing a conventional unit of education, there were some who left high school before graduation and some who left college without receiving their degrees. To some small extent, those persons who thus began jobs with incomplete educational units managed to finish them later on. The Armed Forces has helped hundreds of thousands of men to complete their high school education by obtaining high school equivalency certificates. Night schools are run by almost every public school system, and in most cities it is possible to obtain a bachelor's degree by attending college or university evening and summers. What is the effect of entering before completing a conventional unit on the kinds of jobs obtained upon entry?

The data displayed in Table 11 show the educational attainment for selected groups of respondents at two points in time — at the time of entry into the labor force and at the end of their second jobs (when most respondents had finished their formal education). The top three rows of Table 11 permit a comparison between those who entered before completing their high schooling and did not return to graduate, those who entered without completing high school and subsequently obtained a high school diploma, and those who entered having completed high school and who received no further schooling. No striking differences appear in the average prestige standings of the first jobs for each of these three groups, though a very slight edge (of about 3 prestige points) goes to those who did complete their high schooling. To summarize, for the historical period in question there was scarcely any point to

Table 11. *Prestige scores of first jobs by educational attainment at entry and educational attainment at end of second job, by race*

Educational attainment at		Prestige scores of first jobs for	
Entry	Interview	Whites	Blacks
Some high school	Some high school	25.2 (126)	23.4 (210)
Some high school	High school graduate	30.6 (27)	25.0 (24)
High school graduate	High school graduate	28.0 (263)	25.9 (16)
Some college	Some college	32.4 (69)	28.5 (43)
Some college	College graduate or more	33.6 (9)	30.0 (1)
College graduate or more	College graduate or more	45.5 (73)	39.2 (21)

finishing high school for either whites or blacks before entering the labor force as far as impact upon the prestige level of the first job was concerned.

Quite a different set of results obtain for completing college, however, as the last three rows of Table 11 indicate. Persons entering the labor force after receiving their BA's enter at a much higher level, of the order of 12 prestige scores points higher, than those who had some college and interrupted their college education. Apparently the BA is much more important as a credential than the high school diploma.

Table 12 is an attempt to discern the effect of using differing means of finding a first job on the prestige level of that job. The entries in the table are average prestige scores of first jobs for the combinations of educational attainment by the means used, as designated in row and column headings respectively. At the bottom of Table 12, we show the results of an analysis of variance calculation of the proportion of the variance in occupational prestige accounted for uniquely by educational attainment and means used. Although, as might be expected, education explains a lot more of the variance in the first job's occupational prestige, there is still a significant amount of the variance that is accounted for by the means used, 6.6 % for whites and 4.8 % for blacks.

Scanning the entries in the table it appears that the major effect of means employed to find jobs occurs for the better educated groups. College graduates who rely on the informal help of friends or relatives obtain first jobs with considerably lower prestige standings than those who rely on direct application ("other means"), employment agencies and advertisements. This finding probably reflects the fact that jobs of a professional sort (*e.g.* teachers, engineers, and so on) are usually offered on a wider labor market and employers rely upon universalistic means to obtain properly qualified employees.

Table 12a. *Prestige scores of first jobs by means of finding jobs, by educational attainment and race*

Means of finding first job	Elementary school or less		High school graduates		College graduates	
	Whites	Blacks	Whites	Blacks	Whites	Blacks
Friends	25.0 (66)	22.3 (115)	27.9 (71)	27.9 (46)	41.5 (10)	63.1 (1)
Family	23.2 (106)	20.7 (132)	28.1 (84)	24.2 (4)	36.7 (11)	23.5 (2)
Public agencies	22.8 (4)	26.7 (5)	31.9 (12)	29.0 (10)	54.3 (1)	49.5 (2)
Private agencies	28.7 (2)	17.3 (2)	35.6 (9)	27.9 (2)	67.8 (3)	52.4 (1)
Adver-tisements	25.3 (11)	21.8 (8)	31.8 (17)	30.1 (110)	51.9 (2)	—
Other means	26.1 (77)	22.8 (99)	29.4 (102)	26.4 (66)	55.9 (34)	43.7 (10)

Table 12b. *Analysis of variance*

Source	Whites	Blacks
F-ratio for education **	56.04 * d.f. = (7,617)	22.58 * d.f. = (7,545)
F-ratio for means of getting first job	9.42 * d.f. = (5,619)	5.26 * d.f. = (5,547)
Variance explained by education	36.15 %	20.66 %
Variance explained by means	7.62 %	4.81 %

* All significant beyond .001.
** Education is broken into eight categories in this analysis of variance.

11. *Effects of entry factors on subsequent occupational attainment*

The rationale that supports investment in the research efforts reported here lies in the belief that where and how a person enters the labor force has a lasting impact upon subsequent occupational career. From the previous research, perhaps the strongest evidence that this is the case comes from Blau and Duncan's finding that the prestige levels of the first jobs reported by their sample had appreciable and independent effects upon the standings of their occupations at the time of the interview. However, since Blau and Duncan allowed the respondents to designate what they thought were their first full-time jobs, it is possible that respondents reported instead those jobs held during the early part of their careers which they thought launched them onto the path leading to their current positions. The data we have gathered in this study, being more detailed about all jobs held in the early stages of entry into the labor force as well as defining an entry point for everyone in a uniform way, can more precisely pinpoint the subsequent effects of the entry jobs.

Table 13. *Average prestige scores and durations of first through fifth jobs, by race* *

	Average values for	
	Whites	Blacks
A. Prestige scores of:		
First jobs	29.3 (843)	24.8 (734)
Second jobs	31.3 (811)	26.6 (696)
Third jobs	32.7 (750)	26.4 (634)
Fourth jobs	34.6 (639)	28.0 (541)
Fifth jobs	34.7 (533)	28.1 (422)
B. Prestige score of job held ten years after entry into labor force	37.5 (773)	28.3 (670)
C. Duration in months of:		
First jobs	29.6 (849)	39.7 (736)
Second jobs	33.4 (813)	35.1 (700)
Third jobs	35.9 (750)	40.7 (638)
Fourth jobs	32.5 (642)	39.4 (543)
Fifth jobs	34.3 (534)	35.1 (424)

* Case bases decline for higher order jobs because some respondents had fewer jobs than the order in question.

From Table 13 we can discern that there is a gradual improvement in prestige standing with each successive job. On the average, the shift upward in prestige for subsequent jobs does not amount to very much with each job shift, although the cumulative effect is an increase of 5.4 prestige points for whites and 3.3 points for blacks. Most striking is the finding that the difference between blacks and whites increases with each additional job, from 4.5 points for the first job to 6.6 points for the fifth job.

Table 13 also contains the average prestige scores of jobs held by our respondents ten years after entry into the labor force. We will use this measure as a dependent variable in our analysis because so many of both black and white respondents have had only a small number of job shifts and hence using higher order jobs as dependent variables means losing too many cases. The great majority of our respondents have been in the labor force for more than ten years, and a decade seems to be a reasonable amount of time to allow for several adjustments between the individual and his employment. Note that the average prestige scores of jobs held ten years after entry are higher than the averages for fourth or fifth jobs. This seeming anomaly may be a function of the fact that persons getting relatively good jobs early in their careers may be less likely to change. Hence the higher order jobs could represent attempts on the part of persons with less attractive positions to better themselves.

The bottom section of Table 13 contains average durations of the first through fifth jobs. Note that these numbers remain relatively unchanged with each successive job, although blacks consistently hold their jobs longer than whites at each order of job held.

The prestige scores of adjacent jobs tend to be moderately related. The average correlation between adjacent jobs for whites being .419 and for blacks .385. This finding, taken together with the data of Table 13, indicating a general increase in prestige scores as a worker progresses from one job to the next, means that there is a moderate tendency for one job to be similar to the next in scores, although later jobs are likely to be slightly higher than their predecessors.

Table 14. *Relative effects of educational attainment and prestige of previous jobs on higher order jobs, by race*

	Dependent variable is prestige score of							
	2nd job		3rd job		4th job		5th job	
	Whites	Blacks	Whites	Blacks	Whites	Blacks	Whites	Blacks
Total variance explained	31.8	25.9	31.9	24.8	38.3	32.1	28.2	21.0
Unique variance explained by educational attainment	11.9	10.6	5.6	4.9	2.2	2.0	1.9	1.7
Unique variance explained by prestige of previous jobs	4.1	6.2	6.8	7.9	14.4	10.7	7.6	16.0
Common variance to education and prestige of previous jobs	15.8	9.1	19.5	12.0	21.7	12.5	15.6	13.3

Table 14 presents evidence that a man's early jobs establish him upon a career line which tends to persist over time. The results of multiple regression analysis are given there with each successive job as the dependent variable and educational attainment and the prestige scores of previous jobs (a cluster of variables in the case of higher order jobs) as independent variables. The first two columns pertain to the second jobs held by respondents, showing that for both blacks and whites about one-fourth of the total variance in the prestige scores of the second job are accounted for by these two factors, slightly more so in the case of whites than is true for blacks. The unique effect of educational attainment is much larger than that of the first job for both blacks and whites. For later jobs, the findings are quite different. The importance of educational attainment declines and the importance of the prestige of previous jobs increases in importance. Thus, for the fifth job, the total variance explained has increased slightly, but the unique contribution of education has shrunk to almost nothing (less than 2.0 % for whites and blacks) while the unique variance attributed to previous jobs has increased to 10.7 % for blacks and whites respectively.

In other words, the point at which educational attainment counts is early in the career line. Beyond the second job, labor force experience, as indexed by the prestige levels of previous jobs, begins to count for more and more until by the fifth job, the unique effect of educational attainment has dwindled to almost zero. Indeed, the causal model implied in these findings is one in which social class background and educational attainment, modified positively or negatively by race, have a fairly strong influence on the prestige levels of the first and second jobs. Beyond that point, job experiences begin to count more heavily while background factors and educational attainment decline in importance.

The analysis presented in Table 15 bears upon the interpretation presented in the last paragraph. A multiple regression analysis is shown there using the prestige scores of the third jobs held by respondents as the dependent variables, with background factors and the prestige of the first two jobs as independent variables. The total amount of the variance explained is 33 % for whites and 27 % for blacks [9], a finding which follows the usual pattern of our being better able to predict the behavior of whites than of blacks. However, the important finding to note in Table 15 is that the prestige standings of the first two jobs account uniquely for almost twice as much variance as the unique contributions of any one of the other factors and as much as all of them taken together. In addition, the contributions of combination of variables containing the prestige standings of the first two jobs tend to account for more variance than the corresponding combinations omitting this factor.

12. *Accounting for prestige of occupations held a decade after entry*

The analysis presented in the last section of this report was centered around the chains of jobs held by our respondents. As a glance at the case bases in Table 13 would indicate, there are many respondents who have not chang-

9. Note that the addition of the background variables of social class and pre-entry work experience increases the total variance explained by 0.8 % in the case of whites and 2.2 % in the case of blacks, as a comparison of Table 16 with Table 15 indicates. Thus, social class blackground and pre-entry work experience do not add very much to the explanation of the prestige standings of the third jobs held by our respondents.

Table 15. *Prestige scores of third job after entry by background factors and prestige of previous jobs, by race*

Independent factors				Proportion of variance uniquely explained for	
Social class	Pre-entry jobs	Education (respondent)	Prestige of first two jobs	Whites	Blacks
+	0	0	0	0.1	1.2
0	+	0	0	0.7	1.0
0	0	+	0	3.8	4.1
0	0	0	+	6.3	6.2
Subtotal for single factors:				*10.9*	*12.5*
+	+	0	0	0.1	0.0
+	0	+	0	0.4	1.4
+	0	0	+	0.2	1.3
0	+	+	0	1.0	-0.5
0	+	0	+	0.7	0.3
0	0	+	+	6.3	6.2
Subtotal for factors two a a time:				*8.7*	*8.7*
+	+	+	0	0.4	0.1
+	+	0	+	-0.4	0.1
+	0	+	+	1.3	4.3
0	+	+	+	0.7	0.1
Subtotal for factors three at at time:				*2.0*	*4.4*
+	+	+	+	4.9	1.4
Total variance explained				*32.8*	*27.0*

ed jobs enough to have as many as three jobs between their entry into the job market and the time when they were interviewed. Furthermore, for some individuals, the first three jobs may occupy as little as the first year or so of experience in the labor force, while for others the third job may have been the one they currently held when interviewed, spanning as much as twenty years of labor force experience with the three jobs.

In an attempt to raise the case base as much as possible and to standardize the period of exposure to labor force experience, we chose to concentrate on the job held by respondents a decade after their entries into the labor force. Since our respondents are all in the age group thirty to thirty-nine the preponderance have been in the labor force at least a decade; the only group who are left out where those who entered the labor force later than twenty years of age and who were not ten years older when we interviewed them (and also a small number who were without jobs at the time ten years after they entered).

Table 16a. *Prestige scores of job held ten years after entry by means used to find first job, by race and educational attainment*

Means of finding first job	Less than high school		High school graduate		College graduate	
	Whites	Blacks	Whites	Blacks	Whites	Blacks
Friends	30.5 (60)	24.1 (100)	38.7 (67)	31.0 (53)	50.5 (7)	63.1 (1)
Family	29.8 (65)	24.1 (100)	38.2 (67)	27.3 (43)	46.7 (8)	—
Public agencies	29.2 (4)	25.4 (5)	43.1 (11)	27.6 (42)	57.2 (11)	60.1 (1)
Private agencies	20.8 (2)	17.3 (2)	52.8 (7)	25.8 (2)	49.7 (3)	78.3 (1)
Advertisements	28.1 (7)	25.2 (6)	37.3 (18)	37.6 (13)	62.7 (24)	—
Other means	31.1 (64)	26.5 (82)	38.3 (108)	31.2 (61)	—	57.7 (6)

Table 16b. *Analysis of variance*

Source	Whites	Blacks
F-ratio for education**	32.36 d.f. = (7,525)	28.91* d.f. = (7,454)
F-ratio for means used	3.91* d.f. = (5,525)	9.88* d.f. = (5,454)
Unique variance, education	32.36 %	29.35 %
Unique variance, means used	3.91 %	7.16 %

* All significant beyond .001.

** An eight-category description of education is used in this analysis of variance.

First we will consider the impact of two factors which might have some effect on later prestige but are essentially qualitative and so difficult to enter into a multiple regression analysis. In Table 16, we consider the effect of means used to find first jobs on occupational prestige a decade after entry, for each of six educational attainment levels. The result of an analysis of variance for Table 16 is shown on the bottom of that table. The F-ratio indicates that both educational attainment and means used uniquely explain statistically significant amounts of the total variance in occupational prestige. However, the means used account for only 3.9 % of the variance for whites and 7.2 % for blacks, quite small amounts when compared to the unique effects of education, being 23.9 % for whites and 13.9 % for blacks. The means used to obtain first jobs are relatively more important for blacks, another reflection of the importance of post-entry job experience for this group. This may further indicate that blacks need more skill in locating jobs than whites, especially those jobs which lead into a career line of rising occupational attainment.

A more important factor in the prestige standing of occupations a decade later is the industry in which the first job was found. Tables 17a and 17b

Table 17a. *Prestige scores of jobs held ten years after entry by industry of entry job, by race and education*

Industry of first job	Less than high school		High school graduate		College graduate	
	Whites	Blacks	Whites	Blacks	Whites	Blacks
Agriculture	26.3 (83)	21.0 (129)	31.2 (54)	26.5 (15)	44.2 (7)	—
Construction	32.2 (27)	23.0 (45)	36.0 (54)	28.7 (19)	60.5 (2)	—
Durables manufacture	31.5 (32)	22.3 (44)	37.4 (65)	26.2 (43)	41.9 (10)	—
Non-durables manufacture	30.3 (33)	24.3 (41)	41.4 (39)	29.6 (33)	38.1 (7)	60.1 (2)
Transportation	30.9 (14)	27.6 (12)	34.9 (36)	24.7 (40)	34.5 (5)	36.7 (1)
Wholesale and retail trade	29.1 (46)	22.3 (71)	38.9 (85)	29.4 (53)	55.1 (6)	—
Finance	31.5 —	22.3 —	35.9 (10)	44.0 (10)	21.8 (4)	—
Services and public administration	25.0 (27)	25.1 (46)	31.9 (20)	28.8 (43)	30.9 (35)	36.8 (12)

Table 17b. *Analysis of variance*

Source	Whites	Blacks
F-ratio for education**	41.02* d.f. = (7,579)	26.68* d.f. = (7,497)
F-ratio for industry	8.50* d.f. = (7,579)	5.82* d.f. = (7.497
Unique variance, education	30.96 %	25.26 %
Unique variance, industry	6.41 %	5.51 %

* Significant at .001.

** An eight-category description of education is used in this analysis of variance.

indicate that industry classification uniquely accounts for 6.4 % of the variance for whites and 5.5 % of the variance for blacks. It should be noted that the industry typology used is a very gross one, being the very first digit of the three digit Census occupational code [10]. Especially heterogeneous are

10. The fact that the industry classification was a very gross one means that the variance estimates for the effects of industry constitute lower bounds of the effect than a finer classification would yield.

the industry codes for services and the two codes for manufacturing, each of the three covering specific industries varying very widely in their technical complexity and corresponding skill demands on workers.

That industry of first jobs should make a significant contribution to prestige scores of jobs held a decade later is a further substantiation for the ideas put forth earlier concerning the importance of first jobs taken by individuals. These jobs serve as take off points on career lines conditioned by the prestige levels of those jobs, the industries in which they are embedded, and by the educational attainments and race and class backgrounds of the persons involved. So college graduates will on the whole tend to go further than high school graduates; but college graduates entering some types of industries will do better than those entering others with perhaps a more restricted range of opportunities. For the purposes of this report, however, all we can do is to point out a possible line of further analysis. The technical problems of classifying industries according to some sensible scheme which would facilitate analysis along these lines are too much to tackle in this paper.

As the final set of empirical findings of this report, Table 18 presents a multiple regression analysis in which background, educational attainment and prestige of first job are used to explain prestige of job held a decade after entry into the labor force. The total variance explained is 32.4 % for whites and 27.3 % for blacks. Several points are of interest here. First of all, class background uniquely accounts for little of the variance. Apparently the effects of class background operate through fostering or retarding educational attainment, but beyond the entry period its effects fade out. Secondly, the factors of high importance are those which relate to educational attainment and work experience. For whites, educational attainment and pre-entry job experiences are important, while for blacks, the prestige level of first jobs is more important than educational attainment. Thirdly, the patterning of unique effects for variables taken one at a time also holds for combinations of two or more variables. Combinations which contain the potent variables of education and pre-entry work experiences for whites tend to account for more unique variance, while combinations which contain educational experiencc and the prestige level of first jobs are important for blacks.

Table 18 adds more credence to the line of interpretation that has been developed in the last two sections of this report. While social class background helps to get an individual into a more or less favorable position *vis-à-vis* entry into the labor force, the qualifications of the individual, as indexed by his educational attainment and his early work experiences, have fairly strong effects on his occupational attainment during his thirties.

13. *Summary*

The findings of this report provide ample evidence of the importance of the period of entry into the labor force if we are to come to an understanding of

Table 18. *Prestige scores of job held ten years after entry by means used to find first jobs, by race and educational attainment*

Independent factors				Proportion of variance uniquely explained for	
Social class	Pre-entry jobs	Education (respondent)	Prestige of first job	Whites	Blacks
+	0	0	0	0.4	0.6
0	+	0	0	0.7	0.4
0	0	+	0	6.7	6.9
0	0	0	+	1.6	5.9
Subtotal for single factors:				*9.4*	*13.8*
+	+	0	0	0.1	-0.2
+	0	+	0	1.4	1.7
+	0	0	+	0.0	0.7
0	+	+	0	4.6	1.0
0	+	0	+	0.4	0.1
0	0	+	+	2.3	4.1
Subtotal for factors two at a time:				*8,8*	*7,2*
+	+	0	+	2.2	0.8
+	+	0	+	0.2	0.3
+	0	+	+	0.8	2.5
0	+	+	+	6.7	1.0
Subtotal for factors three at a time:				*9.9*	*4.6*
+	+	+	+	4.3	1.7
Total variance explained:				*32.4*	*27.3*

the American occupational system. Of course, this statement has appeared many times in the literature over the past thirty years. With this report we have contributed more detailed data on the processes which make the entry period important — the chain of events involved in the conversion of class background into educational attainment, the effects of one job in a chain on its successors and so on.

The strong statistical patterning of our findings does not immediately suggest that the entry period is one of uncertainty and "floundering". In a statistical sense, the data "hang together" enough to say that we can account for much of what we call success or failure. Of course, from the point of view of the individual going through the experience of entering the labor force, knowing full well that his first moves may set him upon a path toward career lines of restricted mobility, the feeling of uncertainty and of "floundering" may indeed be very strong, and for good cause.

Our findings also cast some important light on the different ways in which social class backgroun and race function in conditioning occupational attainment. We found that the primary role of class background was to affect markedly the respondent's access to education and also to a less important degree, to pre-entry work experiences. However, once the individual enters the labor market, the unique effects of social class background almost disappear, virtually all of its explanatory power being confounded with and hence mediated through the educational attainment of the individual. In contrast, race acts persistently throughout the entry period and continues to affect occupational careers throughout. Race is important in determining access to education and continues to exert a consistently strong effect thereafter. In every one of the tables presented, blacks are seen as disadvantaged compared to whites of the same educational attainment. This effect of race, moreover, grows in power as the individual spends more time in the labor force, so that whites and blacks are further apart in occupational attainment the longer they are working.

These findings provide evidence concerning the systematic way in which blacks are disadvantaged in the occupational system. They receive less education; while at school they have fewer opportunities to take on full-time or part-time employment; once they enter the labor market, they are less able to transform educational attainment into occupational attainment; the longer they work, the further behind whites they fall; and, finally, the higher the educational attainment of the black man, the worse off he is compared to whites with similar training.

These patterns add up to a massively discriminating occupational system, one which systematically provides less than equal treatment for blacks, even allowing for the poverty of their social backgrounds and their poorer schooling. This is one of the concrete meanings of institutional racism, a pattern of treatment whose outcomes may not be intended by any particular subsystem nor understood in terms of the prejudices of individuals, yet so pervasive that it can best be viewed as the output of the total society.

REFERENCES

Blau, P.M.; Duncan, O.D.
1967 *The American occupational structure.* New York, John Wiley.

Coleman, J.S.
1967 "Race relations and social change", in: *Symposium on race relations.* Ann Arbor, Mich., University of Michigan.

Davidson, P.E.; Anderson, H.D.
1937 *Occupational mobility in an American community.* Stanford, Calif., Stanford University Press.

Hodge, R.W.; Siegel, P.M.; Rossi, P.H.
1966 "Occupational prestige in the United States: 1925-1963", pp. 322-334 in: R. Bendix; S.M. Lipset (eds.). *Class, status, and power.* New York, Free Press of Glencoe. (2nd eds.)

Lipset, S.M.; Bendix, R.; Malm, T.
1955 "Job plans and entry into the labor market", *Social forces* 33 (3), March: 224-232.

Mayeske, G. *et al.* (eds.)
1969 *A study of our nation's schools.* Washington, DC, US Department of Health, Education and Welfare, Office of Education, pp. 344-360. (Working paper.)

Parnes, H.S. *et al.*
1969 *Career thresholds.* Vol. 1. Columbus, Ohio, Ohio State University, Center for Human Resource Research, pp. 65-80.

Reynolds, L.G.
1959 *The structure of labor markets.* New York, Harper and Bros.

Rossi, P.H.; Hodge, R.W.; Siegel, P.
1973 *The prestige standing of occupations.* (In preparation.)

Sheppard, H.L.; Belistky, A.H.
1966 *The job hunt.* Baltimore, Md., Johns Hopkins University Press.

Simpson, R.L.; Harper, I.
1962 "Social origins, occupational advice, occupational values and work careers", *Social forces* 40 (3), March: 264-271.

Stigler, G.
1962 "Unemployment and job mobility", *Journal of political economy* 70 (5), October: 94-106.

Wisler, C.E.
1969 *Partitioning the explained variance in a regression analysis.* (Unpublished paper.)

RITA PASQUALINI

Career mobility in Italy: The case of construction workers

Ammassari (1967) has suggested a theoretical framework for the interrelationships between increasing functional differentiation, career mobility and occupational choice which he proposed as an alternative to current hypotheses in the relevant sociological literature. In particular, he advanced the hypothesis that societal control over occupational choices will increase with the intensification of the division of labor. Such control — in a society which finds any explicit lack of freedom unbearable — is exercised through social mechanisms tending to maintain the system of occupational stratification in a state of equilibrium with respect to the established interests. These mechanisms are identified as the outcome of several processes that are due to the main or secondary activities of social structure such as the family, neighborhood and/or community of residence, school and labor market.

Career mobility then should be framed historically within a given societal context of economic growth and social change. In a research project [1] now being undertaken at the University of Rome, the attempt is being made to

1. A large research project has been undertaken at the University of Rome on the subject of "Occupational stratification and mobility in Italy": it is directed by Paolo Ammassari, of the Graduate School of Sociology and Social Research, and it will be the first study con cerned with the mobility of occupation in addition to individual occupational mobility.

Empirical research on the subject of occupational mobility in Italy has been rather limited, both in the amount of work and in the scope of the investigations, since the pioneering work of Chessa (1911); demographers' works followed, such as Gini's (1912) and Nora Federici's (1942). Since the war, the only empirical studies on a national scale have been the one by Livi (1950; *cf.* also Luzzatto-Fegiz, 1956) and the one by Lopreato (1965). Other works are limited to a single community or province (Cavalli, 1958; Anfossi *et al.*, 1959; Pagani, 1960, which mainly studies attitudes; Pizzorno, 1960; Leonardi, 1964; Ammassari, 1964; Alberoni and Baglioni, 1965, done in and around Milan; Paci and Ziliani, 1968; Varotti, 1971). Most of these works consider intergenerational mobility; some are studies of immigrant workers from the predominantly rural South to the largely industrialized North of Italy; recent industrial developments in the South have also provided a field of investigation into socio-professional change, and the variety of situations to be found in different Italian regions would justify a study of several different stages in economic development.

test hypotheses derived from a working model of the relationships between social change and economic growth and patterns of upward career mobility developed by Ammassari in later articles (1968; 1969*a*). The investigation deals with three main problems:

1. The social processes which promote, accompany and follow trends in the occupational structure;
2. The effects of changes and trends in the occupational structure on the degree of occupational inheritance and self-recruitment, especially with regard to mechanisms controlling the choice of first job and changes between jobs and occupations;
3. The impact of occupational stratification: the societal prerequisites, correlates and implications of the societal ranking of occupations.

Empirical data is being collected by means of the decennial Italian Census, the periodic statistical sampling of the labor force, and by means of a national sample of 5 000 units to be interviewed. The interview schedule covers the entire occupational career and bears upon several aspects of occupational and social origin, life and attitudes.

The analysis of occupational structure through Census data is of particular importance in the light of a general sociological perspective which frames career mobility in a societal context. In this perspective, individual mobility data (analyzed by survey techniques) has to be supplemented by information on a societal scale.

The use of Census data entails a particular set of methodological problems: problems of ecological correlation with regard to group and individual mobility and the question of the validity and reliability of historical statistical data in the context of a retrospective analysis of the Italian occupational structure and occupational changes since Italy's unification in 1861.

Problems of analysis also arise in connection with the relationship between geographical mobility (internal migration) and occupational mobility. In this context, inter-sectorial mobility plays an important role, particularly with respect to Italian economic development in the last decade. Colin Clark's theory on the development of economic sectors has been found inadequate, and the hypothesis of a "two-step flow of sectorial relocation from agriculture into manufacturing industry" by means of an intermediate stage represented by urban-industrial non-manufacturing occupations has been found to correspond more closely to conditions of occupational mobility in given stages of economic and industrial development (see Ammassari, 1969*b*).

My own specific task within the broader research project [2] is to test this

2. The exact title of my research project on construction workers in Rome is: "Construction industry in Italy: Its developments and dynamics 1951-1970, and its role in the economic development and urbanization process of Italian society."

It is to be followed by a comparative study of construction workers in Detroit, USA. This investigation of the situation of the construction industry and of the building trades is to observe in particular the career mobility of people active in construction who are of Italian

hypothesis within the construction industry. This industry represents the main source of urban industrial non-manufacturing occupations and is thus often considered as a transitional, qualifying stage for migrants passing from agriculture to industry or services, particularly in a region where manufacturing is still non-existent. Construction workers are an interesting subject of investigation along these lines: they have an urban occupation, but in many cases a rural background in working and living experiences. Many of them commute from the village to the large city, many become seasonal or permanent immigrants. The move from rural to urban employment and environment implies various aspects and problems, which will be presented with particular consideration being given to the present situation in Rome.

The production of this particular industry (especially housing and related urban equipment) corresponds to demographic phenomena, above all to the urbanization flow, of which it represents the physical aspect, *i.e.* the development in time and space of urban centers. Its dynamics not only reflect trends in the national economy in general, but partly cause them because construction has an impact on many other industrial sectors; employment in it is the largest single share of any industrial branch in Italy (in 1961 about 1/4), and particularly in the city of Rome, where it represents the main "industrial" activity. It is necessary, therefore, in a study of workers employed in construction, to take into account the altered economic situation in Italy between 1951 and 1968, in particular since 1961 (see Confederazione Generale dell' Industria, esp. 1967). From 1953 to 1963, with short interruptions, Italy had a period of economic expansion; the three years 1964-1966 brought a recession, and in 1967 a new expansionary cycle was beginning; however, employment in construction was no longer increasing very greatly, since technological innovations were improving productivity.

This will help to clarify the different roles played by the sector in different areas and periods of time, corresponding to various stages of industrial development: a detailed analysis of three hypothetical occupational models in construction is presented by Paci (1963).

About ten years ago in Rome, between 1958 and 1962 and up to 1964 (Sannibale, 1964) the construction industry attracted and absorbed, through its lowest ranks, many unskilled immigrants (the majority of these leaving agri-

---

origin. An interesting source of data is the 1970 Detroit Area Study (material made accessible by Robert Cole). Out of 700 randomly sampled respondents, those with at least one work experience in construction have already been examined. Their careers show, in most cases, that work in construction (mostly skilled trades like plumbing, electricity, operating machinery) is much better paid and is considered more desirable than others. Among people of Italian origin, a recurrent pattern is that of agricultural or construction laborers who migrate to the US, becoming construction workers and labor contractors. The specific ethnic character of different building trades will be analyzed on the basis of responses to a questionnaire sent to local labor unions, by means of which data on both geographical and occupational mobility of workers are to be collected.

culture), who often later changed to other urban occupations, physically less demanding and economically more rewarding. The same situation appears in Milan (Cantarelli, 1963) before 1963: agricultural migrants enter construction at the lowest level of skill and often use this employment as a means of access to the technologically more advanced sectors. Such an abridged version of the two-step flow pattern of mobility, limited to the construction industry, has been tested in a recent study done in Rome (Schiattarella, 1969).

While the agricultural origin and the low level of skill appear to be confirmed by various sources and direct investigation, the qualification of workers and upward mobility through employment in construction now appear doubtful: although job security and continuity can hardly be judged over a period of time (1955-1969) which has seen a boom and a recession, followed by partial recovery, the analysis of the level of skill at various ages and a first-hand knowledge of the present situation in Rome reveal a picture that is remarkably different from that of the recent past.

Some recent institutional changes in recruitment (such as the compulsory intervention of labour exchanges) have just emphasized the difference from the former "boom" years, when anyone could get a job simply by presenting himself at a construction site; young workers now avoid entering construction at the lowest skill level, from which they were once promoted step by step, learning on the job, but rather — if they work in the sector at all — get hired as "cottimisti" (*i.e.* paid by job, according to the amount of work executed), and make fast money by long days of hard work. This appears to be economically convenient for this consumption-oriented group as well as for the employer who puts up a building in a fraction of the usual time, and also saves on social security, though paying extra hours and promotional incentives; it is also profitable for the hirer ("capo-cottimista") who is paid an extra dollar for each worker he provides, recruiting manpower on a public square and sub-letting it (an illegal but customary practice).

The aspirations and ambitions of the young do not appear to be oriented towards occupational promotion: they prefer to exploit their physical strength in order to stay on the market as long as they can. Older workers can be found at all levels of skill in similar proportions, except in larger firms, where they may have experienced a longer career, with the gradual promotion that was once the rule. There are fewer and fewer young people at the higher levels of skill (acquired through professional training in special schools), and although inter-sector mobility may be hypothesized, qualification through construction work seems very unlikely.

The sector appears, from recent investigations, to be undergoing a process of involution as far as volume and qualification of manpower are concerned. This also is due to technological changes, whereby the old craft skills are replaced by machine-operation and mounting or assembling work (Petralia, 1968): there is a dearth of the "new" skills, but a plethora of old-fashioned workers, and the sector cannot be seen as the open passage it was ten years ago; new workers will seldom be accepted in it today, especially if they belong to the unskilled ex-agricultural labor force.

An interesting observation can be made on the relationship between construction and agricultural work, as it is done by the same individuals at different times of the year: this mixed-job pattern appears clearly from the shifts in age composition of the labor force between June and November, which appears to differ between the inner and outer belt surrounding Rome: the outer area shows a smaller proportion of younger workers in November, because the cultivators (mostly of olive groves) require labor then, as opposed to the inner belt, which draws young laborers in the summer months.

This finding is related to the remarkably high number of non-resident construction workers in Rome, both commuters and seasonal migrants; a relationship between the level of skill and the area of residence emerges, whereby skilled workers tend to establish themselves in the city or its outskirts, while the less skilled maintain their residences farther out. In the general picture of the integration of the rural workers, through occupational and geographical mobility, into the urban environment, the situation indicates grave difficulties for the low-skilled workers in the construction sector, still tied to agricultural occupations and/or long and taxing commuting trips.

Union experts in the sector indicate a trend towards an older average age for construction workers; young people now tend to be more attracted by other sectors, offering higher job security and better general conditions. The two-step hypothesis of sectorial relocation considers urban non-manufacturing industrial employment as paving the way for jobs in manufacturing industries; in a city like Rome, traditionally non-manufacturing, the move into that sector would, in most areas, involve further geographical mobility, which is not considered in the present study.

BIBLIOGRAPHY

Alberoni, F.; Baglioni, G.

1965 *L'integrazione dell' immmigrato nella società industriale.* Bologna, Il Mulino.

Ammassari, P.

1964 *Worker satisfaction and occupational life: A study of the automobile worker in Italy.* East Lansing, Mich., Michigan State University. (Ph.D thesis.)

1967 "Occupational opportunity structure in advanced societies", in: *Proceedings of the first Italo-Hungarian meeting of Sociology.* Rome, Centro Culturale Italia-Ungheria.

1968 "La divisione sociale del lavoro e i meccanismi di controllo delle scelte professionali", *Revue internationale de sociologie* 4: 1-3.

1969*a* "La mobilità ascendente nella società avanzata", *Rassegna Italiana di sociologia* 10 (1): 43-70.

1969*b* "The Italian blue-collar worker", pp. 3-21 in: N.F. Dufty (ed.). *The sociology of the blue-collar worker.* Leiden, Brill.

Anfossi, A.; Talamo, M.; Indovina, F.
1959 *Ragusa, comunità in transizione.* Turin, Taylor.

Cantarelli, D.
1963 "Provvidenze per la migliore utilizzazione delle forze di lavoro disponibili", in: *Atti del convegno sul tema: La futura disponibilità delle forze di lavoro in Italia*' Rome, Accademia Nazionale dei Lincei.

Cavalli, L.
1958 *Quartiere operaio: I metalmeccanici.* Genova, USSL.

Chessa, L.
1911 *La trasmissione ereditaria delle professioni.* Torino, Bocca.

Confederazione Generale dell'Industria Italiana
1967, other years *Prospettive dell' industria italiana.* Rome.

Federici, N.
1942 "Sul ricambio sociale: Teorie sociologiche e contributi statistici", *Statistica* 2

Gini, C.
1912 *I fattori demografici della evoluzione delle nazioni.* Turin, Bocca.

Leonardi, F.
1964 *Operai nuovi: Studio sociologico sulle nuove forze del lavoro industriale nell' area siracusana.* Milan, Feltrinelli.

Livi, L.
1950 "Sur la mesure de la mobilité sociale", *Population* 5 (1): 65-76.

Lopreato, J.
1965 "Social mobility in Italy", *American journal of sociology* 71 (3): 311-314.

Luzzatto Fegiz, P.
1956 *Il volto sconosciuto dell' Italia: Dieci anni di sondaggi Doxa.* Milan, Giuffré.

Paci, M.
1963 *L'immigrazione di manodopera nel settore dell' edilizia milanese.* Milan, ILSES.

Paci, M.; Ziliani, G.
1968 *Ricerca sulla mobilità del lavoro in Lombardia: Metodologia e risultati generali.* Milan, ILSES.

Pagani, A.
1960 *Classi e dinamica sociale: Primi risultati di un' indagine campionaria in provincia di Milano.* Pavia, Istituto di Statistica dell' Università.

Petralia, R.
1968 "I processi di ammodernamento e riorganizzazione in atto nel settore delle costruzioni", in: *Indagine sulla situazione sociale del paese.* Rome, CENSIS.

Pizzorno, A.
1960 *Comunità e razionalizzazione: Ricerca sociologica su un caso di sviluppo industriale.* Turin, Einaudi.

Sannibale, A.
1964 "Immigrati e problemi del lavoro", chap. 4 in: *Problemi e conclusioni risultanti da un' indagine sul fenomeno migratorio nell' area metropolitana di Roma.* Vol. 4. Rome, IRMOU.

Schiattarella, R.
1969 *Le trasformazioni dell' industria edile italiana.* Rome, University of Rome. (Unpublished thesis.)

Varotti, A.
1971 "Il movimento pendolare nel processo di trasformazione della comunità rurale", *Revue internationale de sociologie* 7 (1-2).

ANDREJ CASERMAN

Pattern of career mobility in post-revolutionary society

1. Introduction

In 1970 the Institute for Sociology and Philosophy of Ljubljana University carried out a research programme entitled "Social Stratification and Mobility in Self-governing Society" in the territory of the Socialist Republic of Slovenia.

The purpose of this research was to obtain optimal knowledge of the channels and social mechanisms regulating individual mobility in Slovenia. We also wanted to discover the processes connected with, or conditioning, the emergence of new social groups. We opted for the so-called "snow-ball" sampling technique, best suited to our aims. In this type of sample, the elite groups in the upper strata are over-represented.

The analysis of the material collected in the course of this research has not yet been completed. The data we have selected for presentation in this paper illuminate the patterns of career mobility in a post-revolutionary society. The problems treated are specific to socialist countries; that is why I would like, first, to describe briefly the main characteristics of the revolutionary and post-revolutionary situation in Slovenia.

2. General characteristics of the post-revolutionary situation in Slovenia

The Socialist Republic of Slovenia is a constituent part of Yugoslavia: one of its six socialist republics. Located in Northwest Yugoslavia, it borders on Italy, Austria and Hungary. Slovenia covers 20 251 km² or 7,9 % of the total surface of Yugoslavia. It has almost 1 800 000 inhabitants speaking Slovene, constituting 8,5 % of the entire population of Yugoslavia. Slovenia is considered to be one of the most developed republics in Yugoslavia: it produces 15 % of the national income. The capital of Slovenia is Ljubljana.

The socialist social order in Yugoslavia is the result of a successful revolution, which took place in the years 1941 to 1945 parallel with the national liberation struggle of all the peoples of Yugoslavia. The revolution was organized and carried out from inside and by its own forces; this is a fact of great importance for the entire postwar social development of Yugoslavia and thus also for the course and special characteristics of processes of social mobility.

In the national liberation war and revolution, Yugoslavia lost 11 %, and Slovenia 13 % of its entire population. The revolution traumatized the whole Slovene nation: various positive and hostile sentiments emerged which exercised considerable influence over most of the relations among individuals and among social groups. Hostile sentiments towards the members of exploiting classes and of bourgeois political parties, positive sentiments towards the members of working classes, are the best known of these sentiments which influenced the direction and range of mobility of social groups and individuals.

Following the victory at the end of the Second World War, several profound social changes took place in Slovenia (and in Yugoslavia, generally). These changes occurred in circumstances where the entire nation was divided into a large group of "victors", a second large group in the population trying to preserve a neutral position at a time of revolutionary dichotomization, and a relatively small group of "defeated". The victorious group consisted of members of the Communist Party of that period and of all the participants in the national liberation struggle, while the defeated group consisted of the survivors of the members of military formations who collaborated with the occupier and members of their families.

The beginning of major mobility shifts in the Slovene social structure coincided with the beginning of the national liberation movement and the revolution, though these shifts are often connected with the postwar social and economic development. Already at the time of the basic political bifurcation a well organized national liberation front developed with its own commanding cadres; the establishment of the partisan army, with its own officers, represents the formation of an important channel of vertical social mobility for numerous young people. This channel of social mobility was preserved after the war, when the partisan army was reorganized into a regular army. Beside the organization of the Communist Party, the system of the liberation front committees also represented an important channel of vertical mobility at the time of the national liberation struggle (NLS). At that time, the liberation front committees represented the differentiated organs of the civil authorities, with departments for the economy, health, education, and social security, etc. After the war these committees formed the basis out of which the present political and administrative system has developed. Thus, participants in the national liberation struggle, and above all members of the Communist Party (CP), began their career mobility in the revolutionary period, that is before 1945.

After the liberation, the new, legitimate wielders of power passed legislation which directly influenced the direction and range of mobility of the entire population. The most important laws concerned:

— Prohibition of the activites of all the prewar political institutions and parties. The Communist Party and associations established in the NLS, or renewing their activities together with the Communist Party, took their place;
— Abolition of the old administrative apparatus; its place was taken by the organs of the new authorities as established during the war.
— Abolition of the old military and police system, which was replaced by the system as developed during the war.
— Separation of Church from State.
— Nationalization of foreign-owned property and the property of domestic collaborators of the occupiers, expropriation of the domestic bourgeoisie.
— Agrarian reform.

On the basis of this legislation, major changes occurred in the social structure of Slovenia, resulting in the Communist Party securing control over the fundamental spheres of social life, those which had to be mastered in order to create the conditions for later changes. All the key-positions, as well as a considerable proportion of lower-ranking positions in the apparatus of the politico-administrative system, in the army, police, judicial system and finance as well as in the mass communication media were occupied by party members. In the spheres of production, education, culture, health, etc., the CP endeavoured to occupy at least the most important executive positions. It is obvious that in order to obtain this, at least two systems of selection had to be developed on the basis of which the promotion of the employed personnel could be carried out, and both of these had a direct influence on career mobility. The promotion of personnel was influenced by: *a*) a system of political criteria favouring the promotion of participants in the NLS and members of the CP; this fact certainly also influenced the considerable increase in the membership of the CP after the war, *b*) a system of professional criteria, upon which depended the promotion prospects of the remainder of the population. However, as with most promotion processes, both selection systems were combined.

3. Specific patterns of career mobility

Method

In accordance with the aims of our research, we also treated such questions as: How was the career mobility of members of the parties opposed to the revolution influenced by their party affilation at the time of the revolution? How does the career mobility of members of the CP and of participants in the NLS compare with the career mobility of their former opponents? Can we establish any discrimination against the defeated in the area of career mobility and if so, to what extent? In the following, we shall try to answer some of these questions.

This paper concentrates on one aspect of intragenerational mobility: the difference between the highest occupation in hierarchical terms held by respondents before 1945 and the highest occupation after 1945. The occupational scale, in terms of which career mobility is analyzed, consists of the following seven occupational categories ordered hierarchically.

1. Leading cadres
2. Specialists with university degrees
3. Employees with secondary school degrees
4. Lower administrative personnel
5. Foremen and similar
6. Skilled workers
7. Semiskilled and unskilled workers.

The starting point for further treatment of data concerning career mobility is a 7 by 7 matrix of transition frequencies (TFM).

Highest occupational category : after 1945 →

before 1945 ↓	1	2	3	4	5	6	7	N
1	a_{11}	a_{12}	a_{13}					
2	a_{21}	a_{22}	a_{23}	a_{24}				
3		a_{32}	a_{33}	a_{34}				
4								
5								
6								
7							a_{77}	
N								Total

The element of the matrix a_{ij} is the frequency showing how many individuals passed from the occupational category i into occupational category j. The numbers a_{ij} are integers or zero.

In order to obtain a better understanding we would like to introduce the following symbols:

The sum of the elements in the main diagonal:

$D(0) = a_{11} + a_{22} + a_{33} + a_{44} + a_{55} + a_{66} + a_{77}$

The sum of the elements of the first and second side diagonal over the main diagonal:

$D(-1) = a_{12} + a_{23} + a_{34} + a_{45} + a_{56} + a_{67}$

$D(-2) = a_{13} + a_{24} + a_{35} + a_{46} + a_{57}$

Further sums of side diagonals over the main diagonal, by analogy:

D(-3), D(-4), D(-5), D(-6).

Similarly we mark the first side diagonal under the main diagonal: D(+1), the second side diagonal under the main diagonal: D(+2), and by analogy also D(+3), D(+4), D(+5), D(+6).

Let us have a look at all these sums once more:

$$
\begin{aligned}
D(-6) &= a_{17}\\
D(-5) &= a_{16} + a_{27}\\
D(-4) &= a_{15} + a_{26} + a_{37}\\
D(-3) &= a_{14} + a_{25} + a_{36} + a_{47}\\
D(-2) &= a_{13} + a_{24} + a_{35} + a_{46} + a_{57}\\
D(-1) &= a_{12} + a_{23} + a_{34} + a_{45} + a_{56} + a_{67}\\
D(0) &= a_{11} + a_{22} + a_{33} + a_{44} + a_{55} + a_{66} + a_{77}\\
D(+1) &= a_{21} + a_{32} + a_{43} + a_{54} + a_{65} + a_{76}\\
D(+2) &= a_{31} + a_{42} + a_{53} + a_{64} + a_{75}\\
D(+3) &= a_{41} + a_{52} + a_{63} + a_{74}\\
D(+4) &= a_{51} + a_{62} + a_{73}\\
D(+5) &= a_{61} + a_{72}\\
D(+6) &= a_{71}
\end{aligned}
$$

The distribution of values for D(x), x = —6, ..., —1, 0, +1, ..., + 6, is the basis for investigation of the chosen aspects of career mobility.

This distribution will be used to describe:

1. The influence exercised on career mobility by active participation in NLS. Career mobility will be compared for two groups: participants and non-participants in NLS.

2. In the process of further analysis these two groups will be subdivided according to the membership in CP and thus we will obtain four groups:

a) Members of CP who are also members of the Association of Veterans: (CP and AV)

b) Members of CP who are not members of the Association of Veterans and who did not participate in NLS: (CP)

c) Members of the Association of Veterans who are not members of CP: (AV)

d) People who are members of neither of the two organizations: (CP nor AV).

Our sample included 2 240 respondents of both sexes. The small number of respondents in our tables is due to the fact that most of the people working before and during World War II have been retired and are thus not considered in this analysis.

Results

By presenting the mobility distributions of respondents, arranged according to the criterion of their participation in the NLS, Table 1 enables us to observe the direction of mobility shifts for the members of both groups (see below). The comparison of both distributions in Table 1 leads us to the conclusion that the members of both groups, *i.e.* participants and non-participants in NLS, shift upwards on the scale of occupational hierarchy. Downward mobility was relatively small for both groups. This is understandable. Heavy

Table 1. *Distribution of respondents (of both sexes) according to participation in NLS and mobility achieved after the war in relation to prewar occupational position*

	Participants in NLS %	Participants in NLS cum%	Non-participants in NLS %	Non-participants in NLS cum%
D(—6)	-	-	-	-
D(—5)	-	-	-	-
D(—4)	-	-	-	-
D(—3)	-	-	0.7	0.7
D(—2)	2.2	2.2	0.7	1.4
D(—1)	2.2	4.4	3.7	5.1
D(0)	33.0	37.4	44.0	49.1
D(+1)	16.2	53.6	14.9	64.0
D(+2)	14.6	68.2	11.9	75.9
D(+3)	12.4	80.6	13.5	89.3
D(+4)	7.6	88.2	6.0	95.3
D(+5)	9.2	97.4	2.2	97.5
D(+6)	2.6	100.0	2.2	99.7
(N)	(185)		(134)	

casualties, considerable political emigration in 1945, and, above all, the renewal of old industries and the development of new ones are factors which created opportunities for upward mobility for the entire employed population (see Table 2).

Table 2. *Direction of mobility shifts of members of both groups: NLS and non-NLS*

	Participants in NLS	Non-participants in NLS
Immobility in percent	33.0	44.0
Downward mobility in percent	4.4	5.1
Upward mobility in percent	62.6	50.8
M (mean of mobility distribution)	1.69	1.20
(N)	(185)	(134)

Nonetheless, these two groups did not enjoy quite the same opportunities for career mobility. The values of the diagonal ratio in Tables 1 and 2 show that 33 % of the respondents who participated in the national struggle remained, after the war, in the same occupational categories as they had been in before the war, while 44 % of the respondents who had not participated in the national liberation struggle remained in the same occupational categories. The opportunities for upward career mobility were fulfilled by 62.6 % of respondents who had participated in the national liberation struggle and by only 50,8 % of those who had not. Also, the arithmetical means of the distributions (see Table 2) demonstrate the more favourable opportunities for upward career mobility of the NLS group (M = 1.69) as compared to the non-NLS group (M = 1.20). On the other hand, our data, which show that members of the other groups also succeeded in achieving a significant level of upward

Table 3. *Distribution of respondents according to membership in organizations and extent of mobility shift achieved after the war in relation to the highest pre-war occupational position*

	Members of CP and AV		Members of CP		Members of AV		Non-members of CP or AV	
	%	cum%	%	cum%	%	cum%	%	cum%
D(—6)	-	-						
D(—5)	-	-	-	-	-	-	-	-
D(—4)	-	-	-	-	-	-	-	-
D(—3)	-	-	-	-	-	-	0.7	0.7
D(—2)	-	-	-	-	3.8	3.8	1.5	2.2
D(—1)	-	-	-	-	5.0	8.8	4.5	6.7
D(0)	20.4	20.4	28	28	40.0	48.8	50.0	56.7
D(+1)	16.1	36.5	0	28	18.8	67.6	14.9	71.6
D(+2)	18.3	54.8	20	48	10.0	77.6	11.2	82.9
D(+3)	15.1	69.9	16	64	11.3	88.9	11.9	94.7
D(+4)	9.7	79.6	20	84	6.3	95.2	4.5	99.2
D(+5)	16.1	95.7	8	92	2.5	97.7	0.7	100.0
D(+6)	4.3	100.0	8	100	2.5	100.0	-	-
(N)	(93)		(25)		(80)		(134)	

career mobility despite their unfavourable position in the post-revolutionary period, also support the proposition that the process of post-war expansion and intense industrialization modified and diminished the less favourable social position of members of those groups who did not participate in the national liberation struggle (see Table 4).

Table 4. *Direction and extent of mobility shifts of members of socio-political organizations*

	Members of CP and AV	Members of CP	Members of AV	Non-members of CP or AV
Immobility in percent	20.4	28	40	50
Downward mobility in percent	0	0	8.8	6.7
Upward mobility in percent	79.6	72	51.4	43.2
M (arithmetical mean of mobility distribution)	2.43	2.56	1.13	0.85
(N)	(93)	(25)	(80)	(134)

In Tables 3 and 4, each of the groups (NLS and non-NLS) is further subdivided. In this way we can observe the "mobility" behaviour of the above-mentioned four groups:

— The CP and AV group has the smallest number of individuals who, after the revolution, remained in their previous occupational categories (20.4 %) and the largest number of those who achieved a positive vertical career mobility shift (79.6 %). Downward mobility does not exist in this group at all.

— The (AV) group shows some downward mobility; after the war, 40 % remained in the same occupational position as held before their joining the NLS, while 51.2 % moved upwards.

— The (CP) group is more successful as concerns career mobility.

— The (CP nor AV) group's behaviour was explained above.

The higher level of upward career mobility of the (CP) group and of the members of both organizations (CP and AV) is not surprising. The mobility process investigated principally occurred immediately after the revolution and at the very beginning of the changes in the social structure described in the beginning of our paper. In these changes the dominant role played by the political system in social life, was also reflected in the domination of the political hierarchy, in the politically defined aims of social development and in the politically determined selection system. This dominant role was established and maintained by the Communist Party, through its institutional structure and its cadres. In order to achieve this, party cadres had first to occupy all the key positions in the system: this could not be effected unless new criteria were established alongside the classic selection criteria for the regulation of mobility. We need hardly emphasize that these were the criteria developed by the revolution.

The above data account for the patterns of social mobility in the early post-revolutionary period. Subsequently, political selection criteria have become less and less relevant and are gradually replaced by education, skill and performance criteria.

AVRAHAM ZLOCZOWER

Occupation, mobility and social class

Occupational mobility and the decomposition of the working class

Social stratification and social mobility are usually conceptionalized as multidimensional phenomena. Empirical practice relies however, more often than not, exclusively upon occupational categories. Partly this is simply a matter of convenience. Occupation is — in modern society — a fairly reliable indicator of social status in general, at least among adult males; it correlates highly with other variables such as income, education and prestige (Reissman, 1960, p. 158). Partly this practice reflects a somewhat exaggerated belief in the accuracy of occupational criteria as a measure of social class: "The study of occupations provides a measure of class which is comparatively solid and reliable, which even the unsophisticated can recognize with some precision, which seems to establish a straightforward consciousness of a common identity, susceptible to statistical analysis and capable of experimental replication" (Davies and Encel, 1965, p. 23).

One need not share this faith in the reliability of occupational categories (for a skeptical note *cf.* Zymelman, 1969, p. 107), or in their validity as indicators of class structure at the macro-sociological level (*cf.* Wiley's critique, 1967, p. 530), in order to recognize that the trends of occupational transformation in advanced industrial societies may, by diversifying the markets for labor services, lead to segmentation among the suppliers of these services and thus to brake or even reverse the trends toward the unification of the working class as a social and political force.

In broad outline the occupational transformation common to advanced industrial societies is clearly discernible. It includes a high differentiation of skill in the process of production, the growth of nonmanual occupations, expansion of employment in the tertiary sector and the decline of self-employment. The distribution of the labor force in the occupational structure is increasingly determined by the educational system (Blau and Duncan, 1967, p. 180); the relative prestige of typical occupations is apparently very similar in different countries (Hodge *et al.*, 1966), and inter-generational occupational mobility is ubiquitous (Lipset and Bendix, 1959). Is this convergence compatible with the persistence of divergent patterns of social stratification and political organization? The degree of symmetry between occupational differentiation and other dimensions of social stratification has, no doubt, changed in the course of time and must be assumed to vary still from country to country. The extent of variation and the direction of change remain largely unexplored, unknown and for that reason controversial (*cf.* Weinberg, 1969). Few valid and reliable criteria have become established as guide marks for estimating the bias of using the occupational structure of a society as an indicator of its class structure at a given time. Is occupation today a better indicator of social status in the United States than in Britain? Is there a greater correspondence today, between manual employees and the "working class" in Britain, than there was fifty years ago? Is the manual-nonmanual cleavage, which is said to have divided the classes in the past, being eroded through upwards nivelation of incomes, rising educational standards, mass consumption and the democratization of political processes? Does this inevitably lead to the *embourgeoisement* of the working class, to the destruction of its distinctive *milieu* and to the emasculation of its politics? Must the process of occupational mobility, whereby some men rise in social status and others fall, under these conditions necessarily weaken the cohesion of the working class (Lipset and Bendix, 1959, p. 70)?

Shils (1961, p. 125) seems to express the dominant view that class conflict is, as a result of these trends becoming "more open and more continuous [...] but also more domesticated and restricted by attachment to the central value system". Scarcely two decades ago the United States were still considered to be a curious exception in the, otherwise universal, pattern of political development during the process of industrialization. Capitalistic expansion and technological development failed to produce receptivity for socialist ideology in the American working class. The workers became organized, but their organizations did not challenge capitalism or the legitimacy of the economic, social or political order in America. The proliferation of quantitative studies on occupational mobility voided one of the most pervasive explanations of this "deviant case": the data failed to confirm the claim that America was endowed with singularly high rates of occupational mobility.

Nowadays America has ceased, in the eyes of many observers, to be an exception. She is, rather, coming to be regarded as the prototype of political development in the advanced stages of industrialization.

"In fact, writes Seymour Martin Lipset, history has validated a basic premise of Marxist sociology at the expense of Marxist politics. Marxist sociology assumes that cultural superstructures, including political behavior and status relationships, are a function of the underlying economic and technological structure. Hence, the most developed industrial society should also have the most developed set of political and class relationships. Since the United States is the most advanced society technologically, its superstructure should be more likely to correspond to the social structure of a modern industrial society than the 'less' developed economies of Europe. In addition, one might argue that the United States has been most likely to develop the pure institutions of a capitalist industrial society. Hence, as an unpolitical Marxist sociology would expect, instead of European class and political relationships holding up a model of the United States future, the social organization of the United States has presented the image of the European future" (1964, pp. 271-272).

Lipset does not base his prediction, on the continuing evolution of European politics in the direction of the American model, exclusively on economic and technological trends (*cf.* Goldthorpe, 1964, for a critique of "evolutionary para-Marxism" of that type). Working class militance in the past, he argues, was only partly caused by economic deprivation. An equally important factor was the exclusion of the working class from effective political participation. This led to the identification of government and the state with the propertied classes (for a similar interpretation *cf.* Dahrendorf, 1959, pp. 213-218). This premise is less at odds with the Marxist tradition than the conclusions which Lipset derives from it, namely that the development of purer types of capitalist societies in Europe, which permit the "continued political struggle between representatives of the haves and have-nots" (1964, p. 294), eliminates the roots of working class opposition to private ownership over the principal means of production.

The very fact that socialist parties, which by tradition are identified with the working class and with opposition to the regime, are attaining executive power in many European countries is, according to Lipset, a measure of the transformation in the political culture which has already taken place. These parties will continue to depend for political support mainly upon the relatively under-privileged strata. But, as Lorwin (1968, p. 346) pointed out: "Socialist militancy [is] a victim of socialist success, itself made possible by economic growth [which] facilitated the compromises which reconciled groups to each other in most of the liberal democracies." Working class support for socialist parties will, according to this analysis, increasingly become conditional upon the provision of concrete and specific benefits. Socialist parties in Europe will accordingly come to resemble more the Democratic party in America than their own image of yesterday.

Current European politics give credence to this interpretation. The ideological controversy between socialist and non-socialist parties has lost its former vehemence. On many issues the differences between them have been reduced to mere nuances and, above all, they appear united in rejecting communism and other forms of "left-wing extremism". The socialist parties have more difficulties defending their hold on the manual working class against encroachments from the *bourgeois* parties than against dissidence on the left. But on the whole the manual workers have remained loyal to the moderate socialist parties. If, according to Marx, "the working class is revolutionary — or it is nothing", then indeed the trend of European politics may signify that its working class is becoming what, in spite of their electoral weight, America's workers have, in Marx' sense of class, always been: nothing.

A somewhat discordant element in this prospective decomposition of the working class as a social and political force in Europe, may however be discerned in the political continuity among the upwardly mobile in Europe, which contrasts sharply with the pattern of political reorientation which prevails in America. We turn now to these differences.

The importance of not being a manual worker

The domestication of class conflict does not diminish the importance of occupational class and its correlates as a factor in politics. In many ways the opposite seems to be true (Lipset, 1963, p. 230). The rough categorization of the occupational hierarchy into manual and nonmanual occupations coincides, even in America with the major political fission. Support for the Democratic party, which is usually regarded as progressive and more sympathetic to Labor than the Republican party, is strongly associated with manual occupation. Nonmanuals, on the other hand, tend to support the Republican party which has a conservative, pro-business image.

The significance of this cleavage in the occupational structure is demonstrated even better by the political consequences of mobility accross the manual-nonmanual line than by the correlation between occupation and political orientations. Mobility of this type seems to create discontinuities which affect value-orientations more drastically than occupational mobility which does not involve crossing this boundary (*cf.* Blau, 1957, p. 398; 1965, pp. 488-489).

Social mobility implies, within any interest- or status-theory of political behavior, a probable modification of previous orientations and the transfer of political allegiance. But in contrast with Europe, where upward occupational mobility leads to a rather moderate shift from "left" to "right", nonmanual Americans of manual origins become, apparently, "excessively" and "demonstratively" middle class in their orientations. The American upwardly mobile conform, in the aggregate, *more* to the political norms of the middle class than the second generation nonmanuals (Lipset and Zetterberg, 1956).

Aside from the long-run trend in favour of conservative politics which these consequences of upward occupational mobility imply, this pattern has aroused interest because it suggests that the upwardly mobile in America compulsively over-conform to the norms of their class of destination. This notion fits well into the interactionist approach to mobility processes. Social mobility in this view consists in a change of social *milieu*. Since a person's values, attitudes and behavior are shaped by his social environment, a change of *milieu* may lead to protracted maladjustment and disorientation. As a consequence there may develop an element of status-anxiety which possibly expresses itself in the form of over-conformity to the perceived norms of the new social environment (Simpson, 1970, p. 1003). Over-conformity came to be regarded as one of the unapplauded consequences of occupational mobility in America (Tumin, 1957, p. 34).

The persistence of the European pattern has been documented for Italy (Lopreato, 1967), West Germany (Segal, 1967), Britain (Abramson and Books, 1971) and the Scandinavian countries (Rokkan, 1967; Valen and Katz, 1967). Support for a uniquely American pattern may be found in the finding that among American males only 29.9 percent of former union members identify themselves as working class, compared with 44.4 percent of the current members and 37.7 percent of those who never were members of a union (Hodge and Treiman, 1968, p. 543). A critical re-appraisal by Kenneth H. Thompson (1971), found fault mainly with the scantiness of the evidence and deprecates the difference between America and Europe in this respect. His own data show that although upwardly mobile males may not vote Republican to a *greater* extent than the stationary males, they "tend to be politically indistinguishable from middle class stables and much more Republican as a group than are the working class stable men" (Thompson, 1971, p. 229).

Apparently Thompson regards this as an argument against the thesis of over-conformity and as evidence that the process of acculturation may be smoother in America than in Europe. But data on the distribution of electoral preference and class identification in different statistical aggregates, do not measure the incidence of compulsive over-conformity. The minority of manual workers who vote Republican, may reflect a higher incidence of over-conformity to the dominant middle class values than the Republican majority among the upwardly mobile.

In any event the upwardly mobile differ in America, by adopting, to a far greater extent than their counterparts in Europe, the political orientations of their "class of destination". The pathological implications of the theory of over-conformity have not prevented the authors of recent cross-national comparisons of the consequences of occupational mobility (Lopreato, 1967; Simpson, 1970; Abramson and Books, 1971), from treating the European pattern as a sort of cultural lag.

Joseph Lopreato (1967) for instance, reiterates the customary notion of status-politics and over-conformity: "The likelihood of retaining political links with the class of origin [...] *a*) increases with the degree of status-discrepancies, namely rejection — real or imagined — by the old-timers in the class of destination; *b*) decreases with the strength of 1. the emphasis on achievement and, 2. the tendency toward emulation" (1967, p. 592).

According to this interpretation there is, in America, a greater congruence between occupation and other dimensions of social stratification. The European middle classes are still "keenly sensitive to the nuances of class behavior, and the occupationally successful children of the working class may find it particularly trying to gain the social recognition and acceptance that their economic achievement would warrant'' (Lopreato, 1967, p. 592). In America, on the other hand, occupational achievement is, in comparative perspective, practically the only legitimate claim to social status. The manual-nonmanual line has accordingly in America, but not in Europe, the features of a *gate* in Kurt Lewin's terminology: ''The constellation of the forces before and after the gate region are decisively different in such a way that the passing or not passing of a unit through the whole channel depends to a high degree upon what happens in the gate region. This holds also [...] for the social locomotion of individuals'' (Lewin, 1959, p. 199).

The troublesome problem of over-conformity is handled by Lopreato in a manner which minimizes the implication of social pathology. Lopreato reverses the customary interpretation of cause and effect in the relationship of psychological stress and over-conformity. In orthodox usage over-conformity is one of a variety of possible responses to stress; Lopreato turns over-conformity into a response to psychological relief:

''The experience of social success is likely to give the achiever enormous satisfaction and a deep sense of psychological relief. So profound indeed is the sense of relief [...] that the achiever is quite likely to develop [...] a cult of gratitude' [...] toward the social order [...] Such gratitude is then expressed through an 'over-conformity' to the prescribed behavior of the middle class, specifically by voting disproportionally for the party that is the loudest in proclaiming the reality of the American Dream and the old American virtues: self-reliance, individualism, and faith in the existing social order'' (Lopreato, 1967, p. 592).

Exposure to psychological stress is, according to this line of reasoning, greatest among the manual workers in America, not among the upwardly mobile. Lopreato refers explicitly to Merton's theory of structured strain in the American working class (Merton, 1957). By internalizing the pervasive ''norm of success'', the manual workers are in America saturated with a vital component of middle class values. Accordingly they forfeit self-respect far more than their European colleagues who are, to some extent, sheltered by working class traditions and socialist ideology from these values (*cf.* Parkin, 1967).

Presumably the theories of Lopreato and Lipset are complementary. One would therefore expect that the transformation of the ''traditional'' class structure in Europe will not only diminish the closure of its middle class and enhance the relevance of occupational achievement, but also weaken the defenses of the working class against self-derogation. The refractory pattern of political continuity among the occupationally mobile ought to disappear and a more drastic shift in political orientations toward the class of destination ought to become typical.

This hypothesis might be tested by ordering the European countries according to their proximity to the American model. Some European societies have advanced economically and politically further in the American direction than others. Presumably these countries will also have gone furthest in diminishing the relevance of status criteria which are not related to occupational achievement. We would then predict, firstly, a greater similarity in the political orientations of the upwardly mobile with their class of destination in the advanced European countries than in the more backward ones; secondly, a trend toward the continuing diminution of the political links between the upwardly mobile and their class of origin in these advanced European societies.

Unfortunately, the paucity of reliable data prevents a systematic test of this kind. No doubt such an order would place "northern non-Latin Europe" closer to the American pole of the continuum than, say, France or Italy. The strength of communist parties in Italy and France has been explained much in these terms (Lipset, 1964; Lorwin, 1958, p. 342). In the Scandinavian countries however, "all evidence indicates that social class explains more of the variation in voting and *particularly more of the working class voting* than some decades ago. This has occurred simultaneously with the disappearance of traditional class barriers. As equality has increased the working class voters have been more apt to vote for the workers' own parties than before" (Erik Allardt as quoted by Lipset, 1964, p. 279).

The erosion of the traditional class barriers indicates an approach toward the American model. This has not however resulted in a corresponding change in the pattern of political re-orientation among the mobile. The growing political homogeneity of the working class (which is here defined according to occupation), is not matched to the same degree by the homogenization of the middle class. This signifies that the upwardly mobile retain to a large extent the political orientations of their class of origin. Stein Rokkan explicitly calls attention to this fact:

"Family loyalties in politics have weighed very heavily even for the upward mobile. [...] Movement into the working class appears to have brought about the largest number of generational shifts in political allegiance. This is just another reflection of the basic change toward increasing uniformity of party support in this stratum. Movement into the middle class has produced much more mixed results : surprisingly few shifts *away from* Socialism and curiously many shifts to Socialism, at least among those of working class origins" (Rokkan, 1967, pp. 432-433).

Similar trends prevail, apparently, in Western Germany and in Britain. Segal (1967) has shown that in Germany 52.5 percent of middle class, non-Catholic individuals without union affiliation but of working class origin, support the Socialists, compared with only 18.6 percent of those with similar characteristics but of middle class origin. Abramson and Books (1971) found that, contrary to their expectation, the downwardly mobile orient themselves in Britain more according to their class of destination than the upwardly mobile. Only 28 percent of the upwardly mobile expressed preference for the Conservative party. The fathers of at least half of these voted Conservative themselves (Abramson and Books, 1971, pp. 421-422).

These scattered data cannot replace a systematic comparison of European societies; they do, however, cast doubt on the thesis that advanced technology and political democracy necessarily strengthen the middle class as a normative reference group. There remain, if this analysis is correct, some rather important aspects of social stratification in the United States, which do not serve as a model for developments in Europe. This seems to be connected with the political articulation of the working class in Europe. This class has become in Europe, but not in America, a "force or mechanism that operates to produce certain social attitudes" (Marshall, 1938, p. 97), not only among those individuals who "belong" to a certain social stratum, who interact with each other socially and who share a common fate in the market, but also among individuals and groups who do not, situationally, partake in the life of this stratum. The working class in Europe has aroused to some extent that charismatic responsiveness which, according to Shils (1965) is elicited by power over order: "The attribution of charismatic qualities occurs in the presence of order-creating, order-disclosing, order-discovering power as such; it is a response to great ordering power" (Shils, 1965, p. 204).

An essential aspect of revolutionary working class tradition consists, after all, in the claim that this class represents a tremendous, creative power; a class which possesses not only the capacity to resist the awesome power of the State and the mysterious forces of the market, but also a class which has the will and the ability to impose its own conception of a just social order upon society; a class which in addition to its moral appeal also proclaims itself as harbinger of greater efficiency in the use and development of economic resources.

The growth of the economic and political organizations identified with the working class in many European countries is a growth in real power over order. It may, to some extent, compensate the politics of compromise with the existing social, economic and political order. Locomotion within the hierarchy of occupational status may, under these conditions, reinforce rather than extinguish the charismatic response to the working class and its organizations as a referent of political values.

An example of this may be seen in Israel, where an initially strong charismatic response to the socialist working class traditions was modified, but not destroyed, by conditions which combine an advanced technology, the approximation of industrial maturity and parliamentary democracy.

Occupational mobility in Israel

It may appear bizarre to introject Israel, which is exceptional in so many ways, into a discussion of global trends. Questions of scale alone, pose numerous problems, let alone such complications as the fact that Israel has been engaged in more or less continuous war with its neighbors. This military effort has, no doubt, left its mark on all institutional arrangements, including the system of social stratification.

Yet, the Jewish community in Israel has developed into a highly industrialized society. Like other advanced societies, Israel has developed a highly differentiated occupational structure. About 85 percent of the Jewish labor force is engaged in non-agricultural occupations; about 75 percent of the non-agricultural labor force consists of wage earners, almost equally divided into manual and nonmanual occupations; a very high proportion are professionals and the tertiary sector is more developed than in most other countries (*cf.* Ben-David, 1965).

Like the United States, Jewish Israel has no "feudal traditions" and its middle class can hardly be said to be "permeated by an upper class atmosphere" (Lopreato, 1967, p. 592). As a society of immigrants, social origin seems to carry less weight as a claim to social status than country of origin, ethnic community, period of immigration and occupation. Unlike the United States, Israel has a highly organized working class and a tradition of militant socialism. A socialist party, which attracts nearly 40 percent of the votes, has been at the helm of government since 1948, while an additional 10-15 percent of the votes were regularly given to parties on its left, which were, until recently in more or less permanent opposition (*cf.* Eisenstadt, 1967).

The following analysis is based on a study which was carried out in 1964 on a sample (N = 643) of the male, Jewish residents of Haifa, aged 25-55. Haifa is Israel's major harbor and a center of heavy industry.

The occupational distribution of the sample (which corresponds closely with the census data of 1961) signifies a radical break with the traditional occupational distribution of the Jewish population in the diaspora.

In terms of inter-generational mobility it constitutes an outstanding example of that pattern of proletarization which Marx is said to have predicted, but which failed to become the dominant pattern in the advanced stages of industrialization: within a single generation, an urban middle class, consisting of merchants and artisans, was transformed into a class of wage earners, concentrated in manual occupations.

The major criterion according to which the redistribution of these sons of the middle class into Israel's emerging industrial occupational structure was accomplished, is a universalistic one: the level of education (*cf.* Table 2). Father's occupation and employment status do however assert themselves to some extent. More than twice as many sons of manual wage earners became themselves manual wage earners, although they had a complete high school education, than sons of the nonmanual self-employed.

About 44 percent of the sample population began their occupational career before immigrating to Israel. The occupational re-distribution was already initiated abroad. Most affected were the sons of merchants (the largest occupational category in father's generation). Only 35 percent continued, abroad, their father's occupation. The remainder moved, if they had a high school education, into other nonmanual occupations; otherwise they were, already before migrating, pushed into manual occupations (*cf.* Table 3).

This incipient trend was intensified by the process of migration itself (*cf.* Table 4). Immigration to Israel resulted in a further drastic curtailment

Table 1. *Occupational distribution*

Occupation	Fathers %	Sons %	Sons in each occupational category who are self-employed %
(N = 100 %)	(643)	(643)	25.0
Nonmanual			
Professional and administrative	5.1	13.8	13.5
Clerical	7.9	22.1	7.1
Business and sales	51.0	11.2	84.7
Manual			
Artisans	19.8	6.5	100.0
Foremen and technicians	0.6	6.1	0.0
Skilled, semi- and unskilled	7.6	34.6	12.7
Casual laborers	2.5	4.7	3.3
Unemployed and unknown	5.4	0.9	-

Table 2. *Proportion of sons who are manual wage earners according to education and according to father's occupation and employment status*

Father's occupation and employment status	Son: Completed high school — *Manual wage earners* (N)	%	Son: Did not complete high school — *Manual wage earners* (N)	%
Nonmanual self-employed	(130)	17.7	(217)	46.5
Nonmanual wage earner	(34)	20.6	(28)	43.0
Manual self-employed	(32)	6.3	(114)	60.8
Manual wage earner	(18)	39.0	(51)	70.8

Table 3. *Occupation before immigration to Israel, according to education and father's occupation*

Father's occupation	Son's occupation before immigration							
	Son completed high school				*Son did not complete high school*			
	(N)	Profes-sional %	Sales %	Manual %	(N)	Profes-sional %	Sales %	Manual %
Professional, administrative and clerical	(10)	70	10	20	(21)	29	9	62
Sales	(49)	55	31	14	(108)	14	37	49
Manual	(19)	58	10	32	(75)	13	9	77

Table 4. *Occupation before immigration to Israel and occupation in Israel (1964), according to education*

Occupation prior to immigration	Occupation in Israel							
	Completed high school				*Did not complete high school*			
	(N)	Profes-sional %	Sales %	Manual %	(N)	Profes-sional %	Sales %	Manual %
Professional, administrative and clerical	(46)	87	4	9	(34)	50	12	38
Sales	(18)	61	17	22	(48)	15	42	44
Manual	(15)	27	7	67	(125)	13	6	81

of opportunities for engaging in the traditional sales occupations and, particularly during the pre-State era, also forced many of the educated into manual occupations.

For this stage there exist comparable data. The census of 1961 included questions on occupation abroad as well as on present occupation. This information was gathered from a 20 percent sample of the population (*cf.* Israel Central Bureau of Statistics, 1965). No significant differences were found between our sample and the census data.

Arrival in Israel and the period of entry into its labor market coincide with the nadir of the occupational career of the sample population. Thereafter the trend toward proletarization is reversed. Almost all subsequent intra-generational mobility consists in moves out of manual occupations into non-manual ones and from wage earning to self-employed status. Economic expansion changed the conditions in Israel's labor market and permitted the absorption of a growing proportion of the high school graduates into non-manual occupations directly upon entry to the market (*cf.* Table 5).

Before political independence had been achieved in 1948, a third of the high school graduates who had held nonmanual positions abroad and 50 percent of the graduates who commenced their work career in Israel, had entered the labor force as manual workers. By 1953 enough nonmanual openings had become available to assure practically all high school graduates the non-manual status they had occupied abroad; only 22 percent of the graduates, who had no work experience abroad, began thereafter their career in Israel in manual occupations. As the supply of nonmanual positions increased, the chances of finding nonmanual employment improved considerably, also for those who did not have a completed high school education. Table 6 documents the exodus from manual occupations in the course of the occupational career of our sample.

This table is divided into four periods and shows the proportion of manuals, nonmanuals and new entrants to the labor force, who held a nonmanual position at the end of each period. The table shows that *a*) the chances of maintaining nonmanual status improve from period to period; *b*) new entrants to the labor force were (with education controlled), more likely to enter non-manual positions than incumbents of manual positions; the tendency for new entrants to move directly into nonmanual positions increases over time; *c*) mobility from manual to nonmanual occupations declines monotonically from period to period.

These patterns reflect the transformation of Israel's economy after the establishment of the State. Until the Second World War the economy of the Jewish community in Palestine had provided few opportunities for employment in nonmanual occupations, although the supply of qualified manpower, including trained professionals, was very large (*cf.* Ben-David, 1965, pp. 49-50). There emerged a highly cohesive working class, comprising a strong, articulate component of intellectuals, which was committed to collectivistic

Table 5. *Percent entering Israel labor force as nonmanuals, according to education and occupation abroad*

Education and occupation before immigration	Period of entry into labor force					
	Up to 1947		*1948-1952*		*1953 and after*	
	(N)	%	(N)	%	(N)	%
Nonmanual						
Completed high school	(27)	67	(26)	81	(11)	100
Did not complete high school	(22)	27	(45)	38	(14)	57
Did not work abroad						
Completed high school	(70)	50	(27)	41	(39)	72
Did not complete high school	(117)	18	(65)	25	(28)	35
Manual	(42)	7	(69)	12	(32)	22

Table 6. *Percent who were in nonmanual occupations at the end of each period, according to occupation in Israel at the beginning of each period*

Education and occupation at the beginning of each period	Percentwho were nonmanual at the end of each period							
	1 *1938-1947*		*2* *1947-1952*		*3* *1952-1958*		4 *1958-1964*	
	(N)	%	(N)	%	(N)	%	(N)	%
Finished high school								
Nonmanual	(25)	100	(62)	100	(114)	97	(146)	98
Not in Israel labor force	(54)	50	(61)	57	(34)	77	(17)	82
Manual	(25)	40	(41)	37	(53)	19	(55)	11
Did not complete high school								
Nonmanual	(19)	79	(34)	92	(91)	91	(129)	93
Not in Israel labor force	(81)	12	(175)	23	(56)	27	(17)	35
Manual	(70)	16	(129)	15	(247)	12	(267)	4

values and propagated militant socialist ideas. After the establishment of the State there began a period of rapid industrialization and the expansion of bureaucracies and public services. The initial equalization through proletarization was halted and there commenced a process of increasing occupational differentiation in which educational level played a crucial role. This led to a more "advanced" type of occupational stratification and the devaluation of manual occupations in the hierarchy of prestige (*cf.* Lissak, 1965, pp. 55-58).

Israel has a dual economy. A large proportion of the wage earners (including professionals, who in Israel are rarely independent practitioners), are employed in public or semi-public institutions. By 1964 only 18 percent of the high school graduates in the sample were still manual wage earners. It may be of some interest that new entrants to the labor force, who as new arrivals in Israel, should have been in an inferior bargaining position, made more use of the opportunities for nonmanual employment than the veterans (*cf.* Table 6). This may be a sign that the cleavage between manual and routine nonmanual occupations was not very great in Israel. The newcomers, presumably still oriented toward the values of their country of origin, may have resisted the prospective "proletarization" by accepting nonmanual jobs which were not attractive enough to induce veteran manual workers to change occupation. The great majority of newcomers who entered nonmanual jobs remained wage earners. The same is true for the veterans with a complete high school education who moved from manual to nonmanual employment. The opportunities for establishing a business or an independent workshop were utilized mainly by veteran manual workers who lacked the educational background for clerical employment in the expanding bureaucracies. Of the 336 respondents in the sample population who lack a high school education and who were at some time manual wage earners in Israel, 23.5 percent established themselves as proprietors and only 10.7 entered salaried white-collar positions. By 1964, 36.8 percent of the 133 respondents without a complete high school education, who had arrived in Israel before 1948, had ceased to be wage earners.

Class, mobility and ideology

We shall proceed now to the ideological orientations of the sample population. This will be confined to the presentation of two sets of variables. The first consists of subjective social class identification; the second is the cross-classification of attitudes toward alternative types of socio-economic systems ("Definitely Socialist", "Moderately Socialist", "Anti-Socialist" and "Free enterprise") and toward the *Histadrut*, the General Federation of Labor in Israel. Attitudes on these issues are related to one of the major ideological cleavages in Israel, which separates the "left" from the "right".

Class identification was determined through a cafeteria-type question which included labels such as "Upper class", "Bourgeoisie", "Middle class", "Intelligentsia", "Working intelligentsia", "Labor class", "Working class", "Proletariat", "Lower class" and the opportunity for the respondents to coin their own term. Previous research had established the significance of these labels in the context of Israel. The great majority of the sample chose one of the following four labels: "Middle class", "Working intelligentsia", "Labor class", and "Working class". In order to make the data more manageable we combined the categories "Labor class" and "Working class" together with their synonyms into a single category, which henceforth will be designated as "Working class". Table 7 shows the distribution of working class identification according to education, occupation and employment status.

Each of these factors contributes independently to the identification of the sample with the working class. Combined they form a consistent pattern. It should be noted that the alternative labels (which are not shown in Table 7) follow a similar pattern. The "Middle class" is the characteristic label chosen by the nonmanual self-employed and is typically chosen by the minority of manual self-employed and the nonmanual wage earners without a high school education who do not identify with the working class. Nonmanual wage earners who have a complete high school education refer to themselves as "Working intelligentsia". The middle class label retains in Israel the connotation of *petit bourgeois*. The salariat, when given the opportunity, prefers to identify itself by some term which signals association with, rather than distantiation from the working class.

Class identification is apparently determined more by present position and market situation than by social origin. The predominantly middle class origin of the majority of the sample has not prevented extensive identification with the working class. The career pattern in Israel does, however, leave its mark. Identification with the "Middle class" is dominant mainly among those who never were manual wage earners in Israel (*cf.* Table 8).

The upwardly mobile, who in the past had been manual wage earners in Israel, continue to identify to a considerable extent with the working class.

The second variable is the cross-classified response toward socialism and toward the *Histadrut*. The attitude toward socialism was obtained through a directed, open-end question. The attitude toward the *Histadrut* is derived from a battery of questions: a list enumerating various institutions (*e.g.* parliament, government, the courts, religious law, ethnic associations (specifically named), voluntary associations (specified), specified political parties, various interest groups (including the *Histadrut*), was presented to the respondents. They were asked to identify those institutions which, in their opinion, acted in their (the respondent's) interest and which affected their interests negatively. The cross-classification was attained by combining "Definitely Socialist" and "Moderately Socialist" into a single category and treating the remainder as a non-Socialist residual. As "*Pro-Histadrut*" we

Table 7. *Percent "Working class" according to occupation, education and employment status*

Occupation and education	Employment status: *Wage earners* (N)	%	*Self-employed* (N)	%
Completed high school				
Nonmanual	(134)	20.9	(31)	9.7
Manual	(40)	55.0	(14)	35.7
Did not complete high school				
Nonmanual	(86)	55.8	(52)	34.6
Manual	(223)	78.0	(57)	56.1

Table 8. *Percent "Working class" according to education, employment status, occupation in 1964 and occupational history in Israel*

Occupation (1964) and occupational history	Completed high school *Wage earners and self-employed* (N)	%	Did not complete high school *Self-employed* (N)	%	*Wage earners* (N)	%
Never were manual wage earners	(143)	18.2	(30)	23.3	(50)	50.0
Were formerly manual wage earners						
1964: Nonmanual	(21)	23.8	(22)	50.0	(36)	63.9
1964: Manual self-employed	(14)	35.7	(57)	56.2	-	-
Presently (1964) manual wage earners	(40)	55.0	-	-	(221)	78.7

designated all respondents who had named the *Histadrut* among the institutions which they regarded as championing their interests. Those who failed to mention the *Histadrut*, or who regarded its activities as detrimental to their own interests, were classified as "*Non-Histadrut*".

Table 9 helps to clarify the political connotations of the polar ideological types. We call political "negativism" the expression of antagonism toward political parties in general ("I am against parties", "I am against all parties") and claims that government, parliament or the courts and the legal institutions act against the respondent's own interests. As political "support" we interpret expressions of support for any political party or for political parties in general, provided the laws of the state, parliament and the government were not mentioned as negative factors. The unequivocal association between political negativism and the rejection of both socialism and the *Histadrut* on one hand and the association between attitudes favoring socialism and the *Histadrut* and political "support" on the other, indicates that positive attitudes toward socialism and toward the *Histadrut* signify rather generalized support for the existing political and social order in Israel.

If these ideological constructs are valid indicators of a major class-based ideological cleavage in Israel (Antonovsky, 1963, pp. 21-28), and if positive attitudes toward the *Histadrut* and toward socialism are an attribute of the working class, while their rejection is a major component of middle class values, then the association between these middle class values and political negativism indicates a significant reversal of the typical relationship between social stratification and some aspects of "alienation". Studies of "Western" societies have consistently shown that identification with political institutions varies directly with social class (Shils, 1965, pp. 199-213). This relationship appears to be inverted in Israel.

Table 10 shows that these ideological types indeed vary with social class. The classificatory scheme in this table was constructed by combining objective market criteria (educational level and employment status) and subjective identification with the "Middle class", the "Working intelligentsia" or the "Working class":

Class 1 (N = 140): "*Middle class*"; *a*) self-employed (63 %), all levels of education; *b*) wage earners (37 %), high school graduates only.

Class 2 (N = 82): "*Working intelligentsia*"; *a*) self-employed (7 %), all levels of education; *b*) wage earners (93 %), high school graduates only.

Class 3 (N = 111): "*Working class*"; *a*) self-employed (55 %), all levels of education; *b*) wage earners (45 %), high school graduates only.

Class 4 (N = 86): "*Middle class*" (77 %); "*Working intelligentsia*" (23 %); only wage earners who did not finish high school.

Class 5 (N = 222): "*Working class* "; only wage earners who did not finish high school.

The only category in which the majority (57.5 %) clearly rejects both socialism and the *Histadrut*, is Class 1, which consists of individuals whose subjective identification ("Middle Class") corresponds objectively with their market situation. Only 12 percent of this class support both socialism and the

Table 9. *Orientation toward political institutions according to ideological types*

Orientations toward political institutions	Ideological types		
	Pro-Histadrut Pro-Socialist	*Mixed*	*Non-Histadrut Non-Socialist*
	%	%	%
	—	—	—
(N = 100 %)	(175)	(248)	(220)
Political support	59.5	46.5	17.3
Neutral	32.0	35.4	45.8
Political negativism	6.5	17.7	36.8

Table 10. *Ideological types according to social class*

Social class	(N)	Pro-Histadrut Pro-Socialist	Mixed	Non-Histadrut Non-Socialist
		%	%	%
	—	—	—	—
Class 1	(140)	11.5	30.9	57.5
Class 2	(82)	24.5	36.7	39.0
Class 3	(111)	33.4	32.4	34.2
Class 4	(86)	31.5	46.7	22.2
Class 5	(222)	39.5	44.2	22.6

Histadrut. At the opposite pole, in Class 5, only 23 percent reject, while 40 percent support both socialism and the *Histadrut*.

Israel's middle class does not, like its American "counterpart", symbolically represent the dominant values of its society. "Membership" in this class does not signify proximity to and participation in Israel's central political institutions. Dissociation from the *Histadrut*, that powerful organization, which in many ways carried out the functions of a State during the period of the British Mandate and which still maintains many of these functions, implies distantiation from the vital center of Israel's institutional structure (Eisenstadt, 1967, pp. 38-43).

Israel's institutions, perhaps more than those of any society outside the communist world, were created by the working class. The values of this heritage remain a compelling factor in its system of stratification. But Israel is not, and never considered itself to be, a dictatorship of the proletariat. The emancipation of the working class is not considered an accomplished fact, but a task for the future. The ideological spectrum within the working class, how this desirable state is to be realized, ranges from militant revolutionary to faintly pink evolutionary doctrines. The evolutionary trend has always dominated. Thus, although the largest Socialist party never lost control over the *Histadrut* and has formed every government since the existence of the State, the workers still have the privilege of considering themselves exploited.

The perception of distributive injustice is, therefore, common and varies inversely with social class. In all strata, the class which is most frequently named as getting more than its just share is the *bourgeoisie*. Almost all who perceive distributive injustice at all, designate the "Working class" as getting less than its just share. Within each class there is a positive association between the perception of distributive injustice and support of socialism and the *Histadrut* (*cf*. Table 11).

Amelioration of the market situation and occupational mobility do not therefore mean conversion to middle class values. We have already seen that the occupationally mobile tend to retain their identification with the working class. The relationship between mobility and political orientation can however be documented directly. Our respondents were asked to compare themselves with their fathers and to evaluate whether their own lot had "generally" improved, or if they were worse off than their fathers. Specific probes were used to find out whether the perceived changes were predominantly of an economic nature, or whether social prestige was involved (*cf*. Table 12).

The sons of nonmanual fathers, whatever their own occupation, education and employment status, differ consistently from the sons of manual fathers. Only 29 percent of the former, but 43 percent of the latter, consider themselves better off than their fathers. An even greater contrast is shown when the employment status of both father and son is controlled (*cf*. Table 13).

28 percent of the self-employed sons of self-employed fathers, but 64 percent of the self-employed sons of wage earning fathers, claim inter-generational

Table 11. *Ideological types and social class according to the perception of distributive injustice*

Social class and the perception of distributive injustice	(N)	Pro-Histadrut Pro-Socialist %	Mixed %	Non-Histadrut Non-Socialist %
Class 1				
Do not perceive distributive injustice	(83)	7.2	25.4	67.5
Perceive distributive injustice	(56)	17.9	39.3	43.0
Class 2				
Do not perceive	(49)	18.3	38.8	42.9
Perceive	(33)	33.3	33.3	33.3
Class 3				
Do not perceive	(47)	25.6	34.0	40.3
Perceive	(64)	39.0	31.3	29.7
Class 4				
Do not perceive	(42)	21.5	40.5	38.0
Perceive	(44)	40.9	52.1	5.8
Class 5				
Do not perceive	(65)	32.4	43.0	24.6
Perceive	(157)	33.9	44.6	21.6

Table 12. *Subjective comparison with father (economic dimension) according to occupation and education*

Father's occupation and inter-generational change (subjective evaluation)	Son's education and occupation				
	Total	*Completed high school*		*Did not complete high school*	
		Nonmanual	Manual	Nonmanual	Manual
	%	%	%	%	%
Father nonmanual	(408)	(129)	(36)	(99)	(144)
Deterioration	52.6	55.0	52.9	51.5	51.5
No change	14.7	15.5	11.2	13.1	16.0
Improvement	29.4	24.0	36.1	33.3	29.9
No reply	3.2	5.4	-	-	2.8
Father manual	(214)	(33)	(16)	(37)	(128)
Deterioration	37.9	30.3	56.5	40.6	34.7
No change	11.7	12.2	-	5.4	14.9
Improvement	43.0	42.5	37.6	51.5	41.5
No reply	7.5	15.2	6.3	2.7	7.0

Table 13. *Subjective comparison with father (economic dimension), according to employment status*

Employment status	(N = 100%)	Inter-generational change (subjective evaluation)		
		Deterioration %	*No change* %	*Improvement* %
	—	—	—	—
Father self-employed Son self-employed	(131)	56.5	15.3	28.4
Father self-employed Son wage earner	(339)	54.0	14.0	32.0
Father wage earner Son wage earner	(103)	37.0	14.6	48.5
Father wage earner Son self-employed	(25)	24.0	12.0	64.0

improvement. Apparently, the gap between manual and nonmanual occupations on one hand and between wage earning and self-employed status on the other hand, is perceived as greater during the parental generation than at present. Since Israel is a society of immigrants, this reflects to some extent the differences in Israel's social stratification compared to the countries of origin, which in Haifa are mainly European countries.

The sons of manual fathers and of wage earners are more likely to be satisfied with their own achievements in Israel, even if they did not become occupationally mobile, than the sons of nonmanual or self-employed fathers, even when the latter escaped the pressure toward proletarization and retained, or regained their status of origin. These results indicate that in the social consciousness restratification in Israel is perceived as a process of nivellation, whereby the economic and social distance between the middle class and the working class was reduced. The lot of the working class has improved, while the lot of the middle class has — at least in its self-perception — deteriorated. The American pattern of political re-orientation as a consequence of upward mobility has been explained as an attitude of appreciation toward the social order which made individual achievement possible (Lopreato, 1967). This may not be a specifically American response, although the virtues to which the social order appeals may vary from society to society. In Israel too, the experience of social success and individual satisfaction is associated with faith in the existing social order (*cf.* Table 14).

The order itself is, however, apparently defined as evolving in the direction of socialism. Within each class the subjective experience of inter-generational amelioration (comparison with father "in general") is associated with support of socialism and the *Histadrut*. The experience of downward mobility in this sense, enhances political negativism and susceptibility to the counter-ideology of the middle class, which feels itself frustrated in the attempt to stop, or reverse the trend toward socialism.

This pattern repeats itself when we introduce a direct measure of individual satisfaction. This measure was constructed through a battery of questions concerning different positions occupied by the respondents. Each respondent was asked to define his location in alternative categories pertaining to occupation, education, employment status, income bracket, wealth, sector of employment (private, public, co-operative), social class, industrial branch, period of immigration, age, party commitment, ethnic group, ideological commitment, religious observance and past or present "national service". On each item we asked the respondent how his particular location affected his social status and which aspect of status was involved, income or prestige. By subtracting the number of status-liabilities, *i.e.* the factors which are perceived as affecting socio-economic status negatively, from the status assets, we were able to assign each individual a score. This score is apparently a fair measure of status satisfaction. The score averaged in our population +2.2 and ranged from —6 to +10. It correlates highly with education, occu-

Table 14. *Social class, inter-generational change (subjective evaluation) and ideological orientation*

Social class and inter-generational change* (subjective evaluation)	(N)	Pro-Histadrut Pro-Socialist %	Mixed %	Non-Histadrut Non-Socialist %
Class 1				
Deterioration	(46)	4.3	34.7	61.0
Improvement	(44)	13.6	29.5	57.0
Class 2				
Deterioration	(25)	16.0	36.0	48.0
Improvement	(28)	32.2	35.7	32.0
Class 3				
Deterioration	(37)	29.8	40.6	29.8
Improvement	(37)	29.8	29.8	40.6
Class 4				
Deterioration	(29)	17.3	58.8	24.1
Improvement	(29)	48.4	34.5	17.3
Class 5				
Deterioration	(86)	26.8	46.6	26.8
Improvement	(65)	41.6	40.0	18.5

* Excludes those who declared that no inter-generational change has occurred in their case. These fit consistently, within each class, between those who claim deterioration and those who claim inter-generational improvement.

pation and our classificatory scheme of social class. We designate a score of —6 to 0 as an index of low statisfaction, +1 to +2 we label as "medium" and +3 or higher as high satisfaction. In Table 15 each class is partitioned accordingly.

Satisfaction, we note, is greatest in Class 1, the consistent "Middle class". It is lowest in Class 5, the consistent "Working class". But within each class there is a positive association between satisfaction and working-class ideology. Support of socialism and the *Histadrut* does not feed on dissatisfaction.

In Israel, like in the United States, upward mobility and a positive self-image foster conformity with the dominant value system and enhance the legitimacy of the political institutions and the social order. Only in Israel, it is the working class, rather than the middle class, which is identified with this order. This may be a "false consciousness", but if someone would devise a scale of measuring the degree of "falseness", perhaps it would turn out that the consciousness of the working population in Israel is a shade less "false" than that of the United States. We would of course expect a similar association between satisfaction and identification with the working class in the communist countries, where the working class is the ultimate referent of all social virtue (*cf.* Parkin, 1969, pp. 356-357). In Western Europe, even the moderately socialist parties represent a challenge to the legitimacy of at least some aspects of the social order. No matter how revisionist they may be, to some extent they enhance the dignity and the self-esteem of the working class. As Crosland has pointed out, by attaining executive power, socialist parties destroy the image of the middle class as the pillar of law and order (Crosland, 1956, pp. 232-237). The integration of the upwardly mobile into the middle class and the consequent political re-orientations of individuals who were brought up in a working class *milieu*, varies, we suggest, inversely to the strength of the political parties associated with the working class, and on the extent to which these parties continue to stress their links with this class, once they have become powerful. This point has been stated most eloquently by the authors of the study on the *Affluent worker in the class structure*:

"If the working class does in the long term become no more than one stratum within a system of "classless inegalitarianism", offering no basis for or response to radical initiatives, then this situation will not be adequately explained either as an inevitable outcome of the evolution of industrialism or as reflecting the ability of neo-capitalism to contain the consequences of its changing infrastructure by means of mass social-psychological manipulation. It will to some degree also be attributable to the fact that the political leaders of the working class *choose* this future for it" (Goldthorpe *et al.*, 1969, p. 195).

Conclusion

If our analysis is correct and if it is proper to generalize from the special Israeli case, then the transformation of the occupational structure, as the result of

Table 15. *Social class, status satisfaction and ideological orientation*

Social class and status satisfaction	(N)	Ideological orientations: *Pro-Histadrut Pro-Socialist* %	*Mixed* %	*Non-Histadrut Non-Socialist* %
Class 1				
Low or medium satisfaction	(61)	9.8	29.4	60.6
High satisfaction	(78)	12.8	32.1	55.1
Class 2				
Low or medium satisfaction	(36)	16.7	36.1	47.2
High satisfaction	(46)	30.4	37.0	32.6
Class 3				
Low or medium satisfaction	(70)	34.3	31.4	34.3
High satisfaction	(41)	31.7	32.1	34.1
Class 4				
Low or medium satisfaction	(50)	26.0	52.0	22.0
High satisfaction	(36)	38.9	38.9	22.2
Class 5				
Low satisfaction	(79)	24.0	35.5	29.3
Medium satisfaction	(77)	30.0	48.0	22.0
High satisfaction	(66)	48.5	37.9	13.6

advanced economic development, need not destroy the potency of the working class as a normative reference group for the upwardly mobile.

The proximity of the middle class to the central value system, rather than the willingness to accept, socially, the upwardly mobile, determines whether these will orient themselves politically and ideologically in accordance with middle class values.

Where economic expansion and social progress are believed to be overwhelmingly the result of individual initiative and private enterprise, the upwardly mobile will be encouraged to interpret their success as a consequence of their own, individual effort. They will affirm the validity of the social order which permits these qualities to unfold and identify with the class which seems to represent these values.

Where, however, economic and social progress are believed to be the result of a collective effort, where the working class believes itself hindered in producing and reproducing all human qualities necessary for the performance of highly differentiated functions, where it is convinced that only concerted political action can secure access for its sons to positions through which these functions are exercised, the upwardly mobile in the occupational structure are more likely to interpret their own success as a result of this collective, political effort and to retain their political and ideological ties with their class of origin.

REFERENCES

Abramson, P.R.; Books, J.W.
1971 "Social mobility and political attitudes", *Comparative politics* 3, April: 403-428.

Antonovski, A.
1963 "Ideology and class in Israel", *Ammot* 2, August: 21-28.

Ben-David, J.
1965 "Professionals and unions in Israel", *Industrial relations* 5, October: 48-66.

Blau, P.M.
1957 "Occupational bias and mobility", *American sociological review* 22 : 392-399.
1965 "The flow of occupational supply and recruitment", *American sociological review* 30: 475-490.

Blau, P.M.; Duncan, O.D.
1967 *The American occupational structure.* New York, Wiley.

Crosland, C.A.R.
1961 *The future of socialism.* London, Jonathan Cape.

Dahrendorf, R.
1959 *Class and class conflict in industrial society.* Stanford, Calif., Stanford University Press.

Davies, A.F.; Encel, S.
1965 *Australian society: A sociological introduction.* Melbourne, F.W. Cheshire.

Eisenstadt, S.N.
1967 *Israeli society.* London, Weidenfeld and Nicolson.

Goldthorpe, J.H.
1964 "Social stratification in industrial society", pp. 97-122 in: P. Halmos, (ed.). *The development of industrial society.* Keele, Sociological review. (Monograph No. 8.)

Goldthorpe, J.H. *et al.*
1969 *The affluent worker in the class structure.* Cambridge, University Press.

Hodge, R.W. *et al.*
1966 "A comparative study of occupational prestige", pp. 309-321 in: R. Bendix; S.M. Lipset (eds.). *Class, status and power.* New York, Free Press of Glencoe.

Hodge, R.W.; Treiman, D.J.
1968 "Class identification in the United States", *American journal of sociology* 73: 535-547.

Israel Central Bureau of Statistics
1965 *Labour Force, Part 4: Occupation abroad. Population and housing census of 1961.* Jerusalem.

Lewin, K.
1959 "Group decision and social change", pp. 197-211 in: E.E. Maccobi *et al.* (eds.). *Readings in social psychology.* London, Methuen.

Lipset, S.M.; Zetterberg, H.
1956 "A theory of social mobility" pp. 155-177 in: *Transactions of the Third World Congress of Sociology.* Vol. 3. London, Hereford Times.

Lipset, S.M.; Bendix, R.
1959 *Social mobility in industrial society.* Berkeley, Calif., University of California Press.

Lipset, S.M.
1963 *Political man.* Garden City, NY, Doubleday/Anchor.
1964 "The changing class structure and contemporary European politics", *Daedalus* 93, Winter: 271-303.

Lissak, M.
1965 "Patterns of change in ideology and class structure in Israel", *Jewish journal sociology* 7: 46-62.

Lopreato, J.
1967 "Upward social mobility and political orientation", *American sociological review* 32: 586-592.

Lorwin, V.R.
1958 "Working class politics and economic development in Western Europe", *American historical review* 63: 338-351.

Marshall, T.H.
1938 "The nature of class conflict", pp. 97-111 in: *Class conflict and social stratification.* Ledbury, Play House.

Merton, R.K.
1967 "Social structure and anomie", pp. 185-214 in: *Social theory and social structure.* New York, Free Press of Glencoe.

Parkin, F.
1967 "Working class conservatives: A theory of political deviance", *British journal of sociology* 18: 278-290.
1969 "Class stratification in socialist societies", *British journal of sociology* 20: 355-374.

Reissman, L.
1960 *Class in American society.* New York, Free Press of Glencoe.

Rokkan, S.
1967 "Geography, religion and social class: Cross-cutting cleavages in Norwegian politics", pp. 367-444 in: S.M. Lipset; S. Rokkan (eds.). *Party systems and voter alignments.* New York, Free Press of Glencoe.

Segal, D.R.
1967 "Classes, strata and parties in West Germany and the United States", *Comparative studies in society and history* 10: 66-84.

Shils, E.A.
1961 "Centre and periphery", pp. 117-130 in: *The logic of personal knowledge: Essays presented to Michael Polanyi.* London, Heinemann.
1965 "Charisma, order and status", *American sociological review* 30: 199-213.

Simpson, M.E.
1970 "Social mobility, normlessness and powerlessness in two cultural contexts", *American sociological review* 35: 1002-1013.

Weinberg, I.
1969 "The problem of the convergence of industrial societies: A critical look at the state of a theory", *Comparative studies in society and history* 11: 1-15.

Wiley, N.
1967 "America's unique class politics: The interplay of the labor, credit and commodity markets", *American sociological review* 32: 529-541.

Thompson, K.H.
1971 "Upward social mobility and political orientation: A re-evaluation of the evidence", *American sociological review* 36: 223-235.

Tumin, M.M.
1957 "Some unapplauded consequences of social mobility in a mass society", *Social forces* 36: 32-37.

Valen, H.; Katz, D.
1967 *Political parties in Norway.* Oslo, Universitetsforlaget.

Zymelman, M.
1969 "Productivity, skills and education in manufacturing industries", pp. 103-138 in: United Nations Industrial Development Organization, *Planning for advanced skills and technologies.* New York, United Nations.

Discussion

Introduction

In response to the preceding papers, a number of points were raised during the Workshop, which had not been explicitly dealt with in the papers read or which were differently evaluated by the discussants. Since open and controversial issues of crucial importance were expounded in the course of the discussions, we felt that a number of the statements should also be made available to a wider public *. We have grouped the contributions selected under three main headings: 1) Stratification theory and mobility research; 2) On the use of occupational prestige scales in mobility analysis; 3) Issues in the study of career mobility.

W.M./K.U.M.

1. Stratification theory and mobility research

Investigations of social mobility and the criticisms directed against them operate within particular theoretical frames of reference in regard to stratification, which are closely connected with diverse political orientations. John Goldthorpe characterizes three approaches — liberal, neo-Marxist and ethically socialist — and discusses their implications for empirical research (1.1). That the nation-state may be an unwarranted assumption is argued by Reinhard Bendix (1.2) who also assails current stratification research for its lack of an

* Our main selection criteria were that the statements be either of general concern for mobility research or related to the central themes of at least one published paper. It has been intended that the texts retain their character of intervention in a discussion and of spontaneous reaction. Therefore the contributions have not been revised or condensed. All authors, however, kindly corrected the transcripts for lapses of grammar or meaning.

evolutionist perspective, *i.e.* its disjunction from theories on societal development (1.3). In a comment on the paper by Zloczower, Goldthorpe critically evaluates one influential developmental assumption in mobility studies which he calls "para-evolutionary Marxism" (1.4). In several statements the historical changes in what is defined as equality of opportunity and the seemingly futile attempts to reduce inequalities are being discussed in relation to the political efforts invested (1.5). Finally, the controversy over the consequences of various concepts of inequality for inferences about facts is summarized (1.6).

1.1. *Inequality and mobility: three perspectives*

John H. Goldthorpe: The context that I want to set out first is that of two clearly contrasting approaches to the study of social stratification and mobility which have emerged during the sessions of the Workshop. Basically, one could label the two approaches, for convenience, the liberal approach and the Marxist or neo-Marxist. I don't insist on these labels, you can change them if you wish. Essentially, it seems to me in the case of what I shall call the liberal approach, one operates with a model of stratification that is really based on the idea of continuous distributions — of income, of education, of prestige, of authority, of autonomy, etc. In this perspective, obvious problems for research are changes in the shape of these distributions, that is, increases or decreases in inequality, and studies of the mobility of individuals and groups through time between positions in these various distributions or composite versions of them. In contrast to this, in what I shall label the Marxist approach, one has not the hierarchical or continuous model of stratification, but rather a dichotomous model in which two classes are seen as opposed, as in conflict with each other. In this case, one obvious problem for investigation would be the various manifestations within the society of class conflict, in the industrial or political fields or in these together. Or, conversely, in the absence of any such overt manifestations of conflict, the focus of interest would be on various social mechanisms and processes which are seen as suppressing, either overtly or covertly, the conflict which is inherent in the system: analysis, for example, of various forms of social psychological manipulation or suppression by more obvious direct means; also analyses of the role of ideology, the creation of false consciousness, etc. And from this point of view, obviously, the concern with social mobility in the sense of the liberal approach is of relatively little interest. It would be very difficult to fit this kind of concern into the Marxist model of the class structure.

It seems to me that in this rather stark confrontation of these two approaches, whatever ideological excitement this may create, the likely outcome for sociological research — if that is one of one's concerns — is not particularly promising. Insofar as British sociologists have made any distinctive contribution in this field it is by working out, in a rather traditionally British sleepwalking and non-doctrinaire manner, some alternative perspectives and approaches, which combine elements of both the other approaches and at the same time reject elements of both of them.

For instance, whereas in the liberal approach the general concern has been to try to demonstrate the way in which, with economic development, inequalities in the various distributions which are seen as constituting stratification have diminished, the concern of many British social investigators, in the years both before and after the War, has been with investigating, for example, the distribution of income or the differential distribution of educational opportunity, chiefly to the end of pointing out that inequalities have remained remarkably stable. So the general position of British sociologists would be to reject the rather optimistic, liberal view that there is inherent in the process of industrial development some levelling and equalizing tendency. But, at the same time, the dominant view among British sociologists would also be that these distributions of income, educational opportunity, etc., are of importance, and that inequality is a rather basic concept in the analysis of social class. They would not be inclined — as perhaps some exponents of the neo-Marxist approach might be — to play down the degree of differentiation of income, educational opportunity, authority, autonomy, etc., within the bulk of the employed, non-property-owning labor-force.

As a second example, I think that the general drift of the political motivation of social mobility research in Britain — even when carried out on conventional lines as, say, by Prof. Glass — has not been to try and legitimate the liberal ideology of the "open society". On the contrary, the concern of the Glass research was to investigate critically the idea of the open society, and the results of the research enabled, in fact, very powerful criticisms to be made, since the general drift of findings was that a remarkable rigidity, at least at the top and bottom of the occupational distribution, seemed to exist. Subsequently, most of the discussion going on in this field, largely stemming from data on persisting class differentials in educational opportunity, has been in a similarly critical vein. The point that has been emphasized is that despite the attempt through educational policy to create formal equality of educational opportunity, this is still far from being realized, and that so far as one can see, class differentials have been remarkably untouched. At the same time, though, and again in contra-distinction to the Marxist approach, the ideological position of most British sociologists would be one that gave great political importance to increasing the amount of openness in the society, to levelling inequalities of opportunity — because there would be fairly general recognition of the close relationships between inequalities of opportunity and inequalities of condition. Apart from anything else, there would be some, at least residual, faith in the working of the market system to the effect that if, through increasing equality of opportunity of access to valued occupations one could reduce the restrictions on the supply side of the labour market that at present prevail, this in itself would have a levelling effect — for example, on the distribution of income. Again, I emphasize the concern with inequalities, and the reduction of inequalities, *within* the body of the employed labour-force; that is, of course, the very large majority of the population.

A third point: I think that British sociologists would reject the idea, found frequently in the writings of the members of the liberal school, that there is, again as a kind of automatic process, in advanced industrial societies, a blurring of the lines of stratification in subcultural and relational terms; and, especially, they would question the idea of the *embourgeoisement* of the working class. But at the same time, once more in opposition to the Marxist perspective, there would be, at least among many British sociologists, a rejection of the idea of the working class — even the British working class, the largest proportionately of any — as being the historic agent of revolution. The argument here would be that there is among the British working class a conspicuous absence of revolutionary consciousness and that this has generally been the case historically. Related to this would be — a general skepticism about the utility of the idea of false consciousness, this being seen simply as a device to "save" the Marxist theory and not a notion with any great explanatory value.

In this case, then, one has a basic model of stratification which is different from either the liberal model or the neo-Marxist model. Like the liberal model, it is a hierarchical model, represented in terms of distributions, and not a dichotomous one. But, on the other hand, stratification is not seen simply as a phenomenon of socio-economic status or of prestige. It is seen as a phenomenon of power and advantage. *This* is what ultimately is distributed and what one can measure, although often only indirectly, through looking at such things as distribution of income, authority, educational life chances, and so on. And because the structure of power and the advantage it comprises has inherent in it important self-maintaining properties, it is unlikely that the structure of stratification will be radically changed in an egalitarian direction simply by the inherent working-out of any logic of industrialism. It probably will only be changed, if at all, through purposive and forceful action of a political character.

I don't want to argue that the British sociologists to whom I refer are automatically superior in their analysis to the other two groups simply by virtue of taking a "middle" position. But what I would wish to argue is that, at least so far as British society is concerned, *their* interpretation of the nature of social stratification is one which can produce more empirically supportable propositions than any other. Nor would I want to claim that British sociologists are any more insightful or clever than other sociologists in producing their model. I think the explanation is a rather different one. Among British sociologists there is a tendency to treat actual political practice far more seriously than in either of the two other approaches I've outlined. In the liberal approach, there is some tendency to see politics reduced to a kind of epiphenomenon of technological and economic development. In the Marxist approach, there is a tendency to devalue politics other than of a revolutionary kind, which, in modern Western societies, usually is not happening very effectively. In contrast, one may point to the lack of reliance on the part of most British sociologists on the outcome of historical processes to validate their socio-political values. It is, I think for this reason, if for any at all, that their interpretations of class-structure become less distorted, more empirically sound. That is to say, because they are not dependent on empirical findings, because they are not dependent upon what the course of history shows, to validate the socio-political stance which they adopt. If you want to label this stance, I suppose it is the kind of ethical socialism which is generally in disrepute with both liberals and Marxists. But it seems to me to have at least this advantage: that from this position one can contemplate quite a wide variety of empirical findings — possibly with dismay — but without the feeling that one's valued position has, by their very existence, been undermined.

1.2. *The nation state as frame of reference for inequality*

Reinhard Bendix : I find myself at odds with both contrasts and even with the English pattern that sort of mediates between the two. I shall put my skeptical comments in an over-simplified fashion that runs the risk of misunderstanding. I hope you will allow for the exaggeration; it ought to insure that I will be brief and make the point sharply. I should add that I am as troubled by my own studies of mobility as I am by those in the Marxist tradition and by what John Goldthorpe called the liberal version of a distributive system. There is a set of assumptions that I never see spelled out in any of these traditions.

One of the assumptions is the idea of classes as nation-wide phenomena. The assumption seems to be that we are all talking about national societies. I challenge the implicit contention that you have the degree of integration in a national society that would allow you to speak of nation-wide classes of any kind, upper class, workers, capitalists, whatever. This contention tends to be promoted for technical reasons, for example, in very sophisticated fashion in studies of prestige which Prof. Goldthorpe has criticized very well. The one thing which Prof. Goldthorpe didn't challenge in his paper is the notion that the prestige differences that you find are of a society-wide dimension. I'm not sure.

Secondly, I detect the implicit assumption of societies as closed systems, that the stratification of societies is unaffected by their position within an international context. With these queries or worries out of the way, let me say a few positive things which have occurred to me as I've watched my colleagues undertake studies in this area which I myself have not really followed up in recent years.

The literature has tended to drift toward what is most accessible, namely the impact of inequality on individuals or groups of individuals. You all are well aware of the simple phenomenon that there is a life career of restrictive opportunities which is a by-product of aging. The more choices you have made the fewer choices you will be able to make henceforth. In this respect people find that they are all in the same boat. As they get older the choices they have made in the past predetermine and restrict the choices they will have an opportunity to make subsequently. Of course, the major stratifying factor in this experience is that people's starting points vary tremendously, that actually family background alone, quite apart from anything else, is a very important determining factor to begin with. And once they are launched on their occupational careers every job held for any length of time adds elements of further restriction as well as elements of further opportunities.

In this respect one of the curious omissions in current mobility research is the other side of the coin. It is always asked, and legitimately asked, what is the impact of family background on this life-career of diminishing opportunities at different levels of the social hierarchy? What isn't asked is the other question — perhaps it was a more conservative question or affected by a conservative ideology: what is the capacity of families to maintain themselves over time in the same privileged position? The capacity of families to transmit their privileges or prestige over time used to be one of their major concerns. One should not need the reminder that a mobility factor is built into the social structures that we have had since the French Revolution, namely that families find it exceedingly difficult to transmit their accumulated privileges to the next generation. I agree this is a guess based on personal impression; it is based on a certain amount of evidence — *cf.* a book that is rarely cited by sociologists in recent years, namely Robert Michels, *Umschichtung der herrschenden Klassen nach dem Ersten Weltkrieg*. The evidence wasn't very good, but the kind of question Michels asked has simply dropped from sight.

I'd like to say one other thing. If you question that classes or strata are nation-wide and that you have a very effective hierarchy of ranks covering the entire society, then one is prompted to ask: what really are the mechanisms by which a society is subdivided — and this is where the non-competing groups come in — such that groups within the working class, groups within the capitalist class or whatever groups you wish to name, are indeed capable of monopolizing opportunities for their members to the exclusion of others, whether through organizational devices, legal devices, through influence-peddling or what not. They do this in terms of family background and intermarriage, they do it in linguistic terms — especially in countries in which more than one language is spoken, and even where the same language is spoken in terms of different kinds of accents and dialects. The way in which groups are capable of maximizing opportunities for their members — and by that I mean excluding others from the enjoyment of these opportunities — is neglected in the analysis of stratificational research. I suspect this is due to the fact that, tacitly, we have thought about strata and prestige hierarchies in society-wide or nation-wide terms. Perhaps we ought to do less of that and rather analyze the mechanisms where power and domination and exploitation and all the other things that Marxists are fond of talking about come in very directly. I don't think you investigate these mechanisms of monopolization if you think of it in society-wide terms. I would urge that these things might be investigated at lower levels of comprehensiveness.

1.3. *The lack of an evolutionist perspective*

Reinhard Bendix: One assumption of 19th century theory that has almost disappeared from research on social stratification is the assumption of an evolutionary tendency in society. Even the people who speak of dichotomous tendencies of classes, for example, in the Marxist tradition, are no longer speaking of it in the original Marxian sense. Marx thought he was predicting something. Ossowsky, who thinks of himself as a Marxist, does not say this is a prediction. He says this is an image of the society and that is quite a different thing.

Now Marx thought there was an actual polarization that he could predict. But when you have a social-psychological approach to this dichotomy then of course it is as old as the ancient religions, as Ossowsky points out. The distinction between rich and poor and all that goes with it is a very ancient notion. Let me try and put it this way: there was once, and Marx still used it, the old classic division of land, labor and capital. This is no longer used but I am not so sure that we have an alternative simplification. One cannot talk about stratification of society in other than simplified terms. But what we have instead are mixtures of thoughts, an analysis with recollections from the 19th century tradition which drops off certain implications, such as the developmental one, which were integral to it at one time and have now largely disappeared.

In other words, we are at a point in stratification research where we must indeed examine the assumptions with which we start. A knowledge of ideas in this respect is an indispensable methodological tool. Not because I am interested in antiquarian research, but because I just don't see how you can get a hold of the assumptions that we make implicitly, unless we confront these survivals from the 19th century with the realities of today.

1.4. *Social mobility and economic development: "Para-evolutionary Marxism"*

John H. Goldthorpe: I am not quite sure wether I should comment on Mr. Zloczower's paper or on what he said introducing it. I shall try to do a little of both. It might be useful and relevant to our earlier discussion this morning if I said something of how I see work of the kind that Mr. Zloczower's paper represents, fitting into the general development of mobility studies. In the recent past, and I think in several papers that have been submitted to the Workshop, the suggestion has been made that there is some fairly close relationship between more conventional kinds of occupational and social mobility studies and a liberal ideology, of chiefly American provenance. It has been suggested, for example by Mr. Kreckel, if I understand him correctly, that one can interpret the ideological bases of much of this research as having to do with the defense of the notion of the open society. I would not want to deny that this has been the case. At least in certain American studies, one could show this relationship fairly clearly. Furthermore, I think it is evident enough that the idea of increasing social mobility in association with economic growth was an important element in the kind of liberally oriented political sociology which has been advanced mainly by American writers. This sort of approach, which I tend to associate chiefly with Lipset, seems to me a rather strange kind of what could perhaps best be described as "para-evolutionary Marxism". It is an attempt — Mr. Zloczower has the crucial quotation* — to demonstrate, as Lipset puts it, that history, at least in Western Europe, has validated a basic premise of Marxist sociology at the expense of Marxist politics. That is to say, the general proposition was that economic development together with technological change and closely related social structural change might concomitantly have a crucial impact on the nature of organization and political action, such that the revolutionary potential in Western European society would steadily decline. However, I think that one should stress that, from the first, arguments of this kind were rejected, and not only from a Marxist position but also from a position which has opposed both this evolutionary para-Marxism and Marxism proper. The position which I wish to note refused to see politics reduced to a mere epiphenomenon of technological and economic change.

I think that, in this respect, Mr. Zloczower's paper fits into this counter-tradition fairly clearly. The points in it which I would want to emphasize are those I see as being most significant from this point of view. First, of course, by looking at Israel, he is examining a highly industrialized society which still manages to maintain a form of equality which is, at least arguably, of a socialist kind. But secondly, and more importantly, he is able to show that in an interesting way Lipset's hypothesis can be generalized from liberal capitalism to a more socialistic society, in the sense that in the latter case also, upward mobility can be an important source of positive commitment to the regime and downward mobility can be associated with a high degree of alienation. Only, in this inverted case, the upwardly mobile, the committed groups, tend to be primarily working class or people mobile into the working intelligentsia, whereas the alienated groups tend to be primarily middle class groups. But then, thirdly, and this is the most important point of all, there is the way in which Mr. Zloczower brings out the importance of the relative strength and character of political parties themselves in shaping the political culture of the society. They thus in effect determine the way in which mobi-

* *Cf.* S.M. Lipset, "The changing class structure and contemporary European politics" *Daedalus* 93, Winter, pp. 271-272.

lity and present class-position will be interpreted subjectively by the social actors who are mobile or immobile as the case may be. It seems to me that this is the element which is generally lacking in much earlier discussion of the political consequences of social mobility. In this earlier approach, which I think Lipset's work largely typifies, the assumption generally was that economic development, as related to social structural change, was the crucial independent variable. This determined patterns of mobility and then, subsequently, the experience of mobility shaped patterns of political action and commitment. I think it is important, following Mr. Zloczower's paper, to see that this is an unduly simplified view; that the whole nature of the polity as it exists at any time — the dominant political culture — can be an influence on the way in which people interpret their mobility and class-position, and thus on the way in which they define their relationship to a regime. In these respects my own predilections or prejudices are entirely the same as Mr. Zloczower's.

But in one other respect I would want to differ. I would want to challenge the, what I call liberal, interpretation of social mobility rather more radically than I think he does. If I understand the paper correctly, and what he said just now also, it seems that he would accept the liberal argument that there has generally been an increase in the degree of occupational mobility, attendant upon economic growth. This, I think, is a plausible hypothesis but I maintain that it is still one for which there is no empirical confirmation, and moreover that equally plausible counter-hypotheses can be advanced. Most people here will be aware of the difficulties in demonstrating the economic growth — more social mobility link. The methodological ones have been pointed out by Dudley Duncan; but, over and above that, I would say that if one looks at the scraps of evidence relevant to this hypothesis that *are* available (I admit that they are very inadequate) they seem to point in the direction of no influence on the rate of intergenerational mobility and of loosening of the tie between the occupational position of father and son. And, moreover, I think that if one does take the, as it were, political economy view of this matter, although not the Marxist view, one can suggest alternative hypotheses which would be to the effect that one should not expect an increase in social or at least occupational mobility attendant upon economic development. Prof. Ammassari pointed out, in the paper that has been circulated*, that simply because one can demonstrate the intensifying division of labour as part of economic growth and the adoption of more universalistic criteria in allocating individuals to occupations, it doesn't follow from this that the degree of intergenerational mobility will increase. One has, as it were, on the other side of the argument, to recognize the fact that systems of social stratification are systems of differential power and advantage and therefore contain an inherently self-maintaining force; the power and advantage of the

* Paolo Ammassari, "Occupational opportunity structure in advanced societies", in : *Proceedings of the first Italo-Hungarian meeting of sociology*, Rome, Centro Cultural Italia-Ungheria, 1967.

superior strata can be systematically used to maintain the control they exercise over the more favoured occupational positions.

If one looks at attempts by economists to explain the occupational distribution of income, one finds that most of the purely economic theories in effect break down, because there is no way of taking into account the restrictions on the supply side of the labour market. Economists have had to adopt the device of "non-competing groups" in the labour market to explain why the marginalist theories of income distribution look strange when compared with what one observes to be the case. Now, if one thinks about this notion of non-competing groups in the labour market, the major non-competing groups are in fact what sociologists would call social strata. And the restriction on the supply side of the labour market is simply what sociologists call inequality of occupational opportunity. To a degree, then, one can conceive existing inequalities of condition, at least in terms of income, as being closely related to existing inequalities in access to differentially rewarded occupations. Inequalities of opportunity and inequalities of condition serve to mutually maintain each other. It seems to me that, rather than supposing an increase in occupational mobility brought about merely by economic growth, development of the occupational structure, etc., one ought to ask rather more critically: under what conditions do we have historical evidence of *any* large change in intergenerational (or other) mobility? I think one would probably come up with the answer that this happens only under rather special conditions indeed; *e.g.* what Mr. Zloczower describes of the early days of Israel.

Again, as a more limited example, one of the few changes that show, historically, in differential earnings within the British occupational structure (which, overall, has displayed a quite remarkable historical stability) is the decline of the position in the income distribution of clerks. And this, it seems, is attendant on the universalization of primary education (so that literacy became no longer, as it had been earlier in the 19th century, a fairly rare attribute) and thus, on the "opening" of the occupation of clerk to considerable "upward" recruitment. Apart from developments of this rather special kind, I would want to maintain, contrary to the liberal view, that we have no very strong theoretical expectation that there *should* be any large increase in inter-generational occupational mobility associated with economic development. So I would rather query the suggestion that, if I understood Mr. Zloczower correctly, what were previously classes in the Marxist sense, are now ceasing to be so in consequence of occupational mobility. I think this implies some kind of secular historical trend, for which there is not, as far as I know, very strong evidence.

1.5. *The meaning of inequality of opportunity*

Thomas Luckmann: In all of today's contributions there was talk of the distribution of opportunities, restrictions, inequalities, etc. I would add one assumption to the tacit assumptions with which one ought to feel at least slightly uneasy and which were mentioned by Prof. Bendix: the assumption that opportunities are the same things for individuals in the aggregate, at various historical periods, in various societies, even on various regional levels. Education, prestige, power, etc., usually listed as examples of differential opportunities, may mean so substantially different things to different people at different times in different regions that I would be a bit uneasy about generalizing from *our* conception of them. We have a certain assumption as to the kind of education we want to have for our children, and we feel uneasy if somebody else's children do not have equal access to it. But we have to make this assumption explicit for any historical perspective in mobility studies that transcend two or three generations.

Like everybody else I am sure that there must be some sound basis for the following assumption: there is a hard core of aspirations in terms of which the quality of social opportunities can be defined for large periods and for all strata. I cannot imagine very easily anybody being terribly mad at being denied the opportunity to starve permanently, for example, although I suppose even this has happened. But these are rather extreme possibilities and, as I said, I am sure there is a hard core of what one could define as an anthropological — to use the German term — *Infrastruktur* or the substructure of what turns out to be the structure of opportunities, historical opportunities for concrete people in concrete historical periods. But this is an assumption that I have not really seen spelled out either in this discussion or in much of the literature on the topic.

John H. Goldthorpe: I think that in the British literature on the sociology of education and educability the distinction that you just made has in effect become implicit. The general history of work in this field is really one of growing awareness of the inadequacy of the idea of equality of opportunity understood in a formal sense, *i.e.* in the sense of access to secondary education without economic constraints, etc., which, for example, the 1944 Education Act in Britain tried to ensure. Of course, creating this formal equality of opportunity of access to various kinds of secondary education did very little indeed to diminish class differentials in the actual attainment of this, in part for reasons of the kind indicated by Luckmann relating to the whole problem of how parents and children themselves interpreted opportunity, to the relationships between the opportunities offered and the latter's own felt expectations and aspirations. This emerged as a problem of at least as great, if not greater importance, than simply legal and institutional changes within the educational system. It is true that people continue to speak of problems of equality of opportunity or inequality of opportunity and sometimes make the distinction between formal equality of opportunity and real equality of opportunity. But I think I agree with Prof. Luckmann that the idea of real equality of opportunity is not a very satisfactory term, and that perhaps we ought to say what we mean here in a rather more precise and less misleading manner.

Reinhard Bendix: The thing that has impressed me the most in the British contribution to this field is the inherent instability of what is conceived of as a restriction of opportunity. I find it has a dampening effect on my aspirations to observe that the tremendous impulse of an emancipatory type has a way of being washed out once it has been achieved. I call your attention to the obvious example of the franchise. What a tremendous agitation went into the development of the universal franchise and what tremendous disillusionment has set in once it was granted. Because people discovered that the restriction which they had done everything under the sun to remove proved not to be very effective as a means of removing other restrictions which then loomed much larger.

T.H. Marshall has put this into a scheme by speaking of the British cases as a succession of legal, then political and then social rights. He used these terms in a technical sense which I don't want to spend time on here. The idea was that you have a succession of redistributions affected by the overcoming of previous restrictions. I believe that this perspective has a tremendous advantage in that it provides a historical perspective for the analysis of social mobility or the distribution of opportunities. But it is disheartening at the same time: one of the interesting studies that is going forward tries to apply this scheme to the administration of welfare (I don't know how that would be in Britain); you define certain people as unequal in X, Y and Z. Then you set up machinery in order to equalize X, Y and Z and you find out that A, B and C haven't been taken care of. Plus the fact that the machinery used to equalize X, Y and Z has become an obstacle to the very goal that prompted you to initiate this measure in the first place. I think if some of our Marxist friends would — if I may be permitted a little whimsical remark — employ some of their dialectical interests in the analysis of this kind of process we might get more illumination on why it is so extremely difficult for institutional and political measures to be effective, even when the auspices are good, politically speaking. To explain the obstacles solely by talking about exploitation and dichotomy of classes, etc., I find too gross for the phenomenon that I'd like to see explained.

John H. Goldthorpe: I would agree for my conception of the modern society's system of stratification as being a structure of a number of correlated modes of power and advantage. It would follow that the more powerful and advantaged groups can always use the resources which make up their power and advantage to preserve their privileged position. One can give examples of this happening in many different areas. Although no one has done a detailed study of this, I think that in the British educational system it could be shown that, to a quite considerable extent, the advances in "formal" equality of opportunity — the attempt to move away from streaming, from the tripartite system towards a more comprehensive system of education, etc. — have in various ways been nullified by the activities of particular interest groups using their various forms of power and advantage in the society, their wealth and general economic resources, their position of prestige, etc. So I would agree with you that it is not only through the mechanism of the family that inequalities are preserved.

Where I might disagree with some writers of neo-Marxist persuasion (certainly in Britain, if not in Germany) is on the supposition that, because the system has this nature, that therefore any kind of reduction of inequality or modification of the stratification system through such political institutions as we possess is impossible. I think this an unduly pessimistic notion — at least for Britain. One can point to a number of instances during the last Labour Government, for example, where the government *could* have made some impact — I don't know how great — on the existing structure of inequality, *if* it had had the nerve and the political will to take more decisive action. It may well be that to try and achieve this in the manner of "piecemeal social engineering" is not possible because of problems of the kind that Prof. Bendix has referred to; *i.e.* that one changes a little bit here, and there is a sort of recuperation there. It may be that far wider-reaching reforms, say, of the educational system, or of the taxation system, or of the system of industrial relations would have been necessary than any that were even contemplated. But I see no reason for supposing that through determined political action, at least within the British system, quite substantial changes could not be made in the structure of inequality.

Of course, there is always the question that Harold Laski was very fond of raising at LSE (London School of Economics) in his day, of whether the capitalists would tolerate this, or whether there would be a rebellion of capitalists, a strike of capital, a flight of capital, or whatever. Obviously, there would be *some* reaction of this kind, which might then necessitate still more radical governmental intervention in the management of the economy than perhaps had been initially planned. But I would expect that, given the nature of the British political culture, given the tremendous legitimacy which political institutions and governmental authority have in Britain, there would be a far better chance of establishing successful democratic socialism in Britain than in almost any other country. The remarkable thing is that this has never been attempted; and, in my opinion, the interesting sociological problem here has to do with the character of the leadership of the Labour Party, which is a remarkably neglected topic in Britain. There has been not only a lack of will, but even a lack of interest, in seeing how far radical socialist reforms could be pushed through via democratic processes. There may well be constraints there, but all I am saying is that in Britain a Labour Government has never banged its nose up against these constraints. Therefore, we cannot know where or what they are.

1.6. *The structure of inequality*

Daniel Bertaux: The so-called concept of "inequality" seems to me highly doubtful, to say the least. It seems to postulate one thing which, on the contrary, should be checked: that all kinds of jobs are of the same "nature", of the same quality, and that "inequalities" appear mainly, not in the production but in the distribution process, when sharing the cake (no wonder the middle class likes this conception of society!). But let us imagine a slave plantation. Can you compare the work of the slaves, the so-called "work" of the guards, priests and accountants, and the (non) "work" of the proprietors? Does it have any meaning to say that there is inequality between say, the slaves and the guards? Or the slaves and their masters?

Peter M. Rossi: I don't see how you can *not* say it. They are obviously so acidly unequal. They are unequal in a variety of ways: in terms of material rewards, in terms of prestige, in terms of authority, in terms of control over life and death, and so on. Surely it must be possible to say that some have more money than others, and some have more power than others, and so on. You must not go against common sense to make a point.

Daniel Bertaux: I am not saying they are equal; on the contrary! I am trying to find a concept which would express their situation of *opposition*, of exploitation-and-domination, where the wealth of the rich and the poverty of the poor are only results of the *same* process: the *appropriation*, through persuasion and violence, of the products of work by a small "ruling" class. Maybe you know the cynical saying which goes: "La richesse c'est l'argent des autres, l'amour c'est la femme des autres, le pouvoir c'est la peau des autres." Why does everybody know this except the "sociologists"?

Anyway, if you consider this as a mere *hypothesis*, you just cannot use concepts which implicitly *postulate* a continuum, a continuous dimension along which people would nicely be ranked.

John H. Goldthorpe: I think the distinction which Bertaux is making is between the classification of individuals or units along some continuum, as one can do in the case of, say, income or presumably position within a bureaucratic hierarchy and, on the other hand, the kind of classification where one either has "yes" or "no". I suppose the classical Marxist distinction between people who own the means of production and people who do not own the means of production is an obvious example of this latter case. I can see that distinction.

If you wish to define categories in terms of whether they do have a certain attribute, which is "owning the means of production", or whether they do not have this attribute, then obviously this gives rise to a dichotomous outcome to which the term inequality might not be appropriate. However, what I would want to ask is — let us grant that one can develop classifications in terms of possession or non-possession of some attribute, or of being on one side or the other of a particular relationship — but how consequential are these? This is my challenge to the whole kind of Marxian analysis. All right, make that division and then tell us what follows from it for, say, behaviour within an industrial enterprise, for political behaviour, for work relationships, for political relationships.

It seems to me that the reason why people have perhaps more frequently been forced into analyses in terms of some continuum like income or authority or whatever, is that — at least in modern society — one can make rather more hypotheses about actual social behaviour in relationships which can be empirically confirmed, if one starts out from that kind of classification. Take, for example, voting behaviour or participation in political parties and make the dichotomous distinction — what can you say from that? If one makes some distinction on the basis of continua or combinations of continua I think one can make some propositions that can be empirically confirmed. I think this is at least the challenge: if you want to make the dichotomous distinction, then do something with it in terms of explanatory propositions!

Daniel Bertaux: Agreed, agreed! Only, there are no *direct* relations between the deep structure (of determinations) and the surface phenomena which are the only observable things. On the contrary, there are a number of *mediations* which it is, I think, our task to analyze.

Specifically, it is well possible that the deep social structure is actually dichotomous, but that the empirical consequences of this deep structure "look" continuous in terms of rewards, prestige, etc. To take an analogy: the Earth is round, but it looks flat to us. If you start observing the stars, etc., with the postulate that the Earth is flat, you will build instruments which most probably will prevent you from observing the phenomena by means of which you could realize that the Earth is actually round. This is exactly the case with "stratification theories" based on empirical results of prestige scales, for instance.

I agree with you that the Marxist tradition has not been able so far to develop the understanding of the mediations between the deep (class) structure, and the various empirical phenomena of social life, but this is changing now; and I believe that this approach is far more fertile than the empirical approach, which is content with an empirical look at things: with this kind of approach you would look through the window and swear that the Earth is flat!

John H. Goldthorpe: But we could do something by observing the sun, you know, and ships, and the sea, and things like that. And that would settle the issue.

I can see no way in which Bertaux, or anyone else for that matter, can make their points about ultimate determinations other than by deriving, logically, hypotheses that would follow from that position, and then observing empirically whether these are validated or not.

2. On the use of occupational prestige scales in mobility studies

The following contributions mainly relate to the papers of John H. Goldthorpe (see p. 17-73) and Kaare Svalastoga (see p. 75-85). A short list of questions raised in this debate may help to give a structure to the text: What is the sociological meaning of prestige ratings of occupations? On which dimensions(s) should prestige be measured? What is the relationship between prestige and more material aspects of inequality as, *e.g.* income distributions? What is the value of prestige ratings in studies of social (resp. occupational) mobility? To what extent is the prestige of a person determined by his occupation?

Peter M. Rossi: I'd like to make some remarks about Mr. Goldthorpe's paper. There were a couple of points which I thought terribly important. Perhaps the most important one is the interpretation of prestige ranking as ratings of general goodness. There is a great deal of empirical data to indicate that that is the case. It certainly seems to be the case that no matter how one defines prestige operationally — and it has been operationally defined in a variety of ways — the consistency of results using one method as compared to another leads one to believe that there underlies the results one particular dimension rather than a series of separate dimensions.

For example, the occupational prestige studies which have been done in the United States since 1925 have used as a criterion for operationalization how desirable the job was from the point of view of the individual. In 1943, Smith* used the question of where the person should be seated (this would be the guest-speaker at a luncheon or dinner which honored some prestigeful person), and that sounds very much like deference, if I understand deference. The 1947 NORC (National Opinion Research Center) study asked in a very contradictory sort of way: "In your opinion, what is the general social standing of an occupation?" Our 1964 study, which has yet to be published, also used the question of the social standing of an occupation as the first criterion, we replicated, using nine additional criteria as, for instance: What is the social worth of an occupation? How interesting is the occupation's activity? How desirable is the occupation to pursue? How tough is it? How hard is the work involved in the occupation? and several other questions which I cannot even remember. The relationships among the results are so great — of the order of .8 and above, and usually about .9 or sometimes hovering around .99 —

* M. Smith, "An empirical scale of prestige status of occupations", *American sociological review*, 8 April, 1943, pp. 185-192.

that they look like tautologies. It is very difficult to conceive of this set of definitions as meaning anything but some kind of generalized rank order reference for occupations, which one might call general goodness of occupations.

I don't want to get too much into the second part of Mr. Goldthorpe's paper where he presents a very beautiful example of an attempt to separate various dimensions of ratings along the lines of prestige, and so on. I think that this is a direction in which one could go, provided that one does not get results, the way we did, which indicate that those dimensions are not easily separated. That means that what we conceive of as deference, what we conceive of as social standing, what we conceive of as the perception of an occupation in terms of its income, in terms of its contribution to society, in terms of its functional worth — to steal from Barber — are really alternative manifestations of some kind of generalized and highly agreed-upon rank order of occupation in terms of which some occupations are considered as very good, others as mediocre, and others as bad.

Sugiyama Iutaka: Well, my problem is this: Mr. Goldthorpe is really trying to do what some years ago we were discussing in terms of what socio-economic status meant. As a measure, occupation was replaced by education and income which were thought to be better indicators. But after several studies and correlations we find now that occupation is the best discriminator after all, and many people therefore started to use occupation as a single measure. In fact, the indexing or scoring of the four dimensions (standard of living, prestige in the community, power and influence over other people, value to society), or n dimensions, that we may introduce will perhaps not add as much to our understanding. I'd like to know, for instance, whether these four dimensions which Mr. Goldthorpe distinguishes in his paper are correlated in the same way that Prof. Rossi suggested for his American study. If that's the case, I don't think, Mr. Goldthorpe, you have a point there.

Kaare Svalastoga: May I be allowed to join in the discussion as I have done some work in this area. Prior to my book on social mobility in Denmark*, I made several pretests on the prestige problem. One of them tried various questions as suggested by Prof. Rossi. For example, we presented one group of university students with the question: "How would *you* evaluate the prestige or standing of this set of occupations according to your best estimate?" The other group got the question: "How do you think that the population of Denmark ranks these positions?" We found that the university students tended more frequently to put the cards in the same box when asked to use their *own* evaluation. They said: "I am of course egalitarian and I consider

* K. Svalastoga, *Prestige, class and mobility*, Copenhagen, Gyldendal, 1959.

all equal." Whereas when they were using the other criterion, the general opinion among the population of Denmark, they said: "Well, they are old-fashioned and therefore I'd expect them to rank everybody from ambassador to streetcleaner." That seems to me to suggest that the interpretation of prestige as generalized desirability is wrong. Why should these students, when asked to use their own value, say: "They are all equal to me"? Why should they be more likely to do that under the self-evaluation criterion than under the Denmark-total-population criterion, if it had to do with the question of desirability? It seems to me that you would have expected a similar behavior in both circumstances, as a certain occupation should not become less valuable to the person. Whether he used one or the other criterion, he would be likely to resemble the general population of Denmark in regard to desirability, so that it is because these questions have to do with rank order, with something related to deference rather than desirability, that we get this kind of result. Another indication is the fact that there are certain studies that have used the question: "What is the most interesting occupation?", etc., and have not had very high correlations with the standard prestige measures, because frequently the "journalist" will come out at the top of their list.

Paul Duncan-Jones: Could I say a word or two about John Goldthorpe's paper? I think John Goldthorpe has done a very effective and persuasive demolition job and at the end rather half-heartedly tries to save something from the wreck. And I'd like to nibble at what he tried to save. First, Duncan says (and John Goldthorpe mentioned this) if in fact you are using — or proposing to use — occupation as a proxy for income, why don't you actually go out for income? This would be reasonable, and I want to ask whether in fact Duncan's demonstration is as persuasive as one might have thought.

In Duncan's exercise he used, as far as I remember, about 40 occupations which were all pretty salient and of which most members of the population would have some sort of image. The Rossi-Hodge-Siegel study means that we now have ratings for a very much larger number of American occupations and one could use this data to see whether these correlations hold up anywhere near so well as the correlations between income and education and occupational ratings when one has a much more representative collection of occupations, many of which will be less salient. Apart from that possible use of these ratings, there are, in my opinion, two other possible uses: in the first, outlined by John Goldthorpe, one can use this kind of rating to ask about people's movements from a certain position, that would generally be regarded as less desirable, to a position generally regarded as more desirable, or vice versa. I suppose this is a reasonable way of rephrasing the thing.

And this seems rather a poor kind of apology for what one might have thought one was studying when one was studying social mobility. I suppose there is room for disagreement as to how poor an apology it is. John Goldthorpe suggested that in fact this is a way of looking at *occupational* mobility and that we ought not to bring social mobility into it. I think this notion about occupational mobility is a bit of a red herring and one can question whether there *is* such a subject as occupational mobility. It seems to me that in practice, one doesn't actually study movements between occupations but movements between groups of occupations that have been given certain scores. And this means that either by scoring or by grouping you have introduced some external criterion into the analysis: you are either studying some quite specific aspect of occupational mobility — and one wants a definition of what that aspect is — or you are using occupation as a proxy for something. And whether you say it is an aspect of occupational mobility or whether you say it is used as a proxy is, I think, a bit arbitrary. And so I think it would be nice to bring this back to talk about social mobility rather than occupational mobility, because it seems if one is going to use ratings of this kind for studies of movements between occupations, then one is doing something like a study of social mobility — or else one isn't doing anything very much.

There is, I think, a third possible use or interpretation of these ratings: one could get these to fit into a model of social mobility where one was concerned with motivations for occupational choice and where the public image of an occupation might be regarded as one of the most relevant things. But there one is getting into considerable complexities because occupational and vocational choice has been extensively studied and one knows that many other factors enter into it besides this. I don't know whether anybody would think this interpretation was worth pursuing.

Donald Hayes : I have not published this, so you'll have to take my word for it but I have been interested in the ordering of occupations by their income. My interest is in the subjective side of elitism and egalitarianism as a kind of individual attribute. The way I have been studying elitism is to give people a list of familiar occupations and ask them to do two things with the list: for their own country, estimate the actual median income for each of these ten occupations and then make a personal assignment of income which you consider "just and fair" to the same ten occupations. Various measures of the income inequality are calculated. My interest is not so much in the rank order, which happens to coincide with previous published results by NORC and others, but rather with the inequality represented in their answers. I have had an opportunity to do this now in a number of countries with small samples and although I would'nt trust my life on the results, I'll give you some preliminary findings.

We have samples of Israelis, Chileans, French Canadians, English Canadians, Mexicans and Englishmen and all sorts of US samples. The instrument was designed to facilitate this kind of cross-national and longitudinal research and is simple to translate and administer in approximately ten minutes. It is true, there is a remarkable degree of agreement between these samples concerning the rank-ordering of occupations by income (coefficients of concordance exceed .94). But that misses the most interesting feature of the comparison — it seems to me — despite the high agreement on how occupations should be *ranked* by income, there is substantial disagreement on what sizes of income gaps there are or should be between occupations. If you look at the share of income assigned to a low ranking occupation like a garbage collector — my Israeli sample gave a much larger share of the total income pie to this occupation than any other sample I have, with the sole exception of radical student groups in the United States. By the same token, the Israelis gave to high ranking occupations a much smaller share than in any other sample. At the opposite end of the inequality continuum is my Chilean sample of moderate to radical left Allende supporters, who described the actual income distribution of Chile as being the most unequal of all samples measured to date. The interesting fact is not that Chilean radical students and conservative North American businessmen agree on occupational ranking, so much as the evidence of the relative inequality they perceive in their own country and the degree of inequality they describe as "just and fair" — the differential in income they find acceptable and tolerable. Every sample from every country expresses the view that the actual income distribution ought to be cut greatly, but what looking at *relative* inequalities does is to permit you to note the striking differences between samples — like the Chilean radicals and North American business elites. The income distribution these Chilean radicals described as "just and fair" is a great deal more inequitable than the present level of actual income differentials in the United States. This suggests that a person's egalitarianism-conservativism may be more a function of the actual levels of inequality within his own country rather than some position along some absolute trans-societal dimension. And so I'd like to ask Prof. Rossi in particular: of all the studies you do, does their technique permit you to assess inequality — how large gaps there are between occupations? Does your method preclude the possibility of measuring this dimension of prestige?

Peter M. Rossi (in answer to Prof. Hayes): The problem with cross-national comparisons of occupational prestige that we have done so far, myself and my colleagues, were that we had to live with data that were collected by other people. Hence the data are not standardized in such a fashion that one can make sense out of the variance. In effect, what we found really is that doctors are by and large more highly regarded than garbage-collectors, but that distances between them cannot be ascertained in any kind of standardized metric.

The way you are going about it is obviously the way to do it. A standardized instrument gives one more assurance that the variance that you compute will be somewhat identical in meaning. In the analysis of the American occupational material there are differences of a rather interesting variety in the variances and means that are given to occupation by various subgroups of the population. One finds, for example, that ratings of working class persons in America have smaller variances and higher means in the occupational prestige rating than those of persons in the upper middle class level of society. What working class persons are doing in effect is restricting the social distance among occupations. The average social distance among occupations is smaller for working class persons, as they see it, as compared to the upper middle class, as they see it, who are putting more social distance between themselves and, in that fashion, among all occupations. That, however, does not — as you pointed out — affect very much the correlation between the average rank-orders or average prestige scores given by working class as compared to the upper middle class, the correlation being way above .95. The correlation is only one of the measures that one can use and I am quite sure that one is dazzled by these correlations. We rarely get above .3 and when we get somewhere above .9, God has been so good to us one cannot be ungrateful and question this gift. But you are perfectly right, one should question this gift: God is never without some degree of spite in his gifts, and examination of the variances is the direction in which one must go.

John H. Goldthorpe: I'll try and deal with the points that have been raised more or less in the order in which they were raised. First of all, there is the question that Prof. Rossi and Dr. Iutaka raised about whether, in fact, we are likely to discover, in the way that we are working, something other than a very high correlation between the ratings of occupations on the different dimensions that we have singled out. Well, in the pilot study which we report here and in two other pilot studies of a similarly very small nature, we did in fact discover that among the respondents as a whole — in the sense of looking at the average respondent — they *did* discriminate in using the four criteria or dimensions which we included. In other words, these dimensions or criteria were not treated as synonymous, although one should not exaggerate the quantitative difference that persists between them. This, of course, cannot be taken as at all decisive, until we have analyzed in the same way the results of a much larger inquiry with some 150 respondents which we are engaged on at present. I should say here that I agree with Prof. Rossi that the method of analysis of variance is an extremely valuable one for this purpose. I say this to point out that the credit for applying it should go largely to my colleague Dr. Hope and not to me.

The next point is one that Paul Duncan-Jones raised. I'd agree with him entirely that there are dangers in using studies of occupational mobility, based on what I would want to regard as a measure of general occupational goodness, as proxies for studies of social mobility. I think that this is what has often been done in the past, and it has produced results which are probably fairly reliable and valuable from the point of view of analyses of social mobility in gross terms. But we should now try to move beyond this. My own view is that if one has an interest in studies of social mobility *per se*, one would certainly want to move away from basing studies of social mobility on occupational classifications depending on so-called prestige-ratings. However, I think I would be rather more optimistic than Paul Duncan-Jones as to the possible value of looking at studies of *occupational* mobility *per se*. I think this is an interesting investigation, perhaps if one sets it not within a social-mobility frame of reference but if one looks at the question of occupational mobility more from the point of view of access to occupations — of restrictions of labor supply into occupations which may be associated not only with, as it were, barriers corresponding to lines of status or class demarcation, but also with rigidities and barriers that run vertically in a situs kind of way. These seem to me to be the issues more in the context of the sociology of the labor-market and the sociology of occupational distribution, than in the context of social mobility, but, nonetheless, ones which would repay investigation, and for which some scale based directly on the popular evaluation of the general "goodness" or desirability of occupations, would be worthwhile.

The central question of our paper is whether in fact prestige ratings do act as a valid measure of prestige in a sociologically classical sense. I recognize the point which Prof. Svalastoga made — I can, in fact, think of one or two other studies in which it is possible to argue that for some reason or other the respondents did not adopt a "general goodness" frame of reference (I am not sure if this necessarily means they adopt a prestige frame of reference; there are a number of other possibilities). But I still feel that the evidence from most large-scale inquiries makes it difficult to believe that there is a valid measure of prestige in the sense of probabilities of deference, acceptance and derogation. And the other more general consideration here is whether in fact in modern industrial societies one does have integrated, stable prestige structures at all. Prof. Rossi said he wasn't quite sure what deference meant, because he never experienced it. I think he is probably not alone in this. I think that increasingly in modern society it is questionable whether in fact prestige relationships, in the sense of relationships of deference, acceptance and derogation, do exist as abiding features of the structure of social relationships. I was very much influenced here by Shils' paper in which he suggested that in modern industrial societies prestige relationships are tending increasingly to be intermittent, fleeting, transient. They occur in some contexts and then they disappear. This is one way in which modern societies differ rather significantly in terms of social stratification from, say, feudal societies. Those were the main points that I had to deal with, I think.

Sugiyama Iutaka: I am more preoccupied with analysis than with the collection of data. I think that there is quite a lot to be said for thinking about the analysis before we collect the data, and the point is, that if you use the four dimensions separately, the statistical analysis which you can make is limited. Now, if we assume that the four dimensions discerned in Goldthorpe's paper are really different dimensions, do you think that it's going to pay off, and I am now just asking in terms of pay-off of different analyses for prestige to be used as a dependent variable of standard of living or power, etc.?

John H. Goldthorpe: Well, the answer is, I don't really know. But I think it's worth making the effort to put oneself in a position to find out. When we talked to various other people involved in our mobility project about the general problem of occupational grading and classification as a basis for mobility analysis, the general view was that the greater the variety of occupational classifications one can reasonably try out, the better. So, this was part of an attempt to look at some ways in which one might produce rather different occupational classifications. My own point of view is that it is chiefly interesting as at least a basis for trying to look at occupational mobility other than unidimensionally, but it's not terribly adequate. What I would also like to do is to find out how far these cognitive maps of occupations and the taxonomies that are based upon them would match up to the kinds of taxonomies one might produce on the basis of objective data — that is, income data, on educational qualification, etc.

Daniel Bertaux: Prof. Goldthorpe has made a very good critique of the traditional prestige scales, but in a way he is now falling back on a psycho-sociological position that he has so rightly criticized. You see, what you are studying, Prof. Goldthorpe, is of course not standard of living or power and influence of occupation, but the image in the heads of people of standard of living, of power, of influence and so on. Now, I wish you would get interested in the determination of these images. For this you would have to study the institution in charge of producing the so-called ideology in society like the press, literature, or novels which constantly produce new images of society. I wish there were more studies on this. Then, on the other hand I would like to see some so-called materialist studies of standard of living, I mean of the real standard of living, of all these occupations, of the power and influence of all these occupations, the real power and influence of value to society (I believe it's possible to define the values of society in an objective way) and of qualifications, of course, and to compare them to the prestige ratings, and then try to explain the discrepancy. And I think it's necessary — it would not be necessary if you limit yourself to a study of occupational prestige — but it *is* necessary, if you are going to study mobility, because mobility is a physical phenomenon, a material phenomenon, people are moving from one place to another, it's not only an ideological phenomenon. And if you now study the thinking in a materialist perspective at a certain point you are going to mix an ideological level and a materialistical level.

John H. Goldthorpe: Well, I agree with some of that. Certainly, I would be very interested in knowing how cognitive maps of occupations are generated. But I think, first of all, one must know what they are, and the extent to which they vary between different social groups and categories. The problem would be differently posed, if, for example, one found that there is no difference in the kind of cognitive maps held by people differentially located in the social structure. I would expect to find quite marked differences. But first of all, one needs to know precisely what it is one would like to explain before one can devise ways of explaining it. Secondly, as I said before, I would like to be able to match up these cognitive maps, however variable, with data of an objective character. In Britain one is greatly handicapped here by the nature of census data.

Kaare Svalastoga: As far as I have been able to see from the literature on prestige, it seems to me possible to say that prestige is a function of not more than the following four factors, of which two seem to me to be dominantly important and two not so important. And of the four factors, the two more important ones are related to the occupation itself, the first being its difficulty, and the second the responsibility attached to it. And the two that are not related to the occupation itself, are thirdly the level of information or ignorance that is present in the population judging the position. In general, we found in a Danish study that the more ignorant people were regarding a certain position, the more likely they were to place it towards the middle. And the fourth factor, I have termed ideology; it shows itself in Denmark, for instance, by the fact that those who are against military investments reduce the placing of the captain in the army, in general put him closer to the middle, and it shows itself, for instance, in Holland by the fact that Catholics do not place the Protestant ministers as high as Protestants themselves do. But I will in the following assume that the two dominant factors, the first and the second — for a Danish sample, I have been able to show that they are quite dominant giving a multiple-correlation of about .9 with prestige scores — are actually the main factors and I will be concerned with only one of them and that is their responsibility component. Because, you see, the practical situation frequently is this: we have thousands of occupations, but it's usually very hard to judge in terms of prestige more than a couple of hundred. So, hence we need an estimation procedure and for the difficulty component, for the difficulty determinant of prestige, it seems to me that education is very adequate. But the problem is how shall we get at the responsibility component, and it's much more of a problem since both I myself and such an authority on this, as C. Wright Mills*, we would tend to agree that among those two, responsibility is the more important factor, is the heavier factor. In my paper I have surveyed the various avenues you could go towards finding a good estimate

* C. Wright Mills, *The power elite*, New York, Oxford University Press, 1956.

of the responsibility attached to an occupation, since I plan to use my measure of responsibility for a rather large sample, the Metropolitan Longitudinal Project, and need a method that can be rather conveniently used for many people. It's not so easy for me to use, for instance, Drake's interesting method for the measurement of responsibility, to which I devoted some space in my paper. But I have rather settled for a certain derivation from a model due to Simon and by working on Simon's model I finally arrived at the conclusion that for a person who owns an enterprise, the size of that enterprise is all that I need to know. Because his responsibility will then be assumed to be a function of the size of his enterprise. But if the person is an employee, I have to be informed about the size of the enterprise and the hierarchical level to which the employee belongs. And if I have those two pieces of information and further, if I am able to make fairly reasonable estimates of certain parameters — I think you will see the estimates that I have crudely guessed at in my paper — then I can get a measure of responsibility. And it seems to me that it would have the advantage that we measure responsibility in a way that should be feasible to carry through even in survey research.

Avraham Zloczower: I would like to address the question to both Prof. Svalastoga and Prof. Goldthorpe. I am quite intrigued by Prof. Goldthorpe's attempt to purify occupational categories from those elements which are not related to social prestige. Most of those who have criticized the excessive reliance on occupation as a measure of social class have argued that the occupational hierarchy is almost exclusively a measure of social prestige and very inadequate as a measure of the hierarchy of power. Now Prof. Goldthorpe seems to turn the tables and argues that the current schemes of occupational classification do not measure social prestige adequately and proposes a method of classification better suited to this purpose. I think this is a very laudable endeavour, but I wonder whether he goes along with Prof. Svalastoga who has stated quite unequivocally that he considers a person's prestige to be determined overwhelmingly by his occupation. I quite understand the use of occupation as a general indicator of a person's socio-economic status, because once we know a person's occupation we have a good idea of his probable income, access to power and, certainly, standing in the community. But to what extent is it true that the most important single item of information on the distribution of social prestige in a given society is its occupational structure? In a country like the US for instance, do we not learn more about a person's prestige when we know that he is black or white than by pinpointing his occupation? Why concentrate on occupation as an indicator of prestige? Is it really the best available source of information on the distribution of social prestige?

Kaare Svalastoga: Yes! I would simply say that we are in a situation where the rate of technological change is high; and where increasingly it becomes important for each nation to utilize its talents to the full and hence it seems to me the most likely trend in regard to all race discrimination is that it will be disappearing regardless what people want to do with it and hence I would say occupation is the only thing worth considering in the long run and even in the short run.

John H. Goldthorpe: My answer is rather different. I do not think that prestige, as I understand it, is a very important component in modern systems of social stratification; and so, from the point of view of studying stratification or mobility, I am not much interested in indicators of prestige, because, following Shils' argument, I do not believe that prestige is an important mode of power and advantage in the modern type of society — at least in modern British society, with which I'm chiefly concerned. It may be that in certain contexts in American society this is different, and — I am sure of this — in certain forms of historical society it was different. So, my position is that whether one is interested in occupational mobility or more generally in social mobility, one would not primarily be interested in the prestige aspect, one would be more concerned with the question of power and social advantage that are indicated by income, educational chances, authority, and things of this kind.

3. Issues in the analysis of career mobility *

In the last years, the prevailing mode in the analysis of the intragenerational mobility processes consisted in attempts to predict an individual's occupational status at a given point of his career by individual attributes as his status of origin, intelligence score, his educational attainment, etc. Different models of statistical analysis have been used to estimate the relative weight of such independent variables. In their papers Iutaka/Bock and Müller apply path analysis models and Rossi/Ornstein variance analysis models.

The questions raised in this context related first to a comparison of the different statistical models (see 3.1), then more basically probed the adequacy of these models itself, *e.g.* for studying the impact of education on later occupational attainment (see 3.2). It was also argued that in most mobility studies the analysis applied mainly to the individual level and has almost exclusively been focussed on characteristics of jobs. More attention should be paid to structural determinants and institutional constraints (see 3.3) and to value orientations of the individuals which may lead to specific "job projects" (see 3.4).

* The contributions reproduced in this section relate specifically to the papers by Rossi/Ornstein, Iutaka/Bock, Müller and Pasqualini.

3.1. *Path analysis and variance analysis in the study of the intragenerational mobility process*

Walter Müller: I'd like to bring the discussion around to a comparison and to an evaluation of the differential utility of the statistical techniques of path analysis and the extensions of variance analysis that Prof. Rossi and Prof. Ornstein propose in their paper. It seems to me that the two methods are not as different from each other as they seem to be at first glance. In extracting unique variance from zero order variance Rossi and Ornstein isolate effects of single variables and combinations of them controlling for the effects of other variables. This is quite similar to the calculation of direct and indirect effects in path analysis. Pointing to the differences of the two methods one could say that in path analysis one formulates explicitly a model of dependency according to which the variables introduced are assumed to be acting. One further accepts some restricting assumptions such as for instance non-correlation of error terms. The path coefficients, then, are valuable only for the particular model under study and if the underlying assumptions are correct. In the analysis proposed in the paper of Rossi and Ornstein, the formulation of a model of explanation is less explicit, but still the values of the unique variances are valid only for the model of dependence of variables which has been used. If one adds a further variable to a set of independent variables all of the unique variances may alter quite considerably.

Michael Ornstein: Perhaps it would be appropriate for me to comment on the differential utilities of this kind of variance analysis and path analysis. You are using a model in both cases. One gets less out of the variance model in some ways, because it is difficult to see what the processes are. However, a path analysis of this data would just be so complicated that one could not use it. Using variance decomposition, for example, I could use dummy variables — four variables for education — so I don't have to make any assumptions about the linearity of education. To insert four variables for education into a path analysis would make it absolutely impossible.

They are different models, with path analysis being a process model. What this regression model does is to take the individual in time and look back at what variables have impact on him at the final point. You can then isolate the effect of family background, controlling on other variables. I find that with very complicated data this is the only thing one can do. It seems to be significantly better than just looking at the regression coefficients, which is the normal thing to do. For example, if you want to enter industry of job, and you have a number of dummy variables, and there is no obvious order of the industry, what you normally do is some sort of analysis of the variance technique or a regression technique with dummy variables. By taking the unique variance of that whole set of variables you can discover what the impact of industry as a whole really is. Whereas it is almost impossible to do that in a path analysis. Looking at the regression coefficient of each industry one by one really does not tell you what the whole impact is.

3.2. *On education as a variable in the study of the status attainment process*

Roger Girod: My question is whether this kind of analysis (variance analysis or path models) is the best for observing the influence of education. Because the picture is very different when you take the distribution of people from different kinds of schools. Some schools prepare their students very specifically for certain types of jobs, while the students of other schools go into various types of jobs. This is a very important point.

Michael Ornstein: This does not occur in the United States.

Roger Girod: I'm sorry, but it does. I can take, for instance, the description of the careers of those who come from the very best schools, the Ivy League, and I find that these schools prefer very specific kinds of students and that these individuals are later incorporated in the top level activities as a rule. But if I take the Census monographs of the United States, I observe that there is no very high correlation between the level of education and job distribution. And my question is, how to relate your data to the *Education of the American population** of Folger and Nam, for instance. Because the coefficient of correlation there is very low and even decreasing.

I have a second point: it would be important to observe the concrete use made of education in adult life. Because through the statistical level of education you get an approximative indication not so much of what people did learn as from what social milieu they are coming. It seems one more indicator of their origin, not of education as such. It would be far better to go into the field and to check what remains in the minds of people of a specific type of education. How far is their social prestige concretely influenced by their previous education.

Peter M. Rossi: Let me speak first of the type of schools; at first glance it looks as if that would be a very important question. But there has just been an enormous amount of research on types of schools in the United States, particularly on colleges. There certainly are colleges and universities as different as, for instance, Harvard and Johns Hopkins, and the University of Mississippi and other places of this sort. However, those differences are virtually all taken up, not in the effect of the school so much as in the selectivity of the school. The characteristics of the individuals who go to a certain school account for most of the effects that such schools have. Secondly, those elite

* J.K. Folger and C.B. Nam, *Education of the American population*, New York, Washington, DC, Government Printing Office, 1967.

schools represent so small a portion of the total college graduate population. The Ivy League schools, for example, graduate each year something of the order of perhaps 25 000. The graduating class of the colleges and universities in the United States now is 1 500 000. So that if we look for Ivy League men in our sample of 1 500 we might find one. In a much larger sample it may be worthwhile to put that in, but not in our case. The major differences in the sample would occur between those who are college graduates and those who are not, rather than within college graduates or within high schools. There are also elite high schools, but again they account for so small a proportion of the population. It would be an important factor if you were studying, for example, recruitment to high political positions or recruitment to the highest echelons of large business enterprises or elite law firms. But as far as this research is concerned it isn't worthwhile being more precise

3.3. *Individualistic versus structural perspective*

Daniel Bertaux: I have been listening to all the findings of Rossi and Ornstein with the perspective in mind that people don't choose jobs, but that jobs choose people; and it fits rather perfectly. Let me give you an example: Mark Granovetter has done a study of how managers were looking for new jobs and finding them, in 1968 in the Boston area. He found that not only do they almost *always* find a new job through friends or "relations", but very often *it is the job which finds them:* they were sitting in their office, not thinking about quitting, when "they were offered" something interesting. This example leads to a new conception which is radically opposite to the common sense (or common non-sense) one: that it is not people who find jobs but (even if people desperately look for jobs) *it is the jobs which find people.*

Peter M. Rossi: But the material of that study is really concerned with professional and technical workers who are beyond their first jobs in their career, and in a period of very high demand for professional and technical workers in the Boston metropolitan area which has a very heavy dependence on the electronic industry. What the employers were apparently doing was stealing from each other. And that reflects itself very neatly in the data.

Daniel Bertaux: If the general rule was that people choose their jobs, how do you explain your findings that many of them stay *for a long time* in hard, health-destroying, little-paid jobs?

Michael Ornstein: Probably that they can't find others!

Daniel Bertaux: Yes. But *why* can't they? It would be too easy to say : "because they are unskilled", and thus implicitly to put the blame on them. „Unskilled" people can find good jobs if they have the proper connections, while some skilled or highly skilled people cannot find jobs corresponding to their so-called skills. One should not look for the cause *in the individuals*, where it seems to lie; the question is, are they or are they not useful to the industrials, is their work needed to help some capital grow? It is *this* logic which decides whether people will have a job or not; and they have absolutely no control over it, they are powerless in face of it. (Even the business leaders, who seem to have all the power, are merely *enacting* a logic which is totally beyond their power: they *must* make money, they *must* make their capital grow, they have no other choice.)

So when I say that "jobs find people", jobs are actually only the observable part of a whole machinery.

Michael Ornstein: It may be of interest to you that one finds, looking at the time people need to find their first jobs, for whites the expected pattern: if they only have little education it takes them a longer time to find a job. For blacks the reverse occurs: highly qualified blacks may take as long or longer to find their first jobs as those with some high school. That seems to imply a sort of structural distortion of the labor market during this period, where there is a willingness to accept blacks with low levels of skills and whites with high levels of skills.

3.4. *Occupational mobility and "job projects"*

Pasqualini, in her paper, combines an individualistic and a structural perspective. She notes that in Italy under the economic boom of the early 60's a two step model of (individual) occupational mobility could be observed: unskilled rural-urban migrants went through work in the construction sector to more qualified jobs. This mobility pattern changed considerably as the economic situation of the country changed.

John H. Goldthorpe (to Pasqualini): Can your method of analysis take into account the notion of what I would call the "job project"? A worker who starts in agricultural employment or in a poorly paid job in a depressed area, or who is a recent immigrant to the country in question, might move into some occupation like brick-laying or building or transportation to tide him over till he can find better paid, more secure factory work. In such a case, the first occupational move might not involve any increase in wages. Rather, it is made simply to give the person a better position to take up later opportunities for better paid and more secure employment which might otherwise not have come his way. Can your method of analysis deal with this kind of process where an individual is looking at least two moves ahead? Your ultimate interest is, after all, in the factual processes of mobility.

Rita Pasqualini: Yes. I wanted to do research of this type precisely because it is a common-sense proposition that you leave the country and enter the building industry in order to get even further. You don't enter construction for its own sake, but only because it helps you prepare yourself for a better position. Even limiting myself to the study of construction workers, I have found that they just leave their jobs as soon as something better offers itself.

John H. Goldthorpe: I'd like to know if Mike Ornstein's methods would allow this kind of process to be observed in the data that you, Prof. Rossi, have collected?

Peter M. Rossi: With the occupational prestige scores which we used, occupations from different sectors of industries, involving different types of skills, were all thrown together. We have not quite figured it out yet, but we think that another mode of analysis should be applied, in addition, to these data. Perhaps we should go back to the occupational categories themselves and look at the interchanges among particular occupations. But that would require the classification of occupation in some form beyond the *ca* 400 or 500 occupational titles which are listed in the Census. One of the directions which we have gone into and which has not turned out to be very productive was the categorization of occupations according to value-inventories. John Holland, who is also at Johns Hopkins, has worked out a mode of classifying mainly professional occupations according to the types of interest and skills involved in them. He is now trying to extend that to the total occupational structure, so that one would then be looking at the ways in which individuals shift from one occupation to another, depending on the similarity of skills and interests that could be indulged in those occupations. But that is on a very, very primitive level at the moment. For example, he classifies all working class occupations into one category.

John H. Goldthorpe: It seems to me that this is rather basic if you want to follow Mike Ornstein's suggestion and look at the actual processes that are involved in job changing. I was struck by the general conclusions of his work which support the kind of old-fashioned micro-economic view of labor markets. The more recent work in the area is concerned with reviving the Marshallian idea of "equal net advantages" and a distinction is that between economic rewards, such as wages, on the one hand, and non-economic or intrinsic rewards on the other. It seems to me that the crucial question is the extent to which there is, as it were, a conscious calculation and choice, within given contraints, between these basically different types of work rewards — extrinsic and intrinsic.

This would raise one difficulty that you do have with the measures you are using: you have not got a measure of occupations by intrinsic rewards. You have only some indirect kind of measurement of intrinsic rewards of occupations in the prestige measure. There is now some quite interesting work being done at Cambridge on the operation of the local labor market which brings out a point suggested in our work: for many manual workers there is often quite a sharp dilemma between taking work which pays more or work which offers more intrinsic rewards. Now, if you would look at the exemplary list of occupations, with scores, that you give (*cf.* p. 286 above) you have assemblers and barbers with about 10 points difference between them. Well, at least I think if one were looking at the British situation, any sort of aggregate score of this kind would conceal quite marked differences: assemblers would be far better paid than barbers, but barbers would generally regard themselves as having higher intrinsic satisfaction in their work than assemblers. And this might well be, for someone who was a barber, a crucial dilemma in occupational choice. If, for example, he married, he might be under pressure, via his new familial roles, to increase his earnings. Should he stay as a barber in a job from which he derives some measure of intrinsic satisfaction or should he stop being a barber and go to work on a car assembly line and perhaps increase his income substantially at the cost of having to endure less rewarding work? If you really want to revive a sort of micro-economic model of the labor market, then somehow this whole business of net advantages of occupation has to be taken into account. And some measure is needed to balance the purely economic one of wages.

Michael Ornstein: I think that's a good point. The other thing we have not done is to attempt to look at life styles. We are not, for example, considering transitions from white-collar to blue-collar positions, etc. That type of analysis is problably much more difficult to carry on. My other reason to believe that wages are really the dominant factor in people's job changing — at least for our sample — was that wages take up an absolutely incredible amount of variance. I would be very surprised if anything else will add much to that. But, again, this was a very specific historical context in a specific society.